wm 31.1 YEO

Ethnicity and the Dementias

Second Edition

Ethnicity and the Dementias

Second Edition

Edited by

Gwen Yeo and
Dolores Gallagher-Thompson

Routledge
Taylor & Francis Group
New York   London

Routledge is an imprint of the
Taylor & Francis Group, an informa business

Routledge
Taylor & Francis Group
270 Madison Avenue
New York, NY 10016

Routledge
Taylor & Francis Group
2 Park Square
Milton Park, Abingdon
Oxon OX14 4RN

© 2006 by Taylor and Francis Group, LLC
Routledge is an imprint of Taylor & Francis Group, an Informa business

Printed in the United States of America on acid-free paper
10 9 8 7 6 5 4 3 2 1

International Standard Book Number-10: 0-415-95405-3 (Softcover) 0-415-95404-5 (Hardcover)
International Standard Book Number-13: 978-0-415-95405-1 (Softcover) 978-0-415-95404-4 (Hardcover)
Library of Congress Card Number 2006000043

Library of Congress Cataloging-in-Publication Data

Ethnicity and the dementias / Gwen Yeo, Dolores Gallagher-Thompson, editors.--
2nd ed.
   p. ; cm.
   Includes bibliographical references.
   ISBN 0-415-95404-5 (hb : alk. paper) -- ISBN 0-415-95405-3 (pb : alk. paper)
   1. Dementia--United States--Cross-cultural studies. 2. Minorities--Mental
health--United States. 3. Psychiatry, Transcultural--United States. I. Yeo, Gwen. II.
Gallagher-Thompson, Dolores.
   [DNLM: 1. Cross-Cultural Comparison--United States. 2. Dementia--ethnology--
United States. 3. Minority Groups--psychology--United States. WM 220 E84 2006]

RC521.E86 2006
616.8'3--dc22   2006000043

Visit the Taylor & Francis Web site at
http://www.taylorandfrancis.com

and the Routledge Web site at
http://www.routledge-ny.com

Contents

The Editors

Gwen Yeo, Ph.D., AGSF, a gerontologist, is the founding director of Stanford Geriatric Education Center at Stanford University School of Medicine, which helped develop the field of ethnogeriatrics. Most of her recent work focuses on educational resources in ethnogeriatrics. In addition to over 60 publications in gerontology and ethnogeriatrics, she is a consultant to universities, the chair of the Ethnogeriatrics Committee of the American Geriatrics Society, and the section editor of the Ethnogeriatrics and Special Populations of the *Journal of American Geriatrics Society.*

Dolores Gallagher-Thompson, Ph.D., ABPP, is a professor of research in psychiatry and behavioral sciences at Stanford University School of Medicine. A clinical researcher and practicing geropsychologist for over 20 years, she has published extensively on behavioral interventions for depression among older adults. Her recent work focuses on interventions for unique problems faced by culturally diverse family caregivers. She is a founding and current member of the multi-ethnic Stanford Geriatric Education Center, on committees of the Alzheimer's Association, and co-editor-in-chief of *Clinical Gerontologist: The Journal of Aging and Mental Health.*

Contributors

Patricia Areán, Ph.D., is an associate professor of psychiatry and the director of the Over 60 Research Program at the University of California–San Francisco. Her research is focused on the development of cognitive behavioral therapies for depressed elders, with a particular emphasis on minority populations and medically frail older adults. In addition, her most recent work demonstrates the efficacy of problem-solving therapy, an innovative treatment designed for depression among older adults with concurrent mild cognitive impairment.

Soledad Argüelles, Ph.D., is a clinical psychologist with a specialization in geropsychology, and a program professor with the Fischler School of Education and Human Services at Nova Southeastern University, North Miami Beach, Florida. She combines clinical, research/educational, and technology issues in her psychotherapy practice, advises/teaches graduate students, and contributes to presentations, journal articles, and book chapters. Her special interests lie in the areas of cultural diversity and clinical issues, especially as it impacts the elderly, including issues of acculturation, immigration trends, and family dynamics.

Trinidad Argüelles, M.S., is the recruitment coordinator in the Center on Aging at the University of Miami's Miller School of Medicine. Her special interest in aging was inspired by sharing her childhood with four grandparents and four great grandparents, all very different individuals. She received her master's degree in industrial and organizational psychology with an emphasis on cognitive aging, and a certification in gerontology. She is also a member of numerous community organizations devoted to aging and a leader in translation, older immigrant workers' retraining, and recruitment and retention of older adults in research projects.

Patricia Lanoie Blanchette, M.D., M.P.H., is the founding chair of the department of geriatric medicine and the geriatric medicine fellowship program at the John A. Burns School of Medicine at the University of Hawaii–Mānoa. She is a member of the national board of the Alzheimer's Association and the chair of its Program Committee and has won numerous awards and honors for her geriatric teaching and leadership.

Joan M. Detry Burke, Ed.D., is the project director and social research associate in the Center for Aging and Diversity at the Institute on Aging at the University of North Carolina–Chapel Hill where she oversees the planning, organization, and implementation of large research projects on Alzheimer's disease and other dementia related disorders.

Mary H. Burleson, Ph.D., is an associate professor in the department of social and behavioral sciences at Arizona State University—West. She is a biosocial psychophysiologist who studies the dynamic interplay among stress, emotion, sexuality, physiological outcomes, and health in both heterosexual and lesbian women.

David W. Coon, Ph.D., is a geropsychologist and an associate professor in the department of social and behavioral sciences at Arizona State University—West. He was on the research team of the National Institute on Aging (NIA)-funded Resources for Enhancing Alzheimer Caregiver's Health (REACH) project, studying interventions with Latino, African American, and Anglo caregivers of dementia patients and has published widely from that research. He has also worked extensively with lesbian, gay, bisexual, and transgender (LGBT) organizations, including running a support group for LGBT caregivers of people with dementia.

C. Munro Cullum, Ph.D., ABPP/ABCN, is a board-certified clinical neuropsychologist and director of neuropsychology at the University of Texas Southwestern Medical Center, Dallas, where he is a professor of psychiatry and neurology, the chief of psychology, and holds the Pam Blumenthal Distinguished Professorship in Clinical Psychology. His primary interests are in the early detection, differential diagnosis, and characterization of neurocognitive functioning in dementia and normal aging. Additional interests include neuropsychological assessment of neuropsychiatric disorders in adults.

Colin A. Depp, Ph.D., is a postdoctoral fellow in geriatric psychiatry in the Advanced Center for Interventions and Services Research at the University of California–San Diego. He is a clinical geropsychologist, trained at the University of Louisville and the Palo Alto Veteran's Healthcare System.

Malcolm Dick, Ph.D., is a neuropsychologist with the Alzheimer's Disease Research Center and a project scientist at the Institute for Brain Aging and Dementia at the University of California–Irvine. He has published widely in neuropsychological assessment, especially with ethnic minority populations and is author of the Cross-Cultural Neuropsychological Test Battery (CCNB).

Cordula Dick-Muehlke, Ph.D., is the executive director of Adult Day Services of Orange County, California.

Peggye Dilworth-Anderson, Ph.D., is the director of the Center for Aging and Diversity at the Institute on Aging and professor of health policy and administration at the University of North Carolina–Chapel Hill. Her research interests include minority aging, family caregiving and aging, health disparities, dementia and caregiving, and long-term care. She has published extensively on caregiving among African American families.

Elizabeth S. Edgerly, Ph.D., is the chief program officer with the Northern California and Northern Nevada chapter of the Alzheimer's Association. She is a licensed clinical psychologist specializing in geropsychology and staffs the Medical Scientific Advisory Council of the Northern California Alzheimer's Association. Edgerly is the national spokesperson for the Alzheimer's Association Maintain Your Brain program, which focuses on implementing research about reducing the risk of Alzheimer's into practice.

Linda Gerdner, Ph.D., R.N., is an assistant professor at the University of Minnesota–Twin Cities School of Nursing and a fellow in ethnogeriatrics at the Stanford Geriatric Education Center at Stanford University in Palo Alto, California. Her research focuses on the perception and care of Hmong elders with chronic confusion and memory impairment (i.e., dementia) for the purpose of developing and evaluating culturally responsive family caregiver training programs. She received a grant (K01 NR008433) from the National Institute of Health/National Institute of Nursing Research (NIH/NINR) to support these efforts.

Brent E. Gibson, Ph.D., is an assistant professor in the School of Family Studies at the University of Connecticut–Storrs. His research focuses on the ways in which race, ethnicity, and culture influence family caregiving processes and outcomes. He is also interested in understanding how relationship quality (both past and present) between caregivers and care recipients affects people's experiences of caregiving.

Rita Hargrave, M.D., is a board-certified geriatric psychiatrist at the Martinez Veterans Administration Outpatient Clinic and an assistant professor of psychiatry at the University of California–Davis. Her research and publications focus on neuropsychiatric disorders in ethnic elders with dementia, caregiver issues in African American elders with dementia, affect recognition deficits in dementia, and cognitive deficits and depressive disorders among elders with hypertension and diabetes. She is a member of the Affiliated Core Faculty at Stanford Geriatric Education Center and co-chair of the American Board of Psychiatry and Neurology Committee for Geriatric Psychiatry Recertification.

Levanne Hendrix, Ph.D., G.N.P., is a nurse practitioner with Sunrise Homes. She has worked as a consultant with Indian Health Center of Santa Clara Valley, Inc., and conducted research with urban American Indian elders in San Jose, California. She is a member of the Affiliated Core Faculty at Stanford Geriatric Education Center. Her research interests include long-term care and American Indian aging.

Nancy Hikoyeda, Ph.D., is the director of the San Jose State University gerontology program and a member of the Affiliated Core Faculty of the Stanford Geriatric Education Center. Her areas of expertise include ethnogerontology and ethnogeriatrics. She has written and co-authored articles and chapters about Asian/Pacific Islander American Elders and their families. Her areas of interest include ethnicity and end-of-life issues, long-term care policy, and health literacy.

Ladson Hinton, M.D., is the Education Core director at the University of California–Davis Alzheimer's Disease Center and an associate professor in the department of psychiatry and behavioral sciences in the School of Medicine at the University of California–Davis. He received postdoctoral training in health services research and medical anthropology and is board certified in geriatric psychiatry. His research interests include cultural and ethnic variation in illness meanings and experience, family caregiving, help-seeking processes, and barriers to care. He has worked extensively with Latinos and Asian American populations.

Lori L. Jervis, Ph.D., is a medical anthropologist and an assistant professor of psychiatry in the American Indian and Alaska Native programs in the Health Sciences Center at the University of Colorado–Denver. Her research interests include the cultural phenomenology and assessment of cognitive impairment among American Indian elders, as well as cognitive, psychiatric, and behavioral disorders in nursing homes.

Daniel Jimenez, M.A., is a research associate in the Older Adult and Family Center at Stanford University and a graduate student at the Pacific Graduate School of Psychology, Palo Alto, California. His Cuban heritage has inspired him to focus on conducting research involving the health and well-being of elderly Latinas.

Laurie Leung, Ph.D., is a staff psychologist at Napa State Hospital, Napa, California. Her research and clinical interests include minority mental health and neuropsychological assessment.

Lan-Joun (Dora) Liou, M.S.W., M.A., is the supervisor of Senior Day Services and Social Services at Yu-Ai Kai, the Japanese American Community Senior Services organization in San Jose, California. Her responsibilities there include grant administration.

Weiling Liu is a clinical psychology Ph.D. student at the Pacific Graduate School of Psychology, Palo Alto, California. She works on research projects on caregiving for memory-impaired or demented family members of specific populations. Her clinical research interests include minority mental health, health psychology, and telemedicine.

Susan Long is interested in minority mental health and health care delivery, and crafting culturally sensitive outreach strategies for Asian Americans in mental health.

R. Scott Mackin, Ph.D., is a clinical neuropsychologist and an assistant professor of psychiatry at the University of California–San Francisco. His research focuses on the use of neuropsychological assessment in the differential diagnosis of dementia, identifying the cognitive sequelae of late-life depression, and evaluating the ecological validity of neuropsychological tests.

Spero M. Manson, Ph.D., (Pembina Chippewa), is a professor of psychiatry and the head of the American Indian and Alaska Native programs in the Health Sciences Center at the University of Colorado–Denver. Over the last 18 years, Manson and his colleagues have acquired a research portfolio in excess of $63 million, involving collaboration with over 102 Indian and Native communities. He has published 160 articles and chapters on the assessment, epidemiology, prevention, and treatment of alcohol, drug, mental, and physical health problems across the developmental life span of Indian and Native people.

Barbara Masterson, R.N., is the wellness coordinator at Yu-Ai Kai, the Japanese American Community Senior Services organization in San Jose, California. She is also co-facilitator of the Caregiver Support Group.

Melen McBride, Ph.D., R.N., is an associate director of Stanford Geriatric Education Center at Stanford University School of Medicine. She has written and lectured extensively on issues relating to Filipino elders in the United States and their health issues.

T.J. McCallum, Ph.D., is an assistant professor of psychology at Case Western Reserve University, Cleveland, Ohio. He is a clinical geropsychologist interested in assessing and improving mental health among older adults, cognitive behaviorally based stress reduction programs for the treatment of elder depression, and cognitive enhancement among older adults. His research focuses on the role of cultural beliefs in the stress and coping process and the impact of those beliefs on mental and physical health outcomes.

Julián Montoro-Rodriguez, Ph.D., is a social gerontologist interested in examining the interrelationships between formal and informal support systems and optimal adaptation and adjustment to developmental changes for older adults. His research focuses on issues relating to racial, ethnic, and cultural variations in the psychological experience of caregiving among family caregivers of dementia patients. He is interested in expanding theoretical models of service utilization to better understand the disparities in health service utilization of minority elders and their families.

Ailee Moon, Ph.D., is an associate professor in social welfare in the School of Public Affairs at the University of California–Los Angeles. She is active in gerontological research, particularly in the areas of elder abuse, mental health, service utilization, and dementia caregivers. She was a recipient of the John A. Hartford Foundation's Geriatric Social Work Faculty Scholar, funded to study cultural and noncultural factors in elder abuse assessment and intervention. She has published two books on Korean Americans and over 70 articles, book chapters, and research reports.

Wesley K. Mukoyama, L.C.S.W., is the executive director of Yu-Ai Kai, the Japanese American Community Senior Services organization in San Jose, California. He also serves as a co-facilitator of the Caregivers' Support Group, which meets weekly at Yu-Ai Kai.

Dan Mungas, Ph.D., is a professor in the department of neurology in the School of Medicine at the University of California–Davis and director of the University of California–Davis Alzheimer's Disease Center. His research on neuropsychological assessment has resulted in authorship of the Spanish and English Neuropsychological Assessment Scales (SENAS) and numerous publications.

Vyjeyanthi S. Periyakoil, M.D., is fellowship trained in both geriatrics and palliative care. She is a clinical assistant professor and a senior research scholar in the department of medicine at Stanford University School of Medicine. She serves as the associate medical director of Palo Alto Veterans Administration Hospice and Palliative Care Clinic and as the co-director of Stanford Geriatric Education Center. Her research interests are death with dignity in diverse ethnic populations and psychological states in terminal illness, and she has written numerous articles on Asian Indian elders in the United States.

Jeff A. Small, Ph.D., is an associate professor in the School of Audiology and Speech Sciences and a qualified health researcher in the recently established Centre for Research on Personhood in Dementia at the University of British Columbia, Vancouver. His research focuses on identifying language behaviors associated with a positive sense of self and with successful communication in interactions between persons with dementia and their caregivers. He recently developed a communication training program, Training in Communication Enhancement for Dementia (TRACED), for family caregivers of persons with dementia.

Theresa Sullivan, M.S., is the director of organizational development with the Alzheimer's Association, where she oversees the program operations of seven chapter offices in Northern California. She has worked in the field of caregiving and dementia for 20 years and was formerly the program director at Family Caregiver Alliance, where she was responsible for overseeing the Bay Area Caregiver Resource Center and the Ethnic Outreach Programs.

Father Hank Swift Cloud-LeBeau, M.Div., is a member of the Lakota/Sioux tribe and has served urban Indian congregations in San Jose,

California. He is a leader in the populations and a spokesperson for Indian issues.

Melissa Talamantes, M.S., is a gerontologist who teaches in the department of family and community medicine at the University of Texas Health Science Center–San Antonio. Her primary research interests, work experience, lecturing, and writing relate to caregiving, elder mistreatment, and end-of-life issues affecting Mexican American older adults and their families.

Evelyn L. Teng, Ph.D., is a professor in the department of neurology at Keck School of Medicine at the University of Southern California, Los Angeles. She is the primary author of the Cognitive Abilities Screening Instrument (CASI) and has worked and published extensively, using the CASI in diverse populations.

Hui-Qi Tong, M.D., is a psychiatrist in training from FuDan Medical School, Shanghai, People's Republic of China and a Ph.D. candidate in clinical psychology at the Pacific Graduate School of Psychology, Palo Alto, California.

Carolee Giao Uyen Tran, Ph.D., is an assistant clinical professor in the School of Medicine at the University of California–Davis. A native of Vietnam who immigrated to the United States with her family in 1975, she is a clinical psychologist with a private practice where she sees ethnically diverse elderly patients and their families. She has published on topics pertaining to Vietnamese refugees, including domestic violence and psychiatric illnesses.

Jane Nha Uyen Tran, M.S.W., is a social worker in the coordination of care/social services department with Kaiser Permanente in San Francisco. She worked on the research team studying Vietnamese family caregivers of dementia patients and has co-authored articles and chapters on Vietnamese elders in the United States.

Laura Trejo, M.S.G., M.P.A., is the general manager of the City of Los Angeles Department of Aging. She was one of the founders of *El Portal*, the pioneer program providing support services for Latino families struggling with dementia and has provided leadership and advocacy for aging services for diverse ethnic populations.

Peng Chih Wang, Ph.D., is a postdoctoral fellow at Stanford University School of Medicine/Palo Alto Veterans Administration Health Care System. His research interests include Chinese American caregiver stress and chronic illness management. His clinical interests include minority mental health and older adult depression and suicidal ideation.

Xa Xavier Xiong, B.A., D.C., M.D., is a resident at the Fox Valley Family Medicine Residency Program in Appleton, Wisconsin. He is committed to helping Hmong elders with mental health disabilities.

Deu Yang, L.P.N., is a dedicated advocate of health care issues for members of the Hmong community. She became a nurse in 1997, and, for the past 7 years, she has worked closely with elder Hmong and their family. Deu helped develop and implement the personal care assistant (PCA) program to help family care for elders at home.

Edie Yau, M.A., is the director of diversity for the Northern California and Northern Nevada chapter of the Alzheimer's Association. She oversees the multicultural outreach programs such as the Asian American Dementia Care Network, African American outreach, and Latino outreach programs in the Greater San Francisco Bay Area and provides education to volunteers, staff, and the board of the Alzheimer's Association on issues of diversity in the workplace.

Preface

During the Gerontological Society of America meetings in 2003, my colleague and coeditor Dolores Gallagher-Thompson told me, "We really need to do a second edition of *Ethnicity and the Dementias*. So much new information is available since we did it in 1996." And she was right. In every topic area, the current state of knowledge is substantially deeper than it was a decade ago when the original edition of this volume was developed.

This second edition, like the first, focuses primarily on populations in the United States. The first edition included a few chapters that are still relevant and have not been included in this second edition, for example, the chapter "Variations in Dementia Characteristics by Ethnic Category," the analysis of data from the California Alzheimer's Disease Diagnostic and Treatment Centers. This edition, likewise, not only updates all the chapters on assessment and working with families, but also adds new chapters summarizing the management of dementia and working with families, and on working with Hmong, Korean, Vietnamese, and lesbian, gay, bisexual, and transgender families from diverse ethnic populations. One section that is not included is an overview of the demographic projections for the growth of the older ethnic populations. We assume readers interested in ethnicity and dementia realize that older Americans are becoming increasingly diverse, and are aware that the elders from the four ethnic minority populations are projected to represent one third of all U.S. elders by mid-century.

We are extremely fortunate to have experienced researchers and clinicians from diverse disciplines and ethnic backgrounds as authors for this edition, reviewing the latest findings in each of their specialty areas. Their expertise will be obvious to the reader, and it is with pleasure that we present their work to you.

Gwen Yeo, Ph.D., AGSF

Stanford University
Stanford, California

PART I

Risk of Dementia

CHAPTER 1

Prevalence of Dementia Among Different Ethnic Populations

GWEN YEO

As background for the information in the chapters that follow, it is appropriate to review briefly the available English-language literature on the prevalence of dementia and its subtypes, with emphasis on the United States. As is the case with all topics included in this volume, available data on various populations have increased dramatically since they were reviewed in the first edition. Interpretation of this literature is difficult for many reasons; the most obvious reason is the lack of comparability between studies, because each uses different eligibility criteria, such as age, and different measures of dementia. Various screening instruments and various test batteries are used, some validated with the study populations and some not.

Because there are no national data sets on the prevalence of dementia in the United States or in other countries, available information comes from studies in individual communities. Readers will note the great inconsistencies in the amounts of available data related to individual populations. While some ethnic groups have many available data sets, others, such as most of the Asian subpopulations in the United States, are completely devoid of data on dementia prevalence.

International Comparisons

Suh and Shah (2001) suggested that there is a chronological progression of incidence and types of dementia as societies become more developed. They suggest that societies move from conditions of high mortality with low incidence of dementia to situations in which the mortality is still relatively high and there are more older people; therefore, there is more dementia, especially vascular dementia (VaD). In their third condition, the authors suggest that in more developed societies, mortality rates fall, and with the growing older populations comes somewhat higher incidence of Alzheimer's disease (AD) but decreased incidence of VaD, contributing to an overall lower incidence. Some confirmatory evidence exists, such as a slight reduction in the higher VaD rates in Japan since the 1980s (White et al., 1996), but because little or no data exist on rates of dementia in many societies, the theory is difficult to confirm.

A few published studies include international comparisons using the same methodologies. One is the comparison between self-identified African Americans in Indianapolis and Yoruba elders from Ibidan, Nigeria (Hendrie et al., 1995, 2001). The age standardized prevalence rates of all dementias for people 65 years of age and over was 2.29% (1.41% for AD) for the Ibidan sample and 8.24% (6.24% for AD) for African Americans in Indianapolis, including those residing in nursing homes.

The Indo–U.S. Cross-National Dementia Epidemiology Study compared the frequency of dementia in rural areas in India and Pennsylvania. Using a 0.5 cutoff on the Clinical Dementia Rating Scale, in Ballabargh, India, 1.36% of adults aged 65 and over had any of the dementias (1.07% with AD); in Pennsylvania, 14.9% of those 65 and over had dementia (13.0% with AD) (Chandra et al., 1998; Ganguli et al., 2000).

Prevalence in North America

Table 1.1 summarizes prevalence data from available well-designed population-based studies of ethnic populations in the United States from 1990. A large number of studies compared dementia rates in African Americans with non-Latino/Hispanic Whites, and most, but not all, found that African Americans have higher rates of AD. In most studies, significantly higher rates of VaD were found among African Americans. This is an important finding, because the risk of VaD can be substantially reduced by controlling blood pressure and other cardiovascular risk factors.

Two carefully designed studies explored the rates of dementia in Hispanic/Latino populations. Researchers conducting a New York City study found that Dominican and Puerto Rican elders had higher rates of AD than non-Hispanic Whites (Gurland et al., 1999). From the Sacramento Area Latino Study on Aging (SALSA), rates of dementia among the largely Mexican American sample were reported to be roughly the same as those reported in studies of non-Latino Whites. Major risk factors for dementia in the SALSA study were stroke and diabetes (Haan et al., 2003). In a study of east coast and west coast AD centers, researchers found that Latinos who have AD have significantly earlier onset of the disease than do non-Hispanic Whites (Clark et al., 2005).

The only data on any Asian or Pacific Island population in the United States are from two studies of older Japanese Americans. In both the Seattle and the longitudinal study of Japanese men in Hawaii, rates of AD were found to be in the same range as other studies of Whites, but the rates of VaD were much higher in Hawaii (Graves et al., 1996; White et al., 1996). Earlier studies in Japan and some other Asian countries also found higher rates of VaD (Larson & Imai, 1996).

There are no large-scale studies of prevalence in American Indian populations, but one study with a very small sample in the Cree nation in Manitoba, Canada, found a much lower prevalence of AD but a similar overall rate of dementia compared to a nearby English-speaking community (Hendrie et al., 1993).

There has been considerable interest in the role of Apolipoprotein E (APOE) as a possible genetic explanation for differences in AD between groups. So far, the findings indicate the following:

1. The frequency of the APOE4 allele that has been found to increase the risk of AD may vary in different ethnic populations. For example, there is some indication that American Indians have fewer APOE4 alleles (Henderson et al., 2002), but this has yet to be confirmed in a major study.
2. Compared to non-Hispanic Whites, the link between APOE4 and AD is weaker in African Americans, stronger in Japanese, and possibly weaker among Latinos, but the evidence is mixed (Manly & Mayeux, 2004).

Less education has consistently been recognized as a risk factor for AD. In several studies, if differences in education levels were controlled, differences in rates of AD or total dementia among ethnic populations were reduced or disappeared altogether (Gurland et al., 1999). Literacy levels and quality of education are now being recognized as even more important factors than total years of education in explaining ethnic differences (Manly & Mayeux, 2004).

Table 1.1. Prevalence of Dementia in Studies with Ethnic Minority Populations in the United States

Population/Location	Ages	Alzheimer's Disease	Vascular Dementia	Total Dementia	Nh?[a]	Non-latino Whites[c] Total Dementia	Source
African American							
Indianapolis, IN	65+	6.2%[b]		8.2%[b]	Yes		Hendrie et al., 1995
Manhattan, NY	65–74			9.1%	Yes	2.9%	Gurland et al., 1999
	75–84			19.9%		10.9%	
	85+			58.6%		30.2%	
Piedmont Area, NC	68+			7.0%	No	7.2%	Fillenbaum et al., 1998
Piedmont Area, NC	65+			16.0%	No	3.05%	Heyman et al., 1991
East Baltimore, MD[e]	65+	3.9%	2.7%	7.2%	No	3.8%	Folstein et al. 1991

	Age	Men[b]	Women[b]	Total	Nursing home[a]	Comparative[c]	Reference
Asian American							
Japanese American men, HI	71+	5.4% (4.7%)[b]	4.2% (3.8%)[b]	9.3% (7.6%)[b]	Yes		White et al., 1996
Japanese American, King County, WA	65+	4.46%	1.85%	6.3%	Yes		Graves et al., 1996
Latino/Hispanic							
Dominican[d] and Puerto Rican, Manhattan, NY	65–74 75–84 85+			7.5% 27.9% 62.9%	Yes	2.9% 10.9% 30.2%	Gurland et al., 1999
Mexican American,[d] Sacramento Area, CA	60+			4.8%	N/A		Haan et al., 2003

[a] Does the study include nursing home/institutionalized populations?
[b] Age standardized prevalence rate.
[c] Prevalence in non-Hispanic White population if the study includes comparative data.
[d] Ethnic background of majority of subjects.
[e] Population identified as "non-White" but generally interpreted to be African American.

There are many questions about ethnic differences in dementia prevalence that have yet to be explored, such as the great variability found in some countries with relatively homogenous populations (e.g., Korea) (data not presented here) and if the dramatically lower rates among less-developed societies such as Nigeria and rural India are due only to differential survival rates. In the United States, there is a crucial need to know the status of dementia in populations for which we have no data at all, such as Asian Americans other than Japanese as well as American Indians.

References

Chandra, V., Ganguli, M., Pandav, R., Johnston, J., Belle, S., & DeKosky, S. T. (1998). Prevalence of Alzheimer's disease and other dementias in rural India: The Indo–U.S. study. *Neurology, 51,* 1000–1008.

Clark, C. M., DeCarli, C., Mungas, D., Chui, H., Higdon, R., Nuñez R. et al. (2005). Earlier onset of Alzheimer Disease symptoms in Latino individuals compared with Anglo individuals. *Archives of Neurology, 62,* 774–778.

Fillenbaum, G. G., Heyman, A., Huber, M. S., Woodbury, M. A., Leiss, J., Schmader, K. E. et al. (1998). The prevalence and 3-year incidence of dementia in older black and white community residents. *Journal of Clinical Epidemiology, 51,* 587–595.

Folstein, M. F., Bassett, S. S., Anthony, J. C., Romanoski, A. J., & Nestadt, G. R. (1991). Dementia: Case ascertainment in a community survey. *Journal of Gerontology: Medical Sciences, 46,* M132–M138.

Ganguli, M., Chandra, V., Kamboh, M. I., Johnston, J. M., Dodge, H. H., Thelma, B. K. et al. (2000). Apolipoprotein E polymorphism and Alzheimer disease: The Indo–U.S. cross-national dementia study. *Archives of Neurology, 57,* 824–830.

Graves, A. B., Larson, E. B., Edland, S. D., Bowen, J. D., McCormick, W. C., McCurry, S. M. et al. (1996). Prevalence of dementia and its subtypes in the Japanese American population of King County, Washington state. The Kame Project. *American Journal of Epidemiology, 144,* 760–771.

Gurland, B. J., Wilder, D. E., Lantigua, R., Stern, Y., Chen, J., Killeffer, E. H. P. et al. (1999). Rates of dementia in three ethnoracial groups. *International Journal of Geriatric Psychiatry, 14,* 481–493.

Haan, M. H., Mungas, D. M., Gonzalez, H. M., Ortiz, T. A., Acharya, A., & Jagust, W. J. (2003). Prevalence of dementia in older Latinos: The influence of Type 2 Diabetes Mellitus, stroke, and genetic factors. *Journal of American Geriatrics Society, 51,* 169–177.

Henderson, J. N., Crook, R., Crook, J., Hardy, J., Onstead., L., Carson-Henderson, L. et al. (2002). Apolipoprotein E4 and tau allele frequencies among Choctaw Indians. *Neuroscience Letters, 324,* 77–79.

Hendrie, H. C., Hall, K. S., Pillay, N., Rodgers, D., Prince, C., Norton, J. et al. (1993). Alzheimer's disease is rare in Cree. *International Psychogeriatrics, 5,* 5–14.

Hendrie, H. C., Ogunniyi, A., Hall, K. S., Baiyewu, O., Unverzagt, F. W., Gureje, O. et al. (2001). Incidence of dementia and Alzheimer's disease in 2 communities: Yoruba residing in Ibadan, Nigeria, and African Americans residing in Indianapolis, Indiana. *Journal of the American Medical Association, 285,* 739–747.

Hendrie, H. C., Osuntokun, B. O., Hall, K. S., Ogunniyi, A., Hui, S. L., Unverzagt, F. W. et al. (1995). Prevalence of Alzheimer's disease and dementia in two communities: Nigerian Africans and African Americans. *American Journal of Psychiatry, 152,* 1485–1492.

Heyman, A., Fillenbaum, G., Prosnitz, B., Raiford, K., Burchett, B., & Clark, C. (1991). Estimated prevalence of dementia among elderly black and white community residents. *Archives of Neurology, 48,* 594–598.

Larson, E. B., & Imai, Y. (1996). An overview of dementia and ethnicity with special emphasis on the epidemiology of dementia. In G. Yeo & D. Gallagher-Thompson (Eds.), *Ethnicity and the dementias.* Washington, DC: Taylor & Francis.

Manly, J. J., & Mayeux, R. (2004). Ethnic differences in dementia and Alzheimer's disease. In N. B. Anderson, R. A. Bulatao, & B. Cohen (Eds.), *Critical perspectives on racial and ethnic differences in health in late life.* Washington, DC: National Academies Press.

Suh, G. -H., & Shah, A. (2001). A review of the epidemiological transitions in dementia—cross-national comparisons of the indices related to Alzheimer's disease and vascular dementia. *Acta Psychiatrica Scandinavica, 104,* 4–11.

White, L., Petrovitch, H., Ross, G. W., Masaki, K. H., Abbott, R. D., Teng, E. L. et al. (1996). Prevalence of dementia in older Japanese-American in Hawaii: the Honolulu-Asia aging study. *Journal of the American Medical Association, 276,* 955–960.

PART II

Assessment of Dementia in Diverse Populations

CHAPTER 2

Overview of Psychiatric Assessment with Dementia Patients

R. SCOTT MACKIN, COLIN DEPP, PATRICIA AREÁN, AND DILIP JESTE

Anna is a 64-year-old Latina spousal caregiver for her husband, Hector, who has shown signs of Alzheimer's disease for approximately four years. With help from their four children, she provides care for her husband, whose functioning and mental status has deteriorated to the extent that he needs prompting and assistance with bathing. During a routine appointment with Hector, Anna bursts into tears, describing an incident when her husband grabbed her hair while she was helping to bathe him. Anna complained that Hector's personality was "becoming strange" and different from the way he used to be, a vibrant and amiable person who never became violent. According to Anna, her husband appeared to reach for things that were not there and often arose in the middle of the night to wander the house. Although adamant about her and her family's desire to retain Hector in the home, Anna was confused and highly distressed by his personality changes and wondered if they were going to become worse.[1]

It is estimated from population studies that up to 80 to 90% of older people with dementia manifest one or more psychiatric symptoms (Lyketsos et al.,

2002; Sink, Covinsky, Newcomer, & Yaffe, 2004), which commonly include symptoms of depression (Gilley, Wilson, Bienias, Bennett, & Evans, 2004; Verdelho, Henon, Lebert, Pasquier, & Leys, 2004), anxiety (Teri et al., 1999), agitation (Senanarong et al., 2004), delusions and hallucinations (Bassiony & Lyketsos, 2003), and aberrant motor behavior (Steinberg et al., 2003). The progression of these symptoms is variable; however, it is apparent that some symptoms can be transient while others may be persistent. Further, these symptoms can be intertwined, such that depression may increase the risk of aggression, and vice versa. These psychiatric symptoms have serious effects on patients, including reduced quality of life (Novella et al., 2001), increased nursing home placements (Chan, Kasper, Black, & Rabins, 2003), greater disability (Forsell & Winblad, 1998; Griffiths et al., 1987), and higher rates of morbidity from medical illness and suicide (Arfken, Lichtenberg, & Tancer, 1999; Bruce et al., 2004; Gallo & Lebowitz, 1999; Hughes, Ross, Mindham, & Spokes, 2004; Katz, Striem, & Parmelee, 1994; Teri et al., 1999). Psychiatric symptoms have also been shown to negatively affect caregivers of patients with dementia (Garre-Olmo et al., 2002; Pang et al., 2002) and are commonly linked to caregiver depression and distress (Danhauer et al., 2004; Drinka, Smith, & Drinka, 1987).

Although results of some studies have led some to suggest that the prevalence of psychiatric diagnoses differs among ethnic groups for individuals with Alzheimer's disease (Iwata, Turner, & Lloyd, 2002), among older adults without dementia (Ayalon & Young, 2003; Myers et al., 2002), and across other age groups (Brown, Schulberg, & Madonia, 1996; Flaskerud & Hu, 1992; Jones & Gray, 1986; Strakowski et al., 1995; Strakowski, McElroy, Keck, & West, 1996; Strakowski, Shelton, & Kolbrener, 1993), there is no consistent indication as to which psychiatric symptoms are more frequent among ethnic minorities with dementia. Furthermore, observed differences in the prevalence of symptoms may be attributable to a variety of factors, including cultural differences in the presentation and reporting of psychiatric illness, communication barriers, diagnostician bias, genetic factors, and heterogeneity in risk factors, socioeconomic status, and education (Adebimpe, 1981; Baker, 2001; Bell & Mehta, 1980, 1981; Fabrega et al., 1994; Mukherjee, Shukla, Woodle, Rosen, & Olarte, 1983; Steffens, Artigues, Ornstein, & Krishnan, 1997; Strakowski et al., 1996). The degree to which psychiatric assessment procedures moderate proposed ethnic differences in patients with dementia is particularly relevant for further study.

The purpose of this chapter is to discuss a strategy for assessing psychiatric symptoms in patients with dementia. Specifically, we will describe how to conduct a clinical interview with patients and their families, summarize information to be derived from these interviews, rule out reversible causes of psychiatric symptoms, and work with interpreters. Additionally, a brief review of some structured behavioral rating scales that have been found to be helpful in determining the severity of psychiatric symptoms will be provided.

A Strategy for the Assessment of Psychiatric Symptoms

Our approach to assessing psychiatric symptoms in patients with dementia is standard in most geriatric psychiatry assessment units. The assessment typically involves a review of recent medical evaluations, an interview with the identified patient, and a separate interview with a caregiver. The interviews generally take place either in a psychiatry clinic or at the identified patient's residence. We prefer to assess the patient in his or her milieu, as the potential for observing problematic behavior is more likely in that setting, and the assessor can get a better sense of patient strengths and weaknesses, because patients with dementia often act differently in the home than they do in unfamiliar settings.

Medical Causes of Psychiatric Symptoms

One of the most important pieces of information to evaluate is whether or not the psychiatric symptoms are caused or exacerbated by medical comorbidities. Simply by virtue of their age, patients with dementia are vulnerable to medical illnesses that can also cause psychiatric symptoms. As is the case in all dementia evaluations, when conducting psychiatric interviews with patients with dementia, it is important to rule out potentially reversible causes that, in themselves, may be causing or contributing to the psychiatric symptoms. When these medical conditions are properly treated, psychiatric symptoms typically dissipate. For instance, many causes of reversible dementia have been linked to the manifestation of psychiatric symptoms, including hypothyroidism (Davis, 1989; Haberfellner, Rittmannsberger, & Windhager, 1993; Heinrich & Grahm, 2003), vitamin B_{12} deficiency (Durand, Mary, Brazo, & Dollfus, 2003; Hector & Burton, 1988; Petrie & Ban, 1985), medication effects, neurosyphilis (Kohler, Pickholtz, & Ballas, 2000; Rundell & Wise, 1985), and normal pressure hydrocephalus (Lying-Tunell, 1979; Pinner, Johnson, Bouman, & Isaacs, 1997). Furthermore, physical functioning may heavily influence psychiatric symptoms. For example, apathy or aggression may arise from bodily pain, sleep disorders, or sensory limitations, all of which can be difficult to detect in a noncommunicative patient. A thorough medical evaluation should be done in all cases of new-onset psychiatric symptoms in order to facilitate management of these symptoms.

Assessing Caregiver Safety

Another important piece of information to obtain in the course of the initial assessment is to determine if the environment is safe for the patient and the caregiver. Patients with dementia, particularly those with greater cognitive impairment, can exhibit agitation or aggressive behavior that can be dangerous to themselves or others, in addition to unsafe behaviors related to cognitive decline. In any caregiving situation, it is incumbent on the clinician to assess for the presence of safety risks to determine if interaction with adult protective services (APS) or other external support services is warranted.

In the event that the environment is not safe for the patient or caregiver, and a referral to either APS or to an assisted-living facility is warranted, it is important to convey this information very carefully to the family and patient. This is particularly true when working with ethnic minorities, as they may be more likely to distrust providers (Miranda, Lawson, & Escobar, 2002). Therefore, an explanation about how APS works and an open discussion regarding the circumstances under which a referral could occur will be most useful to family members in the event that community service intervention appears to be necessary. Given the possibility of this type of reporting, adherence to standard practice of explaining the limits of confidentiality and the legal mandates for providers is underscored.

Suggestion to place an individual in an assisted-living facility can also be met with resistance from minority group members, often due to cultural beliefs about the importance of retaining family members in the home (Stevens et al., 2004; Yaffe et al., 2002). As such, these suggestions should be prefaced by explaining safety issues, with an open discussion of the various levels of care that exist and the pros and cons of each of these levels of care. Oftentimes, a motivational interviewing approach, much like those used in substance abuse, can be helpful in this regard. This approach involves allowing the caregiver time to consider the information, being available to discuss concerns in an atmosphere that promotes caregiver choice, and permitting the caregiver to "set the pace" of the intervention.

Preparing the Patient and Caregiver for the Interview

Few specific guidelines are available on how the assessment of psychiatric symptoms should be adapted for ethnically diverse patients and their caregivers. For the clinician, information regarding background knowledge of the cultural influences on the patient and caregiver, such as described in this volume and in the online "diversity toolkit" provided by the Alzheimer's Association (www.alz.org), can be helpful in assessing the cultural significance of psychiatric symptoms and subsequently determining the contributors to these symptoms.

The most effective way to gather information about psychiatric symptoms of a patient with dementia is to conduct a clinical interview that involves both open-ended questions and structured assessment tools with both the patient and the caregiver. We first discuss the types of open-ended questions to be asked, followed by briefly reviewing useful standardized measures.

Open-Ended Interview

For most patients, and ethnic minorities in particular, it is generally useful to begin the interview with a discussion of the purpose, how the interview will be conducted (a combination of open-ended questions and structured assessments), and how the information will be integrated to facilitate decision making regarding the management of psychiatric symptoms.

We often start our interviews by asking either the patient or caregiver (whoever is in the best position to offer information) about the problematic symptoms, which includes obtaining a detailed description of symptoms, severity and onset, and if specific antecedents or patterns have been identified. It is important to establish antecedents of psychiatric symptoms, as they can significantly affect treatment or care. As an example, the third author saw an 86-year-old Japanese American man who was brought in by his daughter because he was having visual hallucinations. Particularly striking about this case was the fact that the patient was blind. The patient had been diagnosed with Lewy-body dementia 2 years prior; however, the hallucinations were becoming more detailed and increasingly more intense and frightening. In addition, the man was exhibiting greater anxious symptomatology. Upon ascertaining the potential antecedents to these symptoms, which included an advancing underlying dementing illness, it was determined that his anxiety had also worsened significantly after the death of his wife. While the team was aware that the hallucinations were most likely due to the dementing process, it is also likely that the sudden change in anxiety was due to the death of his wife and his feelings of isolation and confusion now that he was alone in the home for periods of time without someone to provide structure. Placement in an assisted-living facility, coupled with pharmacotherapy, significantly reduced the severity of the patient's anxiety.

The clinical information to be gathered in a psychiatric interview with ethnic minority patients with dementia is similar to that gathered in traditional interviews; however, special care must be taken to clarify the meaning of symptom reports. Take, for instance, the Latino culture. It is often difficult to differentiate anxiety from depression among many Latinos, because in this culture, the term *nervios* (nerves) can apply to both depression and anxiety. Other ethnic differences in the manifestation of psychiatric symptoms have commonly been reported (Ayalon & Young, 2003; Iwata et al., 2002; Myers et al., 2002). More research in this area is clearly needed, but clinicians should be aware of possible ethnic group differences in reporting psychiatric symptoms that may influence diagnosis and should clarify with the patient or caregiver in the event that there is uncertainty.

Beyond history regarding psychiatric symptoms, information regarding patients' past educational and employment histories, where they grew up and their acculturation level, personal and family histories of psychiatric and substance use disorders, and when they were first diagnosed with dementia, is also helpful. Medical information is also obtained, as is the ability to perform activities of daily living. Any recent changes in medication and diet are also determined. Following the completion of open-ended questions, standardized measures of psychiatric status are administered.

Standardized Rating Scales for Psychiatric Symptoms

Rating scales can be particularly useful in delineating the specific behaviors and their impact on the caregiver, ensuring that important symptoms are asked about and allowing for comparison to normative samples. Furthermore, they can be extremely useful in differential diagnosis and to assess change in response to treatment over time (Forester & Oxman, 2003). A number of brief standardized scales for the assessment of psychiatric symptoms of dementia exist (see Table 2.1). Many of these scales have been translated in other languages and assessed for their reliability in culturally diverse patients with dementia.

These scales are typically administered to an informant, in either a self-report, structured, or semistructured interview format, because patients with diminished insight or memory problems can be poor historians of psychiatric problems. The use of informant rating scales can also provide a more accurate rating of symptoms than clinician-rated scales, such as the Brief Psychiatric Rating Scale (Overall & Gorham, 1962), that require that the behaviors in question occur in the presence of the clinician, which may not be realistic (e.g., nighttime wandering).

Some scales target specific symptoms (e.g., depression), while others encompass multiple domains. Some scales include measures of caregiver distress in relation to specific or global symptoms. Further, these scales differ in the duration of time to administer, number of items, and responsivity to changes. Therefore, it is essential that the clinician become aware of the properties and purposes of the instrument as they relate to the circumstances of the evaluation and the normative data available in ethnic

Table 2.1 Selected Scales for Assessing Neuropsychiatric Symptoms of Dementia

Scale	Administration Format and Time Required	Number of Items	Domains Assessed	Selected Studies Examining Psychometric Properties in Other languages
Neuropsychiatric Inventory (NPI)	Caregiver report or clinician interview (10 min)	12	Delusions, hallucinations, agitation/aggression, depression/dysphoria, anxiety, elation/euphoria, apathy/indifference, disinhibition, irritability/lability, nighttime disturbances, eating, motor disturbance	Spanish: Vilalta-Franch et al. (1999), Hinton et al. (1999); Chinese: Leung et al. (2001); Tawainese: Fuh et al. (2001); Korean: Choi et al. (2000)
Behavioral Pathology in Alzheimer's Disease Rating Scale (BEHAVE-AD)	Clinician interview (20 min)	26	Delusions and hallucinations, activity disturbances, aggression, diurnal variation, and mood disturbances	Spanish: Harwood et al. (2001); Chinese: Leung et al. (2001); Korean: Suh & Son (2001)
Revised Memory and Behavior Problems Checklist (RMBPC)	Caregiver report (20 min)	24	Memory problems, disruptive behavior, depression	Spanish: Harwood et al. (2001); Chinese: Fuh et al. (1999)
Cohen-Mansfield Agitation Inventory (CMAI)	Caregiver report (15 min)	29	Wandering, aggression, verbal disruptiveness, hoarding, and negativism	Chinese: Choy et al. (2001); Korean: Suh (2004)
Center for Epidemiological Studies Depression Scale (CES-D)	Self-report (5–10 min)	20	Well-being and dysphoria	www.rcmar.ucla.edu/mmreflist_cesd.phplanguages
Geriatric Depression Scale (GDS)	Self-report (5–10 min)	15 for the short version; 30 for the long version	Dysphoric mood, withdrawal–apathy–vigor, hopelessness, cognitive symptoms, and anxiety	www.stanford.edu/~yesavage/GDS.html

groups. Perhaps even more importantly, although these instruments have been translated into other languages, they often need to be administered and interpreted by an individual who is fluent in that language. Selected instruments and their properties in ethnic groups and different languages are described next.

Neuropsychiatric Inventory The Neuropsychiatric Inventory (NPI; Cummings, 1997) is a semistructured interview for use with the caregiver to rate the severity and frequency of 10 neuropsychiatric symptoms during the past month (delusions, hallucinations, agitation/aggression, depression/dysphoria, anxiety, elation/euphoria, apathy/indifference, disinhibition, irritability/lability, nighttime disturbances, eating, motor disturbance). This instrument takes about 10 min to administer. Caregivers also describe their own distress in relation to these symptoms. The content and concurrent validity, as well as between-rater, test–retest, and internal consistency reliability have been reported in English-language settings, showing the instrument to be valid and reliable (Cummings et al., 1994).

A Spanish version of the NPI was validated in Spain (Vilalta-Franch et al., 1999) and further validated among Mexican American respondents (Hinton, Haan, Geller, & Mungas, 2003). A Spanish self-report version of this scale (NPI-Q) has also shown good psychometric properties and convergence with the interviewer version (Boada, Cejudo, Tarraga, Lopez, & Kaufer, 2002). The Chinese version of the NPI (the CNPI) shows high internal validity among 62 patients with dementia (Leung, Lam, Chiu, Cummings, & Chen, 2001) in China, as well as among 95 Taiwanese patients with Alzheimer's disease (Fuh, Liu, Mega, Wang, & Cummings, 2001). A Korean version has also been developed using a sample of 141 patients with mixed dementias (Choi et al., 2000), showing high test–retest reliability and similar frequency of symptoms to the original NPI validation study (Cummings, 1996).

Behavioral Pathology in Alzheimer's Disease Rating Scale The Behavioral Pathology in Alzheimer's Disease (BEHAVE-AD) scale (Reisberg & Franssen, 1989) was developed to be used in prospective clinical trials of medications to treat behavioral symptoms of Alzheimer's disease. The BEHAVE-AD takes about 20 min to administer by a clinician. Twenty-five symptoms are assessed, under domains including delusions and hallucinations, activity disturbances, aggression, diurnal variation, and mood disturbances. This scale is available in a Spanish version (Harwood et al., 2001) and a Korean version (Suh & Son, 2001), although specific reliability and validity information for these versions could not be located.

Revised Memory and Behavior Problem Checklist For the Resources for Enhancing Caregiver Health (REACH) study, the Revised Memory and Behavior Problems Checklist (RMBPC) was translated and backtranslated into Spanish (Wisniewski et al., 2003). This scale contains 24 items asking about the frequency of specific behaviors over the past week, including memory, disruptive behavior, and depression. The caregiver is then asked to rate his or her degree of distress in relation to each symptom. In the validation study of this instrument (Teri, 1997), the reported alphas were .84 and .90, and subscale alphas ranged from .67 to .89, using a sample of 201 caregivers. In light of its usage in the REACH project, the RMBPC is among the best-validated instruments in the Spanish language. A report of the use of this instrument in a Taiwanese sample is also available (Fuh et al., 2001).

A separate, Spanish-language, briefer version of the RMBPC was devised (Harwood et al., 2001). This scale includes the Depression (nine items) and Disruption (eight items) scales of the original instrument and omits the Memory Problems section, in order to focus on behavioral pathology. This measure was backtranslated and tested on a sample of 27 caregiver-patient dyads. Greater reliability was found for the Depression subscale (Cronbach's alpha = 0.87) than the Disruption subscale (Cronbach's alpha = 0.60).

Cohen-Mansfield Agitation Inventory Agitation and behaviors associated with more severe dementia can be assessed with the Cohen-Mansfield Agitation Inventory (CMAI; Cohen-Mansfield & Billig, 1986). Twenty-nine different agitated behaviors in patients with dementia are queried, taking 10–15 min. This scale is the most common observer-rated scale of agitation, is frequently used for patients in institutions, and shows high test–retest reliability (Koss et al., 1997). Specific behaviors include wandering, aggression, verbal disruptiveness, hoarding, and negativism. A Korean version is available, the CMAI-K (Suh, 2004), that was validated among 257 institutionalized Korean patients with dementia and showed good reliability (Cronbach's alpha = 0.88) and concurrent validity with the Korean BEHAVE-AD scale. A Chinese version was validated among 164 patients with dementia, although this measure was shown to have differing psychometric properties among residential and institutionalized patients (Choy, Lam, Chan, Li, & Chiu, 2001).

Depressive Symptoms

Among patients with mild cognitive impairment or early-stage dementia, depressive symptoms are perhaps the most common psychiatric symptom encountered. Clinician-rated measures of depression in dementia include the Cornell Scale for Depression in Dementia (CSDD; Alexopoulos, Abrams, Young, & Shamoian, 1988) and the Montgomery Asberg Depression Rating Scale (MADRS; Montgomery & Asberg, 1979). The CSDD is a 19-item instrument with a maximum score of 38 points. A cutoff score of 7 or greater has been used to discriminate depression among patients with Alzheimer's disease. Although the overall factor structure of the Spanish CSDD is similar, reduced loadings of the physical complaint item were found (Ownby, Harwood, Acevedo, Barker, & Duara, 2001). The MADRS has become a popular clinician-rated instrument for the assessment of depression in dementia, yet we identified few indications of its reliability or validity in mixed ethnicity samples.

Two of the most commonly used self-report instruments to measure depression in older people are the Center for Epidemiological Studies Depression Scale (CESD; 20 items; Radloff, 1977) and the Geriatric Depression Scale (GDS; Yesavage et al., 1982). Both of these instruments were used in the REACH studies and are available in many different languages (CESD: www.rcmar.ucla.edu/ mmreflist_cesd.phplanguages; GDS: www.stanford.edu/~yesavage/GDS.html). Note that even though these self-report measures are carefully translated, it is important to gauge the literacy level of caregivers, particularly those who are older and less acculturated, prior to interpreting scores.

The Use of Interpreters

At times, situations will arise in which neither the patient nor the caregiver can speak the language of the provider and an interpreter is needed. Despite the extensive literature on procedures to be utilized in translating psychiatric measures of use with different ethnic groups (Alegria et al., 2004; Knudsen et al., 2000; Matias-Carrelo et al., 2003; Rubio-Stipec, Bird, Canino, & Gould, 1990; Serrano-Duenas, Martinez-Martin, & Vaca-Baquero, 2004; Verhey et al., 2004), there is a paucity of research focusing on the use of interpreters while conducting psychiatric interviews with patients with dementia. The use of interpreters with these patients is, nonetheless, quite common despite evidence to suggest that psychiatric interviews conducted in this way may obscure clinically relevant information (Marcos, 1979; Sabin, 1975). Common problems in using an interpreter are the tendency for an interpreter to translate the interviewer's question and the patient's answer inaccurately and to edit the information relayed by the patient.

Given the frequent necessity of using an interpreter to conduct psychiatric interviews with patients with dementia, and the evidence to suggest that these types of interviews may obscure clinically meaningful information, clinicians should attempt to minimize threats to the validity of these assessments through careful consideration of several issues. These issues include properly selecting an interpreter, preparing the interpreter and patient with dementia for the psychiatric interview, considering the advantages and disadvantages of using a family member as a translator, and structuring the physical environment for the interview.

Choosing an Interpreter   Whenever possible, a trained medical interpreter should be selected not only on the basis of the languages that he or she speaks but also on his or her training in clinical methods (Kapborga & Bertero, 2002; Phelan & Parkman, 1995). Using an interpreter who understands the rationale behind asking questions as the clinician poses them and the importance of communicating responses as given by the patient reduces the possibility that they may interject information that would alter a patient's responses, or paraphrase a response in such a way as to lose important clinical details. This is particularly true when conducting psychiatric interviews with patients with psychotic symptoms or patients with dementia. In these cases, one should inform the interpreter that the patient's report may not make sense (Phelan & Parkman, 1995) and instruct the interpreter not to attempt to normalize or condense (Farooq & Fear, 2003) the patient's report, as that could obscure clinically relevant material. Clinicians should ask patients to clarify responses and ask for word-by-word translation if necessary to clarify meaning, and they should meet with translators after the assessment for feedback and for the opportunity to clarify responses (Farooq & Fear, 2003).

Pros and Cons of Using Families to Translate   For cases for which a trained interpreter cannot be utilized, family members may be suitable to serve as translators. While there are several advantages to this type of situation (e.g., family members typically know the patient well, are trusted by the patient, and are motivated to help the patient), there are also several potential limitations that can arise. First, the examiner should be aware that family members might be prone to unknowingly distort a patient's responses when their impressions, values, or opinions become part of the translation. This may be particularly relevant when working with populations in which family members may have concerns about the patient being identified as mentally ill or fear of the mental health system (Alvidrez, Azocar, & Miranda, 1996). Second, it should not always be assumed that a patient would feel comfortable discussing problems, particularly psychiatric symptoms, with family members present. Last, family members may attempt to minimize the patient's symptoms in an effort to present the patient in the most socially desirable manner, even if this contradicts the purpose of the evaluation. It is especially important to avoid using young children as interpreters, because they are less likely to be familiar with much of the vocabulary needed for this task (in one or both languages), and they may be distressed by the experience.

Preparing the Interpreter and Patient for the Interview To prepare an interpreter for the psychiatric interview, the clinician should provide him or her with an overview of the purpose of the evaluation, topic areas that will likely be covered, and how long the interview will last (Phelan & Parkman, 1995). The interpreter should be informed that the patient may have cognitive impairments that could affect his or her speech or thought process in order to stress the importance of the need to report exactly what the patient says instead of adding, condensing, omitting, or normalizing a patient's responses (Farooq & Fear, 2003). These cautions are particularly relevant when working with family members. After the translator is prepared in this manner, he or she should be encouraged to point out any potential culturally sensitive factors that may have been proposed for the interview (Phelan & Parkman, 1995). In closing, the confidentiality of the interview should be stressed to the interpreter. To prepare the patient for the interview, it is equally important to clearly identify the interpreter's role for the patient, which includes describing the purpose of the interpreter and explaining confidentiality of information (Phelan & Parkman, 1995). If possible, this should be done prior to, or immediately after, the introduction of the interpreter, aided by a family member for interpretation, if necessary. Because patients with dementia may lack the cognitive capacity to understand the purpose of the interpreter, clinicians should pay close attention to any behavioral signs that may indicate discomfort regarding the presence of the interpreter. If the patient appears to be uncomfortable in the presence of the interpreter, attempts to reassure the patient should be undertaken before the interview begins.

Preparing the Environment for the Interview During the interview, there are several steps that a clinician should undertake to minimize potential difficulty arising from the translation. First, a clinician should utilize simple language and avoid using jargon or technical words (Farooq & Fear, 2003). A clinician should talk directly to the patient and not address the interpreter. To facilitate this, the clinician should sit directly across from the patient in order to maintain eye contact with the patient, with the interpreter sitting to one side (Farooq & Fear, 2003; Phelan & Parkman, 1995).

Putting the Information Together

When synthesizing information obtained in a psychiatric interview with ethnically diverse patients with dementia, clinicians often must evaluate information from multiple sources, which is frequently contradictory (i.e., the patient denies symptoms, and the caregiver reports symptoms). In these cases, the clinician should derive a clinical judgment based on what he or she believes to be the most accurate information. The use of structured and unstructured interviewing techniques will often assist clinicians in determining the most accurate source of information based on inconsistencies that may arise through multiple interviewing techniques. Additionally, an analysis of the severity and types of cognitive impairment present will guide this decision, as will an analysis of how long a caregiver has known a patient and how often the caregiver interacts with the patient. Clarifying culturally significant responses that may obscure clinically relevant information is paramount in this process.

Summary and Conclusions

Psychiatric symptoms are prevalent in patients with dementia and cause significant distress, disability, and diminished quality of life for both patients and their caregivers. Research is just beginning to explore the impact of cultural variability on psychiatric symptom presentation, but it seems clear that ethnically diverse patients and caregivers may be "exposed" to these symptoms for longer periods of time due to their lower usage of respite and residential treatment facilities. Psychiatric assessment with ethnically diverse patients with dementia requires a thorough evaluation of symptoms as well as an evaluation of safety issues and medical history. A combination of clinical interview and standardized measures of psychiatric symptoms is the most effective means of minimizing inaccurate diagnosis due to cultural differences in symptom reporting. Although the use of culturally validated and translated measures is recommended, the use of interpreters is often necessary. By preparing the patient and the interpreter for a psychiatric interview and by structuring the environment, interpreters are more likely to be utilized effectively in the psychiatric interview. Finally, a growing body of resources is available for the clinician to use to gain an understanding of the intricacies of dementia and caregiving in the context of diverse cultural groups. It is extremely important that the clinician working with all caregivers become competent in psychiatric evaluation, because correctly identifying and subsequently treating psychiatric problems in dementia can have a major positive impact on the health and well-being of caregiver and care recipient.

Note

1. Names have been changed in this patient excerpt.

References

Adebimpe, V. R. (1981). Overview: White norms and psychiatric diagnosis of black patients. *American Journal of Psychiatry*, 138(3), 279–285.

Alegria, M., Vila, D., Woo, M., Canino, G., Takeuchi, D., Vera, M. et al. (2004). Cultural relevance and equivalence in the NLAAS instrument: Integrating etic and emic in the development of cross-cultural measures for a psychiatric epidemiology and services study of Latinos. *International Journal of Methods in Psychiatric Research*, 13(4), 270–288.

Alexopoulos, G. S., Abrams, R. C., Young, R. C., & Shamoian, C. A. (1988). Cornell Scale for Depression in Dementia. *Biological Psychiatry*, 23(3), 271–284.

Alvidrez, J., Azocar, F., & Miranda, J. (1996). Demystifying the concept of ethnicity for psychotherapy researchers. *Journal of Consulting and Clinical Psychology*, 64(5), 903–908.

Arfken, C. L., Lichtenberg, P. A., & Tancer, M. E. (1999). Cognitive impairment and depression predict mortality in medically ill older adults. *Journals of Gerontology. Series A, Biological Sciences and Medical Sciences*, 54(3), M152–M156.

Ayalon, L., & Young, M. (2003). A comparison of depressive symptoms in African Americans and Caucasian Americans. *Journal of Cross Cultural Psychology*, 34(1), 111–124.

Baker, F. M. (2001). Diagnosing depression in African Americans. *Community Mental Health Journal*, 37(1), 31–38.

Bassiony, M. M., & Lyketsos, C. G. (2003). Delusions and hallucinations in Alzheimer's disease: Review of the brain decade. *Psychosomatics*, 44(5), 388–401.

Bell, C. C., & Mehta, H. (1980). The misdiagnosis of black patients with manic depressive illness. *Journal of the National Medical Assocication*, 72(2), 141–145.

Bell, C. C., & Mehta, H. (1981). Misdiagnosis of black patients with manic depressive illness: Second in a series. *Journal of the National Medical Association*, 73(2), 101–107.

Boada, M., Cejudo, J. C., Tarraga, L., Lopez, O. L., & Kaufer, D. (2002). Neuropsychiatric inventory questionnaire (NPI-Q): Spanish validation of an abridged form of the Neuropsychiatric Inventory (NPI). *Neurologia*, 17(6), 317–323.

Brown, C., Schulberg, H. C., & Madonia, M. J. (1996). Clinical presentations of major depression by African Americans and whites in primary medical care practice. *Journal of Affective Disorders*, 41(3), 181–191.

Bruce, M. L., Ten Have, T. R., Reynolds, C. F., III, Katz, I. I., Schulberg, H. C., Mulsant, B. H. et al. (2004). Reducing suicidal ideation and depressive symptoms in depressed older primary care patients: A randomized controlled trial. *Journal of the American Medical Association*, 291(9), 1081–1091.

Chan, D. C., Kasper, J. D., Black, B. S., & Rabins, P. V. (2003). Presence of behavioral and psychological symptoms predicts nursing home placement in community-dwelling elders with cognitive impairment in univariate but not multivariate analysis. *Journals of Gerontology. Series A, Biological Sciences and Medical Sciences*, 58(6), 548–554.

Choi, S. H., Na, D. L., Kwon, H. M., Yoon, S. J., Jeong, J. H., & Ha, C. K. (2000). The Korean version of the neuropsychiatric inventory: A scoring tool for neuropsychiatric disturbance in dementia patients. *Journal of Korean Medical Science*, 15(6), 609–615.

Choy, C. N., Lam, L. C., Chan, W. C., Li, S. W., & Chiu, H. F. (2001). Agitation in Chinese elderly: Validation of the Chinese version of the Cohen-Mansfield Agitation Inventory. International *Psychogeriatrics*, 13(3), 325–335.

Cohen-Mansfield, J., & Billig, N. (1986). Agitated behaviors in the elderly. I. A conceptual review. *Journal of the American Geriatrics Society*, 34(10), 711–721.

Cummings, J. L. (1996). Neuropsychiatric assessment and intervention in Alzheimer's disease. *International Psychogeriatrics*, 8(Supp. 1), 25–30.

Cummings, J. L. (1997). The Neuropsychiatric Inventory: Assessing psychopathology in dementia patients. *Neurology*, 48(5 Supp. 6), S10–S16.

Cummings, J. L., Mega, M., Gray, K., Rosenberg-Thompson, S., Carusi, D. A., & Gornbein, J. (1994). The Neuropsychiatric Inventory: Comprehensive assessment of psychopathology in dementia. *Neurology*, 44(12), 2308–2314.

Danhauer, S. C., McCann, J. J., Gilley, D. W., Beckett, L. A., Bienias, J. L., & Evans, D. A. (2004). Do behavioral disturbances in persons with Alzheimer's disease predict caregiver depression over time? *Psychology and Aging*, 19(1), 198–202.

Davis, A. T. (1989). Psychotic states associated with disorders of thyroid function. *International Journal of Psychiatry in Medicine*, 19(1), 47–56.

Drinka, T. J., Smith, J. C., & Drinka, P. J. (1987). Correlates of depression and burden for informal caregivers of patients in a geriatrics referral clinic. *Journal of the American Geriatrics Society*, 35(6), 522–525.

Durand, C., Mary, S., Brazo, P., & Dollfus, S. (2003). Psychiatric manifestations of vitamin B12 deficiency: A case report. *Encephale*, 29(6), 560–565.

Fabrega, H., Jr., Mulsant, B. M., Rifai, A. H., Sweet, R. A., Pasternak, R., Ulrich, R. et al. (1994). Ethnicity and psychopathology in an aging hospital-based population. A comparison of African-American and Anglo-European patients. *Journal of Nervous and Mental Disease*, 182(3), 136–144.

Farooq, S., & Fear, C. (2003). Working through interpreters. *Advances in Psychiatric Treatment*, 9, 104–109.

Flaskerud, J. H., & Hu, L. T. (1992). Relationship of ethnicity to psychiatric diagnosis. *Journal of Nervous and Mental Disease*, 180(5), 296–303.

Forester, B. P., & Oxman, T. E. (2003). Measures to assess the noncognitive symptoms of dementia in the primary care setting. *Primary Care Companion to the Journal of Clinical Psychiatry*, 5(4), 158–163.

Forsell, Y., & Winblad, B. (1998). Major depression in a population of demented and nondemented older people: Prevalence and correlates. *Journal of the American Geriatric Society*, 46(1), 27–30.

Fuh, J. L., Liu, C. K., Mega, M. S., Wang, S. J., & Cummings, J. L. (2001). Behavioral disorders and caregivers' reaction in Taiwanese patients with Alzheimer's disease. *International Psychogeriatrics*, 13(1), 121–128.

Gallo, J. J., & Lebowitz, B. D. (1999). The epidemiology of common late-life mental disorders in the community: Themes for the new century. *Psychiatr Services*, 50(9), 1158–1166.

Garre-Olmo, J., Lopez-Pousa, S., Vilalta-Franch, J., Turon-Estrada, A., Hernandez-Ferrandiz, M., Lozano-Gallego, M. et al. (2002). Carer's burden and depressive symptoms in patients with Alzheimer's disease. State after twelve months. *Revista de Neurologia*, 34(7), 601–607.

Gilley, D. W., Wilson, R. S., Bienias, J. L., Bennett, D. A., & Evans, D. A. (2004). Predictors of depressive symptoms in persons with Alzheimer's disease. *Journals of Gerontology. Series B, Psychological Sciences and Social Sciences*, 59(2), P75–P83.

Griffiths, R. A., Good, W. R., Watson, N. P., O'Donnell, H. F., Fell, P. J., & Shakespeare, J. M. (1987). Depression, dementia and disability in the elderly. *British Journal of Psychiatry*, 150, 482–493.

Haberfellner, E. M., Rittmannsberger, H., & Windhager, E. (1993). Psychotic manifestation of hypothyroidism. A case report. *Nervenarzt*, 64(5), 336–339.

Harwood, D. G., Barker, W. W., Ownby, R. L., Bravo, M., Aguero, H., & Duara, R. (2001). The Behavior Problems Checklist-Spanish: A preliminary study of a new scale for the assessment of depressive symptoms and disruptive behaviors in Hispanic patients with dementia. *International Psychogeriatrics*, 13(1), 23–35.

Hector, M., & Burton, J. R. (1988). What are the psychiatric manifestations of vitamin B12 deficiency? *Journal of the American Geriatrics Society*, 36(12), 1105–1112.

Heinrich, T. W., & Grahm, G. (2003). Hypothyroidism presenting as psychosis: Myx-edema madness revisited. *Primary Care Companion to the Journal of Clinical Psychiatry*, 5(6), 260–266.

Hinton, L., Haan, M., Geller, S., & Mungas, D. (2003). Neuropsychiatric symptoms in Latino elders with dementia or cognitive impairment without dementia and factors that modify their association with caregiver depression. *Gerontologist*, 43, 669–677.

Hughes, T. A., Ross, H. F., Mindham, R. H., & Spokes, E. G. (2004). Mortality in Parkinson's disease and its association with dementia and depression. *Acta Neurologica Scandinavica*, 110(2), 118–123.

Iwata, N., Turner, R. J., & Lloyd, D. A. (2002). Race/ethnicity and depressive symptoms in community-dwelling young adults: A differential item functioning analysis. *Psychiatry Research*, 110(3), 281–289.

Jones, B. E., & Gray, B. A. (1986). Problems in diagnosing schizophrenia and affective disorders among blacks. *Hospital and Community Psychiatry*, 37(1), 61–65.

Kapborga, I., & Bertero, C. (2002). Using an interpreter in qualitative interviews: Does it threaten validity? *Nursing Inquiry*, 9(1), 52–56.

Katz, I. R., Striem, J., & Parmelee, P. (1994). Psychiatric-medical comorbidity: Implications for health services delivery and for research on depression. *Biological Psychiatry*, 36(3), 141–145.

Knudsen, H. C., Vazquez-Barquero, J. L., Welcher, B., Gaite, L., Becker, T., Chisholm, D. et al. (2000). Translation and cross-cultural adaptation of outcome measurements for schizophrenia. EPSILON Study 2. European Psychiatric Services: Inputs linked to outcome domains and needs. *British Journal of Psychiatry Supplement*, 177(39), S8–S14.

Kohler, C. G., Pickholtz, J., & Ballas, C. (2000). Neurosyphilis presenting as schizophrenialike psychosis. *Neuropsychiatry, Neuropsychology, and Behavioral Neurology*, 13(4), 297–302.

Koss, E., Weiner, M., Ernesto, C., Cohen-Mansfield, J., Ferris, S. H., Grundman, M. et al. (1997). Assessing patterns of agitation in Alzheimer's disease patients with the Cohen-Mansfield Agitation Inventory. The Alzheimer's Disease Cooperative Study. *Alzheimer Disease and Associated Disorders*, 11(Supp. 2), S45–S50.

Leung, V. P., Lam, L. C., Chiu, H. F., Cummings, J. L., & Chen, Q. L. (2001). Validation study of the Chinese version of the neuropsychiatric inventory (CNPI). *International Journal of Geriatric Psychiatry*, 16(8), 789–793.

Lying-Tunell, U. (1979). Psychotic symptoms in normal-pressure hydrocephalus. *Acta Psychiatrica Scandinavica*, 59(4), 415–419.

Lyketsos, C. G., Lopez, O., Jones, B., Fitzpatrick, A. L., Breitner, J., & DeKosky, S. (2002). Prevalence of neuropsychiatric symptoms in dementia and mild cognitive impairment: Results from the cardiovascular health study. *Journal of the American Medical Association*, 288(12), 1475–1483.

Marcos, L. R. (1979). Effects of interpreters on the evaluation of psychopathology in non-English-speaking patients. *American Journal of Psychiatry*, 136(2), 171–174.

Matias-Carrelo, L. E., Chavez, L. M., Negron, G., Canino, G., Aguilar-Gaxiola, S., & Hoppe, S. (2003). The Spanish translation and cultural adaptation of five mental health outcome measures. *Culture, Medicine and Psychiatry*, 27(3), 291–313.

Miranda, J., Lawson, W., & Escobar, J. (2002). Ethnic minorities. *Mental Health Services Research*, 4(4), 231–237.

Montgomery, S. A., & Asberg, M. (1979). A new depression scale designed to be sensitive to change. *British Journal of Psychiatry*, 134, 382–389.

Mukherjee, S., Shukla, S., Woodle, J., Rosen, A. M., & Olarte, S. (1983). Misdiagnosis of schizophrenia in bipolar patients: A multiethnic comparison. *American Journal of Psychiatry*, 140(12), 1571–1574.

Myers, H. F., Lesser, I., Rodriguez, N., Mira, C. B., Hwang, W. C., Camp, C. et al. (2002). Ethnic differences in clinical presentation of depression in adult women. *Cultural Diversity & Ethnic Minority Psychology*, 8(2), 138–156.

Novella, J. L., Jochum, C., Jolly, D., Morrone, I., Ankri, J., Bureau, F. et al. (2001). Agreement between patients' and proxies' reports of quality of life in Alzheimer's disease. *Quality of Life Research*, 10(5), 443–452.

Overall, J., & Gorham, D. (1962). The Brief Psychiatric Rating Scale. *Psychological Reports*, 10, 799–812.

Ownby, R. L., Harwood, D. G., Acevedo, A., Barker, W., & Duara, R. (2001). Factor structure of the Cornell Scale for Depression in Dementia for Anglo and Hispanic patients with dementia. *American Journal of Geriatric Psychiatry*, 9(3), 217–224.

Pang, F. C., Chow, T. W., Cummings, J. L., Leung, V. P., Chiu, H. F., Lam, L. C. et al. (2002). Effect of neuropsychiatric symptoms of Alzheimer's disease on Chinese and American caregivers. *International Journal of Geriatric Psychiatry*, 17(1), 29–34.

Petrie, W. M., & Ban, T. A. (1985). Vitamins in psychiatry. Do they have a role? *Drugs*, 30(1), 58–65.

Phelan, M., & Parkman, S. (1995). How to work with an interpreter. *BMJ*, 311(7004), 555–557.

Pinner, G., Johnson, H., Bouman, W. P., & Isaacs, J. (1997). Psychiatric manifestations of normal-pressure hydrocephalus: A short review and unusual case. *International Psychogeriatrics*, 9(4), 465–470.

Radloff, L. (1977). A self-report depression scale for research in the general population. *Applied Psychological Measures*, 1, 385–401.

Reisberg, B., & Franssen, E. (1989). Stage specific incidence of potentially remediable behavioral symptoms in aging and AD: A study of 120 patients using the BEHAVE-AD. *Bulletin of Clinical Neuroscience*, 54, 95–112.

Rubio-Stipec, M., Bird, H., Canino, G., & Gould, M. (1990). The internal consistency and concurrent validity of a Spanish translation of the Child Behavior Checklist. *Journal of Abnormal Child Psychology*, 18(4), 393–406.

Rundell, J. R., & Wise, M. G. (1985). Neurosyphilis: A psychiatric perspective. *Psychosomatics*, 26(4), 287–290, 295.

Sabin, J. E. (1975). Translating despair. *American Journal of Psychiatry*, 132(2), 197–199.

Senanarong, V., Cummings, J. L., Fairbanks, L., Mega, M., Masterman, D. M., O'Connor, S. M. et al. (2004). Agitation in Alzheimer's disease is a manifestation of frontal lobe dysfunction. *Dementia and Geriatric Cognitive Disorders*, 17(1–2), 14–20.

Serrano-Duenas, M., Martinez-Martin, P., & Vaca-Baquero, V. (2004). Validation and cross-cultural adjustment of PDQL-questionnaire, Spanish version (Ecuador) (PDQL-EV). *Parkinsonism & Related Disorders*, 10(7), 433–437.

Sink, K. M., Covinsky, K. E., Newcomer, R., & Yaffe, K. (2004). Ethnic differences in the prevalence and pattern of dementia-related behaviors. *Journal of the American Geriatrics Society*, 52(8), 1277–1283.

Steffens, D. C., Artigues, D. L., Ornstein, K. A., & Krishnan, K. R. (1997). A review of racial differences in geriatric depression: Implications for care and clinical research. *Journal of the National Medical Association*, 89(11), 731–736.

Steinberg, M., Sheppard, J. M., Tschanz, J. T., Norton, M. C., Steffens, D. C., Breitner, J. C. et al. (2003). The incidence of mental and behavioral disturbances in dementia: The cache county study. *Journal of Neuropsychiatry and Clinical Neurosciences*, 15, 340–345.

Stevens, A., Owen, J., Roth, D., Clay, O., Bartolucci, A., & Haley, W. (2004). Predictors of time to nursing home placement in White and African American individuals with dementia. *Journal of Aging and Health*, 16(3), 375–397.

Strakowski, S. M., Lonczak, H. S., Sax, K. W., West, S. A., Crist, A., Mehta, R. et al. (1995). The effects of race on diagnosis and disposition from a psychiatric emergency service. *Journal of Clinical Psychiatry*, 56(3), 101–107.

Strakowski, S. M., McElroy, S. L., Keck, P. E., Jr., & West, S. A. (1996). Racial influence on diagnosis in psychotic mania. *Journal of Affective Disorders*, 39(2), 157–162.

Strakowski, S. M., Shelton, R. C., & Kolbrener, M. L. (1993). The effects of race and comorbidity on clinical diagnosis in patients with psychosis. *Journal of Clinical Psychiatry*, 54(3), 96–102.

Suh, G., & Son, H. (2001). Reliability and analysis of symptom category scores of the Behavior Pathology in Alzheimer's Rating Scale: Korean version (BEHAVE-AD-K). *Journal of Korean Geriatric Psychiatry*, 5, 50–57.

Suh, G. H. (2004). Agitated behaviours among the institutionalized elderly with dementia: Validation of the Korean version of the Cohen-Mansfield Agitation Inventory. *International Journal of Geriatric Psychiatry*, 19(4), 378–385.

Teri, L. (1997). Behavior and caregiver burden: Behavioral problems in patients with Alzheimer disease and its association with caregiver distress. *Alzheimer Disease and Associated Disorders*, 11(Supp. 4), S35–S38.

Teri, L., Ferretti, L. E., Gibbons, L. E., Logsdon, R. G., McCurry, S. M., Kukull, W. A. et al. (1999). Anxiety of Alzheimer's disease: Prevalence, and comorbidity. *Journals of Gerontology. Series A, Biological Sciences and Medical Sciences*, 54(7), M348–M352.

Verdelho, A., Henon, H., Lebert, F., Pasquier, F., & Leys, D. (2004). Depressive symptoms after stroke and relationship with dementia: A three-year follow-up study. *Neurology*, 62(6), 905–911.

Verhey, F. R., Houx, P., Van Lang, N., Huppert, F., Stoppe, G., Saerens, J. et al. (2004). Cross-national comparison and validation of the Alzheimer's Disease Assessment Scale: Results from the European Harmonization Project for Instruments in Dementia (EURO-HARPID). *International Journal of Geriatric Psychiatry*, 19(1), 41–50.

Vilalta-Franch, J., Lozano-Gallego, M., Hernandez-Ferrandiz, M., Llinas-Regla, J., Lopez-Pousa, S., & Lopez, O. L. (1999). The Neuropsychiatric Inventory. Psychometric properties of its adaptation into Spanish. *Revista de Neurologia*, 29(1), 15–19.

Wisniewski, S. R., Belle, S. H., Coon, D. W., Marcus, S. M., Ory, M. G., Burgio, L. D. et al. (2003). The Resources for Enhancing Alzheimer's Caregiver Health (REACH): Project design and baseline characteristics. *Psychology and Aging*, 18(3), 375–384.

Yaffe, K., Fox, P., Newcomer, R., Sands, L., Lindquist, K., Dane, K. et al. (2002). Patient and caregiver characteristics and nursing home placement in patients with dementia. *Journal of the American Medical Association*, 287(16), 2090–2097.

Yesavage, J. A., Brink, T. L., Rose, T. L., Lum, O., Huang, V., Adey, M. et al. (1982). Development and validation of a geriatric depression screening scale: A preliminary report. *Journal of Psychiatric Research*, 17(1), 37–49.

CHAPTER 3

Neurocognitive Assessment of Dementia in African American Elders

RITA HARGRAVE

Background

The U.S. Census Bureau predicts that in the coming years the number of African American elders will continue to grow more rapidly than the number of White elders (Farrar, 2000). Despite this well-documented epidemiological trend, there are limited data on the prevalence, symptomatology, and clinical course of dementia in African American elders. Recent studies indicate that as compared to White elders, African American elders have a higher prevalence of dementia, particularly Alzheimer's disease and vascular dementia (Farrar, 2000; Taylor & Doraiswamy, 2004; Baker, 1996). Several theories have evolved to explain the increased risk for dementia among African Americans, including ethnic differences in socioeconomic status, ethnic differences in rates of comorbid illnesses that influence cognitive status (e.g., cardiovascular disease), and greater lifetime exposure to chronic stress by ethnic minority elders (Schwartz et al., 2004).

Despite recent technological advancements in the diagnosis and management of dementia, African American elders encounter serious obstacles to obtaining comprehensive neurocognitive assessment. One of the most pervasive barriers to care is the reduced reliability and sensitivity of neuropsychological assessment instruments when used with ethnic minority elders (Baker, 1996). Most cognitive screening instruments are less accurate in detecting dementia in African American populations, and they are more likely to lead to overdiagnosis among African Americans (Anthony, Le Resche, Niaz, Von Korff, & Folstein, 1982; Callahan, Hui, Musick, Unverzagt, & Hendrie, 1996; Cohen & Carlin, 1993; Fillenbaum, Hughes, Heyman, George, & Blazer, 1988; Gurland, Cross, Teresi, & Barrett, 1992; Mast, Steinberg, MacNeill, & Lichtenberg, 2001).

Reliable, accurate neuropsychological testing is a cornerstone of dementia assessment, management, and treatment planning. In clinical settings, cognitive assessment begins with the administration of a brief screening instrument such as the Mini-Mental State Examination (MMSE; Folstein et al., 1975). This initial screening process is followed by more sensitive, comprehensive assessments using neuropsychological batteries. But the majority of cognitive assessment instruments (both screening instruments and neuropsychological batteries) have not been validated for ethnic minority populations and are significantly affected by cultural and socioeconomic variables.

The nature of the dynamic interaction between ethnic background, cultural experience, and neuropsychological test performance is not well understood (Ardilla, 1995). Studies show that ethnic minority elders (including those who have dementia and those who do not) compared to White elders obtain lower scores on many cognitive screening measures (Bohnsteadt & Kohatsu, 1994; Gurland et al., 1992; Manly et al., 2004; Murden, Kaner, & Bucknam, 1991; Ripich & Ziol, 1997; Welsh et al., 1995). Some authors suggest that differences in cognitive test performance may be related to ethnic differences in sociodemographic variables, such as overall health status and early-life or life-course disadvantages concerning education (Jacobs et al., 1999; Manly, Jacobs, Touradji, Small, & Stern, 2002). Other investigators suggest that ethnic minority elders may be more susceptible to medical conditions that adversely affect cognitive performance (Wu & Liang, 2003; Yaffe et al., 2003). A recent study proposes that ethnic differences in cognitive test performance may be the result of higher levels of chronic stress associated with race/ethnicity that are not fully described by other sociodemographic factors (Schwartz et al., 2004). Several researchers identified structural problems with neuropsychological tests that are problematic for ethnic minority elders, including the lack of appropriately translated and culturally normed instruments, educational and socioeconomic diversity within ethnic populations, and additional sources of measurement bias inherent within the cross-cultural test-taking situation (Mahurin, Espino, & Holifield, 1992).

Validity of Testing

The validity of cognitive assessment in African American and other ethnic minority elders is affected by a complex network of social, environmental, and psychological variables. These variables include: degree of acculturation, literacy and education, ethnic difference in cognitive test performance, stereotype threat, and measurement bias in neuropsychological test instruments.

Acculturation

Acculturation is an important psychosocial variable that may affect the performance of ethnic elders on screening tests for dementia (Taussig & Ponton, 1996). Acculturation is described as the degree to which people actively participate in the language, values, and practices of their own ethnic community as compared to those of the dominant culture (Landrine, 1996; Padilla, 1980). The effect of acculturation on cognitive test performance among African American elders was examined by using the African American Acculturation Scale (Landrine, 1994, 1995). The African American Acculturation Scale is a self-report measure consisting of 33 items assessing 10 factors of African American culture. Manly et al. (1998c) reported in their study of African Americans aged 20–65 years old that subjects with lower levels of acculturation to the dominant culture obtained lower scores on tests of general information and naming. These findings are supported by a study of older African Americans that found that lower levels of acculturation were associated with lower scores on tests of verbal and nonverbal abilities, even after adjustments for age, education, and gender (Manly et al., 1998a).

In a study of older African Americans in Florida, Lucas (1998) found that lower degrees of acculturation accounted for a significant portion of variance in scores on a wide array of neuropsychological measures, including the verbal intelligence quotient (IQ; measured by Wechsler Adult Intelligence Scale), the Boston Naming Test, and delayed recall of stories from the Wechsler Memory Scale—Revised (Lucas, 1998). Other investigators suggested that the lower scores on the Consortium to Establish a Registry for Alzheimer's Disease (CERAD) battery obtained from older African Americans may also be related to reduced acculturation levels (Fillenbaum, Unverzagt, Ganguli, Welsh-Bohmer, & Heyman, 2002). These results support the hypothesis that the unique lifetime cultural experience of African American elders may influence their performance on cognitive assessment tests and compromise the validity of dementia screening procedures.

Education and Literacy

The interrelationship among ethnicity, education, and risk for cognitive impairment is in a growing area of cross-cultural geriatric mental health research. Mehta et al. (2004) and Gurland et al. (1997) proposed three theories to explain the association between low levels of educational attainment and poorer performance on cognitive tests. The first theory is that poor performance on cognitive tests is the result of a lifetime history of diminished cognitive abilities and cognitive reserve. The second theory is that people with lower educational attainment are more likely to experience various aspects of socioeconomic deprivation, such as poor nutrition, alcohol abuse, and inadequate health care. The final theory is that lifetime exposure to rich educational experiences creates a cognitive reserve that exerts a protective effect against cognitive deterioration in older people (Mehta et al., 2004).

The connection between *cognitive reserve* and dementia risk is a fertile area for neuropsychological and neurobiological research. Cognitive reserve is a neurobiological construct that represents a measure of the brain's synaptic density or complexity (Manly et al., 2003). Functional and structural brain imaging studies suggest that cognitive reserve consists of discrete neural substrates, probably involving a complex network of processes that support neuroplasticity of the aging brain. Correlates of cognitive reserve include education, intelligence, and occupational level (Whalley, Appleton, & Starr, 2004).

Recent studies suggest that higher levels of educational attainment and greater cognitive reserve predict reduced risk for Alzheimer's disease (Katzman, 1993; Scaremeas, 2004; Stern, Tatemichi, Tang, Wilder, & Mayeux, 1994). Other investigators report that lower levels of education were found to be associated with increased risk for dementia, rapid cognitive decline, and increased rates of mortality (Callahan et al. 1996; Gurland et al., 1997; Stern et al., 1994; Unverzagt, Torke, & Rediger, 1996). Thus, higher educational attainment (a proxy measure of greater cognitive reserve) may be protective process for the aging brain against the development of dementia (Katzman, 1993; Stern et al., 1994).

Ethnic Differences in Cognitive Test Performance

Studies of brief screening cognitive instruments and comprehensive neuropsychological test batteries suggest they are both affected by ethnic and cultural factors (Adams & Crain, 1982; Mast et al., 2001; Unverzagt et al., 1996). A number of studies have found that older African Americans, when compared to older White Americans, obtain lower scores on cognitive tests. But is not clear which sociodemographic factors exert the greatest influence on ethnic differences in cognitive test performances. Many investigators report that lower educational attainment is a leading factor in the poorer performance of older African Americans with and without dementia on tests of cognitive function (Callahan et al., 1996; Carlson, Carson, & Kawas, 1998; Shadlen et al., 2001).

Other studies have adjusted cognitive test scores in an effort to correct for differences in education, age, occupation, and relevant medical comorbidity (e.g., hypertension, diabetes). Even after test scores were adjusted for demographic variables, ethnic differences in cognitive performance continued to exist (Escobar, Karno, Forsythe, Landsverk, & Golding, 1986; Fillenbaum et al., 1988; Fillenbaum, Heyman, Huber, Ganguli, & Unverzagt, 2001; Manly et al., 1998a, 1998b; Reynolds, Kauffman, & McLean, 1987; Teresi, Holmes, & Mayeux, 1999; Unverzagt et al., 1996; Welsh et al., 1995). Schwartz et al. (2004) reported that ethnic differences in the cognitive functioning of African American elders and White elders persisted even after adjustments were made for numerous confounding variables. His group analyzed data from the Baltimore Memory Study, a large cohort study of the multilevel determinants of cognitive decline in populations of randomly selected samples of community dwelling people aged 50–70. The study used an extensive cognitive test battery from the Baltimore Memory Study that included the Boston Naming Test, Raven's Colored Progressive Matrices, the Rye Complex Figure copy, the Rye Auditory Verbal Learning Test immediate recall, the Purdue Pegboard, the Stroop Test (A, B, and C forms), and Trail-Making Tests A and B (Schwartz et al., 2004). Ethnic differences in test performance were present in all cognitive domains, including tests that would not be characterized as susceptible to differential item functioning by race/ethnicity. The authors concluded that their results were not due to race/ethnicity-associated measurement errors in the cognitive assessment instruments.

Because the relationship between educational attainment, dementia, and ethnicity remains controversial, researchers are faced with the dilemma of how to address the confounding influence of premorbid education on cognitive assessment for dementia. Many studies that compare neuropsychological test scores on different ethnic groups use covariance or matching procedures to control for differences in educational attainment (Manly et al., 1998b). Many authors feel that dissimilar educational experiences between African Americans and Whites represent a major contribution to the lower scores of African American elders on cognitive testing. Illiteracy rates in the United States are especially elevated among ethnic minority elders (Kirsch, Jungeblut, Jenkins, & Kolstad, 1993). Associated socioeconomic forces (e.g., poverty and racism) present in segregated communities often limited minority elders' access to adequate educational resources or higher levels of occupational status. These social barriers may obscure the individual's native intellect or drive to succeed (Manly, Touradji, Tang, & Stern, 2003). The aftermath of these sociological trends can lead to the underestimation of the individual's premorbid intelligence and interfere with the accurate assessment of cognitive decline in old age. Thus, years of education alone does not fully reflect the discrepancies in the quality of educational experiences between African American and White elders and may account for the persistent racial/ethnic differences in cognitive performance even after groups are matched for years of education (Manly et al., 2002).

More recently, investigators (Manly et al., 2002; Mehta et al., 2004) examined the impact of literacy on performance on cognitive tests. Literacy is considered a correlate of education and may be a more sensitive measure of cognitive reserve than educational attainment (Albert, 1999; Manly et al., 2002, 2003; Mehta et al., 2004). Literacy may more accurately reflect the true quality of the educational experience of ethnic minority elders. But Metha et al. (2004) suggest that an array of socioeconomic variables, including literacy, education, income, and financial adequacy may in large part account for the differences in cognitive testing scores between African American and White elders (Mehta et al., 2004).

Stereotype Threat

Relatively few studies have examined the complex cultural, psychological, and environmental parameters embedded in the cognitive testing environment. Two largely unexplored parameters in neuropsychological testing are cross-cultural test-taking attitudes and motivation during the testing session and participant–examiner interactions. Performance on traditional neuropsychological assessment measures is based on skills that are considered important by the majority culture but may not be considered salient or important within the African American culture (Helms, 1992). African American elders who only had access to segregated, impoverished schools systems may not be as "test-wise" or as familiar with the explicit and implicit structure and language of formal neuropsychological assessment (Manly, Byrd, Touradji, & Stern, 2004).

A handful of studies have attempted to describe the interpersonal dynamics of the cross-cultural pairings of participant and examiner in neuropsychological assessment settings. The ethnicity of the examiners (who are often White) may subtly affect the performance of ethnic elders (Woodard, Godsall, & Green, 1998). Manly et al. (2004) suggested that some ethnic elders compared to White older adults may suffer greater discomfort and loss of self-confidence during testing sessions. This loss of self-confidence may contribute to poorer test performance. This phenomenon is called "stereotype threat and [it] describes the effect of attention diverting from the task at hand to the concern that one's performance will confirm a negative stereotype about one's group" (Manly, Espino, 2004, p. 104) and causes the participant to become diverted from the cognitive task. Research on stereotype threat suggests that the social stigma of intellectual inferiority by certain cultural minorities can influence their performance on standardized tests (Aronson, Good, Keough, Steele, & Brown, 1999). The minority participant becomes overly concerned that his or her cognitive performance will confirm a negative stereotype about his or her (ethnic/racial) group (Manly et al., 2004). Stereotype threat has been hypothesized to account for women having lower scores on tests of mathematics when compared to men and for White men having lower scores on mathematics tests when compared to Asians (Aronson et al., 1999; Spencer & Quinn, 1999). Though the impact of stereotype threat on the cognitive testing of African American elders has not been directly investigated, Manly hypothesized that some minority groups will be more vulnerable to this process than others. Additional research is needed to elucidate the experiential, social, and cultural variables that influence performance on cognitive tests among ethnic minority elders (Manly et al., 2004).

Measurement Bias in Cognitive Assessment Tools

The critical first step in dementia evaluation is to obtain an accurate neuropsychological assessment of premorbid and current intellectual functioning. Sensitive and specific cognitive assessment instruments for dementia are fundamental in the early diagnosis of and treatment planning of the illness. Early diagnosis of dementia and Mild Cognitive Impairment (MCI) is critical to the initiation of treatment with cognitive enhancers (e.g., tacrine [Cognex˚], donepezil [Aricept˚], or rivastigmine [Exelon˚]), which can slow the progression of dementia.

Many have questioned the effectiveness of traditional cognitive assessment instruments in ethnic minority populations. The validity of neuropsychological instruments for African American elders is hampered by factors such as overall lack of normative test data for minority populations, limited consideration of premorbid status, lack of literacy, culture-specific factors related to individual test items, and limited use of comprehensive test batteries (Lowenstein, Arguelles, & Linn-Fuentes, 1994; Parker & Philip, 2004). Studies of cognitive performance of African American elders are hampered by additional methodological problems, including small sample size, the absence of a randomized selection process, and the absence of a comprehensive neuropsychological test battery.

The normative data for cognitive instruments are often based on independently living, community-dwelling White elders with high levels of education. Several investigators caution that normative data based on White elders cannot be generalized to minority elders and to participants with lower educational levels (Bank, Yochim, MacNeill, & Lichtenberg, 2000). However, numerous studies report that cognitive screening instruments for dementia are affected by cultural and ethnic factors (Fillenbaum, Heyman, Williams, & Burchett, 1990; Ford, Haley, Thrower, West, & Farrell, 1996; Gurland et al., 1992), and most have not been cross-validated in large populations of ethnic minority elders. Even dementia screening batteries show reduced sensitivity and specificity when used with African American patients. Fillenbaum's analysis of six commonly used measures for cognitive impairment revealed a high percentage of "false positives" when used for screening large populations of African American patients, other minority elders, and participants with low levels of educational attainment (Fillenbaum et al., 1990).

Specific Cognitive Assessment Instruments

Next, eight cognitive assessment instruments will be presented. Data on the benefits and limitations of these instruments in the assessment of dementia in African American elders will be discussed.

Mattis Dementia Rating Scale

The Mattis Dementia Rating Scale (MDRS; Mattis, 1973) is a 36-item neuropsychological instrument used to screen for cognitive impairment and track cognitive changes in patients with dementia. The MDRS assesses attention, language, reasoning, visual spatial construction, and memory; scores are affected by age and education (Lucas, 1998).

Studies on racial bias in the MDRS reveal inconclusive results. A study by Woodard, Godsall, and Green (1998) revealed no clear evidence of test bias due to race. Based on their comprehensive item analysis of the MDRS, only 4 out of 36 items (palm up/palm down, fist clenched/fist extended, counting distraction 2, and visual recognition) produced differential item functioning based on race after matching participants on the basis of age, education, and gender. The authors (Woodard et al.) proposed that these items could potentially be eliminated from the analysis to produce a modified MDRS total score that would be more stable to the effects of cultural differences and maximize the test's sensitivity to true changes in dementia severity. The results of this study suggest that the MDRS has no appreciable evidence of test bias and minimal item bias because of race, suggesting that the MDRS may be effectively used for African American and non-Hispanic White elders for dementia assessment (Woodard et al., 1998). Consistent with these findings, Vangel and Lichtenberg (1995) and Lichtenberg, Ross, Millis, and Manning (1995) reported that MDRS scores were not significantly affected by race or gender.

On the other hand, Lichtenberg et al. (1995), using multiple regression analysis, reported that MDRS scores were significantly affected by ethnicity even after controlling for age, education, gender, and Geriatric Depression Scale scores. Bank et al. (2000), using a multi-ethnic sample of older adults who did not have dementia, reported that MDRS scores were correlated with gender and race and produced higher mean scores among women and White participants. Though ethnicity did not produce a statistically significant effect on MDRS scores, authors reported a trend toward statistical significance for the influence of race on the MDRS scores (Bank et al., 2000). Because the effect of ethnicity on MDRS scores are inconsistent, further studies are needed to improve the validity of MDRS in ethnic minority populations.

Mini-Mental State Examination

The Mini-Mental State Examination (MMSE) is the most commonly used screening instrument for cognitive impairment (Folstein, Folstein, & Mc Hugh, 1975). It has been used extensively in the testing of African American and other ethnic minority elders. The MMSE is an 11-item instrument that tests a variety of cognitive domains, including orientation, registration, and recall of three words; attention; calculation; language; and constructional apraxia.

MMSE scores are affected by numerous demographic factors, including education, age, ethnicity, and level of functional impairment (Fillenbaum et al., 1988, 1990; Gurland et al., 1992; Murden et al., 1991). Many researchers believe that ethnic differences in education are the primary reason for the lower MMSE scores obtained from African Americans compared to the scores from White Americans. Using age and educationally adjusted normative data, investigators can calculate the appropriate cutoff points for cognitive impairment (Crum, Bassett, & Folstein, 1993; Tombaugh & McIntyre, 1992). The presence of educationally adjusted normative data is an important asset for the MMSE, because African American elders are more likely to have lower educational levels than White American elders.

Though there are ethnic differences in MMSE test performance, it is not clear if this bias is eliminated after the MMSE scores are adjusted for education and socioeconomic status. In some studies, ethnic differences in test performance disappear when the scores are adjusted for education, age, and levels of functional impairment (Brayne & Calloway, 1991; Crum et al., 1993; Escobar et al., 1986; Fillenbaum et al., 1990; Ford et al., 1996; Kuller et al., 1998; Mast et al., 2001; Mungas, Weldon, Haan, & Reed, 1996; Murden et al., 1991; Unverzagt et al., 1996; Welsh et al., 1995). Other studies indicate that African Americans continue to have lower MMSE scores compared to White Americans even after scores are adjusted for educational level (Fillenbaum et al., 1990; Welsh et al., 1995).

Several investigators reported that the specificity and sensitivity of the MMSE are lower when used with African American elders (Fillenbaum et al., 1989; Mast et al., 2001). The MMSE may underestimate the cognitive abilities of African American elders and, consequently, produce higher rates of false-positive cases of dementia (Fillenbaum et al., 1990; Gurland et al., 1992; Mungas et al., 1996; Welsh et al., 1995). Because the MMSE may have poorer specificity for African Americans, many authors have questioned the utility of the MMSE in the assessment of ethnic minority elders (Fillenbaum et al., 1988; Mungas et al., 1996).

Due to the problems of measurement bias associated with the MMSE, investigators employ numerous statistical adjustment strategies to improve the test's validity with ethnic minority elders. Some studies propose that MMSE scores should be adjusted for demographic factors, such as race, education, and age, to avoid overestimating an individual's level of cognitive impairment (Fillenbaum et al., 1990; Gurland et al., 1992; Murden et al., 1991). Based on normative data adjusted for age and education, other studies modify the cutoff point for diagnosing dementia to compensate for the effects of confounding demographic variables (Crum et al., 1993; Gurland et al., 1992; Murden et al., 1991; Tombaugh & McIntyre, 1992).

New approaches are being developed to address the problems of measurement bias in the MMSE for ethnic minority elders. Based on a survey of a population-based sample of White and Hispanic elders (n = 590), Mungas and his colleagues developed a new measure called the statistically adjusted MMSE (MMSAdj; Mungas et al., 1996). The MMSAdj incorporates a statistical adjustment for the effects of age and education. The MMSAdj is defined as raw MMSE score − (0.471 × [education minus 12]) + (0.131 × [age minus 70]) (Mungas et al., 1996). Though the MMSAdj may have a wider range of clinical applications than unadjusted MMSE scores, the authors cautioned that there may be limitations in the generalizability of their results. The utility of the MMSAdj may be compromised if it is used with minority groups other than Hispanic and non-Hispanic White elders (Mungas et al., 1996).

Despite the theoretical benefits of making statistical adjustments to the MMSE, some authors recommend caution when using corrections for demographic factors. They hypothesize that there may be common underlying etiological processes that affect education, socioeconomic status, and aspects of poor health (Anthony et al., 1982; Berkman, 1986). They warn that the cumulative effects of that etiological process would be minimized if the MMSE scores are adjusted.

Blessed Information–Memory–Concentration Test

The Blessed Information–Memory–Concentration (BIMC) test is a 26-item instrument that evaluates orientation, long-term memory, recall, and concentration (Blessed, Tomlinson, & Roth, 1968). With scores ranging from 0–33, the BIMC is comparable to the MMSE in respect to its ability to assess cognitive deficits. There are currently no age-adjusted or education-adjusted norms and no published studies examining the presence of racial bias in BIMC scores.

Blessed Orientation Memory–Concentration Test

The Blessed Orientation Memory–Concentration (BOMC) test, a shortened version of the BIMC, consists of six items with a maximum score of 28 (Katzman et al., 1983). The items on the BOMC include current date (month, year) and time, counting backwards from 20 to 1, reciting the months of the year in reverse order, and recalling a previously repeated five-element address. Performance on the BOMC is highly correlated with performance on the MMSE. Studies have found statistically significant racial bias in the BOMC similar to the bias reported in the MMSE (Fillenbaum, Landerman, & Simonsick, 1998). Welsh et al. (1995) found that the BOMC misclassified 62% of African American participants who did not have dementia as having dementia, as compared to 22% of White participants. Fillenbaum et al. (1989) noted that among African American elders, as compared to White elders, the BOMC demonstrated significantly poorer specificity (38% vs. 79%), resulting in a higher percentage of false-positive cases of dementia in African American patients. Thus, current studies suggest that the BOMC has reduced sensitivity and specificity when used with African Americans.

Short Portable Mental Status Examination

The Short Portable Mental Status Examination (SPMSQ; Pfieffer 1975) is a 10-item measure normed on a community representative sample of African American and non-Hispanic White residents 65 years of age or older. The SPMSQ focuses on orientation but also includes two items on memory and one on concentration.

Welsh et al. (1975) reported that the SPMSQ has less racial bias than many other instruments, and it has cutoff scores adjusted for race and education. Fillenbaum et al. (1989) noted that due to the adjustment for race and education embedded in the dichotomized scoring system, SPMSQ is less likely to misclassify African Americans and elders with low educational attainment as having dementia.

Cambridge Cognitive Examination

The Cambridge Cognitive Examination (CAMCOG) is a brief neuropsychological scale that can be used to detect the cognitive changes of mild dementia and has numerous advantages over the MMSE. Some researchers report that the CAMCOG is more sensitive and specific to cognitive deficits than the MMSE (Roth et al., 1986). The CAMCOG has a wider range of values (0–106) compared to the MMSE (0–30) and, thus, avoids ceiling effects. CAMCOG can also screen for a greater variety of dementia types, including dementia due to Parkinson's disease, stroke, and Lewy-body disease (Hobson & Meara, 1998; Kwa, Voogel, Teunisse, Derix, & Hijdra, 1996; Walker, Shergill, & Katona, 1997). CAMCOG scores must be adjusted for age, but the sensitivity of the test is not affected by education, socioeconomic factors, or depression. Because CAMCOG has not been standardized for minority populations, it is not clear if the scores are affected by race (Lampley-Dallas, 2001).

Consortium to Establish a Registry for Alzheimer's Disease Neuropsychological Battery

The Consortium to Establish a Registry for Alzheimer's Disease (CERAD) was developed to facilitate dementia assessment (Welsh, Butler, Hughes, Mohs, & Heyman, 1991) and includes the following seven measures: Verbal Fluency, Modified Boston Naming, MMSE, Word List Learning, Recall and Recognition, and Constructional Praxis (Fillenbaum et al., 1998; Morris et al., 1989).

In several studies (Fillenbaum et al., 1998; Welsh et al., 1995), it was found that African American elders consistently performed more poorly than White elders on several of the cognitive measures of the CERAD battery. Several authors proposed that cultural or experiential differences may have compromised their performance on specific neuropsychological tests (Welsh et al., 1991). Another explanation is that racial differences in the quality of education may have contributed to racial differences in test performance. Several authors reported that statistical matching on years of formal education does not necessarily take into account differences in the quality of education that was available for African Americans and White Americans (Fillenbaum et al., 2002; Manly et al., 1998). Prior to the desegregation in public schools in the 1950s, the quality of education of African Americans was compromised by a variety of adverse factors including unequal distribution of funds based on race, variable teacher education, shorter length of school year, and lower attendance (Margo, 1990). These issues were particularly relevant for the Fillenbaum study, in which elders were recruited from North Carolina, where in their formative years the African American elders would have been living in segregated communities and attending segregated schools with fewer facilities, inadequate resources, and lower academic standards (Fillenbaum et al., 2001).

Fillenbaum and coworkers comment that numerous discrepancies can arise when an instrument like the CERAD battery, developed from a tertiary care population, is used to construct community-based norms. Her group reported that the published norms for the CERAD battery overestimated the prevalence of dementia in community-based populations. The authors recommended that the composition and selection characteristics of the sample providing the normative data should be comparable to the population on which the test battery is being used (Fillenbaum et al., 2001). Based on this recommendation, the authors developed population means for the CERAD neuropsychological battery using a representative sample of community-dwelling African American ($n = 2,261$) and White American ($n = 1,975$) residents. Fillenbaum and colleagues also suggested that because their study was conducted in the southern part of the United States, other investigators should consider that there may be regional differences in the educational and social experiences of African American elders that may affect the performance of African Americans on neuropsychological batteries in the assessment for dementia. Their study reported that race was not a statistically significant factor in determining the score on any of the seven neuropsychological measures of the CERAD battery after controlling for sex, age, and education.

Other studies have found that there may be ethnic differences on discrete subtests of the CERAD battery. After controlling for education, age, duration of illness, and severity of illness, African American elders scored lower than White Americans on the test of visual naming, constructional praxis, and MMSE. There were no ethnic differences on tests of fluency and word list memory. The authors suggest that cultural or experiential differences may affect performance on specific neuropsychological tests (Welsh et al., 1995).

Boston Naming Test

The Boston Naming Test is a 60-item instrument that provides a detailed examination of naming abilities, well standardized for all ages (Kaplan, Goodglass, & Weintraub, 1983). The test is composed of 60 line drawings of objects ranging from high-frequency vocabulary words (e.g., tree) to rare words (e.g., abacus) that are presented to participants one at a time on cards. The authors of one study reported ethnic differences in performance on the Boston Naming Test (Lichtenberg, Ross, & Christensen, 1994). Because this study utilized a small sample population, the authors recommended that more studies of the clinical application of the test on African American elders be conducted. More research is needed to develop age-adjusted norms and ethnically adjusted norms and to improve the clinical utility of the Boston Naming Test for ethnic minority elders.

Summary

Clinicians should be attentive to the fact that ethnic/cultural factors affect the sensitivity, specificity, and validity of cognitive assessment instruments. Strategies to improve the utility of existing screening instruments for ethnic minority elders have consisted of the adjustment of cut-points, translation, and replacement of culture-specific items (Parker & Philip, 2004). Although these statistical adjustment strategies may reduce the rate of misdiagnosis, Manly et al. (2004) caution that these approaches do not take into consideration the intragroup variability of educational and cultural experiences among African Americans. In the future, tests should be used that are comprised of meaningful, predictive variables that capture the essence of ethnic differences in test performance across cultures (Manly et al., 2004). Development and utilization of more culturally sensitive test instruments would improve the accuracy and validity of diagnostic assessment for dementia for African American elders.

Clinicians need to be aware that educational and cultural experiences of African American elders vary considerably depending on geographic, socioeconomic, and acculturative factors. Future studies are needed to examine the clinical applications of cognitive assessment instruments using larger numbers of African American participants from diverse educational, regional, and socioeconomic backgrounds. Investigators should be encouraged to increase their recruitment of ethnic minority elders to facilitate the development of more effective screening measures for cognitive impairment.

References

Adams, R. L., & Crain, C. (1982). Bias in a neuropsychological test classification related to education, age and ethnicity. *Journal of Clinical and Experimental Psychology, 50*(1), 143–145.

Albert, T. J. (1999). Reading ability, education and cognitive status assessment among older adults in Harlem, New York City. *American Journal of Public Health, 89*, 95–97.

Anthony, J. C., Le Resche, L., Niaz, U., Von Korff, M. R., & Folstein, M. (1982). Limits of the "Mini-Mental State" as a screening test for dementia and delirium among hospital patients. *Psychological Medicine, 12*, 397–408.

Ardilla, A. (1995). Directions of research in cross-cultural neuropsychology. *Journal of Clinical and Experimental Neuropsychology, 17*, 143–150.

Aronson, L. M., Good, C., Keough, K., Steele, C. M., & Brown, J. (1999). When white men can't do math: Necessary and sufficient factors in stereotype threat. *Journal of Experimental Social Psychology, 35*, 29–46.

Baker, F. M. (1996). Issues in assessing dementia in African American elders. In G. Yeo & D. Gallagher-Thompson (Eds.), *Ethnicity and the Dementias* (pp. 59–76). Washington, DC: Taylor & Francis.

Bank, A., Yochim, B. P., MacNeill, S. E., & Lichtenberg, P. A. (2000). Expanded normative data for the Mattis Dementia Rating Scale for use with urban, elderly medical patients. *The Clinical Neuropsychologist, 14*(2), 149–156.

Berkman, L. F. (1986). The association between educational attainment and mental status examination: Of etiological significance for senile dementia or not? *Journal of Chronic Diseases, 39*, 171–175.

Blessed, G., Tomlinson, B., & Roth, M. (1968). The association between quantitative measures of dementia and senile change in the cerebral grey matter of elderly subjects. *British Journal of Psychiatry, 114*, 797–811.

Bohnsteadt, F. P., & Kohatsu, N. D. (1994). Correlates of Mini-Mental Status Examination scores among elderly demented patients. *Journal of Clinical Epidemiology, 47*, 1381–1387.

Brayne, C., & Calloway, P. (1991). The association of education and socioeconomic status with the mini-mental state examination and the clinical diagnosis of dementia in elderly people. *Age and Aging, 19*, 91–96.

Callahan, H. S., Hui, S. L., Musick, B. S., Unverzagt, F. W., & Hendrie, H. C. (1996). Relationship of age, education and occupation with dementia among a community-based sample of African Americans. *Archives of Neurology, 43*, 134–140.

Carlson, B. J., Carson, K., & Kawas, C. (1998). Lack of relation between race and cognitive test performance in Alzheimer's disease. *Neurology, 50*(5), 1499–1501.

Cohen, C. L., & Carlin, L. (1993). Racial and social differences in clinical and social variables among patients evaluated in a dementia assessment center. *Journal of the National Medical Association, 85*, 379–384.

Crum, A. J., Bassett, S. S., & Folstein, M. F. (1993). Population-based norms for the mini-mental state examination by age and educational levels. *Journal of the American Medical Association, 269,* 2386–2391.

Farrar, L. A. (2000). Familial risk for Alzheimer disease in ethnic minorities. *Archives of Neurology, 57,* 28–29.

Fillenbaum, G. G., Heyman, A., Huber, M. S., Ganguli, M., & Unverzagt, F. W. (2001). Performance of elderly African American and white community residents on the CERAD Neuropsychological Battery. *Journal of International Neuropsychological Society, 7*(4), 502–509.

Fillenbaum, G. G., Heyman, A., Williams, K., & Burchett, B. (1990). Sensitivity and specificity of standardized screens of cognitive impairment and dementia among elderly black and white community residents. *Journal of Clinical Epidemiology, 43,* 651–660.

Fillenbaum, G. G., Hughes, H. D., Heyman, A., George, L. K., & Blazer, D. G. (1988). Relationship of health and demographic characteristics to mini-mental state examination score among community residents. *Psychological Medicine, 18,* 719–726.

Fillenbaum, G. G., Landerman, L., & Simonsick, E. M. (1998). Equivalence of two screens of cognitive functioning: The short portable mental status exam and the orientation-memory-concentration test. *Journal of American Geriatric Society, 46,* 1512–1518.

Fillenbaum, G. G., Unverzagt, F. W., Ganguli, M., Welsh-Bohmer, K. A., & Heyman, A. (2002). The CERAD neuropsychological battery: Performance of representative community and tertiary care samples of African American and European American elderly. In F. R. Ferraro (Ed.), *Minority and cross cultural aspects of neuropsychological assessment* (pp. 45–77). Lisse, the Netherlands: Swets & Zeitlinger.

Flicker, C., Ferris, S., & Reisberg, B. (1991). Mild cognitive impairment in the elderly: Predictors of dementia. *Neurology, 41,* 1006–1009.

Folstein, M. F., Folstein, F. S., & Mc Hugh, P. R. (1975). "Mini-Mental State": A practical method for grading the cognitive state of patients for the clinician. *Journal of Psychiatric Research, 12,* 189–198.

Ford, G. R., Haley, W., Thrower, S. L., West, C. A., & Farrell, L. E. (1996). Utility of mini-mental state exam scores in predicting functional impairment among white and African American dementia patients. *Journal of Gerontology, 51,* 185–188.

Gurland, B., Wilder, D., Lantigua, R., Mayeux, R., Stern, Y., Chen, J. et al. (1997). Differences in rates of dementia among ethno-racial groups. In L. Martin & B. Soldo (Eds.), *Racial and ethnic differences in the health of older Americans* (pp. 233–269). Washington, DC: National Academy Press.

Gurland, W. D., Cross, P., Teresi, J., & Barrett, V. W. (1992). Screening scales of dementia: Toward reconciliation of conflicting cross-cultural findings. *International Journal of Geriatric Psychiatry, 7,* 105–113.

Helms, J. E. (1992). Why is there no study of cultural equivalence in standardized cognitive ability testing? *American Psychologist, 47,* 1083–1101.

Hobson, P., & Meara, J. (1998). Screening for "cognitive impairment, no dementia" in older adults. *Journal of American Geriatric Association, 46,* 659–660.

Holzer, T. G., Leaf, P. J., & Myers, J. K. (1983). An epidemiologic assessment of cognitive impairment. *Research on Community Mental Health, 4,* 3–32.

Jacobs, D. M., Albert, S. M., Sano, M., del Castillo-Castaneda, C., Paik, M. C., Marder, K. et al. (1999). Assessment of cognition in advance AD: The test for severe impairment. *Neurology, 52,* 1689–1691.

Kaplan, E. F., Goodglass, H., & Weintraub, S. (1983). *The Boston Naming Test.* Philadelphia: Lea and Febiger.

Katzman, R. (1993). Education and prevalence of dementia and Alzheimer's disease. *Neurology, 43,* 13–20.

Katzman, R., Brown, T., Fuld, P., Peck, A., Shechter, R., & Schimmel, V. (1983). Validation of a short orientation-memory-concentration test for cognitive impairment. *American Journal of Psychiatry, 140,* 481–485.

Kirsch, I. S., Jungeblut A., Jenkins L., & Kolstad A. (1993). Adult literacy in America: The National Adult Literacy Survey. National Center for Education Statistics, US Department of Education. Washington, DC: US Government Printing Office.

Kuller, L. H., Shemanski, L., Manolio, T., Haan, M., Fried, L., Byran, N. et al. (1998). Relationship between ApoE, MRI findings and cognitive function in the Cardiovascular Health Study. *Stroke, 29*(2), 288–298.

Kwa, L. M., Voogel, A. J., Teunisse, S., Derix, M. M., & Hijdra, A. (1996). Feasibility of cognitive screening of patients with ischemic stroke using the CAMCOG: A hospital based study. *Journal of Neurology, 243,* 405–409.

Lampley-Dallas, V. (2001). Neuropsychological screening tests in African Americans. *Journal of the National Medical Association, 93*(9), 323–328.

Landrine, K. E. (1994). The African American Acculturation Scale: Development, reliability, and validity. *Journal of Black Psychology, 20,* 104–127.

Landrine, K. E. (1995). The African American Acculturation Scale II: Cross-validation and short from. *Journal of Black Psychology, 21*(2), 124–152.

Landrine, K. E. (1996). *African American acculturation: Deconstructing race and reviving culture.* Thousand Oaks, CA: Sage.

Larrieu, A., Letenneur, L., Orgogozo, J., Fabrigoule, C., Amieva, H., Le Carret, N. et al. (2002). Incidence and outcome of mild cognitive impairment in a population-based prospective cohort. *Neurology, 59,* 1594–1599.

Lichtenberg, P. A., Ross, T., & Christensen, B. (1994). Preliminary normative data on the Boston Naming Test for an older urban population. *Clinical Neuropsychology, 8,* 109–111.

Lichtenberg, P. A., Ross, T., Millis, S. R., & Manning, C. A. (1995). The relationship between depression and cognition in older adults: A cross-validation study. *Journal of Gerontology: Psychological Sciences, 16,* 623–629.

Lopez, O. L., Jagust, W., Dulberg, C., Becker, J. T., DeKosky, S. T., Fitzpatrick, A. et al. (2003). Risk factors for mild cognitive impairment in the Cardiovascular Health Study Cognition Study: Part 2. *Archives of Neurology, 60*(10), 1394–1399.

Lowenstein, A. T., Arguelles, S., & Linn-Fuentes, P. (1994). Potential cultural bias in the neuropsychological assessment of the older adult. *Journal of Clinical and Experimental Neuropsychology, 16*, 623–629.

Lucas, J. A. (1998). Acculturation and neuropsychology test performance in elderly African American acculturation and neuropsychological test performance among nondemented community elders. *Journal of International Neuropsychological Society, 4*, 77.

Luis, L. D., Acevedo, A., Barker, W. W., & Duara, R. (2003). Mild cognitive impairment: Directions for future research. *Neurology, 61*(4), 438–444.

Mahurin, R. K., Espino, D. V., & Holifield, E. B. (1992). Mental status testing in elderly Hispanic populations: Special concerns. *Psychopharmacology Bulletin, 28*, 391–399.

Manly, J., Byrd, D., Touradji, P, & Stern, Y. (2004). Acculturation, reading level, and neuropsychological test performance among African American elders. *Applied Neuropsychology, 11*(1), 37–46.

Manly, J. J., Jacobs, D., Sano, M., Bell, K., Merchant, C. A., Small, S. A. et al. (1998a). African American acculturation and neuropsychological test performance among nondemented community elders. *Journal of International Neuropsychological Society, 4*, 77.

Manly, J. J., Jacobs, D., Sano, M., Bell, K., Merchant, C. A., Small, S. A. et al. (1998b). Cognitive test performance among non-demented elderly African Americans and whites. *Neurology, 50*, 1238–1245.

Manly, J. J., Jacobs, D., Touradji, P., Small, S. A., & Stern, Y. (2002). Reading level attenuates differences in neuropsychological test performance between African American and white elders. *Journal of International Neuropsychological Society, 8*(3), 341–348.

Manly, J. J., Miller, S. W., Heaton, R. K., Byrd, D., Reilly, J., & Velasquez, R. J. (1998). The effect of African American acculturation on neuropsychological test performance in normal and HIV positive individuals. *Journal of International Neuropsychological Society, 4*, 291–302.

Manly, J. J., Touradji, P., Tang, M. X., & Stern, Y. (2003). Literacy and memory decline in among ethnically diverse elders. *Journal of Clinical and Experimental Neuropsychology, 25*(5), 680–690.

Margo, R. A. (1990) *Race and schooling in the South, 1880–1950: An economic history.* Chicago: University of Chicago Press

Mast, F. J., Steinberg, J., MacNeill, S. E., Lichtenberg, P. A. (2001). Effective screening for Alzheimer's disease among older African Americans. *Clinical Neuropsychology, 15*(2), 196–202.

Mattis, S. (1973). *Dementia Rating Scale professional manual.* Odessa, FL: Psychological Assessment Resources Inc.

McKay, P. F. (2003). The effects of demographic variables and stereotypic threat on Black/White differences in cognitive ability test performance. *Journal of Business and Psychology, 18*, 1–14.

Mehta, S. E., Rooks, R., Newman, A. B., Pope, S. K., Rubin, S. M., & Yaffe, K. (2004). Black and white differences in cognitive function test scores: What explains the difference? *Journal of American Geriatric Association, 52*, 2120–2127.

Miller, H. R., Kirson, D., & Grant, I. (1997). Neuropsychological assessment of African Americans. *Journal of International Neuropsychology Society, 3,* 49.

Morris, H. A., Mohs, R. C., Hughes, J. P., van Belle, G., Fillenbaum, G., Mellits, E. D. et al. (1989). The Consortium to Establish a Registry for Alzheimer's Disease (CERAD). Part I. Clinical and neuropsychological assessment of Alzheimer's disease. *Neurology, 39,* 1159–1165.

Morris, J. C., Storandt, M., Miller, J. P., McKeel, D. W., Price, J. L., Rubin, E. H. et al. (2001). Mild cognitive impairments represent early-stage Alzheimer's disease. *Archives of Neurology, 58,* 397–405.

Mungas, M. S., Weldon, M., Haan, M., & Reed, B. R. (1996). Age and education correction of mini-mental state examination for English- and Spanish-speaking elderly. *Neurology, 36,* 700–706.

Murden, M. T., Kaner, S., & Bucknam, M. E. (1991). Mini-mental State exam scores vary with education in blacks and whites. *Journal of American Geriatric Association, 39,* 149–155.

Nelson, H. E. (1982). *National Adult Reading Test (NART) manual.* Windsor, UK: NFER-Nelson.

Padilla, A. M. (1980). *Acculturation: Theory, models and some new findings.* Boulder, CO: Westview Press for the American Association for the Advancement of Science.

Parker, C., & Philip, I. (2004). Screening for cognitive impairment among older people in black and minority ethnic groups. *Age and Aging, 33*(5), 447–452.

Peterson, S. G., Waring, S. C., Ivnik, R. J., Tangalos, E., & Koikmen, E. (1999). Mild cognitive impairment. Clinical characterization and outcome. *Archives of Neurology, 56,* 303–308.

Peterson, S. J., & Ganguli, J. D. (2001). Practice parameter: Early detection of dementia: Mild cognitive impairment (an evidence-based review). *Neurology, 56,* 1133–1142.

Pfieffer, E. (1975). A short portable mental status questionnaire for the assessment of organic brain deficit in elderly patients. *Journal of the American Geriatric Society, 23,* 433–441.

Reynolds, C. R., Kauffman, A. S., & McLean, J. E. (1987). Demographic characteristics and IQ among adults: Analysis of the WAIS-R standardization sample as a function of the stratification variables. *Journal of School Psychology, 23,* 323–342.

Ripich, C. B., & Ziol, E. (1997). Comparison of African-American and white persons with Alzheimer's disease on language. *Neurology, 48*(3), 781–783.

Rooks, S. E., & Miles, T. (2002). The association of race and socioeconomic status with cardiovascular disease indicators among older adults in the health, aging, and body composition study. *Journal of Gerontology B—Psychological Sciences & Social Sciences, 57B,* 247–256.

Roth, T. E., Mountjoy, C. Q., Huppert, F. A., Hendrie, A., Verma, S., & Goddard, R. (1986). A standardized instrument for the diagnosis of mental disorder in the elderly with special reference to the early detection of dementia. *British Journal of Psychiatry, 149,* 698–709.

Scaremeas, S. Y. (2004). Cognitive reserve: Implications for diagnosis and prevention of Alzheimer's disease. *Current Neurological Neuroscience Reports, 4*(5), 374–380.

Schwartz, G. T., Bolla, K. I., Stewart, W. F., Glass, G., Rasmussen, M., Bressler, J. et al. (2004). Disparities in cognitive functioning by race/ethnicity in the Baltimore Memory Study. *Environmental Health Perspectives, 112*(3), 314–320.

Shadlen, L. E., & Gibbons, L. E. (1999). Alzheimer's disease symptom severity among blacks and whites. *Journal of American Geriatric Society, 47*, 482–486.

Shadlen, L. E., Gibbons, L. E., Rice, M. M., McCormick, W. C., Bowen, J., McCurry, S. M. et al. (2001). Ethnicity and cognitive performance among older African Americans, Japanese Americans, and Caucasians: The role of education. *Journal of American Geriatric Association, 49*(10), 1371–1378.

Spencer, S. C., & Quinn, D. M., (1999). Stereotype threat and women's math performance. *Journal of Experimental Social Psychology, 35*, 4–28.

Steele, C. M. (1997). A threat in the air: How stereotypes shape intellectual identity and performance. *American Psychologist, 52*(6), 613–629.

Steele, C. M., & Aronson, J. (1995). Stereotype threat and the intellectual identity test performance of African Americans. *Journal of Personality & Social Psychology, 69*(5), 797–811.

Stern, G. B., Tatemichi, T. K., Tang, M. X., Wilder, D., & Mayeux, R. (1994). Influence of education and occupation on the incidence of Alzheimer's disease. *Journal of the American Medical Association, 271*, 1004–1010.

Strickland, L. P., Alperson, B., & Andre, K. (2005). Mini-Mental State and cognitive performance in an older African American sample. *Clinical Neuropsychologist, 19*, 87–99.

Taussig, M. K., & Ponton, M. (1996). Issues in neuropsychological assessment for Hispanic older adults: Cultural and linguistic factors. In D. Gallagher-Thompson & G. Yeo (Eds.), *Ethnicity and the Dementias* (pp. 47–58). Philadelphia: Taylor & Francis.

Taylor, S. F., & Doraiswamy, P. M. (2004). Marked increase in Alzheimer's disease identified in Medicare claims records between 1991 and 1999. *Journal of Gerontology A—Biological Sciences & Medical Sciences, 59*(7), 762–766.

Teresi, A. S., Holmes, D., & Mayeux, R. (1999). Use of latent class analyses for the estimation of prevalence of cognitive impairment, and signs of stroke and Parkinson's disease among African-American elderly of central Harlem: Results of the Harlem Aging Project. *Neuroepidemiology, 18*(6), 309–321.

Tombaugh, T. N., & McIntyre, J. (1992). The mini-mental state examination: A comprehensive review. *Journal of American Geriatric Association, 40*, 922–935.

Unverzagt, G. S., & Baiyewu, O. (2001). Prevalence of cognitive impairment: Data from the Indianapolis study of health and aging. *Neurology, 57*, 1655–1662.

Unverzagt, H. K., Torke, A. M., & Rediger, J. D. (1996). Effects of age, education and gender on CERAD neuropsychological test performance in an African American sample. *Clinical Neuropsychology, 10*, 180–190.

Urnverzagt, H. S., Farlow, M., Halk, S., & Hendrie, H. C. (1998). Cognitive decline and education in mild dementia. *Neurology, 50*(1), 181–185.

Vangel, S. J., & Lichtenberg, P. (1995). Mattis Dementia Rating Scale: Clinical utility and relationship with demographic variables. *The Clinical Neuropsychologist, 9,* 209–213.

Walker, A. R., Shergill, S., & Katona, C. L. (1997). Neuropsychological performance in Lewy body dementia and Alzheimer's disease. *British Journal of Psychiatry, 170,* 156–158.

Welsh, F. G., Wilkinson, W., Heyman, A., Mohs, R. C., Stern, Y., Harrell, L. et al. (1995). Neuropsychological test performance in African American and white patients with Alzheimer's disease. *Neurology, 45,* 207–2211.

Welsh, K. A., Butler, N., Hughes, J., Mohs, R., & Heyman, A. (1991). Detection of abnormal memory in mild cases of Alzheimer's disease using CERAD neuropsychological measures. *Archives of Neurology, 48,* 278–281.

Whalley, D. I., Appleton, C. L., & Starr, J. M. (2004). Cognitive reserve and the neurobiology of aging. *Aging Research Review,* 3(3), 369–382.

Woodard, A. A., Godsall, R. E., & Green, R. C. (1998). An analysis of test bias and differential item functioning due to race on the Mattis Rating Scale. *Journal of Gerontology: Psychological Services,* 53B(6), 370–374.

Wu, H. M., & Liang, J. (2003). Impact of diabetes on cognitive function among older Latinos: A population based cohort study. *Journal of Clinical Epidemiology, 56,* 686–693.

Yaffe, K., Lindquist, K., Penninx, B. W., Simonsick, E. M., Pahor, M., Kritchevsky, S. et al. (2003). Inflammatory markers and cognition in well-functioning African-American and white elders. *Neurology, 61,* 76–80.

Yochim, B. P., Bank, A., Mast, B. T., MacNeill, S. E., & Lichtenberg, P. A. (2003). Clinical utility of the Mattis Dementia Rating Scale in older, urban medical patients: An expanded study. *Aging Neuropsychology and Cognition,* 10(3), 230–237.

CHAPTER 4

Assessment of Cognitive Status in Asians

MALCOLM B. DICK, CORDULA DICK-MUEHLKE,
AND EVELYN L. TENG

The capacity to perform culturally and linguistically appropriate cognitive assessments is becoming increasingly important given the aging and increasing diversity of the U.S. population. By 2050, 18.7% of the U.S. population will be 65 or older, an increase of 51% over the 12.4 million this age in 2000 (U.S. Census Bureau, 2004). And, in this same time period, the minority population in the United States will increase to 47% of the total, with Asian and Pacific Islanders being one of the fastest-growing groups (U.S. Department of Commerce, 1999). The number of Asians is expected to triple from 11.2 million in 2000 to 34.4 million in 2050. While information about prevalence of dementia in most Asian minorities in the United States is not available (see chapter 1), in one study (Huang et al., 2003), researchers found nearly 75% of Chinese elders just admitted to a New York City nursing home had significant cognitive impairment.

Designed to provide primary care physicians and other clinicians with the basic knowledge and tools they need to recognize dementia in Asian patients, this chapter begins with a review of factors that make identification difficult, including cultural beliefs, linguistic differences, and challenges to accurate neuropsychological evaluation. Based on this discussion, the authors recommend a two-step approach to cognitive assessment of Asian patients, beginning with a screening that, if positive, is followed by a comprehensive dementia evaluation. Culturally and linguistically appropriate screening tools and neuropsychological test batteries are reviewed with a final caveat that successful identification of dementia among minorities requires a combination of appropriate tools with culturally and linguistically sensitive outreach.

Challenges to Assessing Dementia in Asian Elders

Identifying dementia in Asian elders is challenging for multiple reasons. At the cultural level, both misconceptions about dementia and linguistic limitations interfere with early detection (Elliott, Di Minno, Lam, & Tu, 1996). For example, in a recent telephone survey, 67% of Vietnamese but only 10% of Caucasian respondents strongly agreed with the statement "Alzheimer's disease and other forms of memory problems are a normal part of aging" (Robinson, Abbott, & Smoller, 2002). In addition, dementia may be misattributed to the stress of immigration and acculturation, an imbalance between opposing forms of energy within the body (i.e., "yin" and "yang"), mental illness, or punishment for past transgressions. As Asian languages such as Chinese and Vietnamese lack a word for dementia, other terms that foster misunderstanding, such as "crazy," "stupid," and "slow," have been used to describe cognitive impairment. As a result, dementia is usually identified only in its later stages, when behavioral symptoms can no longer be ignored or managed by families (Chow et al., 2002), but the optimal window for pharmaceutical intervention has already passed.

Underrecognition of cognitive impairment by physicians further compounds the problem. Surprisingly, 40–70% of physicians in primary care (Chodish et al., 2004; Valcour, Masaki, Curb, & Blanchette, 2000) and emergency room settings (Hustey & Meldon, 2002) fail to diagnose mild-to-moderate dementia in older patients. Physicians may miss cognitive impairment for numerous reasons, including insufficient knowledge about dementia (Barrett, Haley, Harrell, & Powers, 1997), time restraints, under-reimbursement that prohibits comprehensive evaluation, unfamiliarity with brief screening tools, and the heterogeneity of dementia. Among Caucasians, the presentation of dementia is influenced by factors such as its etiology and the individual's age, education, and gender. Wide variations occur in the type and course of symptoms as well as their impact on everyday functioning. Little is known about how the clinical presentation of dementia may vary within other cultural groups, and this ignorance further obscures diagnosis (Powell, 2002).

Two other significant barriers to the identification of dementia, which this chapter focuses on, are (a) the paucity of culturally and linguistically appropriate neuropsychological measures and (b) insufficient normative data for existing tests. Culturally fair neuropsychological evaluation has been hindered by ethnocentrism, or a presumption that the Western perspective is universally applicable, and the associated dependence of existing tools on education. In developing tests, researchers must not assume that abilities assessed by neuropsychological measures for English speakers are of equal relevance for other ethnic groups (Fortuny et al., 2005). For example, non-Western cultures may place less emphasis on reading and writing (Salmon, Jin, Zhang, Grant, & Yu, 1995). As many in the current cohort of Asian elders never had the opportunity to attend school (Xu et al., 2003), they would perform poorly on tests involving reading, writing, and other education-based skills. As a result, cognitive impairment may be overdiagnosed when minority individuals with little or no formal education are assessed with tests developed for better-educated English-speaking populations, and when test norms are insufficiently adjusted for lower levels of education (Liu, Teng, et al., 1994).

Some Pitfalls in the Neuropsychological Testing of Asian Populations

To assess cognitive impairment in non-English-speaking populations, researchers have either developed new tools or translated and adapted tests originally developed for English-speaking individuals. While newly developed tools may be more sensitive to linguistic and cultural differences, the validation process is complex, time consuming, and expensive (Xu et al., 2003). It can be particularly challenging to identify sufficient numbers of well-diagnosed individuals from a specific minority group to validate a new test. Consequently, researchers have found it more attractive to translate and adapt existing tests. Although easier and useful for exploring differences related to language, culture, and socioeconomic status, this approach has hidden pitfalls, some of which are discussed below.

Linguistic Differences

Both the availability and complexity of words within a language can make translating and adapting existing tests challenging. A given language may lack the words for a particular test item or response, thus making direct translation impossible. For example, the Visual Naming subtest of the Multilingual Aphasia Examination (Benton & Hamsher, 1978) requires the naming of some body parts, including *shin* and *instep*, but such words just do not exist in the Chinese language. As another example, idiomatic expressions such as the "no ifs, ands, or buts" used in the Mini-Mental State Examination

(MMSE; Folstein, Folstein, & McHugh, 1975) are difficult to translate or adapt, as such sayings have no counterparts in other languages.

Complexity of a language may also influence the difficulty level of test items. For example, reciting the months of the year backwards, a common test item, is easier in the Chinese language than in the English language. In Chinese, this task is similar to counting backwards from 12 to 1, as the months are named Month 1, Month 2, and so forth. Word length may also make tasks easier or more difficult. When translated versions of the Wechsler Adult Intelligence Scale-Revised (WAIS-R) Digit Span (Wechsler, 1981) and Consortium to Establish a Registry for Alzheimer's Disease (CERAD) Animal Fluency (Mohs, Rosen, & Davis, 1983) tests were administered to English-, Chinese-, Spanish-, and Vietnamese-speaking participants, Hispanics scored lowest, while Chinese and Vietnamese scored highest (Dick, Teng, Kempler, Davis, & Taussig, 2002; Kempler, Teng, Dick, Taussig, & Davis, 1998). In Spanish, most of the numbers from one to nine and many animal names are multisyllabic, while in both Chinese and Vietnamese, all the digits and a majority of the animal names are monosyllabic. It is well known that multisyllabic terms are more difficult to retrieve from semantic memory (e.g., Le Dorze, 1992) and to store and manipulate in working memory (Caplan, Rochon, & Waters, 1992).

Brush Versus Pencil

Many neuropsychological tests involve the use of a pencil or pen; however, it cannot be assumed that use of these writing instruments is a universal ability or that drawing tasks are culturally fair. Interestingly, Chinese elders in Shanghai tested with a translated version of the MMSE were better at recalling words than copying designs (Salmon et al., 1989), and some educated participants were reluctant to perform the writing and drawing items (Salmon et al., 1995). One possible explanation rests in the educational experience of these Chinese elders. When they were in school, drawing was considered frivolous and not taught, and writing was performed with brushes that require delicate forms of motor control quite different from those involved in using a pen or pencil. All sensory–motor skills require extensive practice for proficiency. Even a Western concert pianist would have trouble using chopsticks at first. It is as far-fetched to assume that using a pen or pencil is a universal skill as it is to presume Westerners could automatically use chopsticks.

Timed Tasks and Nonverbal Tests

Although highly valued in the United States, where efficiency and competitiveness permeate the society, fast performance may be less important in other cultures. In acquiring norms for the Cross-Cultural Neuropsychological Test Battery (CCNB; Dick et al., 2002), Part A of the Trail Making Test (Spreen & Strauss, 1998) was administered to 54 African American, 70 Caucasian, 71 Chinese, 80 Hispanic, and 61 Vietnamese healthy adults with an average age of 73 years. In this task, the individual is asked to draw a continuous line as quickly as possible to connect 25 sequentially numbered circles irregularly positioned on a sheet of paper. African American, Chinese, Hispanic, and Vietnamese elders were all slower at performing the task than were their Caucasian peers, who took an average of 51 s ($SD = 21$s). Notably, Chinese participants, whose education was comparable to that of the Caucasians, took significantly longer ($M = 76$, $SD = 48$ s). Given these results, the fairness of using timed tasks across ethnic groups is questionable in the absence of culture-specific norms.

It was previously presumed that tests emphasizing nonverbal abilities could minimize the effects of language and culture on test performance, but research has refuted this assumption. Nonverbal measures, which frequently emphasize response speed and are heavily dependent on abilities (e.g., drawing, constructional skills) acquired in school, have been found to be no more (Rosselli & Ardila, 2003) or even less (Anastasi, 1988) culturally fair than verbal tests.

A Two-Stage Approach to Identifying Cognitive Impairment

Detecting dementia early is critical, as pharmaceutical treatment with the cholinesterase inhibitors is most effective while impairments are still mild (van Reekum, Simard, & Farcnik, 1999). Unfortunately, for reasons mentioned earlier, minority elders typically do not seek medical attention for dementia until the later stages. Therefore, it is incumbent on the primary care physician to screen for dementia if there is any suspicion about cognitive impairment during a clinical visit. A practical and cost-effective two-step approach to dementia evaluation (Powell, 2002) can facilitate and simplify the process of identifying cognitive impairment for primary care physicians, whose time and resources are limited. In this approach, individuals suspected to have cognitive impairment are screened with a brief culturally and linguistically appropriate measure. If the screening is positive for impairment, the individual is referred for a standard diagnostic workup that includes additional neuropsychological testing, a neurological examination, brain imaging, and blood analysis. Results of the workup would (a) verify the presence of cognitive impairment, (b) rule out confounding factors (e.g., depression, medication side effects, metabolic disorders) that might account for the cognitive difficulties, (c) establish a differential diagnosis, and (d) provide the basis for treatment recommendations. As space limitations do not permit a comprehensive review of all cognitive measures used with Asian populations, the remainder of this chapter will focus on three screening instruments and two neuropsychological batteries that have cross-cultural applicability.

Three Screening Tests

Mini-Mental State Examination

The MMSE is the most widely used test to screen for and grade the severity of dementia. It takes approximately 10 min to administer, has a score range of 0–30, and assesses seven areas of functioning: orientation, attention, mental manipulation, recent memory, language, praxis, and visual–spatial abilities. The MMSE has been translated into multiple Asian languages, including Chinese (Katzman et al., 1988; Xu et al., 2003), Hindi (Ganguili et al., 1995), and Korean (Lee et al., 2002). Applicability of these translated versions varies based on the extent to which they have been adapted for local languages and cultures. For example, a minimally adapted Chinese version of the MMSE, the CMMSE, has been used in epidemiological studies in Shanghai (Katzman et al., 1988; Zhang et al., 1990) and Beijing (Li et al., 1991). While the CMMSE proved appropriate for testing the more Westernized and educated individuals living in these metropolitan areas, the MMSE required further adaptations to effectively assess cognitive impairment in the less-educated, rural-dwelling individuals who comprise 80% of mainland China's population (Xu et al., 2003). In developing the Chinese-adapted MMSE (CAMSE) for persons with little or no formal education, Xu et al. strove to keep the contents of test items similar to those of the original MMSE while reducing language dependence and increasing sociocultural relevance. For example, in the CAMSE, the elder is asked to name a button rather than a pencil, because an illiterate individual would have little experience with a writing instrument. Similarly, as reading and following the written command "Close your eyes" would be inappropriate for an illiterate individual, the comparable item in the CAMSE involves orally directing the elder to imitate the posture of a man with his arms crossed over his chest, as illustrated in a cartoon.

Hasegawa Dementia Scale-Revised

The Hasegawa Dementia Scale-Revised (HDS-R; Imai & Hasegawa, 1994) and its predecessor, the Hasegawa Dementia Screening Scale (HDSS; Hasegawa, 1983), have been used widely in East Asian countries. The nine-item HDS-R takes several minutes to administer, has a score range of 0–9, and assesses five areas of functioning: orientation, memory, attention, calculation, and category fluency (Imai & Hasegawa, 1994; Kim et al., 2005). Unlike the MMSE, the HDS-R does not require reading, writing, drawing, or the ability to follow commands. Consequently, the HDS-R has greater applicability for individuals with limited education or motor impairments. In addition, it can be administered over the telephone. While both the MMSE and HDS-R proved sensitive to Alzheimer's disease in a study of Korean elders (Kim et al., 2005), the MMSE showed a higher false-positive rate among participants with limited education. While omitting visual–spatial and praxis items has some clear advantages, the lack of these measures in the HDS-R makes it less sensitive for detecting some forms of dementia (e.g., Dementia with Lewy Bodies) that are characterized by motor or perceptual impairments.

Cognitive Abilities Screening Instrument

The Cognitive Abilities Screening Instrument (CASI) was specifically designed for easy cross-cultural adaptation (Teng, 1996; Teng et al., 1994). It takes approximately 20 min to administer, has a score range of 0–100, and includes items from the MMSE, the HDS, and the Modified Mini-Mental State (3MS; Teng & Chui, 1987), plus three additional questions to assess judgment. The 3MS standardized the administration and refined the scoring of the MMSE, expanded the assessment of short-term memory, and added new items to assess long-term memory, category fluency, and abstract thinking, thereby reducing the floor and ceiling effects of the original instrument. Improvements made in the 3MS were incorporated into the CASI. Items in the CASI are grouped under the cognitive domains of attention, concentration, orientation, short-term memory, long-term memory, language, visual construction, category fluency, abstract thinking, and judgment. As each domain score as well as the total score showed continued deterioration with the progression of dementia (Liu et al., 2002), the CASI can be used as a staging as well as a screening tool. Estimated scores for the MMSE, 3MS, and HDS can be derived from subsets of the CASI items, a feature that facilitates comparison with studies that use these other instruments.

Based on the original CASI (CASI E-1.0) developed for a North American English-speaking population (Teng et al., 1994), versions have been developed and validated with English-speaking Chamorros on Guam (CASI E-2.0; Waring et al., 1994), Chinese elders in Kimmen and Taiwan (CASI C-2.0; Liu, Chou, et al., 1994; Liu, Teng, et al., 1994), and Japanese elders in Seattle (Graves et al., 1996), Honolulu (White et al., 1996), and Japan (Yamada et al., 1999). Additionally, preliminary Spanish and Vietnamese versions have been developed and incorporated into the CCNB (Dick et al., 2002). Cutoff scores and associated sensitivity and specificity values have been reported elsewhere (Lin, Wang, Liu, Chen, Lee, & Liu, 2002; Teng et al., 1994).

Age and education have consistently been found to affect scores on the CASI (Liu, Chou, et al., 1994; McCurry et al., 1999; Teng et al., 1994). Cutoff scores were identified by educational level in a large study (Lin et al., 2002) involving 2,096 Chinese elders (65 years of age and older) in Kimmen and Taipei, Taiwan—1,178 diagnosed with dementia and 918 without dementia. In those with no formal education, a cutoff score of <50 yielded a sensitivity of 83% and a specificity of 85%. With 1–5 years of schooling, the cutoff increased to <68, with a sensitivity of 83% and a specificity of 91%. With 6 or more years of education, the cutoff score increased further to <80, with a sensitivity of 89% and a specificity of 90%.

The CASI-Short (Teng et al., 1994), comprised of just four items with a total score range of 0–33, has particular relevance for screening in a managed care environment. The four items—repeating three words, temporal orientation, animal naming for 30 s, and recalling three words—take only a few minutes to administer and the test can be given over the phone. In early studies, the CASI-Short performed as well as the entire CASI, the 3MS, and the MMSE in screening for dementia (Teng et al., 1994). In analyses of data from larger samples of participants with a wider range of education, the CASI-Short was actually better than the other instruments in identifying dementia among persons with very low levels of education (i.e., 0–3 years; Teng, Larson, Lin, Graves, & Liu, 1998). The CASI-Short may have been particularly effective in this group because it assesses areas impaired early in dementia (i.e., recent memory, temporal orientation, category fluency) and does not require reading, writing, drawing, arithmetic, and other abilities gained through schooling. When tests include education-dependent items, unimpaired individuals with little schooling could score worse than well-educated individuals with early dementia, thereby reducing the sensitivity and the specificity of the instruments.

Cross-Cultural Neuropsychological Test Battery

Although the CASI total score has proven to be effective for screening and staging dementia, researchers (Liu et al., 2002; McCurry et al., 1999) have recommended against using subscale score patterns or individual cut-points for screening purposes. Scores for eight of the nine subscales have a limited range of 0–12 points, resulting in substantial floor and ceiling effects. For example, persons with mild dementia score at the floor on the CASI three-item short-term memory task, while adults without dementia perform at the ceiling. Given such limitations, further testing may be necessary to fully evaluate specific cognitive abilities. Two culturally and linguistically appropriate options for an in-depth neuropsychological evaluation are the Alzheimer's Disease Assessment Scale–Cognitive Subscale (ADAS-Cog; Mohs et al., 1983) and the Cross-Cultural Neuropsychological Test Battery (CCNB; Dick et al., 2002).

The ADAS-Cog, specifically designed to assess domains of functioning affected by Alzheimer's disease, has been translated into multiple Asian (i.e., Chinese, Japanese, Korean) and European (e.g., French, German, Greek, Italian, Spanish) languages. Two versions of the ADAS-Cog are available in Chinese: one in which pictures were substituted for words in the 10-item list-learning task (Liu et al., 2002) and the other in which standard procedures are used (Wang et al., 2004). In the standard administration, individuals unable to read the list are taught the words and asked to repeat them during the learning phase of the recall and recognition trials. The two versions were equally effective at discriminating mild from moderate Alzheimer's disease in Chinese elders with varying levels of education.

Developed with particular attention to cultural and linguistic factors that can affect neuropsychological test performance, the CCNB offers an alternative tool for the evaluation of dementia in minority populations. To achieve cross-cultural applicability, the developers (Dick et al., 2002) (a) minimized administration time by limiting the battery to 11 tests, (b) incorporated five well-established measures into the battery to facilitate comparisons between English- and non-English-speaking groups, (c) reduced the effects of education through strategies such as using oral instructions and pictorial stimulus information, (d) included tests appropriate for persons with moderate-to-severe dementia as most minority families delay seeking help, and (e) recommended having the battery administered by a bilingual examiner in the patient's primary language rather than through a translator.

The CCNB includes the CASI as a measure of global mental status and 10 additional tests to assess six cognitive domains: recent memory, attention, language, reasoning ability, visual–spatial skills, and psychomotor speed. In the Common Objects Memory Test (COMT), developed by Dick et al. (2002), the individual is shown 10 photographs of everyday objects to learn across three acquisition trials. A test of free recall is given immediately after each trial, with delayed recall and recognition tests after 5 min and 30 min. Language abilities are assessed with Category Fluency for animal names from the CERAD battery (Morris et al., 1989) and two tests developed by the authors—confrontational naming of body parts and auditory comprehension of multistep commands. To assess visual–spatial skills, the battery includes two well-known tests, WAIS-R Block Design (Wechsler, 1981) and CERAD Figure Drawing (Morris et al., 1989), plus a third developed by the authors, Read and Set Time. In this test, the individual is asked to read the time on three different clocks and to draw the hands of a clock at three specific times. As a measure of reasoning ability, the authors developed a culturally appropriate picture completion test that taps concepts similar to those assessed in the WAIS-R. Additionally, the CCNB includes WAIS-R Digit Span as a measure of attention and Part A of the Trail Making Test to assess psychomotor speed as well as attention.

The entire CCNB was administered to 336 healthy older adults from five ethnic groups: African American, Caucasian, Chinese, Hispanic, and Vietnamese. In the latter three groups, the majority of participants spoke only their native language at home and did not read English. All participants were free of major health problems, cognitive impairment, depression, and functional deficits based on informant report using standardized measures. Participants were 54–99 years old (*M* = 74, *SD* = 8.4) and had 0–22 years of schooling (*M* = 10.2, *SD* = 4.6). Normative data are reported elsewhere (Dick et al., 2002), with major findings highlighted here.

Education contributed significantly to performance on most tests; however, age affected scores only on measures of recent memory and psychomotor speed. Both ethnicity and language affected performance on tests of attention, category fluency, and visual–spatial skills. Notably, the COMT was not affected by ethnicity or education. As a whole, the participants with dementia scored significantly worse than their healthy peers on the entire CCNB. The CASI and COMT proved particularly useful in discriminating healthy from impaired individuals in all five ethnic groups. Consequently, these two tests could form the core of a shorter battery to further reduce administration time. Analyses of data from 80 healthy Hispanics and 39 Hispanics with dementia revealed that a shorter battery of five tests, namely, the CASI, COMT, CERAD Figure Drawing, Auditory Comprehension, and WAIS-R Block Design, was appropriate for diagnostic evaluation in this specific ethnic group. Ongoing research is attempting to identify the essential tests for other groups in order to shorten the battery yet maintain diagnostic accuracy.

Conclusion

Taking into consideration the multiple cultural and linguistic challenges that can interfere with the accurate assessment of cognitive functioning in Asians, this chapter outlined a time- and cost-effective approach to help physicians better identify dementia in this population. When cognitive impairment is suspected, it is critical that the physician or other health-care professional screen the individual for dementia with one of the culturally and linguistically appropriate tools reviewed here in order to facilitate early diagnosis and treatment. If the screening is positive, a comprehensive evaluation, including further cognitive testing with a tool such as the Cross-Cultural Neuropsychological Test Battery, is warranted. Finally, it should be noted that the availability of appropriate assessment instruments will only result in better identification to the extent that tools are paired with culturally and linguistically sensitive outreach.

References

Anastasi, A. (1988). *Psychological testing.* New York: Macmillan.

Barrett, J., Haley, W., Harrell, L., & Powers, R. (1997). Knowledge about Alzheimer's disease among primary care physicians, psychologists, nurses, and social workers. *Alzheimer's Disease & Associated Disorders, 11*(2), 99–106.

Benton, A. L., & Hamsher, K. (1978). *Multilingual aphasia examination.* Iowa City: University of Iowa Hospitals.

Caplan, D., Rochon, E., & Waters, G. S. (1992). Articulatory and phonological determinants of word length effects in span tasks. *Quarterly Journal of Experimental Psychology: Human Experimental Psychology, 45,* 177–192.

Chodish, J., Petitti, D., Elliott, M., Hays, R. D., Crooks, V. C., Reuban, D. B., Buckwalter, J. G., & Wenger, N. (2004). Physician recognition of cognitive impairment: Evaluating the need for improvement. *Journal of the American Geriatrics Society, 52*(7), 1051–1059.

Chow, T. W., Liu, C. K., Fuh, J. L., Leung, V. P. Y., Tai, C. T., Chen, L. -W. et al. (2002). Neuropsychiatric symptoms of Alzheimer's disease differ in Chinese and American patients. *International Journal of Geriatric Psychiatry, 17,* 22–28.

Dick, M. B., Teng, E. L., Kempler, D., Davis, D. S., & Taussig, I. M. (2002). The Cross-Cultural Neuropsychological Test Battery (CCSN): Effects of age, education, ethnicity, and cognitive status on performance. In F. R. Ferraro (Ed.), *Minority and cross-cultural aspects of neuropsychological assessment* (pp. 17–41). Lisse, the Netherlands: Swets & Zeitlinger.

Elliott, K. S., Di Minno, M., Lam, D., & Tu, A. M. (1996). Working with Chinese families in the context of dementia. In G. Yeo & D. Gallagher-Thompson (Eds.), *Ethnicity and the dementias* (pp. 89–108). Washington, DC: Taylor & Francis.

Folstein, M. F., Folstein, S. E., & McHugh, P. R. (1975). "Mini-Mental State": A practical method for grading the cognitive state of patients for the clinician. *Journal of Psychiatric Research, 12,* 189–198.

Fortuny, L. A. I., Garolera, M., Romo, D. H., Feldman, E., Barillas, H. F., Keefe, R. et al. (2005). Research with Spanish-speaking populations in the United States: Lost in the translation—a commentary and a plea. *Journal of Clinical and Experimental Neuropsychology, 27,* 555–564.

Ganguili, M., Ratcliff, G., Chandra, V., Sharma, S., Gilby, J., Pandav, R. et al. (1995). A Hindi version of the MMSE: The development of a cognitive screening instrument for a largely illiterate rural elderly population in India. *International Journal of Geriatric Psychiatry, 10,* 367–377.

Graves, A. B., Larson, E. B., Edland, S. D., Bowen, J. D., McCormick, W. C., McCurry, S. M. et al. (1996). Prevalence of dementia and its subtypes in the Japanese American population of King County, Washington State: The Kame project. *American Journal of Epidemiology, 144,* 760–771.

Hasegawa, K. (1983). The clinical assessment of dementia in the aged: A dementia screening scale for psychogeriatric patients. In M. Bergener, U. Lehr, E. Lang, & R. Schmitz-Scherzer (Eds.), *Aging in the eighties and beyond* (pp. 207–218). New York: Springer.

Huang, Z. –B., Neufeld, R. R., Likourezos, A., Breuer, B., Khaski, A., Milano, E. et al. (2003). Sociodemographic and health characteristics of older Chinese on admission to a nursing home: A cross-racial/ethnic study. *Journal of American Geriatrics Society, 51,* 404–409.

Hustey, F. M., & Meldon, S. W. (2002). The prevalence and documentation of impaired mental status in elderly emergency department patients. *Annals of Emergency Medicine, 39,* 248–253.

Imai, Y., & Hasegawa, K. (1994). The Revised Hasegawa's Dementia Scale (HDS-R)—Evaluation of its usefulness as a screening test for dementia. *Journal of Hong Kong College of Psychiatrists, 4*(Suppl. 2), 20–24.

Katzman, R., Zhang, M., Quang-Ya-Qu, Wang, Z., Liu, W. T., Yu, E., Wong, S. C., Salmon, D. P., & Grant, I. (1988). A Chinese version of the Mini-Mental State Examination: Impact of illiteracy in a Shanghai dementia survey. *Journal of Clinical Epidemiology, 41,* 971–978.

Kempler, D., Teng, E. L., Dick, M. B., Taussig, I. M., & Davis, D. S. (1998). The effects of age, education, and ethnicity on verbal fluency. *Journal of the International Neuropsychological Society, 4,* 531–538.

Kim, K. W., Lee, D. Y., Jhoo, J. H., Youn, J. C., Suh, Y. J., Jun, Y. H. et al. (2005). Diagnostic accuracy of Mini-Mental Status Examination and Revised Hasegawa Dementia Scale for Alzheimer's disease. *Dementia and Geriatric Cognitive Disorders, 19,* 324–330.

Le Dorze, G. (1992). The effects of age, educational level, and stimulus length on naming in normal subjects. *Journal of Speech-Language Pathology & Audiology, 16,* 21–29.

Lee, J. H., Lee, K. U., Lee, D. Y., Kim, K. W., Jhoo, J. H., Kim, J. H. et al. (2002). Development of the Korean version of the Consortium to Establish a Registry for Alzheimer's Disease Assessment Packet (CERAD-K): Clinical and neuropsychological assessment batteries. *Journal of Gerontology, 57,* P47–P53.

Li, G., Shen, Y. C., Chen, C. H., Zhau, Y. W., Li, S. R., & Lu, M. (1991). A three-year follow-up study of age-related dementia in an urban area of Beijing. *Acta Psychiatrica Scandinavia, 83,* 99–104.

Lin, K. -N., Wang, P. -N., Chai-Yih, L., Chen, W. -T., Lee, Y. -C., & Liu, H. -C. (2002). Cutoff scores of the Cognitive Abilities Screening Instrument, Chinese version in screening of dementia. *Dementia and Geriatric Cognitive Disorders, 14,* 176–182.

Liu, H. C., Chou, P., Lin, K. N., Wang, S. J., Fuh, J. L., Lin, H. C. et al. (1994). Assessing cognitive abilities and dementia in a predominantly illiterate population of older individuals in Kinmen. *Psychological Medicine, 24,* 763–770.

Liu, H. C., Teng, E. L., Lin, K. N., Chuang, Y. Y., Wang, P. N., Fuh, J. L. et al. (2002). Performance on the Cognitive Abilities Screening Instrument (CASI) at different stages of Alzheimer's disease. *Dementia and Geriatric Cognitive Disorders, 13,* 244–248.

Liu, H. C., Teng, E. L., Lin, K. N., Hsu, T. C., Guo, N. W., Chou, P. et al. (1994). Performance on a dementia screening test in relation to demographic variables: A study of 5,297 community residents in Taiwan. *Archive of Neurology, 51,* 910–915.

McCurry, S. M., Edland, S. D., Teri, L., Kukull, W. A., Bowen, J. D., McCormick, W. C. et al. (1999). The Cognitive Abilities Screening Instrument (CASI): Data from a cohort of 2524 cognitively intact elderly. *International Journal of Geriatric Psychiatry, 14,* 882–888.

Mohs, R. C., Rosen, W. G., & Davis, K. L. (1983). The Alzheimer's Disease Assessment Scale: An instrument for assessing treatment efficacy. *Psychopharmacology Bulletin, 24,* 627–628.

Morris, J. C., Heyman, A., Mohs, R. C., Hughes, J. P., van Belle, G., Fillenbaum, G. et al. (1989). The Consortium to Establish a Registry for Alzheimer's Disease (CERAD). Part 1. Clinical and neuropsychological assessment of Alzheimer's disease. *Neurology, 39,* 1159–1165.

Powell, A. (2002). On issues pertinent to Alzheimer's disease and cultural diversity. *Alzheimer's and Associated Disorders, 16,* S43–S45.

Reekum, van, R., Simard, M., & Farcnik, K. (1999). Diagnosis of dementia and treatment of Alzheimer's disease: Pharmacologic management of disease progression and cognitive impairment. *Canadian Family Physician, 45,* 945–952.

Robinson, G., Abbott, P., & Smoller, F. (2002). Orange County long-term care multilingual senior needs assessment telephone survey: Preliminary results.

Report. Fullerton: California State University Fullerton, Social Science Research Center.

Rosselli, M., & Ardila, A. (2003). The impact of culture and education on non-verbal neuropsychological measurements: A critical review. *Brain and Cognition, 52*, 326–333.

Salmon, D. P, Jin, H., Zhang, M., Grant, I., & Yu, E. (1995). Neuropsychological assessment of Chinese elderly in the Shanghai Dementia Survey. *The Clinical Neuropsychologist, 9*, 159–168.

Salmon, D. P., Riekkinen, P., Katzman, R., Zhang, M., Jin, H., & Yu, E. (1989). Cross-cultural studies of dementia: A comparison of Mini-Mental State Examination performance in Finland and China. *Archives of Neurology, 46*, 769–772.

Spreen, O., & Strauss, E. (1998). Trail Making Tests. In O. Spreen & E. Strauss (Eds.), *A compendium of neuropsychological tests: Administration, norms, and commentary* (2nd ed., pp. 533–547). New York: Oxford University Press.

Teng, E. L. (1996). Cross-cultural testing and the Cognitive Abilities Screening Instrument. In G. Yeo & D. Gallagher-Thompson (Eds.), *Ethnicity and the dementias* (pp. 77–85). Washington, DC: Taylor & Francis.

Teng, E. L., & Chui, H. C. (1987). The Modified Mini-Mental State (3MS) Examination. *Journal of Clinical Psychiatry, 48*, 314–318.

Teng, E. L., Hasegawa, K., Homma, A., Imai, Y., Larson, E., Graves, A. et al. (1994). The Cognitive Abilities Screening Instrument (CASI): A practical test for cross-cultural epidemiological studies of dementia. *International Psychogeriatrics, 6*, 45–58.

Teng, E. L., Larson, E., Lin, K., Graves, A., & Liu, H. (1998). Screening for dementia: The Cognitive Abilities Screening Instrument–Short Version (CASI-Short). *Clinical Neuropsychologist, 12*, 256.

U.S. Census Bureau. (2004). *U.S. interim projections by age, sex, race, and Hispanic origin.* Retrieved October 18, 2005, from www.census.gov/ipc/www/usinterimproj/

U.S. Department of Commerce. (1999). *Minority population growth: 1995 to 2050.* Retrieved October 18, 2005, from www.mbda.gov/documents/mbdacolor.pdf

Valcour, V. G., Masaki, K. H., Curb, J. D., & Blanchette, P. L. (2000). The detection of dementia in the primary care setting. *Archives of Internal Medicine, 160*, 2964–2968.

Wang, H., Yu, X., Li, S., Chen, Y., Li, H., & He, J. (2004). The cognitive subscale of the Alzheimer's Disease Assessment Scale, Chinese version in staging of Alzheimer's disease. *Alzheimer's Disease and Associated Disorders, 18*, 231–235.

Waring, S. C., Esteban-Santillan, C., Teng, E., Peterson, R. C., O'Brien, P. C., & Kurland, L. T. (1994). Evaluation of a modified version of the Cognitive Abilities Screening Instrument (CASI) for assessment of dementia in elderly Chamorros on Guam. Abstract. *Neurobiology of Aging, 15*(Suppl. 1), S43.

Wechsler, D. (1981). *Wechsler Adult Intelligence Scale-Revised.* San Antonio, TX: The Psychological Corp.

White, L., Petrovitch, H., Ross, G. W., Masaki, K. H., Abbott, R. D., Teng, E. L. et al. (1996). Prevalence of dementia in older Japanese-American men in Hawaii: The Honolulu-Asia Aging Study. *Journal of the American Medical Association, 276,* 955–960.

Xu, G., Meyer, J. S., Huang, Y., Du, F., Chowdhury, M., & Quach, M. (2003). Adapting Mini-Mental State Examination for dementia screening among illiterate or minimally educated elderly Chinese. *International Journal of Geriatric Psychiatry, 18,* 609–616.

Yamada, M., Sasaki, H., Mimori, Y., Kasagi, F., Sudoh, S., Ikeda, J. et al. (1999). Prevalence and risks of dementia in the Japanese population: RERF's Adult Health Study Hiroshima subjects. *Journal of American Geriatrics Society, 47,* 189–195.

Zhang, M. Y., Katzman, R., Salmon, D., Jin, H., Cai, G., Wang, Z. et al. (1990). The prevalence of dementia and Alzheimer's disease in Shanghai, China: Impact of age, gender, and education. *Annals of Neurology, 27,* 428–437.

CHAPTER 5

Neuropsychological Assessment of Hispanics Elders

Challenges and Psychometric Approaches

DAN MUNGAS

Chronic diseases of aging, such as Alzheimer's disease (AD) and cerebrovascular disease (CVD), have enormous impacts on quality of life for patients and their families and also have major societal and economic impacts. The older population at risk for developing these diseases has been growing at a rapid rate, and this growth has been especially rapid in minority groups in general and in Hispanic populations in particular. While the prevalence of dementia in ethnic minority populations has not been well studied, there is some evidence of increased dementia prevalence in community-dwelling Hispanics compared with Caucasians (Gurland et al., 1999; Tang et al., 2001). Absent dramatically improved prophylactic therapies, increased longevity in the general population and in minority groups will result in a corresponding increase in the number of persons with AD and other dementias. As a result, the social and economic costs of dementia will be magnified.

Neuropsychological assessment is recognized as a central component of the clinical evaluation of patients with neurological disorders (American Academy of Neurology Therapeutics and Technology Assessment Subcommittee, 1996), and more recently of mild cognitive impairment

(Petersen et al., 2001), which is thought to represent a transitional stage between normal cognitive function and dementia. Sensitive and accurate clinical assessment of cognitive impairment will become increasingly important as more effective treatments become available for diseases like AD. Improved availability of treatments coupled with demographic trends will converge to create an expanding demand for neuropsychological assessment methods that are appropriate for the increasingly diverse older population. The focus of this chapter is on assessment of one large and important subgroup, Hispanics.

Neuropsychological assessment of Hispanics presents challenges that apply to other minority groups and presents unique challenges. As with other groups, minority status in general is associated with different life experiences and environmental exposures that can complicate assessment of cognition. For example, minority groups as a whole often have less formal education, and there is increasing evidence that the quality of the formal education they receive may be different than that afforded to the majority culture (Manly et al., 1999; Manly, Jacobs, Touradji, Small, & Stern, 2002). These variables have been shown to have a substantial impact on performance on neuropsychological tests. A finding that is counterintuitive on the surface is that these effects are observed on nonverbal and simple psychomotor tasks as well as on more complicated, language-dependent, and seemingly culturally bound tasks. One hypothesis that may help to explain this finding is that education promotes familiarity with the process of being tested and so confers advantages beyond direct enhancement of specific knowledge or skills related to the task.

There are special challenges involved with assessment of older Hispanics. First, language is an important factor. While many older Hispanics are monolingual Spanish speakers, there are also substantial numbers of monolingual English speakers and of bilingual individuals. In addition to linguistic diversity, there is also racial, cultural, and regional diversity. Hispanic ethnicity encompasses many different racial groups, including Caucasians, African Americans, Native Americans, and Asians. Country of origin varies widely from Europe, to the Caribbean region, Mexico, Central America, and South America, and there are substantial cultural and experiential differences both across and within these regions. This diversity is further compounded by incredible diversity of demographic characteristics and level of acculturation within seemingly homogenous groups. In our experience working with predominantly Mexican American Hispanics from northern California, for example, relatively high percentages of this group have no formal education, are monolingual Spanish speakers despite having lived in the United States for much of their lives, and have not assimilated the dominant Anglo culture. However, there are also substantial numbers who have college degrees, speak English only or are fully bilingual, and are well adapted to the dominant culture.

The exceptional diversity of Hispanic elders presents a number of critical challenges for neuropsychological assessment. The ultimate goal of clinical neuropsychological assessment of older patients is to be able to sensitively identify cognitive changes associated with diseases of aging, such as AD, and other diseases that might affect cognition, such as cerebrovascular disease and diabetes. A conceptual model that illustrates the difficulties encountered in this process is presented in the next section.

Determinants of Cognitive Function and Implications for Neuropsychological Assessment

Figure 5.1 presents a model to account for differences in cognitive functioning and cognitive test performance. The core of the model in Figure 5.1 describes how diseases of aging affect brain structure and function, which in turn affect cognitive ability. The primary purpose of neuropsychological assessment is to characterize the direct pathway from disease to brain to cognition, using neuropsychological tests to make inferences about the presence of disease and brain changes affecting cognition. This model shows pathways by which ethnicity and associated demographic diversity can influence cognitive function and might modify or complicate the characterization of the disease–brain–cognition pathway. There are many different pathways by which ethnicity can influence manifest cognitive ability. On one side of the diagram, ethnicity is associated with environmental variables, education for example, that might have a direct effect on development of cognitive skills and knowledge. Different linguistic exposures would also operate at this level. Ethnicity is also associated with environmental factors (such as poverty, reduced access to health

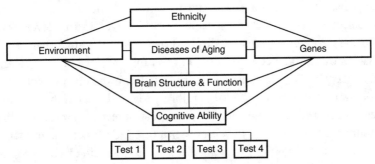

Figure 5.1 Conceptual model for multiple influences on cognition and cognitive test scores.

care, and nutrition) that might indirectly influence cognitive function via mediating effects on diseases of aging and brain structure and function. Ultimately, all of these variables might have direct (nondisease) effects on cognition and may also have indirect effects mediated via an association with disease. The other side of the diagram describes genetic influences, which similarly can operate at multiple levels in the chain from disease to brain to cognition.

There are features of this model that are important to highlight. First, ethnicity is considered to have multiple pathways by which clinical status of older persons is affected. The challenge is to decompose effects of ethnicity into measurable variables that explain ethnic differences. Second, this model explicitly recognizes that diseases such as AD and CVD are not the only determinants of cognitive function, and that genetic and environmental variables have important influences independent of age-associated disease.

For neuropsychological tests to make a contribution in the clinical assessment of cognition of older Hispanics, they must be able to disentangle some of these complex relationships. There are important prerequisites for an effective neuropsychological test. First, it must have a demonstrable relationship with brain structure and function and diseases of aging. Ideally, the test should be sensitive to cognitive effects observed across a broad range of disease progression from normal to demented and to variations in brain structure and function from normal to seriously compromised. Second, nondisease influences on test scores must be understood so that disease effects can be estimated independent of these confounding effects. This is particularly important in one-time, cross-sectional assessments, where tests results are used to make inferences about disease presence, but where longitudinal results are not available to help to separate confounding nondisease effects on baseline scores from disease effects. This can be accomplished by using accurate norms to help define the range of normal performance in the group of interest. However, in the development of norms, researchers must be directed by empirical results that identify variables that influence test scores in the range of normal performance, and consequently, they must be incorporated into the norms. Note that a corollary of this model is that susceptibility to nondisease influences, such as education and language, does not invalidate a test if (a) there is a direct relationship between that test, brain structure, and function, and (b) the extraneous pathways not involving disease and the brain can be accounted for adequately. These are essentially empirical questions that will figure prominently in subsequent discussion in this chapter.

Traditional Approaches to Neuropsychological Assessment of Hispanics

The traditional approach to neuropsychological assessment with minority patients has often used existing neuropsychological tests, typically developed with primarily Caucasian samples, as the starting point. For Hispanics and other linguistic minorities, this process requires translation of the test items and instructions into Spanish or other target languages of interest. The development of empirical norms appropriate to the group of interest is an important next step that enables identification of abnormal test results. Finally, validation against external criteria, a diagnosis of dementia or AD, for example, is often part of the development process.

This approach has been applied most frequently to the screening tests for assessing global cognition. There also have been attempts to create more comprehensive neuropsychological assessment batteries. For example, Ardila and colleagues (Ardila, Rosselli, & Puente, 1993) described a comprehensive battery adapted for use with Spanish-speaking Columbians. Dick, Teng, Kempler, Davis, and Taussig (2002) developed a neuropsychological test battery for use with multiple cultures and languages, and this battery included English- and Spanish-language versions that could be used with Hispanics. Jacobs and colleagues (1997) described development of a Spanish-language neuropsychological test battery that has been used in subsequent studies of dementia in multi-ethnic samples (Gurland et al., 1999; Tang et al., 2001).

These previous approaches to neuropsychological test development have been described and reviewed (Ferraro, 2002) in previous publications and will not be addressed in detail in this chapter. These works have made important advances in the neuropsychological assessment of older Hispanics, but in many respects are early steps in the field, so that a number of important issues have not been resolved, and a number of questions remain. Of particular relevance, issues of psychometric equivalence in different ethnic and linguistic groups and of equivalent validity across groups have been only partially addressed.

Careful and expert translation is generally regarded as a necessary step in multilingual test development but is not sufficient to assure that different-language versions of the test will have the same measurement properties. Measurement equivalence in different ethnic groups tested in the same language is similarly an issue, because individual items and total test scores might have different reliability, validity, and meaning in different groups. There are established psychometric methods for evaluating measurement equivalence. These are typically based in item response theory (IRT; Hambleton & Swaminathan, 1985; Hambleton, Swaminathan, & Rogers, 1991) and covariance structure analysis/structural equation modeling (CSA;

MacCallum & Austin, 2000). Both of these approaches require relatively large sample sizes, and their application in the area of neuropsychological assessment of older minorities in general and Hispanics in particular has been limited by the difficulty in obtaining sufficiently large samples of minority individuals. Studies examining equivalence of validity across ethnic groups have also been limited by practical considerations. Ideally, such studies would involve samples from different ethnic groups recruited using the same methods and clinically evaluated and diagnosed using the same methods. This would facilitate studies that examine whether the neuropsychological tests of interest have the same relationship to clinically relevant external criteria in different ethnic groups. This type of study is resource intensive and difficult to implement. As a result, most of the validation studies of traditional neuropsychological tests applied to Hispanic populations have had small sample sizes, have not directly compared validity across different ethnic groups, and have included comparison between healthy controls and patients with dementia that, while of interest, do not provide stringent tests of the sensitivity of these tests to subtle but clinically relevant changes in cognitive ability.

Spanish and English Neuropsychological Assessment Scales

This chapter presents a somewhat different approach to neuropsychological test development that has been used in the creation and development of the Spanish and English Neuropsychological Assessment Scales (SENAS). The initial steps in the development of the SENAS were described in the first edition of this book (Mungas, 1996), and subsequent steps have been reported in a series of publications (Mungas, Reed, Marshall, & González, 2000; González, Mungas, Reed, Marshall, & Haan, 2001; Mungas, Reed, Crane, Haan, & González, 2004; Mungas, Reed, Haan, & González, 2005a; Mungas, Reed, Tomaszewski Farias, & DeCarli, 2005b).

Goals of SENAS Development

The SENAS development process was initiated in 1992 with an overarching goal of creating psychometrically matched English- and Spanish-language neuropsychological measures of cognitive abilities relevant to the clinical neuropsychological assessment of older persons. A neuropsychological model of cognitive ability was constructed that incorporated domains of semantic memory, episodic memory, attention, abstract thinking, language, and visual-spatial abilities. A test development model was constructed that called for a verbal measure and a nonverbal measure of the first four domains, and two different measures of the language and

Table 5.1 SENAS Scales and Abilities Measured (Executive Function Measures Are Recent Additions)

Ability Domain	Verbal Measure	Nonverbal Measure
Conceptual thinking	Verbal conceptual thinking	Nonverbal conceptual thinking
Semantic memory	Object naming	Picture association
Attention span	Verbal attention span	Visual attention span
Episodic memory	Word list learning—I; word list learning—II	Spatial configuration learning
Nonverbal/spatial abilities		Pattern recognition; spatial localization
Verbal abilities	Verbal comprehension; verbal expression	
Executive function	Category fluency (animals, supermarket test); phonemic fluency (F, L); working memory (digit span backward, list sorting); executive composite	Working memory (visual span backward); executive composite

visual–spatial domains. This model is presented in Table 5.1. During subsequent development, an additional verbal memory measure was added. A more recent addition involved development of measures of two aspects of executive function: working memory and fluency. The goal was to create scales that have matched psychometric characteristics both across and within language versions. That is, the English and Spanish versions of any scale should have the same psychometric characteristics, and any two scales within a specific language version should also be psychometrically matched. The importance of matching across language versions is obvious, because this permits direct comparison of results from the English and Spanish versions. Matching within language versions is equally important, especially for differential deficit analysis, because this permits the accurate identification of different patterns of cognitive impairment (Chapman & Chapman, 1973).

There were additional goals for SENAS scale development. First, there was an explicit attempt to create measures that were sensitive to cognitive differences across a broad range of ability, spanning a continuum from high-ability, highly educated normals, for example, to patients with moderate dementia. Second, linear measurement across this broad ability range was an important consideration. Linear measurement means that a given change in underlying ability results in the same change in test score, regardless of where on the ability continuum this change occurs. Practically, this means that a test does not have floor or ceiling effects that limit sensitivity to change for more intact or more impaired individuals.

Approach to SENAS Development

An important difference between the SENAS and most other approaches to multi-ethnic and multilingual neuropsychological test development was that SENAS scales were new scales rather than adaptations and translations of existing scales. SENAS scales were conceptualized to fit the model for test development for this project (Table 5.1) and were constructed using newly generated items to measure the domains within the model. Another overarching consideration in SENAS development was that item selection and scale construction were empirically based. While a conceptual model guided the design of the instrument, and cultural and linguistic considerations influenced item content and generation, decisions about which items were effective and would be retained were based on empirical data.

The SENAS development followed a sequential, multiple-stage process. In Stage 1, a large number of provisional items were generated for each of the scales proposed for the assessment model. At this stage, there was an explicit attempt to create items that were widely varying in difficulty level so that there would be items that would be challenging for high-functioning normals, items that could be successfully completed by individuals with moderate-level dementia, and items with difficulty levels between these extremes. There was also an explicit attempt to incorporate item content that would be relevant and familiar to predominantly Mexican American Hispanics from northern California as well as items relevant to Caucasians from this region. Item content was also systematically varied to address potential differences related to gender, education level, and rural versus urban backgrounds. In this stage, a large item pool was generated, with the goal that empirical data from subsequent steps would be used to select items from this pool to create final scales.

In Stage 2, the initial item pool was administered to a sample of approximately 200 English-speaking and 200 Spanish-speaking individuals 60 years of age and older. These results were used to establish preliminary estimates of item measurement parameters. They were used to identify items with favorable measurement characteristics for further study and to identify less effective items for elimination from the item pool. About half of the items from the initial item pool were retained for subsequent study. This stage of the development process is described in more detail in Mungas et al. (2000).

In Stage 3, the refined item pool was administered to a new and larger sample of English- and Spanish-speaking Hispanics and English-speaking Caucasians. About half of the scales were administered to a sample that included approximately 650 tested in Spanish (all Hispanics) and about 700 tested in English (350 Hispanics, 350 Caucasians). The remaining scales were administered to a subsample of the overall sample that consisted of 324 tested in Spanish and 385 tested in English (160 Hispanics, 225 Caucasians). These data were used to obtain new estimates of item parameters and, subsequently, to create final English and Spanish versions of scales.

In the most recent phase of development (Stage 4), measures of executive function were added, and additional Hispanic and Caucasian participants are being enrolled and tested along with a new sample of African American participants. The executive function measures assess two aspects of executive function, working memory and fluency, but are not intended to provide a comprehensive assessment of executive abilities. Unlike the earlier SENAS scales, most of the executive function measures are adaptations of tests that are in common use rather than new tests created for the SENAS.

SENAS Administration and Norms

The overall SENAS, including the original 13 scales and the new executive function measures, can be administered in about 4 hr. However, for many applications, smaller subsets of scales can be used to obtain relatively comprehensive assessments in under 2 hr. The SENAS has been used for the neuropsychological assessment component of an epidemiological study of cognitive impairment and dementia in older Hispanics, the Sacramento Area Latino Study on Aging (SALSA), and in this study, an abbreviated group of scales is used. This battery has been designed to be administered by nonprofessionals who receive training in general cognitive testing and specific administration of the SENAS. Most of the test administration in the development process has been accomplished by psychometrist-level testers. The manual for the battery has detailed instructions, and for most of the scales, the instructions and procedures are relatively simple. All scales can be administered to illiterate individuals. Only one scale involves written words as stimuli (Verbal Conceptual Thinking), and the examiner can read the words out loud if the examinee is unable to read.

Test materials are available free of charge from Dr. Mungas. There are extensive stimulus material (much in color) and multiple protocol sheets. All of these elements and the manual are available in pdf format files that are currently being distributed on a CD and can be printed on a color laser printer and collated into test administration kits.

Normative data for the SENAS are currently available for more than 400 Hispanics 60 years of age and older and more than 200 Caucasians in this age group. (Additional normative data will soon be added for more than 200 Hispanics and 200 Caucasians, as well as for more than 200 African Americans.) The normative sample for Hispanics is from northern California and is composed primarily of Mexican Americans. These norms are incorporated into a Microsoft Excel spreadsheet that calculates empirically based adjustments for effects of education, linguistic background, age, and gender, and then generates standard scores that show the obtained scores in comparison with the level expected on the basis of the individual's demographic characteristics. This spreadsheet generates a graphical profile of test results that also shows the standard errors of measurement associated with the obtained scores. This spreadsheet is distributed along with the test stimuli and protocol sheets. The SENAS is being used with Spanish speakers from different regions of the United States, but the research base to date has included individuals from northern California.

Psychometric Properties of SENAS Scales

Modern psychometric methods, including IRT, played a central role in the development of the SENAS. A detailed description of the psychometric methods used for SENAS development was previously published in Mungas et al. (2004) and in an online supplement to that article (http://dx.doi.org/10.1037/1040-3590.16.4.347.supp). Detailed information about psychometric characteristics of scales (not including the more recently added measures of executive function) is also included in that publication. A brief summary of those results follows.

The general model of scale construction specified that all scales, whether from English- or Spanish-language versions, would have similar test information curves, which are IRT-based graphs of scale reliability across the continuum of ability measured by the test. Test information can be directly converted to the standard error of measurement. In this manner, the concept of psychometric equivalence was operationalized. Specifically, this model specified a uniform standard error of measurement (0.30 of the standard deviation) across a range of plus or minus two standard deviations of the combined, diverse development sample of Hispanics and Caucasians. A scale that fits this model will sensitively measure individual differences among approximately 98% of community-dwelling Hispanics and Caucasians.

Results were strongly supportive of the psychometric matching of English and Spanish versions of scales. Matching within language groups was very good for 7 of the 13 SENAS scales. Of the remaining six scales, differences in precision of measurement in comparison with the target model were either minor or confined to high-ability levels for four scales. The remaining two scales did not meet the *a priori* goal for fidelity of measurement but showed levels of reliability similar to those of many neuropsychological tests in common usage. Thus, even for scales that did not meet the ambitious target model, level of reliability was acceptable for many purposes. Traditional internal consistency reliability coefficients (coefficient α) were uniformly high and were quite consistent across linguistic and ethnic groups: for non-Hispanics tested in English, the average coefficient α was 0.85; for Hispanics tested in English, it was 0.86; and for Hispanics tested in Spanish, it was 0.88. Values for the entire battery were generally comparable to or better than reliabilities reported for the current Wechsler intelligence and memory scales (Psychological Corporation, The, 1997).

The correspondence of the dimensional structure of the SENAS to the conceptual model that guided scale development was evaluated as one component of the construct validation of the SENAS. Results from CSA supported construct validity with respect to the six-domain model for the SENAS and provided evidence of a similar dimensional structure in English and Spanish versions of the SENAS. The dimensions underlying the SENAS scales were highly correlated, but a simple one-dimensional model did not adequately account for interrelationships among scales. Correlations among domains were well accounted for by a single second-order dimension representing general cognitive ability. Finally, while scales were correlated with one another, the magnitude of intercorrelations was moderate, and more than 90% of the bivariate correlation coefficients fell in the .30–.70 range. This indicates that individual scales, even those sharing common domains, contributed unique measurement variance.

Item Bias and Measurement of Ability

SENAS development included explicit steps to minimize measurement bias associated with language of test administration. The effects of item-level measurement bias on the overall scale score related to other variables including education, age, gender, and ethnicity was evaluated for one scale, Object Naming, in a separate study described in Mungas et al. (2004). Object Naming was selected because it is a verbal measure that would likely be influenced by cultural experience, so one might expect that cultural and linguistic bias would have important effects. Innovative psychometric methods were used to identify differential item function (DIF; Camilli & Shepard, 1994) associated with the demographic characteristics and to evaluate the net impact of DIF on scale-level measurement. Results showed that DIF had relatively minor effects on the assessment of ability of persons with widely divergent demographic backgrounds. These results are consistent with a previous study (Jones & Gallo, 2002) that showed similar, limited effects of DIF on differences between low and high education groups on ability as measured by the Mini-Mental State Examination. Another study by Jones (2003), however, showed that racial differences between Caucasians and African Americans on a telephone cognitive screening measure were substantially affected by DIF. This highlights the importance of careful empirical evaluation of the appropriateness of neuropsychological tests for use with culturally diverse groups. Unfortunately, this has received almost no attention in the field of neuropsychology.

Relationship to Demographic Variables

A recently published study (Mungas et al., 2005a) examined the relationship of SENAS scales to demographic variables and acculturation in Hispanic ($N = 367$) and Caucasian ($N = 160$) populations. Education had robust effects across SENAS scales, though these effects varied considerably from scale to scale. Measures of semantic memory were strongly influenced by education, whereas education effects on measures of episodic memory were weaker. Age had modest effects for nonmemory abilities, but age effects on verbal episodic memory measures were as strong as were education effects. Gender effects were relatively weak and were present for only a few variables. After controlling for all other demographic variables, episodic memory was better in females, while semantic memory was better in males. English-language proficiency had broad and robust associations with test scores. Spanish proficiency also had important relationships with test scores, with high Spanish proficiency associated with lower test scores; that is, those who spoke Spanish had lower scores overall than those who spoke only English. Interestingly, acculturation effects were limited after controlling for education, English proficiency, and Spanish proficiency, suggesting that these simple and easy to measure variables adequately accounted for acculturation effects in this sample. There were substantial ethnic group differences in simple bivariate analyses comparing means of Hispanics and Caucasians. There were striking education differences between Hispanics and Caucasians, and controlling for education substantially attenuated the Hispanic–Caucasian group differences. Mean ethnic group differences were essentially eliminated by controlling for education, English proficiency, and Spanish proficiency. These results indicate that education and linguistic background are important variables to account for in norms and procedures for identifying cognitive impairment.

External Validity

The relationship of SENAS scores to independent measures of global cognition (Modified Mini-Mental State Examination; Teng & Chui, 1987) and independent function (Informant Questionnaire on Cognitive Decline in the Elderly; Jorm, 1994; Jorm & Jacomb, 1989) was examined in Mungas et al. (2005a). This study examined the relative validity of SENAS scales for use with Hispanic and Caucasian populations with respect to these concurrent measures of cognition and independent function. It should be noted that the SENAS development was based upon linguistic groups, and that English-speaking Hispanics were included with English-speaking non-Hispanics in the data sets used for item and scale calibration. The validation efforts described in this study separated effects of language and ethnicity and, consequently, presented a stringent test of validity and measurement bias. Results showed that all SENAS scales were associated with the concurrent measure of cognitive status independent of effects of demographic variables, many were independently related to functional status, and relationships to cognitive and functional status were essentially the same in Hispanics and Caucasians. A previous study using earlier, provisional SENAS scales similarly showed that SENAS results had the same relationship with another measure of global cognition in Hispanics and Caucasians (Mungas et al., 2000).

Another study with a different sample examined the validity of SENAS scales with respect to a clinical diagnosis of normal cognition (32 Hispanics, 30 Caucasians), mild cognitive impairment (19 Hispanics, 39 Caucasians), and dementia (17 Hispanics, 17 Caucasians; Mungas et al., 2005b). This study included the recently added measures of executive function along with the original SENAS scales. SENAS results were excluded from the process of establishing clinical diagnosis, and so, clinical diagnosis could be used as an independent external validation criterion. Twelve of the 17 SENAS scales examined significantly differed across clinical diagnosis groups, and for 11 of these scales, clinical diagnosis accounted for at least 10% of the variance in the SENAS scale after controlling for demographic (including ethnicity) and linguistic effects. Effects of clinical diagnosis on SENAS scales were similar in the Hispanic and Caucasian populations. A majority of scales discriminated normal from mild cognitive impairment and mild cognitive impairment from dementia, relatively subtle but clinically important discriminations.

Clinical diagnosis was most strongly related to verbal memory, explaining about 35% of the variance, independent of demographic and linguistic covariates. Nonverbal memory and category fluency showed the next strongest relationships, sharing about 20% of the variance. Clinical diagnosis explained 10–15% of the variance of several scales, including verbal and nonverbal measures of semantic memory, verbal abstraction, spatial perception, and working memory. It should be noted that these results refer to incremental variance explained after the effects of demographic variables are subtracted; this is a result that is not often reported, and it is obtained here in the context of a sample that had great demographic diversity.

Verbal Episodic Memory and Object Naming, when used in combination, had diagnostic sensitivity of better than 80%, associated with 80% specificity for discriminating mild cognitive impairment from dementia and for discriminating normal cognition from mild impairment. These sensitivity and specificity values compare well with those previously reported for other well-recognized neuropsychological tests in primarily Caucasian samples. This study is unique in the literature in that it addresses discrimination of clinically relevant stages of cognitive impairment in Hispanics and Caucasians and directly evaluates relative validity in these two ethnic groups.

Conclusions and Future Directions

The SENAS has evolved as part of a systematic test development process over the course of more than a decade. There have been two important guiding principles in this process. First, there has been an emphasis on empirical data and results, and second, state-of-the-art psychometric methods have been applied to this data to develop scales and address clinically relevant and conceptually significant measurement questions. This general approach has resulted in a large dataset that consists of comprehensive measures of cognition in a large and ethnically and demographically diverse sample. This is an important resource that can be used for further empirical studies to more broadly evaluate the validity of the SENAS. Studies in progress at the time of this writing are examining the recently added executive function measures; the psychometric equivalence and validity of SENAS scales in African Americans; the relationship of SENAS scores to quantitative magnetic resonance imaging (MRI) in Hispanics, African Americans, and Caucasians; and the relationship of SENAS scores to measures of reading proficiency in these ethnic groups. While the primary goal of this work is to better define the clinical utility of this test battery in different ethnic groups, this data can also be used to address important measurement questions for multilingual and multicultural applications of neuropsychological tests. Modern psychometric methods are directly relevant to many of the difficult problems associated with the clinical neuropsychological evaluation of diverse elderly individuals. An important goal of the SENAS development project is that it will serve as a resource for further studies to advance our scientific understanding of these measurement problems so that more effective tests can be developed.

References

American Academy of Neurology Therapeutics and Technology Assessment Subcommittee. (1996). Assessment: Neuropsychological testing of adults. Considerations for neurologists. *Neurology, 47,* 592–599.

Ardila, A., Rosselli, M., & Puente, A. E. (1993). *Neuropsychological evaluation of the Spanish speaker.* New York: Plenum Press.

Camilli, G., & Shepard, L. A. (1994). *Methods for identifying biased test items.* Thousand Oaks, CA: Sage.

Chapman, L. J., & Chapman, J. C. (1973). *Disordered thought in schizophrenia.* New York: Appleton Century Crofts.

Dick, M. B., Teng, E. L., Kempler, D., Davis, D. S., & Taussig, I. M. (2002). The cross-cultural neuropsychological test battery (ccnb): Effects of age, education, ethnicity, and cognitive status on performance. In F. R. Ferraro (Ed.), *Minority and cross-cultural aspects of neuropsychological assessment. Studies on neuropsychology, development, and cognition* (pp. 17–41). Lisse, the Netherlands: Swets & Zeitlinger.

Ferraro, F. R. (2002). *Minority and cross-cultural aspects of neuropsychological assessment. Studies on neuropsychology, development, and cognition.* Lisse, the Netherlands: Swets & Zeitlinger.

González, H. M., Mungas, D., Reed, B. R., Marshall, S., & Haan, M. (2001). A new verbal learning and memory test for English- and Spanish-speaking older people. *Journal of the International Neuropsychological Society, 7,* 544–555.

Gurland, B. J., Wilder, D. E., Lantigua, R., Stern, Y., Chen, J., Killeffer, E. H. et al. (1999). Rates of dementia in three ethnoracial groups. *International Journal of Geriatric Psychiatry, 14,* 481–493.

Hambleton, R. K., & Swaminathan, H. (1985). *Item response theory. Principles and applications.* Boston: Kluwer-Nijhoff.

Hambleton, R. K., Swaminathan, H., & Rogers, H. J. (1991). *Fundamentals of item response theory.* Newbury Park, CA: Sage.

Jacobs, D. M., Sano, M., Albert, S., Schofield, P., Dooneief, G., & Stern, Y. (1997). Cross-cultural neuropsychological assessment: A comparison of randomly selected, demographically matched cohorts of English- and Spanish-speaking older adults. *Journal of Clinical and Experimental Neuropsychology, 19*(3), 331–339.

Jones, R. N. (2003). Racial bias in the assessment of cognitive functioning of older adults. *Aging and Mental Health, 7*(2), 83–102.

Jones, R. N., & Gallo, J. J. (2002). Education and sex differences in the Mini-Mental State Examination: Effects of differential item functioning. *Journal of Gerontology B—Psychological Sciences & Social Sciences, 57B*(6), P548–P558.

Jorm, A. F. (1994). A short form of the informant questionnaire on cognitive decline in the elderly (IQCODE): Development and cross-validation. *Psychological Medicine, 24,* 145–153.

Jorm, A. F., & Jacomb, P. A. (1989). The informant questionnaire on cognitive decline in the elderly (IQCODE): Socio-demographic correlates, reliability, validity and some norms. *Psychological Medicine, 19,* 1015–1022.

MacCallum, R. C., & Austin, J. T. (2000). Applications of structural equation modeling in psychological research. In S. K. Fiske, D. L. Schacter, & C. Zahn-Waxler (Eds.), *Annual review of psychology* (Vol. 51, pp. 201–226). Palo Alto, CA: Annual Reviews.

Manly, J. J., Jacobs, D. M., Sano, M., Bell, K., Merchant, C. A., Small, S. A. et al. (1999). Effect of literacy on neuropsychological test performance in nondemented, education-matched elders. *Journal of the International Neuropsychological Society, 5*(3), 191–202.

Manly, J. J., Jacobs, D. M., Touradji, P., Small, S. A., & Stern, Y. (2002). Reading level attenuates differences in neuropsychological test performance between African American and White elders. *Journal of the International Neuropsychological Society, 8*(3), 341–348.

Mungas, D. (1996). The process of development of valid and reliable neuropsychological assessment measures for English- and Spanish-speaking elderly persons. In G. Yeo & D. Gallagher-Thompson (Eds.), *Ethnicity and the dementias* (pp. 33–46). Washington, DC: Taylor & Francis.

Mungas, D., Reed, B. R., Crane, P. K., Haan, M. N., & González, H. (2004). Spanish and English Neuropsychological Assessment Scales (SENAS): Further development and psychometric characteristics. *Psychological Assessment, 16*(4), 347–359.

Mungas, D., Reed, B. R., Haan, M. N., & Gonzalez, H. (2005a). Spanish and English Neuropsychological Assessment Scales (SENAS): Relationship to demographics, language, cognition, and independent function. *Neuropsychology, 19*(4), 466–475.

Mungas, D., Reed, B. R., Marshall, S. C., & González, H. M. (2000). Development of psychometrically matched English and Spanish neuropsychological tests for older persons. *Neuropsychology, 14,* 209–223.

Mungas, D., Reed, B. R., Tomaszewski Farias, S., & DeCarli, C. (2005b). Criterion-referenced validity of a neuropsychological test battery: Equivalent performance in elderly Hispanics and non-Hispanic whites. *Journal of the International Neuropsychological Society, 11,* 620–630.

Petersen, R. C., Stevens, J. C., Ganguli, M., Tangalos, E. G., Cummings, J. L., & DeKosky, S. T. (2001). Practice parameter: Early detection of dementia: Mild cognitive impairment (an evidence-based review). Report of the quality standards subcommittee of the American Academy of Neurology. *Neurology, 56*(9), 1133–1142.

Psychological Corporation, The. (1997). *Wais-III-WMS-III technical manual.* San Antonio, TX: The Psychology Corporation.

Tang, M. X., Cross, P., Andrews, H., Jacobs, D. M., Small, S., Bell, K. et al. (2001). Incidence of AD in African-Americans, Caribbean Hispanics, and Caucasians in northern Manhattan. *Neurology, 56,* 49–56.

Teng, E. L., & Chui, H. C. (1987). The Modified Mini-Mental State (3MS) Examination. *Journal of Clinical Psychiatry, 48,* 314–318.

CHAPTER 6

American Indians, Cognitive Assessment, and Dementia

LORI L. JERVIS, C. MUNRO CULLUM,
AND SPERO M. MANSON

Although many gaps in our knowledge remain, it has become increasingly clear that dementia phenomenology and prevalence differs by ethnic/cultural group. In the United States, for instance, African Americans and Latinos appear to have a higher overall prevalence of dementia than European Americans and Asian Americans—although etiologies vary by group (Manly & Mayeux, 2004). While little empirical research has been conducted to date, American Indians seemingly have a lower prevalence of Alzheimer's disease (AD) but a higher prevalence of non-AD dementias (Henderson et al., 2002; Hendrie et al., 1993; Manly & Mayeux, 2004; Rosenberg et al., 1996). In this chapter, we argue that such claims, while intriguing, may be premature given the limited body of research on American Indians and dementia (Jervis & Manson, 2002). In fact, so little is known about any facet of dementia among American Indians that the field remains essentially wide open. Here, we describe the small literature on American Indians and dementia with a specific focus on the cognitive assessment of American Indians. In this vein, we specifically explore the cultural validity of cognitive testing as well as cultural understandings and the identification of cognitive impairment.

Although American Indian life expectancy increased dramatically in the last half of the 20th century (John, 1996; U.S. Department of Health and Human Services, 2001), our knowledge about dementia in this population is virtually nonexistent. Only a handful of small, non-population-based studies have examined dementia among American Indians, most focused primarily on AD (Henderson, 2002; Henderson et al., 2002; Rosenberg et al., 1996). In one such study, researchers determined that the degree of genetic Cherokee ancestry was associated with a lower frequency of AD (Rosenberg et al., 1996). Other clinically based investigations reported that Cherokee and Choctaw elders had a similar course of illness in AD compared to whites, and that disease course was not associated with blood quantum (Weiner et al., 2003). In terms of biochemical studies, a comparison of the frequency of the apolipoprotein E4 allele, a risk factor for AD, and the tau H2 haplotype revealed lower frequencies among Choctaws compared to whites, and the association between the E4 allele and dementia appeared to be weaker in the Native group (Henderson et al., 2002).

A study of dementia among First Nations' people (the Canadian equivalent of American Indians) compared dementia prevalence among 91 Cree Indians 65 years of age and older from two reserves to 67 non-Natives (with unspecified ethnicity) with low scores on the Community Screening Interview for Dementia, a cognitive screening measure specifically developed with the hope of circumventing cultural and education biases (Hall et al., 1993, 2000). The prevalence of probable dementia was the same (4.2%) for both groups, although the subtypes varied considerably by sample, with non-Natives having more AD and the Cree having more vascular and alcohol-related dementia (Hendrie et al., 1993).

The available evidence, then, suggests that AD may be somewhat less prevalent among American Indians than other U.S. populations. This pattern might partially be explained by genetic contributors and by premature mortality given that, despite improvements, American Indians still tend to die younger than the general population (4.7 years earlier, on average; U.S. Department of Health and Human Services, 2001). Because AD is strongly associated with advancing age, shorter life expectancies would most likely limit the number of AD cases in a population. However, the evidence points to the greater impact of non-AD dementias among this population.

American Indians have high prevalences of several conditions that increase risk for poor cognitive functioning and dementia, such as alcohol abuse and addiction (Beals et al., 2003; Beauvais, 1998; Harris, Albaugh, Goldman, & Enoch, 2003; Kunitz & Levy, 2000; May & Gossage, 2001; Robin, Long, Rasmussen, Albaugh, & Goldman, 1998; Spicer et al., 2003), diabetes (Acton, Burrows, Geiss, & Thompson, 2003; Arvanitakis, Wilson,

Bienias, Evans, & Bennett, 2004; Centers for Disease Control, 2003; Haan et al., 2003), overweight/obesity and cardiovascular disease (Denny, Holtzman, & Cobb, 2003; Gustafson, Rothenberg, Blennow, Steen, & Skoog, 2003; Liao, Tucker, & Giles, 2004), and traumatic brain injury (Langlois et al., 2003; Warner, 2001). Many of these health conditions are near-epidemic among American Indians (Henderson, 2002). Further, American Indians as a group are disproportionately poor (28.4% compared to 12.4% of the U.S. general population) (U.S. Census Bureau, 2002). Important to this discussion is the association of low socioeconomic status with a number of factors that might affect cognitive ability, such as pre- and postnatal complications and health care differences, malnutrition, exposure to environmental toxins, increased risk of neurocognitive trauma, and risky health behaviors (Evans & Kantrowitz, 2002; Harris, Echemendia, Ardila, & Roselli, 2001).

One factor impeding research on the prevalence of dementia among American Indians is our limited knowledge of the validity of standardized cognitive measures and available normative data in this population. Understanding the psychometric properties of cognitive assessment instruments is crucial since cognitive testing is a recommended component of the dementia diagnostic process (Storey, Slavin, & Kinsella, 2002).

Cultural Validity of Cognitive Testing among American Indians

Numerous factors come into play when seeking to determine the cultural validity of cognitive measures with older American Indians. These include the cultural phenomenology of how symptoms are experienced, identified, and conveyed to others; the need for culturally relevant assessment practices; and the tendency for cognitive tests and norms to be based on (and hence most appropriate for) middle-class European Americans.

Cultural Construction of Illness and the Diagnosis of Dementia

More than 4 million people, or 1.5% of the total U.S. population, reported that they were American Indian (AI) or Alaskan Native (AN) in 2000 (U.S. Census Bureau, 2000). The combined AI/AN population is comprised of 556 federally recognized tribes that speak over 200 different languages (Gover, 2000). These tribes represent several culture areas with distinctive characteristics and traditions (Southwest, Southeast, Northeast, Prairie–Plains, Intermontane West and California, Northwest Coast, and Arctic/Subarctic) (Kehoe, 1981). Further, individual tribes (and individual tribal members) have experienced different degrees of acculturation to the dominant U.S. culture. Diversity also exists with respect to geographical variation (e.g., region and rural/urban location) and the political/legal status of a tribe's land base (Jervis and Manson, in press).

Assessment and diagnosis of many disorders, including dementia, can be influenced by culture, defined here as a system of meaning that has been historically transmitted among a group of people and that organizes their way of life (Geertz, 1973; Schneider, 1980). Culturally specific explanatory models of illness affect how symptoms are experienced, configured, understood, and described (Kleinman, 1980). These explanatory models may also identify the actions to be taken to "treat" symptoms (Chesla, 1989; Kleinman, 1978). Explanatory models, therefore, can impact the identification of dementia, because they influence the extent to which symptoms are considered problematic and worthy of help-seeking, as well as how they are described to health-care practitioners.

Empirical reports on American Indians' understanding of dementia are virtually nonexistent. Ethnographic accounts of other U.S. ethnic groups identify diverse understandings of cognitive impairment, as well as similar perceptions that "senility" constitutes an expected part of aging rather than a distinct disease entity (Hinton, Guo, Hillygus, & Levkoff, 2000; Holstein, 2000; Ikels, 2002). Among American Indians, intertribal differences in attitudes about cognitive problems in older people may also vary, with some groups considering impaired cognition to be a part of normal aging and others seeing it as part of the dying process (Kramer, 1996).

Only a few published accounts explore how American Indians view dementia. Henderson (2002) reported three different perspectives on dementia based upon a case study approach with Choctaw elders. The first perspective viewed dementia as part of normal aging; the second maintained that dementia was part of an elder's transition to the next world; and the third combined lay and biomedical explanations. Another study found that among the Pueblo, family caregivers were less embarrassed than expected by the "inappropriate" behavior of the "confused" elders for whom they cared. This may support the notion that American Indian cultural constructions of dementia symptoms differ from those of the dominant U.S. society (Hennessy & John, 1995; John, 2004). Preliminary research by the first author found that Northern Plains tribal elders perceived AD as unusual but some memory loss among older people as normal, with mental acuity judged primarily in relation to an elder's ability to recall details about the distant past (Jervis, in preparation).

These findings, collectively, hint at the complexity surrounding dementia assessment in the American Indian population. Given the cultural and geographical diversity of American Indians, a great deal of work remains in order to understand the cultural constructs of cognitive impairment and dementia among American Indians, and how these cultural views affect dementia detection and diagnosis.

Culturally Relevant Assessment Practices

As with other cultural groups, modifications in clinical assessment methods must be made when dealing with American Indian patients in order to ensure cultural sensitivity and relevance. The notion of cognitive testing may be foreign and anxiety-provoking for some people with different cultural backgrounds than the groups for whom the test was designed, especially when the test is in a second language or refers to unfamiliar cultural information (Parker & Philp, 2004). Attempts to develop more culturally appropriate tests usually involve adaptations of existing clinical measures (e.g., language translations) or the creation of new "culture-free"—or more accurately, "culture-reduced"—cognitive measures, though the latter approach, in particular, presents many inherent challenges.

Some of the more basic recommendations for the clinical evaluation process are inherent to working with members of any ethnic group, such as gaining the client's trust and being sensitive to his or her cultural norms and personal background experiences within that person's life context. Recommended practices specific to some American Indians include avoiding looking directly into the client's eyes and shaking hands "Indian style," which usually refers to a handshake with a lighter grasp (Ferarro, 2001). Other tips for dealing with American Indians include decreasing formality in terms of demeanor, wardrobe, and the testing environment, as well as spending more time than usual establishing rapport (Gardiner & Tansley, 2002; King & Fletcher-Janzen, 2000). All of these factors depend not only on the client's specific tribal background, but importantly, upon his or her degree of acculturation. Some American Indian clients would likely do very well without any of these modifications, while for others, these procedures may be essential to obtain a valid assessment.

Culturally Sensitive and Relevant Neuropsychological Tests

Very little empirical research has been conducted that addresses neuropsychological assessment among older American Indians. The need for measures with known validity, adequate norms, and diagnostic value is especially pressing given the differences in culture and language fluency/ preference among some older American Indians. These differences may be compounded by educational disparities, both in terms of the content and quality of schooling, some of which may result from the boarding school legacy. Here, American Indian children were at times removed from their homes and institutionalized in residential (and often religious) schools that focused primarily on assimilation and vocational skills (Pickering, 2004). Other potential influences upon cognitive styles that may impact assessment outcomes include factors such as rural versus urban residence, though this may be confounded by acculturation, education, and migration between urban and rural areas. Given the combination of unique cultural worldviews, varying degrees of bilingualism and acculturation, and decidedly unique (and arguably substandard) educational histories, the presumption that standardized cognitive measures can be validly and directly applied to all American Indian elders is questionable. This concern is further underscored when factors such as poverty, rurality, and health disparities are considered.

Potential Bias in Cognitive Testing

Cognitive measures may be biased in their application among American Indians in a number of ways. First, a test's psychometric properties may differ across cultural groups (Stewart & Napoles-Springer, 2003). Second, conceptual problems may occur because measures were developed with a group other than that being tested. As a result, instruments may reflect irrelevant interests, concerns, or ways of thinking (Manly et al., 1998; Stewart & Napoles-Springer, 2003). It has been argued that some American Indians think differently than Euro-Americans, with reasoning processes that tend to be more global and holistic and less linear, sequential, and analytic (King & Fletcher-Janzen, 2000). Other research has suggested differences in functional brain organization (Scott, Hynd, Hunt, & Weed, 1979), decision-making strategies, and learning styles among some American Indians (King & Fletcher-Janzen, 2000). Such differences in cognition may have important, but as yet poorly understood, implications for performance on standard cognitive testing. In addition, culturally specific worldviews, local cultural patterns that influence cognitive styles, and linguistic factors (e.g., having English as a second language or lack of fluency in English) may interfere with American Indian elders' ability to perform well on traditional cognitive testing (Jervis & Manson, 2002).

Education

It is well established that most cognitive evaluation measures are influenced by education, with those who completed more years of formal education outperforming those with lower educational levels (Vangel & Lichtenberg, 1995; Whitfield, 1996). For instance, even some tasks on the Mini Mental State Examination (MMSE), arguably the most widely used brief cognitive screening tool, require some formal education and may prove to be difficult for those with little or no formal education. This necessitates careful adjustment of clinical interpretations of such tasks and provision of different normative reference standards for patients with lower educational levels (Albert, 1994). Demographically adjusted norms (i.e., for age, education, and gender) have been developed for many popular neurocognitive tests, including the MMSE (Crum, Anthony, Bassett, & Folstein, 1993; Murden, McRae, Kaner, & Bucknam, 1991), but these have not been widely examined in terms of their utility in American Indian populations. Disentangling a low level of education from cognitive impairment can be difficult, because a low level of education may be associated with lifestyle factors that may impact the risk of dementia (Langley, 2000). While it is standard practice to adjust test scores for years of education, the quantity of formal education does not necessarily equate to educational quality (Manly et al., 1998; Whitfield, 1996). Quality of education, needless to say, is much harder to measure than quantity, but it can be an important factor in assessing a patient's educational background and estimating his or her premorbid level of cognitive functioning. For older, reservation-dwelling American Indians, there may be great disparities in the quality of education related not only to extreme rurality but also to severe poverty and the boarding school legacy. Boarding schools, in particular, reportedly focused primarily on assimilation and menial labor, which gave them a decidedly vocational rather than academic emphasis (King & Fletcher-Janzen, 2000; Pickering, 2000, 2004). Thus, care must be taken when making educational adjustments and interpreting cognitive test scores from American Indian elders; unfortunately, no clear guidance exists about how best to do so.

Language

Standardized tests may underestimate the abilities of individuals with different language experiences in comparison to those for whom the measures were originally developed (King & Fletcher-Janzen, 2000). Cognitive assessment may be affected by language issues in several ways among bilingual individuals, too, including overestimation of an individual's English-speaking ability and varying proficiencies in different aspects of language ability, such as reading, writing, and speaking (Harris et al., 2001). Lower cognitive performance scores may be seen among those for whom English is not the primary language, even in the absence of cognitive impairment (Hohl, Grundman, Salmon, Thomas, & Thal, 1999). Further, even American Indians who speak English as a first language may be relatively less proficient and may exhibit different language patterns than those represented in formal tests (King & Fletcher-Janzen, 2000).

Cognitive Test Norms

In cognitive testing, individual scores are often compared to published norms to help determine the existence and severity of cognitive impairment. The extent to which a given patient is similar to the normative reference group used for a particular test must be considered in making clinical inferences and diagnoses. Thus, caution must be taken when applying existing norms to groups who are substantially different from those for whom the test was normed.

This said, it should not be automatically assumed that separate normative reference groups are needed or that test items are necessarily inappropriate simply because a patient's background differs somewhat from the normative population. For example, investigations of American Indian elders' performance on cognitive measures have shown few differences from the largely white samples on which most popular clinical tests were normed. To illustrate, a sample of 22 older American Indians from a North Dakota reservation performed similarly to an age-matched non-Native sample on a short version of the Boston Naming Test, a widely used measure of language function in persons with known or suspected brain dysfunction (Ferarro & Bercier, 1996). Similar findings were obtained in a group of 51 older members of a North Dakota tribe with respect to several neuropsychological measures, including the Logical Memory subtest (immediate and delayed recall) of the Wechsler Memory Scale-Revised (WMS-R), a popular test of verbal declarative memory, and the Vocabulary and Digit Symbol subtests of the Wechsler Adult Intelligence Scale-Revised (WAIS-R; Ferarro, Bercier, Holm, & McDonald, 2002). The fact that much of this sample was comprised of "Michif" (mixed blood) people (Native and French) who were relatively acculturated might partially explain this lack of variation, however (Ferarro et al., 2002).

A recent investigation to explore the applicability of a standard neurocognitive evaluation for dementia was conducted among 40 American Indian Natives (primarily Cherokee and Choctaw) and 40 age-, education-, and gender-matched European Americans with a clinical diagnosis of AD (Whyte et al., in press). Specifically, the Consortium to Establish a Registry for Alzheimer's Disease-Neuropsychological Battery (CERAD-NB; Morris et al., 1989; Morris, Mohs, Rogers, Fillenbaum, & Heyman, 1988) was examined, a commonly used battery of tests for dementia that taps multiple cognitive domains (i.e., global cognitive function, verbal declarative memory, confrontation naming, verbal fluency, and visuospatial skills). Despite the development and norming of the test in a predominantly European American sample, the American Indian elders did not differ significantly in their performance from the matched non-Native group on any of the CERAD-NB measures, suggesting that within this American Indian sample, the CERAD-NB is clinically useful and, importantly, that different test norms may not be necessary. It is not clear, however, to what extent these findings may generalize to other tribes, as the Cherokee and Choctaw are recognized for their high degree of admixture with non-Native groups (Wright, 1981). Given the diversity of the American Indian population, additional research using neurocognitive tests is necessary in order to further explore the utility and validity of various measures.

Rather than these standardized cognitive tests, some clinicians might be interested in cognitive/intellectual assessment tools that tend to be less culturally influenced than many mainstream tests, including Ravens Colored Matrices and the Culture Fair Test. However, such measures are limited in scope and primarily provide an estimate of overall cognitive ability or "g" and would require supplementation to assess specific cognitive functions such as memory or reasoning. The assessment of multiple areas of cognition (i.e., attention/concentration, language, visuospatial skills, learning and memory, and executive function) is important in a comprehensive evaluation, though tests must be carefully selected with respect to their known psychometric properties and sensitivity to factors such as education and cultural diversity. Unfortunately, little information regarding the appropriateness of many neurocognitive measures in different AI groups is currently available, leaving much research to be done.

Conclusions

As demonstrated in this chapter, the "jury is still out" with regard to the prevalence of dementia in American Indian populations and the appropriateness of existing cognitive measures and norms. Much work remains to determine the most valid and reliable cognitive measures to be used with this group, arguably an important step in the determination of dementia prevalence in the American Indian population. As with other cultural groups, this task is more complex than it first may seem given the geographical and cultural diversity of the American Indian population, as well as the different levels of acculturation among American Indian tribes and individuals. The current "state of the art" in cognitive assessment of culturally diverse groups is to involve well-trained clinical neuropsychologists in the assessment process, because test selection and interpretation are both important aspects of neurodiagnosis. While no universally accepted or validated cognitive measures exist for AI populations, preliminary data suggest that the CERAD neuropsychological battery and the MMSE may be viable options when assessing global cognitive status in American Indians from the Southeastern culture area (especially those who are Cherokee or

Choctaw). The Boston Naming Test, the Logical Memory subtest (immediate and delayed recall) of the WMS-R, and the Vocabulary and Digit Symbol subtests of the WAIS-R may be useful when assessing Ojibwa people, especially those with higher levels of acculturation (Ferarro et al., 2002). It is not known whether these measures would be as useful with members of other tribes or those with lower levels of acculturation to the dominant society. Moreover, although preliminary studies suggest that the use of some standard clinical neuropsychological tools may provide valid data pertaining to the cognitive status of American Indian groups, cautious use of existing norms as general reference guidelines and careful interpretation of results are advised.

In addition, a number of steps can be taken on the research front:

1. As suggested previously, considerable work is needed on cultural validity and assessment tools.
2. As part of this work, a better understanding of contributors and confounders to test performance is needed.
3. Research on the cultural phenomenology of cognitive impairment and dementia among various American Indian groups might aid efforts to determine optimal assessment strategies.
4. A better understanding of contributors, confounders, and cultural phenomenology would discourage overgeneralization from one tribal group to another, which may be important since tribes may have different cultural patterns, genetic makeups, and health practices.
5. It is crucial to recognize how early we are in the process of understanding dementia in this population. Even if it can be definitely shown at some point that American Indians have a lower risk of AD, it will take further research to determine whether this is due to genetic influences, health behaviors, cultural practices, or a combination of factors.

Until these steps are in place, uncertainties will persist with regard to clinical diagnosis, the meaning of individual cognitive test performance, and the epidemiology of dementia in the larger American Indian population.

References

Acton, K. J., Burrows, N. R., Geiss, L. S., & Thompson, T. (2003). Diabetes prevalence among American Indians and Alaska Natives and the overall population—United States, 1994–2002. *Morbidity and Mortality Weekly Report*, 52(30), 702–704.

Albert, M. S. (1994). Brief assessments of cognitive function in the elderly. *Annual Review of Gerontology and Geriatrics*, 14, 93–106.

Arvanitakis, Z., Wilson, R. S., Bienias, J. L., Evans, D. A., & Bennett, D. A. (2004). Diabetes Mellitus and risk of Alzheimer's disease and decline in cognitive function. *Archives of Neurology*, 61, 661–666.

Beals, J., Spicer, P., Mitchell, C. M., Novins, D. K., Manson, S. M., & the AI₁ SUPERPFP team. (2003). Racial disparities in alcohol use: Comparison of two American Indian reservation populations with national data. *American Journal of Public Health*, 93(10), 1683–1685.

Beauvais, F. (1998). American Indians and alcohol. *Alcohol Health & Research World*, 22(4), 253–259.

Centers for Disease Control. (2003). Diabetes prevalence among American Indians and Alaska Natives and the overall population—United States, 1994–2002. *Morbidity and Mortality Weekly Report*, 52(30), 702–704.

Chesla, C. A. (1989). Parents' illness models of schizophrenia. *Archives of Psychiatric Nursing*, 3(4), 218–225.

Crum, R., Anthony, J., Bassett, S., & Folstein, M. F. (1993). Population-based norms for the Mini-Mental State Examination by age and educational level. *Journal of the American Medical Association*, 269, 2386–2391.

Denny, C. H., Holtzman, D., & Cobb, N. (2003). Surveillance for health behaviors of American Indians and Alaska Natives: Findings from the behavioral risk factor surveillance system 1997–2000. *Morbidity and Mortality Weekly Report Surveillance Summaries*, 52(SS07), 1–13.

Evans, G. W., & Kantrowitz, E. (2002). Socioeconomic status and health: The potential role of environmental risk exposure. *Annual Review of Public Health*, 23, 303–331.

Ferarro, F. R. (2001). Assessment and evaluation issues regarding Native American elderly adults. *Journal of Clinical Geropsychology*, 7(4), 311–318.

Ferarro, F. R., & Bercier, B. (1996). Boston Naming Test performance in a sample of Native American elderly adults. *Clinical Gerontologist*, 17, 58–60.

Ferarro, F. R., Bercier, B. J., Holm, J., & McDonald, J. D. (2002). Preliminary normative data from a brief neuropsychological test battery in a sample of Native American elderly. In F. R. Ferarro (Ed.), *Minority and cross-cultural aspects of neuropsychological assessment* (pp. 227–240). Lisse, the Netherlands: Swets & Zeitlinger.

Gardiner, J. C., & Tansley, D. P. (2002). Native Americans: Future directions. In F. R. Ferraro (Ed.), *Minority and cross-cultural aspects of neuropsychological assessment* (pp. 241–261). Lisse, the Netherlands: Swets & Zeitlinger.

Geertz, C. (1973). *The interpretation of cultures.* New York: Basic Books.

Gover, K. (2000). Indian entities recognized and eligible to receive services from the United States Bureau of Indian Affairs. *Federal Register*, 65(49), 13298–13303.

Gustafson, D., Rothenberg, E., Blennow, K., Steen, B., & Skoog, I. (2003). An 18-year follow-up of overweight and risk of Alzheimer's disease. *Archives of Internal Medicine*, 163, 1524–1528.

Haan, M. N., Mungas, D. M., Gonzales, H. M., Ortiz, T. A., Acharya, A., & Jagust, W. J. (2003). Prevalence of dementia in older Latinos: The influence of Type 2 Diabetes Mellitus, stroke, and genetic factors. *Journal of the American Geriatrics Society*, 51, 169–177.

Hall, K. S., Gao, S., Emsley, C. L., Ogunniyi, A. O., Morgan, O., & Hendrie, H. C. (2000). Community Screening Interview for Dementia (CSI'D'); Performance in five disparate study sites. *International Journal of Geriatric Psychiatry*, 15, 521–531.

Hall, K. S., Hendrie, H. C., Brittain, H. M., Norton, J. A., Rodgers, D. D., Prince, C. S. et al. (1993). The development of a dementia screening interview in two distinct languages. *International Journal of Methods in Psychiatric Research*, 3, 1–28.

Harris, C. R., Albaugh, B., Goldman, D., & Enoch, M. A. (2003). Neurocognitive impairment due to chronic alcohol consumption in an American Indian community. *Journal of Studies on Alcohol*, 64, 458–466.

Harris, J. G., Echemendia, R., Ardila, A., & Roselli, M. (2001). Cross-cultural cognitive and neuropsychological assessment. In D. H. Saklofske & H. L. Janzen (Eds.), *Handbook of psychoeducational assessment: Ability, achievement, and behavior in children* (pp. 391–414). San Diego: Academic Press.

Henderson, J. N. (2002). Cultural construction of disease: A "supernormal" construct of dementia in an American Indian tribe. *Journal of Cross-Cultural Gerontology*, 17, 197–212.

Henderson, J. N., Crook, R., Crook, J., Hardy, J., Onstead, L., Carson-Henderson, L. et al. (2002). Apolipoprotein E4 and tau allele frequencies among Choctaw Indians. *Neuroscience Letters*, 324, 77–79.

Hendrie, H. C., Hall, K. S., Pillay, N., Rodgers, D., Prince, C., Norton, J. et al. (1993). Alzheimer's disease is rare in Cree. *International Psychogeriatrics*, 5(1), 5–14.

Hennessy, C. H., & John, R. (1995). The interpretation of burden among Pueblo Indian caregivers. *Journal of Aging Studies*, 9(3), 215–229.

Hinton, L., Guo, Z., Hillygus, J., & Levkoff, S. (2000). Working with culture: A qualitative analysis of barriers to the recruitment of Chinese-American family caregivers for dementia research. *Journal of Cross-Cultural Gerontology*, 15(15), 119–137.

Hohl, U., Grundman, M., Salmon, D. P., Thomas, R. G., & Thal, L. J. (1999). Mini-Mental State Examination and Mattis Dementia Rating Scale performance differs in Hispanic and non-Hispanic Alzheimer's disease patients. *Journal of the International Neuropsychological Society*, 5(4), 301–307.

Holstein, M. (2000). Aging, culture, and the framing of Alzheimer's Disease. In P. J. Whitehouse, K. Maurer, & J. F. Ballenger (Eds.), *Concepts of Alzheimer disease: Biological, clinical, and cultural perspectives*. Baltimore: Johns Hopkins University Press.

Ikels, C. (2002). Constructing and deconstructing the self: Dementia in China. *Journal of Cross-Cultural Gerontology*, 17, 233–251.

Jervis, L. L. (in preparation). Cultural understandings of cognitive impairment among Northern Plains American Indian elders.

Jervis, L. L. & Manson, S. M. (in press). American Indian elders. In R. Schulz (Ed.), *Encyclopedia of aging*. New York: Springer.

Jervis, L. L., & Manson, S. M. (2002). American Indians/Alaska Natives and dementia. *Alzheimer Disease and Associated Disorders*, 16(Suppl. 2), S89–S95.

John, R. (1996). Demography of American Indian elders: social, economic, and health status. In G. D. Sandefur, R. R. Rindfuss, & B. Cohen (Eds.), *Changing numbers, changing needs: American Indian demography and public health* (pp. 218–231). Washington, DC: National Academy Press.

John, R. (2004). Health status and health disparities among American Indian elders. In K. E. Whitfield (Ed.), *Closing the gap: Improving the health of minority elders in the new millennium* (pp. 27–44). Washington, DC: Gerontological Society of America.

Kehoe, A. B. (1981). *North American Indians: A comprehensive account*. Englewood Cliffs, NJ: Prentice Hall.

King, J., & Fletcher-Janzen, E. (2000). Neuropsychological assessment and intervention with Native Americans. In E. Fletcher-Janzen, T. L. Strickland, & C. R. Reynolds (Eds.), *Handbook of cross-cultural neuropsychology* (pp. 105–122). New York: Kluwer.

Kleinman, A. (1978). Concepts and a model for the comparison of medical systems as cultural systems. *Social Science and Medicine*, 12, 85–93.

Kleinman, A. (1980). *Patients and healers in the context of culture: An exploration of the borderland between anthropology, medicine, and psychiatry*. Berkeley: University of California Press.

Kramer, B. J. (1996). Dementia and American Indian populations. In *Ethnicity and the dementias* (pp. 175–181). Washington, DC: Taylor & Francis.

Kunitz, S. J., & Levy, J. E. (2000). Drinking, conduct disorder, and social change: Navajo experiences. New York: Oxford University Press.

Langley, L. K. (2000). Cognitive assessment of older adults. In R. L. Kane & R. A. Kane (Eds.), *Assessing older persons: Measures, meaning, and practical applications* (pp. 65–128). New York: Oxford University Press.

Langlois, J. A., Kegler, S. R., Butler, J. A., Gotsch, K. E., Johnson, R. L., Reichard, A. A. et al. (2003). Traumatic brain injury—related hospital discharges: Results from a 14-state surveillance system, 1997. Washington, DC: Department of Health and Human Services, Centers for Disease Control and Prevention.

Liao, Y., Tucker, P., & Giles, W. H. (2004). Health status of American Indians compared with other racial/ethnic minority populations—selected states, 2001–2002. *Journal of the American Medical Association*, 291(8), 935–937.

Manly, J. J., Jacobs, D. M., Sano, M., Bell, K., Merchant, C. A., Small, S. A. et al. (1998). Cognitive test performance among nondemented elderly African Americans and whites. *Neurology*, 50, 1238–1245.

Manly, J. J., & Mayeux, R. (2004). Ethnic difference in dementia and Alzheimer's disease. In N. B. Anderson, R. A. Bulatao, & B. Cohen (Eds.), *Critical perspectives on racial and ethnic differences in health in late life* (pp. 95–141). Washington, DC: The National Academies Press.

May, P. A., & Gossage, J. P. (2001). New data on the epidemiology of adult drinking and substance use among American Indians of the northern states:

Male and female data on prevalence, patterns, and consequences. *American Indian & Alaska Native Mental Health Research*, 10(2), 1–26.

Morris, J. C., Heyman, A., Mohs, R. C., Hughes, J. P., van Belle, G., Fillenbaum, G. et al. (1989). The Consortium to Establish a Registry for Alzheimer's Disease (CERAD): Part I. clinical and neuropsychological assessment of Alzheimer's disease. *Neurology*, 39, 1159–1165.

Morris, J. C., Mohs, R. C., Rogers, H., Fillenbaum, G., & Heyman, A. (1988). Consortium to Establish a Registry for Alzheimer's Disease (CERAD) clinical and neuropsychological assessment of Alzheimer's disease. *Psychopharmacology Bulletin*, 24(4), 641–652.

Murden, R., McRae, T., Kaner, S., & Bucknam, M. (1991). Mini-Mental State Exam scores vary with education in blacks and whites. *Journal of the American Geriatrics Society*, 39, 149–155.

Parker, C., & Philp, I. (2004). Screening for cognitive impairment among older people in black and minority ethnic groups. *Age and Ageing*, 33, 447–452.

Pickering, K. A. (2000). *Lakota culture, world economy*. Lincoln: University of Nebraska.

Pickering, K. A. (2004). Decolonizing time regimes: Lakota conceptions of work, economy, and society. *American Anthropologist*, 106(1), 85–97.

Robin, R. W., Long, J. C., Rasmussen, J. K., Albaugh, B., & Goldman, D. (1998). Relationship of binge drinking to alcohol dependence, other psychiatric disorders, and behavioral problems in an American Indian tribe. *Alcoholism: Clinical and Experimental Research*, 22(2), 518–523.

Rosenberg, R. N., Richter, R. W., Risser, R. C., Taubman, K., Prado-Farmer, I., Ebalo, E. et al. (1996). Genetic factors for the development of Alzheimer disease in the Cherokee Indian. *Archives of Neurology*, 54(10), 997–1000.

Schneider, D. M. (1980). *American kinship: A cultural account*. Chicago: University of Chicago Press.

Scott, S., Hynd, G., Hunt, L., & Weed, W. (1979). Cerebral speech lateralization in Native American Navajo. *Neuropsychologia*, 17, 89–92.

Spicer, P., Beals, J., Croy, C. D., Mitchell, C. M., Novins, D. K., Moore, L. et al. (2003). The prevalence of DSM-III-R alcohol dependence in two American Indian populations. *Alcoholism: Clinical and Experimental Research*, 27(11), 1785–1797.

Stewart, A. L., & Napoles-Springer, A. M. (2003). Advancing health disparities research: Can we afford to ignore measurement issues? *Medical Care*, 41(11), 1207–1220.

Storey, E., Slavin, M. J., & Kinsella, G. J. (2002). Patterns of cognitive impairment in Alzheimer's disease: Assessment and differential diagnosis. *Frontiers in Bioscience*, 7, 155–184.

U.S. Department of Health and Human Services. (2001). *Trends in Indian health 1998–1999*. Rockville, MD: Author.

U.S. Census Bureau. (2000). *Overview of race and hispanic origin: Census 2000* brief. Washington, DC: Author.

U.S. Census Bureau. (2002). *The American Indian and Alaska Native population: 2000, Census 2000* brief. Washington, DC: Author.

Vangel, S. J. J., & Lichtenberg, P. A. (1995). Mattis Dementia Rating Scale: Clinical utility and relationship with demographic variables. *The Clinical Neuropsychologist*, 9(3), 209–213.

Warner, J. (2001). Divining dementia. *Journal of Neurology, Neuropsychiatry, and Psychiatry*, 71, 289–290.

Weiner, M. F., Rosenberg, R. N., Svetlik, D., Hynan, L. S., Womack, K. B., White, C. I. et al. (2003). Comparison of Alzheimer's Disease in Native Americans and whites. *International Psychogeriatrics*, 15(4), 367–375.

Whitfield, K. E. (1996). Studying cognition in older African Americans: Some conceptual considerations. *Journal of Aging and Ethnicity*, 1(1), 41–52.

Whyte, S. R., Cullum, C. M., Hynan, L. S., Lacritz, L. H., Rosenberg, R. N., & Weiner, M. F. (in press). Performance of elderly Native Americans and Caucasians on the CERAD neuropsychological battery. *Alzheimer Disease and Associated* Disorders.

Wright, J. L. J. (1981). *The Only Land They Knew: American Indians in the Old South*. Lincoln: University of Nebraska Press.

PART **III**

Treatment and Management of Dementia

CHAPTER 7

Overview of Treatment Alternatives for Dementing Illnesses

PATRICIA LANOIE BLANCHETTE

Dementia is a condition resulting in the decline of at least two brain functions severe enough to impair daily function in a previously healthy adult. The most common types include Alzheimer's disease (AD), vascular dementia (VaD), mixed dementia, dementia that may occur with Parkinson's disease or as a result of severe head injury or anoxia, and rarer types of dementia, including Lewy-body dementia (DLB), frontotemporal dementia (FTD), Pick's disease, Creutzfeldt-Jakob disease, and Huntington's disease. Of these, AD is by far the most common, followed in prevalence by VaD or a combination of causes, usually called *mixed dementia*. Because of the complexity and severity of both medical and social problems facing an individual with dementia, a broad and interdisciplinary approach to care is extremely important. An individual diagnosed with dementia is facing a current and possibly progressive decline in his or her ability to function as an adult. Family and loved ones are dealing with the loss of this person functioning in his or her expected social roles. Dementia is rarely a painful condition. However, the array of serious physical and emotional symptoms requiring skilled management is extensive.

Diagnosis

It has been said that dementia is both the most underdiagnosed and most overdiagnosed condition in older people. It is underdiagnosed when severe cognitive losses are erroneously considered to be a normal part of aging. Cultural factors play a large role in this underdiagnosis when loss of functional abilities is considered the social norm. Dementia is overdiagnosed when other potentially reversible conditions are overlooked. In an adult with cognitive losses, a correct diagnosis is both possible and important. Reversible causes of cognitive and functional impairment should be carefully considered. The most common of these include metabolic and hormonal deficiencies, such as hyper- or hypothyroidism, adverse effects from medications, substance abuse, and major depression. Prolonged vitamin B_{12} deficiency due to autoantibodies to gastric mucosal cells that produce intrinsic factor or due to gastrectomy for peptic ulcer disease is not uncommon among today's elders and has been associated with both cognitive and physical impairments. Symptoms due to one of the above conditions can be improved or totally reversed with treatment. Specific diagnosis has been confounded by the absence of "biomarkers" for AD, for example, a blood test, to make the diagnosis of AD with great specificity. However, there are promising studies of potential biomarkers in blood, cerebrospinal fluid (CSF), and urine that could improve the specificity of diagnosis in the future (Molchan, 2005). Improvements in brain imaging, most recently by advances in positron-emission tomography (PET), are proving important in research and, more recently, in clinical diagnosis. Examining the function of the brain and the rate of deposition or removal of brain amyloid should also prove to be important in evaluating new treatments (Waxman, 2005).

Alzheimer's Disease

Once a correct diagnosis has been established, and management for concomitant conditions has been optimized, it is important to begin treatment early with medications that have been approved for the specific treatment of AD. At the time of the writing of this chapter, the U.S. Food and Drug Administration (FDA) had approved drugs in two classes, acetylcholinesterase inhibitors (AChEIs), also called cholinesterase inhibitors (ChEIs), and an N-methyl-D-aspartate (NMDA)-receptor antagonist. While these are not curative, they can improve cognitive and functional symptoms and may slow the progression of the disease. The AChEIs have been shown to be more effective when started early in the disease.

AChEIs

Among the many alterations in the brain in AD, the depletion of the neu-rotransmitter, acetylcholine (ACh), is one of the most profound. Its deple-tion has been correlated to memory impairment, a key feature of AD. As a class, all of the approved AChEIs increase the brain's acetylcholine (ACh) by inhibiting its chemical breakdown by the enzyme acetylcholinester-ase (AChE). Two of the drugs, tacrine and rivastigmine, also inhibit the enzyme butyrylcholinesterase (BuChE). In 1993, the first of this class of drugs to earn FDA approval was Cognex* (tacrine, tetrahydroaminoacri-dine, THA). Approval of this drug was exciting, because it was one of the first substances to demonstrate any effectiveness against AD in method-ologically sound clinical trials. However, Cognex is hepatotoxic, that is, it can raise serum liver enzymes and cause liver damage. Other gastrointesti-nal side effects, such as diarrhea, anorexia, dyspepsia, and abdominal pain, also limit its use, especially now that there are other much better tolerated and safer drugs in this class. In 1996, the drug Aricept* (donepezil) was approved. It was much safer than Cognex. More recently approved drugs in this class include Exelon* (rivastigmine) that was approved by the FDA in 2000 and Reminyl* (galantamine), approved in 2001. In 2005, Reminyl was renamed to Razadyne* to eliminate confusion with another drug with a similar sounding name. The AChEIs differ greatly from each other in terms of chemical structure and metabolism. There is reason to believe that persons who are unresponsive to one drug in the class may derive ben-efit if switched to another (Auriacombe, Vellas, Pere, & Loria-Kanza, 2002) While the cholinergic deficit is most profound in AD, there may also be a cholinergic deficit in other dementias, such as Parkinson's dementia (PD), Lewy-body dementia (DLB), and vascular dementia (VaD). Persons with AD often have concurrent vascular risk factors that can contribute to their symptoms. Interestingly, Exelon (rivastigmine) has been shown to be effec-tive in this situation (Kumar, Anand, Messina, Hartman, & Veach, 2000).

N-Methyl-D-Aspartate-Receptor Antagonist

In 2003, the FDA approved Namenda* (memantine) for moderate to severe AD. Namenda, also known as Axura* or Ebixa* in Europe, is an uncompetitive NMDA-receptor antagonist that appears to work by regu-lating the activity of glutamate, a neurotransmitter involved in information processing, storage, and retrieval (Reisberg et al., 2003). There is evidence that persons with AD who are taking AChEIs may derive additional ben-efit from taking memantine (Tariot et al., 2004).

Antioxidants

Oxidative metabolism, or normal cell function, produces by-products known as free radicals that can cause cell damage. Cells have natural defenses against these free radicals, substances called antioxidants. It has been theorized that free radicals play a role in the neuronal cell damage of AD and that taking supplemental antioxidants, such as vitamin E, may provide a benefit (Sano et al., 1997). However, the safety and risk–benefit ratio of various antioxidant supplements have recently been questioned, and further study is required to firmly establish safety, benefits, and dosages.

Vascular Dementia

Formerly called multi-infarct dementia (MID), VaD is caused by one or more strokes combining to significantly impair at least two areas of cognitive functioning. It is important to note that these strokes may be clinically "silent" in that the person and others do not know that the person has had strokes. The prevalence of VaD is greater among people with a greater prevalence of hypertension, such as in people of African, Asian, and Pacific Islander descent. The importance of making this diagnosis cannot be overstated. VaD is classically thought to manifest as a stepwise decline—that is, sudden declines in function are interspersed with some improvement, then there is a plateau until the next vascular event. However, in population studies of dementia, it was shown that VaD can go completely unsuspected and without the classical events and can be undetectable in neuroimaging (Rasmusson et al., 1996). While the damage that previous strokes have caused might not be reversed, finding that strokes are occurring can lead to identification of the causes of these strokes and prevention of future brain damage. Cardiac arrhythmia, poorly treated hypertension, and hyperlipidemia are some of the more common causes, all of which can be effectively treated.

Mixed Dementia

The most common causes of mixed dementia include a combination of AD and VaD. Without classical features of either insidious onset or progression, as in AD, or a stepwise decline, as in VaD, an accurate diagnosis of either AD or VaD cannot be made. Sometimes the presentation is typical of AD, but neuroimaging studies reveal considerable vascular changes. The diagnosis is sometimes called *AD in the presence of cerebrovascular disease*. Depending on the prevalence of cerebrovascular risk factors, such as diabetes mellitus, hypertension, and hyperlipidemia, in the population under study, mixed dementia may be present in as many as one third of the cases of dementia. AD, VaD, and mixed dementia are by far the most common causes of dementia in the United States.

Lewy-Body Dementia

Dementia with Lewy bodies (DLB) is another form of progressive dementia. It differs from AD in its clinical presentation. Lewy bodies are inclusions found in some brain cells on brain autopsy. Although DLB and AD may be clinically similar, there are several symptoms that may help with the diagnosis. First, in DLB, there may be wide fluctuations in cognitive functioning, excessive daytime drowsiness when nighttime sleep has been adequate, frequent staring into space, visual hallucinations (often seeing very small people), with motor stiffness and poor coordination as prominent early features of the disease. DLB might be confused with Parkinson's disease (PD), except that DLB does not usually respond to treatment for PD. There is no FDA-approved treatment specific for DLB, but because there is an associated cholinergic deficit, AChEIs may provide some symptomatic benefit.

Frontotemporal Dementia

FTD is a group of rare brain diseases, such as Pick's disease, in which specific areas of the brain, the frontal and temporal areas, are much more severely affected than others. FTD usually occurs in people who are 40–64 years of age, as opposed to AD, which can occur in younger adults but has greatly increased prevalence in those over the age of 65. The diagnosis may be suspected by the behavioral symptoms that are most prominent, but because the symptoms overlap with those of AD, the diagnosis of FTD is usually only made with accuracy with neuroimaging studies. Impairment in frontal lobe functioning results in uninhibited behavior (sometimes of a sexual nature), impaired personal hygiene and appearance, and lack of motivation. Impairment in temporal lobe functioning results in memory impairment and problems with speech and language functions. Information about this condition is emerging (www.mayoclinic.com/invoke. cfm?id=AN00541). As in DLB, there is no FDA-approved treatment, but AChEIs may provide some symptomatic benefit.

Symptomatic Treatment

Persons with dementia quite often suffer from one or several symptoms that may greatly benefit from a combination of caregiver training and assistance, attention to the environment or milieu, and specific medications.

Some of these symptoms include sleep disturbances, day/night reversal, motor restlessness, agitation, anxiety, depression, aggressiveness, and psychosis (delusions and hallucinations). While there are no drugs that have been FDA approved for the treatment of these symptoms in dementia, experienced clinicians can greatly improve a person's quality of life by paying careful attention to specific symptoms and timing, and ameliorating or exacerbating external factors. In assessing these behaviors, it is important to optimize social and medication management and to observe the effect of reduction or discontinuation of other medications. In a behaviorally impaired person with dementia, it is important to first discontinue all drugs that could be causing the behavioral symptoms and then optimize the specific disease therapy. Because of the difficulty in caring for persons with behavioral symptoms, it is common for caregivers to have administered an array of over-the-counter (OTC) medications. Often, such as in OTC sleep medications, the drugs are anticholinergic, making the overall symptoms worse. Specific AD drugs, AChEIs and memantine, may improve behavioral as well as cognitive symptoms. In selecting other medications for persons with dementia, it is advisable to select the least anticholinergic drugs possible, because there is a cholinergic deficit in most of these conditions. Examples of medications that can greatly improve the lives of person with dementia include antidepressants, nonsedating anxiolytics, and low-dose antipsychotics. Paranoid delusions are common in persons with dementia and cause great fear and unnecessary suffering. Hallucinations are a common feature of DLB. In both conditions, these symptoms may be greatly relieved with antipsychotic medications, often at very low doses. However, no antipsychotic is currently FDA approved for use in dementia, and many carry important safety warnings. As with any other treatment, using the lowest effective dose, carefully considering the risk–benefit ratio, and discussing the treatment with the patient and legally authorized representatives are important in obtaining informed consent to treatment. Written informed consent might be considered.

Nonpharmacological Treatment

Dementia affects the person with the condition, loved ones, and professional caregivers. AD, for example, has been termed *the long goodbye*, wherein the person's body continues to exist, while the personality and cognitive abilities change markedly over time. It is important to provide support and continuing education and training for both personal and professional caregivers. Because of the interplay of medical and social factors in the diagnosis and management of dementia, it is especially important to interact with the patient, family, other loved ones, and professional caregivers in a culturally competent manner. Several chapters in this text provide excellent techniques and resources for upgrading skills and knowledge in culturally respectful approaches. An ethnogeriatrics online curriculum may also be helpful (www.stanford.edu/group/ethnoger/). Specific techniques that improve the ability to care and the ability to sustain care can be effectively taught and reinforced.

Because the prevalence of dementia increases with age, caregiving spouses and partners are likely to be aged themselves. Children who function as caregivers are often middle-aged, in a "sandwich" situation, supporting their college-aged children or caring for grandchildren while also caring for a parent with a progressive dementia. An increasing number of older people have primary responsibility for the care of young children. Special attention must be paid to ameliorating stress-related conditions in the caregiver, such as hypertension, anxiety, depression, and other chronic illnesses. Getting proper medical care and enough rest, using respite services, and finding knowledgeable support are some of the keys to maintaining the caregiving relationship.

The Alzheimer's Association (www.alz.org) is the best source of support and continuously updated information about dementia, specific training for dealing with troublesome behaviors, and information about other training sources. The association deals with AD and related disorders (i.e., other dementias) and operates a nationwide contact center helpline 24 hr a day, 7 days a week (800-272-3900). There is a nationwide chapter network providing informational materials, operating caregiver support groups, and providing other services. The association staff may also be an excellent source of referral to local professional community providers. When care outside the home is required, it is helpful to be informed on how to select high-quality facilities. Excellent resources for information about dementia care in assisted-living facilities and nursing homes can be found (Zimmerman et al., 2005).

Geriatricians and geriatric care teams may provide invaluable services in diagnosis and both pharmacological and nonpharmacological management of cognitive impairment and troublesome behaviors. They may also be familiar with community resources and be able to advise caregivers on those likely to be most appropriate for their needs. When symptoms such as pain, nausea, and weight loss are prominent, caregivers should also seek out specialists in palliative care, a relatively new discipline providing the interdisciplinary team assistance of a physician certified in palliative medicine and other specially trained providers, such as nurses, social workers, and therapists. The palliative care team specializes in managing both acute and chronic pain and other serious symptoms. Many hospitals have such teams, and the local hospital may be a good source of information about both inpatient and outpatient services. When the disease is moderately to severely advanced, caregivers may be advised to seek out the services of a hospice program. The palliative care team may be an excellent referral source for inpatient and outpatient hospice services in the community.

Alternative and Complementary Treatments

In a book such as this, focused on ethnogeriatrics, it is especially important to consider potentially beneficial alternative and complementary treatments. In a disease such as AD, where the current FDA-approved drugs are beneficial but far from curative, or in other types of dementia, the likelihood exists for patients and families to be victimized by exaggerated claims for products and treatments that range from not beneficial to truly harmful. They also range from free to exorbitantly expensive. Matters are further confused by false testimonials, temporary placebo response, and poorly designed and misleading research studies. Stories abound about persons who were so victimized. The demographic imperative and the personal losses and financial losses suffered by people with dementia in every country make it likely that truly beneficial products or treatments will become widely known and evaluated very quickly. Some considerations in evaluating claims for dietary supplements include unknown safety and effectiveness, inconsistent and unknown purity and consistency of ingredients when the manufacturing is not up to FDA pharmaceutical standards, and unreported or unmonitored serious negative reactions. There is particular reason to avoid products and alternative therapies derived from the brains of animals because of the possible transmission of very serious illnesses, such as the prion disease, bovine spongiform encephalopathy (BSE), also known as *mad cow disease*. There are large numbers of alternative treatments that have been discussed as having potential benefit in dementia. Some of the most commonly mentioned are as follows:

Ginkgo biloba leaf extracts. As in most naturally occurring substances, the extract of ginkgo biloba leaf contains a number of potentially active ingredients. It is important to differentiate the leaf from the ginkgo seeds, as the seeds are toxic. Ginkgo leaves and leaf extracts have been used for centuries, either alone or in combination with other herbal therapies. Ginkgo is widely used around the world and is one of the best-selling herbal products. Claims of benefit in dementia are controversial because of the paucity of well-designed, methodologically sound studies. Some well-designed studies are currently underway. Gingko biloba leaf is thought to work by improving circulation. Because gingko biloba leaf has been used for so long and so widely, benefits, if any, are probably modest. Side effects appear to be few, but it is important to note the mild effect on reducing the ability of the blood to clot. This mild effect in normal adults would be of serious concern in persons with bleeding problems and in those taking blood-thinning medications, such as warfarin and aspirin.

Huperzine A. This is a dietary supplement that is currently undergoing its first U.S. clinical trial in a study launched in 2004. Its safety and efficacy are not yet known. Its mechanism of action is possibly similar to the currently approved AChEIs, so its use concomitantly with those medications is not recommended.

Phosphatidylserine. This is a phospholipid that is a major component of neurons. Past studies using an animal source showed some potential benefit. However, because of a concern about transmission of animal brain diseases, the studies were discontinued. Phosphatidylserine may also be obtained from plant sources, such as soy; however, the ability of the body to use phosphatidylserine derived from plants is not known. Further studies are needed to determine whether dietary supplementation with this phospholipid would be helpful or harmful in preventing or treating AD.

Coral calcium. This is a product that was formerly heavily marketed as a cure for AD and other illnesses. It is a calcium source derived from coral and contains other minerals in addition to calcium. In 2003, the U.S. Federal Trade Commission and the FDA filed a formal complaint against the promoters and distributors for deceptive marketing (www.ftc.gov/opa/2003/06/trudeau.htm).

Future Treatments

A number of different types of treatments for dementia are undergoing careful investigation at this time. Any of these, alone or in combination with currently approved medications, could prove promising. These treatments are based on the amyloid and neurotransmitter pathologies, various hormonal therapies, neuronal growth factors, and immunotherapy. It is possible, even likely, that future treatment will consist of a combination of these. Despite the exciting promise of new treatments, there is considerable social concern about the affordability of treatment that requires several different costly medications for so many people. Prevention would be ideal.

Prevention

While some of the treatments currently being studied show promise, it would be much better for there to be effective prevention for dementia or for there to be methods to dramatically slow progressive degenerative processes, such as in AD and DLB. Cardiovascular risk factors, such as hypertension, diabetes mellitus, and hyperlipidemia have been shown to increase the risk of both AD and VaD, the most common causes of dementia. Keeping the heart healthy can have the added benefit of keeping the brain healthy. Finding ways to slow the progression of AD would yield great personal and societal benefits. The prevalence of AD doubles every 5 years over the age of 65. Slowing the onset of clinical symptoms by 5 years would result in a reduction of the disease prevalence by one half, a significant potential public health benefit. Clues to risk factors are obtained by careful long-term epidemiological or population-based studies. Some of these have already yielded important clues to the prevention of the disease, such as the importance of nutrition in brain health at every age, reducing cardiovascular risk factors, as above, and keeping the brain active with mentally challenging work or play.

Online Sources

Alzeheimer's Association: www.alz.org
Curriculum in Ethnogeriatrics: www.stanford.edu/group/ethnoger/
Federal Trade Commission: www.ftc.gov/opa/2003/06/trudeau.htm
Mayo Clinic: www.mayoclinic.com/invoke.cfm?id=AN00541

References

Auriacombe, S., Vellas, B., Pere, J. J., & Loria-Kanza, Y. (2002). Efficacy and safety of rivastigmine in patients with Alzheimer's disease who failed to benefit from treatment with donepezil. *Current Medical Research and Opinion, 18,* 129–138.

Kumar, V., Anand, R., Messina, J., Hartman, R., & Veach, J. (2000). An efficacy and safety analysis of Exelon˙ in Alzheimer's disease patients with concurrent vascular risk factors. *European Journal of Neurology, 7,* 159–169.

Molchan, S. (2005, July). The Alzheimer's Disease Neuroimaging Initiative. *U.S. Neurology Review,* 30–32. Retrieved March 8, 2006, from http://www.touchbriefings.com/cdps/cditem.cfm?NID=1239.

Rasmussen, D. X., Brandt, J., Steele, C., Hedreen, J. C., Troncoso, J. C., & Folstein, M. F. (1996). Accuracy of clinical diagnosis of Alzheimer disease and clinical features of patients with non-Alzheimer disease neuropathology. *Alzheimer Disease and Associated Disorders, 10,* 180–188.

Reisberg, B., Doody, R., Stöffler, A., Schmitt, F., Ferris, S., & Mobius, H. J., for the Memantine Study Group. (2003). Memantine in moderate-to-severe Alzheimer's disease. *New England Journal of Medicine, 348,* 1333–1341.

Sano, M., Ernesto, C., Thomas, R., Klauber, M. R., Schafer, K., Grundman, M. et al., for The Members of the Alzheimer's Disease Cooperative Study. (1997).

A controlled trial of selegiline, α-tocopherol, or both as treatment for Alzheimer's disease. *New England Journal of Medicine, 336*, 1216–1222.

Tariot, P. N., Farlow, M. R., Grossberg, G. T., Graham, S. M., McDonald, S., & Gergel, I., for the Memantine Study Group. (2004). Memantine treatment in patients with moderate to severe Alzheimer disease already receiving donepezil: A randomized controlled trial. *Journal of the American Medical Association, 291*(3), 317–324.

Waxman, A. D. (2005, July). Functional brain imaging in dementia: The transition from SPECT to PET. *U.S. Neurology Review*, 14–16. Retrieved March 8, 2006, from http://www.touchbriefings.com/cdps/cditem.cfm?NID=1239.

Zimmerman, S., Sloane, P. D., Williams, C. S., Reed, P. S., Preisser, J. S., Eckert, J. K., Boustani, M., and Dobbs, D. (2005). Dementia care and quality of life in assisted living facilities and nursing homes: Foundations for dementia care training program for residential care staff. *The Gerontologist, 45*, 133–146.

PART **IV**

Working with Families

CHAPTER 8

The Family as the Unit of Assessment and Treatment in Work with Ethnically Diverse Older Adults with Dementia

DOLORES GALLAGHER-THOMPSON

Why focus on the family (broadly defined) when working with elders from ethnically diverse backgrounds? It can be more time consuming, add complexities to the interaction, and be more difficult to do, particularly in busy primary care practice settings where appointments are typically between 10 and 30 min in length (Hinton, 2002). Most clinicians are accustomed to working directly with the patient (as long as he or she can communicate with some intelligence) and perhaps one "primary" caregiver, typically the spouse in the case of Caucasian families (Mittelman, Zeiss, Davies, & Guy, 2003). This individual is usually the one who gives the patient's history to help make the diagnosis and who supervises medications. He or she will also take on the role of reporting behavioral and other problems as impairment becomes greater. Most health-care providers refer to this primary caregiver as the "informant," and as the dementia progresses, they often talk directly to that person, ignoring the patient, essentially. Most providers do not treat the caregiver, however distressed he or she may be, but instead focus on the patient's problems and how to resolve them, often with medication for the patient and referral to a specialized agency for

119

patients of dementia and their families, like the Alzheimer's Association, which offers support groups and other services targeted to the caregiver.

Health-care providers typically rely on ethnic minority families for all of these things, plus they are asked to translate when the older person does not speak English. Many papers are written on the pitfalls of using family members for cognitive testing and interpretation of complex concepts (see Purnell & Paulanka, 1998); whenever possible, if bilingual staff are not available, professional translators or interpreters should be used rather than family members, especially for sensitive information, such as dates and locations, or being able to follow commands.

Clinicians may ask themselves the following: why bother to learn new information and develop the skills needed to work with ethnically diverse families? One concrete reason focuses on medical decision making; for instance, in situations in which clinicians believe it may be time to place the person with dementia in a nursing home or some other institutional setting, they may soon find that the process is stalled, and action is not taken. In the case of Hispanic/Latino and Chinese families, for example, key members of the family may live in Mexico, Cuba, Taiwan, Hong Kong, or mainland China (Valle, 1998; Zhan, 2004). They often cannot be physically present at an appointment to discuss such matters, but they are consulted before any important decisions are made. Clinicians who are not aware of this practice may alienate the family by trying to rush a decision before family members are ready, or may seem disrespectful and unaware of how traditional family roles operate in most non-Caucasian cultures.

We argue in this brief chapter that inclusion of the family (broadly defined) is crucial to success—it is not really an option in this time of significant health disparities (La Veist, 2004). Most ethnically diverse individuals prefer to be treated within their family unit rather than solely as individuals; it is likely that greater appreciation of this fact, and accommodation to it in the health-care visit, will result in the reduction of at least some of the barriers that lead to disparities in health-care access (Institute of Medicine, 2002). In subsequent chapters, much more detail will be presented regarding how to work effectively with families from a broad range of ethnic and cultural backgrounds.

Although there are many unique points made in each chapter, one striking similarity across all of them is the admonition to find out just who is in "the family," how they participate in caregiving, and when and how they should be consulted about changes in the treatment process and implementation plan. Other "common factors" across most of the groups discussed in subsequent chapters include: endorsement of concepts like *filial piety* (the responsibility to care for one's elders, which encourages family caregiving until the very end); not wanting to "lose face" or be shamed in front of other family members, and the larger community, by making consistent use of formal services (e.g., adult day care, respite, in-home support services) when seeking such services is construed as a sign of failure or weakness to live up to responsibilities; and extreme reluctance to discuss issues involving transitions (e.g., nursing home placement, end-of-life decision making). Although the reasons that support these beliefs and practices vary from one cultural group to another, they are present in most of the groups written about in this book. These are important issues to keep in mind when working with culturally diverse families, as they clearly affect both the process of making a diagnosis and subsequent treatment planning and implementation. For example, what is the value of giving a referral to a day care program (even if it is a "culturally appropriate" one, which most are not) if the family will almost always reject such a plan, due to their beliefs that they should be "taking care of mom and dad," not some strangers. It would seem a better use of the clinicians' time to know in advance that this is likely to be politely dismissed as a treatment option and to elicit the beliefs that stand in the way, with an eye toward presenting other ways to view the situation. It is hoped that this increased awareness and sensitivity will result in more appropriate use of existing services.

Beliefs such as these also influence family dynamics. The following are illustrations of this process:

1. Ethnic minority caregivers may be reluctant to admit distress related to caregiving when asked directly about it, either to professionals or to other family members, although many studies have shown equal or higher levels of distress among them than among Caucasian care-givers (see Aranda & Knight, 1997). They may be similarly likely to underreport memory and behavioral problems of their loved ones and to interpret them as "normal aging" until the situation becomes severe and help must be sought (Hinton, Frantz, & Friend, 2004).

2. Ethnically diverse caregivers tend to experience higher levels of family conflict than Caucasians, precisely because many more family members are involved in the process. This is found to be related both to intergenerational differences in values regarding aging and care of the elderly and differences in acculturation, including education, socioeconomic status, and degree of exposure to beliefs of the majority culture (see Ishii-Kuntz, 1997; Valle, 1998; Wang & Gallagher-Thompson, 2005). Therefore, clinicians need to inquire about such things as immigration history, if relevant, and differences in values, keeping in mind that while factual information can generally

be asked about directly, inquiries of a more personal nature (such as intergenerational differences in values) should be made in a more indirect manner.

This is related to a point also raised in virtually all the chapters in this section, namely, the importance of understanding roles in the family and how "traditional" versus "modern" the family seems to be in its adherence to a rigid role structure. Although these issues cannot usually be asked about directly, they may be observed in family interactions. Keep in mind that the role reversal when an adult child provides physical, emotional, and financial care to an aging parent with dementia is particularly stressful for most minority caregivers and may be one impetus for seeking help (Janevic & Connell, 2001).

Finally, the term *cultural competency* is commonly used to signify a process that includes modifying one's attitudes and beliefs about diverse groups, and learning new skills for working with them, in order to more effectively treat them. It is a concept of relevance to all groups discussed in this book. The interested reader is referred to sources such as the Stanford Geriatric Education Center's Web site (http://sgec.stanford.edu), where one can complete an online training module in improving communication with older people of different cultures. This is one example of the many resources available through that Web site that address these and related issues. Another valuable resource for clinicians is the *Diversity Toolbox* created recently by the Alzheimer's Association. It is located through the main Web site for their national office (www.alz.org, in the "resources" section). It contains a wealth of information of use to clinicians in multiple languages, such as explanations of what is dementia, the top 10 warning signs, recognizing and managing caregiver stress, managing problem behaviors in the home, and related issues. Many of these can be used as handouts for the family, to improve their understanding of this devastating disease. Other resources are there for professionals, such as presentations of recent research findings made at national meetings and abstracts of relevant published papers.

In summary, caregiving is largely a family responsibility within ethnic minority communities. Inclusion of key family members from the beginning, although perhaps more time consuming and challenging, will lead to better patient and caregiver outcomes. For the clinician to do this effectively, he or she needs to develop awareness of both the unique and common culturally based factors affecting views about dementia and the family's role in providing care, along with development of the needed skill set to provide care in a culturally competent manner. Although this may sound difficult, experience has shown that it is within the grasp of most of us, given a sincere commitment to learning and to improving one's practice, as new information becomes available. Given the ever-increasing diversity of our country, this is likely to be an area of great intellectual and social progress in the decade ahead.

References

Allery, A. J., Aranda, M., Dilworth-Anderson, P., Guerrero, M., Haan, M., Hendrie, H. et al. (2004). Alzheimer's disease and communities of color. In K. E. Whitfield (Ed.), *Closing the gap: Improving the health of minority elders in the new millennium* (pp. 81–86). Washington, DC: Gerontological Society of America.

Aranda, M., & Knight, B. (1997). The influence of ethnicity and culture on the caregiver stress and coping process: A sociocultural review and analysis. *The Gerontologist, 37,* 342–354.

Hinton, L. (2002). Improving care for ethnic minority elderly and their family caregivers across the spectrum of dementia severity. *Alzheimer Disease and Associated Disorders, 16*(Suppl. 2), 50–55.

Hinton, L., Franz, C., & Friend, J. (2004). Pathways to dementia diagnosis: Evidence for cross-ethnic differences. *Alzheimer's Disease and Associated Disorders, 18,* 134–144.

Institute of Medicine. (2002). *Unequal treatment: Confronting racial and ethnic disparities of healthcare.* Washington, DC: National Academy Press.

Ishii-Kuntz, M. (1997). Intergenerational relationships among Chinese, Japanese, and Korean Americans. *Family Relations, 46,* 23–32.

Janevic, M. R., & Connell, C. M. (2001). Racial, ethnic, and cultural differences in the dementia caregiving experience: Recent findings. *The Gerontologist, 41,* 334–347.

La Veist, T. (2004). Conceptualizing racial and ethnic disparities in access, utilization, and quality of care. In K. E. Whitfield (Ed.), *Closing the gap: Improving the health of minority elders in the new millennium* (pp. 87–92). Washington, DC: Gerontological Society of America.

Mittelman, M., Zeiss, A., Davies, H., & Guy, D. (2003). Specific stressor of spousal caregivers: Difficult behaviors, loss of sexual intimacy, and incontinence. In D. W. Coon, D. Gallagher-Thompson, & L. W. Thompson (Eds.), *Innovative interventions to reduce dementia caregiver distress: A clinical guide* (pp. 77–98). New York: Springer.

Purnell, L. D., & Paulanka, B. J. (1998). Purnell's model for cultural competence. In L. D. Purnell & B. L. Paulanka (Eds.), *Transcultural health care: A culturally competent approach* (pp. 7–51). Philadelphia: F.A. Davis.

Valle, R. (1998). *Caregiving across cultures: Working with dementing illness and ethnically diverse populations.* Washington, DC: Taylor & Francis.

Wang, P. C., & Gallagher-Thompson, D. (2005). Resolution of intergenerational conflict in a Chinese female dementia caregiver: A case study using cognitive/behavioral methods. *Clinical Gerontologist, 28*(3), 91–94.

Zhan, L. (2004). Caring for family members with Alzheimer's disease: Perspectives from Chinese American caregivers. *Journal of Gerontological Nursing, 13*, 19–29.

Working with African American Families

CHAPTER 9

Working with African American Families

PEGGYE DILWORTH-ANDERSON, BRENT E. GIBSON,
AND JOAN DETRY BURKE

In order to understand caregiving for patients with dementia among African American families, it is imperative that we consider the multiple contexts within which care takes place. Attention to these contexts highlights the interconnectedness of broader social trends and individual or familial characteristics. In addition, we see the interwoven effects of biological, social–cultural, and psychological factors on caregiving experiences and outcomes. This chapter has six major sections. We begin by discussing population aging in the United States and some specific demographic characteristics of African Americans as a group. These population-level statistics provide the backdrop for understanding caregiving for dementia patients among African Americans. Second, we discuss the structure and composition of African American caregiving networks in order to illustrate how various people (i.e., family members and friends) come together to provide care to an older person with dementia. Third, we cover the more specific social and cultural contexts that shape caregiving for dementia patients among African Americans. We include in this discussion specific cultural values and beliefs that are reflected in caregiving behaviors and outcomes. Fourth, we provide specific strategies for working effectively with African American caregivers of loved ones with dementia. Fifth, we provide a list of resources that provide specific information for and about African

American family caregivers of patients with dementia. We conclude with some summary points and future directions.

Demographic Characteristics of Older African Americans

The age structure of the U.S. population is changing rapidly. Overall, the population is aging. These patterns of demographic change are most dramatic for minority ethnoracial groups and will have important implications for addressing the specific needs and experiences of these caregivers. According to the Administration on Aging (2003), the proportion of people over 65 years of age is growing most rapidly among minority groups; the population of persons over 65 years of age belonging to minority ethnoracial groups was 17.2% in the year 2000, and this is projected to increase to 26.4% by the year 2033. Further, the number of people over age 65 is expected to increase by 77% in the White population, with more dramatic increases of 342% for Hispanics and 164% for African Americans over the same period of time (Administration on Aging, 2003). This trend is, in part, attributable to the increasing life expectancy of the U.S. population; more specifically, the life expectancy of African Americans has increased by 12.8% from 1970 to 2002, and for Whites it increased by only 8.4% for the same time period (National Center for Health Statistics, 2002). This is very relevant to Alzheimer's disease research given that age is a key risk factor for developing the disease; more than 10% of people over 65 years of age and nearly 50% of people over 85 years of age have the disease (Alzheimer's Association, 2003). Thus, the number of people with Alzheimer's disease is expected to increase dramatically over the coming years as the population ages.

Due to factors such as socioeconomic disadvantage and the cumulative effects of oppression, ethnoracial minority elders are more likely to be in poorer health, have higher rates of functional disability, become impaired at an earlier age, and have fewer financial resources, such as pensions, Social Security, and adequate health insurance (Jolicoeur & Madden, 2002; Tennestedt, Chang, & Delgado, 1999). In a survey conducted in 2002, it was found that among the 65-year-old and over population, 39.5% of African Americans rated themselves as in fair/poor health compared to 25.2% of Whites and 71.6% of African Americans experienced difficulty in physical functioning compared to 65% of Whites. Also, the average income for African Americans was $15,642 compared to $22,790 for Whites in 2001 (National Center for Health Statistics, 2002).

Already, larger proportions of ethnoracial minority families are providing care for older family members as compared to European American families: 29% of African American families, 27% of Hispanic families, and

24% of European American families provide care to older family members (National Alliance for Caregiving & AARP, 1997). Ongoing health disparities and increases in numbers of older people in minority ethnoracial groups will continue to place proportionally higher caregiving demands on minority families than on European American families. Furthermore, due to different patterns of socioeconomic status, health status, and cultural norms and beliefs, the experience of caregiving (i.e., the levels of caregiver distress and satisfaction) can differ across ethnoracial groups.

Within most ethnoracial groups in the United States, adult children are more likely to provide care to dependent elders than are other family members, with 42–44% of dependent elders cared for by adult children and less than 40% cared for by spouses (National Academy on an Aging Society, 2000; Center on an Aging Society, 2005). Due to lower fertility rates, the baby boomers, compared to their parents, will have fewer adult children available to care for them should they become dependent in old age (Population Reference Bureau, 2003). In looking to the future, we can expect a greater need for assistance from adult children at a time when there is a shrinking pool of potential family caregivers. Understanding the needs of caregivers and creating appropriate supports and interventions are critically important because family caregiving is a major factor in preventing or delaying institutionalization. The health status of older people is also a significant issue among ethnoracial groups. Two of the main risk factors for Alzheimer's disease are high blood pressure and high cholesterol; having either of these risk factors alone doubles one's likelihood of developing Alzheimer's disease, whereas having both risk factors quadruples one's likelihood (Alzheimer's Association, 2003). In 2000, 65% of African American Medicare beneficiaries had hypertension, the prevalence of which had increased by 4% since 1997. In contrast, 51% of White Medicare beneficiaries had hypertension, with an increased prevalence of 2.1% since 1997 (National Center for Health Statistics, 2002). Vascular dementia is a more common form of dementia among African Americans than among Whites. Contributing to the risk of vascular dementia are hypertension, diabetes, and stroke. African Americans have a 60% higher risk than Whites of developing type 2 diabetes mellitus. The impact of these health disparities on the prevalence of dementia among African Americans is noticeable. The age-specific prevalence of dementia is 14–100% higher than that found among Whites. In addition, first-degree relatives of African Americans who have Alzheimer's disease have a 43.7% cumulative risk of getting the disease (Alzheimer's Association, 2003).

The Structure and Composition of African American Family Caregiving Networks

With the above discussion in mind, it is important that we assess how African American families meet the challenges of caregiving. Meeting these challenges can be understood within the context of the structure and composition of family networks in African American families. Similar to other families, the structure of the African American family is related to the composition of the kin network, which provides an understanding of family resources (Zollar, 1985). Therefore, spouses, adult children, siblings, grandchildren, nieces, and nephews are documented as forming part of the family network of care (Dilworth-Anderson, Williams, & Cooper, 1999; Haley et al., 1995; Young & Kahana, 1995). Research shows that in African American families, kin and non-kin are part of the network. Non-kin network members consist of friends and neighbors who provide care to dependent elders. Lawton, Rajagopal, Brody, and Kleban (1992) reported that the quality of care to older people in African American families did not vary by relationship to the caregiver. Luckey (1994) found that roles and tasks performed by grandchildren, nieces, or nephews assisted the older people as well as the primary caregivers in interacting with formal services. Sharing living arrangements and pooling financial resources are ways in which African American networks have traditionally provided and continue to provide care to members (Franklin, 1997). Caregiving networks among African Americans, therefore, have addressed both simple and complex problems of family and community members.

Additionally, the literature suggests that African American families are more likely than White families to provide care in collectivist versus individualistic caregiving systems (Dilworth-Anderson et al., 1999; Keith, 1995; Pyke & Bengtson, 1996). Collectivism is fostered through cultural values of interdependence, reciprocity (giving back to those who cared for us), and filial responsibility in African American families. Research also suggests that strong cultural values and beliefs about helping and giving support encourage cohesiveness among African American families (Dilworth-Anderson et al., 1999; Jarrett & Burton, 1999; Taylor & Chatters, 1986). These values of collectivism and cohesion, therefore, have shaped both the composition and size of the caregiving network of older African Americans (Burton & Dilworth-Anderson, 1991; Franklin, 1997; Katz, 1993). Strong adherence to cultural values and norms regarding reciprocity and interdependence can also increase the availability of family members to be included in a helping network, reflecting a behavioral response by family members to those values and norms (Lawton et al., 1992). Findings show that this availability also increases the likelihood of having different types of caregivers that play both distinctive and overlapping roles. Taken together, the various roles of family members represent how the larger network is constructed or configured. Thus, the system of care is comprised of individuals who fulfill specific roles (e.g., primary caregiver) through performing tasks and taking on responsibilities that may be discrete or may overlap with the tasks and responsibilities taken on by those in other roles (e.g., secondary caregiver). Although researchers assert that it is more realistic to conceptualize informal caregiving to dependent elders as a process involving various family members (Dilworth-Anderson et al., 1999; Keith, 1995; Piercy, 1998), only a few studies have addressed the issue (Bourgeois, Beach, Schulz, & Burgio, 1996; Taylor & Chatters, 1991; Tennstedt, McKinlay, & Sullivan, 1989). The findings from these studies show that the caregiving duties of secondary and tertiary caregivers both complement and supplement those of primary caregivers.

We believe that the cultural values that once served to foster the strong caregiving networks described above may now be a source of stress for some caregivers. For example, Dilworth-Anderson, Goodwin, and Williams (2004) found that very strong cultural justifications for giving care to dependent family members predicted less positive evaluations of health for African American caregivers. Very weak cultural justifications for caregiving were predictive of poor evaluations of health as well. However, African American caregivers with moderate levels of cultural justifications for providing care evaluated their health the most positively. Another concern that has emerged in recent studies is that older African American caregivers have smaller social networks and fewer social resources as compared to Whites (Ajrouch, Antonucci, & Janevic, 2001; Barnes, Mendes de Leon, Bienias, & Evans, 2004; Miller & Guo, 2000). These findings support those reported earlier that we can no longer assume that large and extended networks still exist in African American families (Jarrett & Burton, 1999; McDonald & Armstrong, 2001; Roschelle, 1997). Jarrett and Burton (1999) and Roschelle (1997), in particular, suggest that characteristics such as age distribution, education, and living arrangements of those in the network can influence the type of support given and received. Roschelle also suggests that, unlike in the past, more African American families will begin to rely on varied combinations of support that include the family and formal services. These findings show that the size and strength of the kin network are being challenged by the needs of multiple generations in the family coupled with declining resources in the network to address the needs of family members (Dilworth-Anderson & Burton, 1999).

Caregiving Experiences among African Americans

Caregiving is often viewed as a balancing act between the needs and resources of care recipients and the needs and resources of caregivers. This balancing act differs across diverse groups; in other words, caregiving experiences are variable and often reflect the culture and social location of the caregiver. In this discussion, we focus on the experiences of African American caregivers, which are often examined through comparative studies. From the available literature comparing caregivers of different ethnoracial groups, a number of differences have been noted when comparing African American caregivers to other groups (Aranda & Knight, 1997; Dilworth-Anderson, Williams, & Gibson, 2002; Haley et al., 2004). These differences are often linked to cultural, religious, and spiritual beliefs and practices that shape the context in which care is provided and how caregivers experience their roles.

For example, in one of the most comprehensive studies on well-being, appraisal, and coping among diverse groups of caregivers, Haley et al. (2004) found that African Americans, as compared to Whites, reported lower levels of psychological distress and used fewer psychotropic medications. They also found that African American caregivers, as compared to Whites, gave more positive appraisals in relation to stress that is associated with behavioral problems of care recipients with dementia. Their findings show that African Americans also reported significantly higher appraisals of the benefits of caregiving. This latter finding supports those by Dilworth-Anderson et al. (2005), which show that African American caregivers, unlike their White counterparts, express positive views about giving and receiving benefits for providing this care. Other researchers (Adams, Aranda, Kemp, & Takagi, 2002; Haley et al., 2004; Sterritt & Pokorny, 1998) found that African American caregivers, when compared to other ethnic groups, reported higher levels of religious and spiritual coping in their caregiving roles. In fact, Sterritt and Pokorny (1998) reported that African American caregivers were more likely to include God as part of their informal support system, and they ranked God or religion as their first source of informal support, followed by family. In addition, higher levels of religiosity have been found to be related to more positive appraisals of caregiving (Gallagher-Thompson et al., 2000; Haley et al., 1996; Picot, Debanne, Namazi, & Wykle, 1997; Roff et al., 2004).

A growing body of literature is providing more insights into the effects of caregiving on African Americans. Despite being faced with fewer resources than White caregivers, African American caregivers have more positive appraisals of the role and higher levels of religiosity (i.e., more engagement in religious activities and greater reliance on faith in caregiving). The research by Haley and colleagues (2004) and Roth, Haley, Owen, Clay, and Goode (2001) shows that African American caregivers deal with chronic stress in their caregiving roles, but they also express very positive views and feelings about what they are doing. In other words, they are affected emotionally less by caregiving than are White caregivers. When compared with White female caregivers, African American female caregivers report lower levels of anxiety and upset about care recipients' problem behaviors and higher levels of satisfaction and rewards in the caregiving role (Foley, Tung, & Mutran, 2002; Roff et al., 2004; White, Townsend, & Stephens, 2000). The literature also suggests that the combination of cultural values and positive appraisals coupled with economic constraints helps to explain why African Americans spend a longer time in the community than do Whites prior to nursing home admission.

Findings by Dilworth-Anderson and colleagues (2004), however, provide a few notable cautions on the health implications of positive appraisal, fewer negative effects of caregiving, and long-term home care among African American caregivers, especially for their physical health. In a longitudinal study, they found that cultural justifications for caregiving had a curvilinear effect on psychosocial health with very weak and very strong cultural justifications for caregiving being predictive of poor psychosocial health. They suggested that caregivers may be providing care because of a very strong identification with cultural values and beliefs and are doing so out of a sense of duty, expectation, and obligation. They further suggested that these caregivers might be experiencing role engulfment (Skaff & Pearlin, 1992) or role captivity (Aneshensel, Pearlin, & Schuler, 1993). For caregivers with low levels of cultural beliefs and values, the authors assert that they may be providing care out of necessity, because there may not be anyone else available to provide care. Because we view such findings as rooted in strong cultural beliefs that affect appraisals and coping, we believe the concept of "John Henryism" (James, Hartnett, & Kalsbeek, 1983) can provide some interpretive insight. This concept is a synonym for prolonged, high-effort coping with difficult psychological stressors. In the case of African American caregivers, getting the job done, as a caregiver, is more often associated with poor physical health outcomes, as compared to poor psychological outcomes. Getting the job done is also associated with positive appraisals of caregiving, feeling less burdened, and relying more on spiritual beliefs to deal with chronic stress in caregiving as compared to White caregivers.

Cultural and Social Context of African American Caregivers' Responses to Dementia Caregiving

The often complex and mixed messages about how and why African American caregivers are affected by their caregiving experiences can be explained by cultural and social factors. Culturally speaking, evidence shows that cultural norms and beliefs can help shape a group's perceptions of disease and illness (Klonoff & Landrine, 1994; Nelson, Geiger, & Mangione, 2002). In this discussion, culture is defined as a set of shared symbols, beliefs, and customs that shape individual and group behavior. It provides guidelines for speaking, doing, interpreting, and evaluating one's actions and reactions in life (Goodenough, 1999). Dementia, for example, is defined and perceived differently among diverse cultural groups (Dilworth-Anderson & Gibson, 2002; Henderson & Gutierrez-Mayka, 1992). In assessing different cultural realities regarding dementia, Roberts, Akinleye, Hipps, and Green (2005) found that African Americans as compared to Whites were more likely to report that stress, mental illness, God's will, alcohol abuse, smoking, and exposure to toxins were causes of Alzheimer's disease. In addition, African Americans were more likely to suggest that lifestyle changes, such as lowering stress levels, being physically active, and eating nutritious foods can prevent Alzheimer's disease. These findings suggest that the reality of dementia held by other cultural groups in understanding the labels and meanings that are assigned to dementia direct and structure caregiving. Findings also show that compared to Whites, African American caregivers derived higher levels of day-to-day and spiritual meaning from caregiving to elders with dementia (Farran, Miller, Kaufman, & Davis, 1997).

Caregiving occurs within a particular social context that includes cultural, familial, and religious values and norms, which in turn influences a caregiver's decision to provide care. Caregivers' reasons and explanations for caregiving include affection, gratification, reciprocity for past kindness and care, family responsibility or duty, and moral obligation (Dilworth-Anderson et al., 2002; Noonan, Tennstedt, & Rebelsky, 1996). In general, researchers describe Hispanic families and African American families as holding strong cultural values and norms for members of the extended family who care for an older relative (Mausbach et al., 2004; Nkongo & Archbold, 1995; Sterritt & Pokorny, 1998). In addition, religious and spiritual beliefs and practices (also shaped by one's cultural context) can be used as coping resources in caregiving and can lead to differences in caregiving experiences between ethnoracial groups. Gallagher-Thompson and colleagues (2000) explained lower levels of socioeconomic status as being associated with positive appraisals of caregiving for African Americans by suggesting that difficulties faced by people with lower socioeconomic status, combined with their increased religiosity, contribute to an enhanced ability to frame difficulties more positively. That is, past hardships and strong faith may lead to increased resilience among African American caregivers. Religiosity, therefore, can provide partial explanation for African Americans' more positive appraisals of caregiving when compared to Whites (Roff et al., 2004).

Examples of Social and Cultural Responses to Care of Those with Dementia

In an ongoing study on "Perceiving and Giving Meaning to Dementia" in diverse groups by Dilworth-Anderson (2003–2007), funded by the Alzheimer's Association, preliminary findings show that families of individuals with Alzheimer's disease and other forms of dementia recognized and defined memory loss problems based on cultural and social interpretations of the patients' behavioral changes. For example, in this study, African American family members, unlike White families, often noticed that their older relatives were exhibiting increasingly problematic behaviors, such as forgetfulness, repetition during conversations, difficulty performing familiar tasks, disorientation, and changes in personality but they did not associate these problems with any dementia. They often defined symptoms using words related to forgetting behaviors; emotional descriptions such as sadness, depression, and loneliness; and physical indicators such as lapses in acceptable personal hygiene and physical deterioration.

Family members also displayed some reservation in giving meaning to the symptoms they noticed. This caution in assigning labels such as "Alzheimer's disease" and "dementia" may have been due in part to some difficulty in differentiating between early signs of dementia and the patient's normal behavior. For instance, one caregiver retold an incident in which her mother refused to attend a family function but later cried because she did not want to be left alone. The caregiver reported that

> I thought my mother was honestly jerking my chain…and the reason why as they both said my mother was extremely witty. My mother is the type of person, if she could mess with you, she would…. So it was real difficult in the beginning to separate…. And that has been the biggest part of the problem…. Some days it's hard to distinguish if she is just messing with you or is she really not understanding or comprehending what she is actually doing.

In many cases, the hesitancy in assigning meaning to symptoms was due to a belief that the behaviors were simply a sign of normal aging.

African American families often attributed, as evidenced in the following quotes, that while some families may have sincerely misinterpreted the symptoms, others exhibited a sense of denial about acknowledging a more serious problem:

> … that's the last thing I thought about. I agree everybody forget somethin'. That's the farthest thing from my mind was Alzheimer's…because I mean to me we didn't see Alzheimer's. I just saw momma forgettin' stuff, then it just kept on gettin' a little bit worse and worse.

> Yeah and for me I associated it with, you know, you are getting older. [Sort of laughs.] I mean I've seen people get old, you know what I'm saying…. Those are one of the things that you associate with old age. You know, you don't give a name like Alzheimer's to start off with. I mean. You know what I mean.

> We talked about her but we kind of just like passed it. Just—you know—yes, you know, so-so and so yeah she'll be all right. You know, it's just a stage….I took the day off work the next time and I took her [to the doctor]. And that's when [the doctor diagnosed] dementia. And I came back and I told Aunt, and she said, "Yeah that's old age, she's just forgetful." And we left it at that.

The lack of knowledge related to dementia prompted one caregiver to ask:

> How do we convince or make Black people know that Alzheimer's is real? How do we convince them? Because most of them have this preconceived idea in their mind, "this cannot happen to us." But then when you hear another group talk about it on different colors, they well accept the idea, but it's just we don't accept it.

Effective Strategies to Support Families

In light of the above discussions in the different sections of the chapter, several important suggestions for intervention strategies can be gleaned from this information:

- Interventions are needed that address the family unit of informal caregivers. The lone primary caregiver is not a typical cultural way of providing care in African American families. Instead, it is the network of care that is the sustaining caregiving structure in African American families.

- Workforce and economic issues need to be addressed in all interventions for African American caregivers.
  - A large proportion of African American caregivers are adult children who are employed but have limited resources.
- Interventions that link and bridge the resources of the African American family, church, and formal organizations are needed.
  - The place of religion and spirituality are very important to African Americans. Finding ways to bridge the strength of the family and that of the church has a long-standing tradition in the African American community. Linking these traditions to institutions and formal support would be innovative.
- Interventions are needed that adjust for the cultural implications of affective outcomes among African American caregivers.
  - Some caution should be taken when applying existing findings that African Americans experience fewer negative psychological effects of caregiving than do other ethnoracial groups. Emotional expressions for this group when caring for parents are much less acceptable than having physical health problems or complaints while providing care.
- The final and most important suggestion for intervention strategies is to have an awareness and education campaign that provides the intergenerational African American community with information about dementia within a trustworthy, culturally competent framework. In addition, placing dementia within the discussion of other related chronic diseases (e.g., diabetes and hypertension) that are common within this community is critical in this framework.

Discussion and Conclusions

Caregiving to elders with dementia in African American communities is provided by the extended family. Thus, the family and not the lone primary caregiver, as in the past, is still the unit of care in African American families. This unit of care includes kin and non-kin. Adult children, particularly adult daughters, provide the majority of hands-on care, but multiple family members may be involved in providing other instrumental and emotional support for dependent elders. Most caregivers positively appraise their caregiving role and perceive it as an expression of their cultural values and beliefs. Another important finding about African American caregivers is their strong use of religion and spirituality as coping mechanisms. These mechanisms are rooted in a historical memory of how best to face, survive, and adapt to adversity and hardships (Franklin, 1997; Taylor & Chatters, 2004).

Although emerging research evidence shows that the church provides a low level of support to family caregivers, we believe that the Black church can serve as a bridge through which African American caregivers can have access to formal services. By working with local churches, formal service agencies can gain credibility in the eyes of African American caregivers, and so will facilitate access to the African American community and its caregivers. With outside assistance, these caregivers may be able to provide better care for their dependent older family members and receive help for them. African American caregivers, however, still underutilize formal care, which might help reinforce the high level of informal care family caregivers provide. A marked problem in assisting African American caregivers is their traditional reluctance to use formal assistance.

In addition to religious beliefs, cultural values and norms help shape and influence family caregiving in African American families. Thus, coping strategies, rooted in a culture that stresses religion and spirituality, help buffer the effects of stress. Some findings (Dilworth-Anderson & Boswell, in press) show that spirituality assisted caregivers by giving them strength; it defined and reinforced their Christian duties of honoring their mothers and fathers by giving back to them the care that they received when they were young. It also gave them the faith that they could "carry on," and it provided them with a sense of gratification and a positive attitude that they fulfilled their roles to their dependent parents. Another important finding was that the majority of caregivers in their respective families shared meanings about the role of spirituality in helping them as caregivers. This finding also suggests that when different caregivers in the same family share strong spiritual beliefs about their caregiving, they are less likely to experience role conflict and, possibly, feelings of burden or stress. Most importantly, this finding of shared spiritual beliefs and caregiving shows that African American caregivers have given meaning to their sense of coping—it is spiritual. This spiritual way of coping with caregiving may serve to help interpret the consistent finding in the literature that African American caregivers experience less depression than is found among their White counterparts (Dilworth-Anderson et al., 2002).

Notwithstanding some of the positive findings reported in this chapter, a note of caution should be made. In the face of emerging evidence, the size and strength of the kin network are being challenged by the needs of multiple generations in the family coupled with declining resources in the network to address the needs of family members (Dilworth-Anderson & Burton, 1999). Further, the African American church, as in the past, does not provide the level and type of care to dependent elders and caregivers as expected and expressed in the broader society. Additionally, there is a need to reexamine the belief that African Americans are coping well in the caregiving role. We purport that new measures and a deeper understanding are needed to assess how this cultural group is allowed to cope with stress and burden. We assert that the prolonged, high-effort coping among African American caregivers may not be associated with negative psychological outcomes but instead is associated with poor physical health outcomes.

Several key categories of intervention strategies are suggested in this chapter to address the needs of African American caregivers. Together, these strategies reflect attention to culturally nuanced caregiving beliefs and practices among African Americans. Attention to cultural nuances is critical to providing relevant and appropriate services to meet the needs of caregivers from diverse groups. We use the phrase *culturally nuanced* to reflect the reality that there is great commonality across ethnoracial groups in norms, beliefs, and practices related to caregiving, but there are slight differences (cultural nuances) across groups in the meanings associated with these norms and beliefs as well as in the ways in which they are expressed through behavior. For example, all ethnoracial groups for which there are data have cultural norms and expectations regarding the care of older family members, and these norms are given as reasons for providing care. Thus, African Americans are not culturally distinct in terms of their beliefs about duty, expectation, and reciprocity in caregiving. However, as illustrated by the findings of Dilworth-Anderson and colleagues (2005), as discussed above, the degree to which these cultural beliefs affect caregiving behavior can differ across groups, reflecting cultural nuance. Therefore, when developing interventions and other services for caregivers, it is important to be aware of the possibility of cultural nuances in beliefs and behavior. With respect to African American caregivers, we suggest four major cultural nuances that should guide interventions: strong adherence to expectations that family members (especially adult daughters) will provide care (often with the help of the extended support network) to dependent elders; high levels of religiosity and inclusion of God in the support network; greater acceptability of physical symptoms than psychological symptoms related to chronic stress; and culturally nuanced meanings assigned to specific illnesses and their symptoms (e.g., dementia and forgetfulness).

We believe that a final clarification is necessary so that researchers and practitioners are not discouraged from pursuing studies and interventions with diverse groups. It is not necessary to know all of the culturally nuanced beliefs and behaviors of a population before studying or serving them. Of course, the more one knows about a particular group the better. However, we propose that the starting place is knowledge that cultural nuances exist and are important in shaping caregiving experiences and outcomes. From this place of broader cultural understanding, specific nuances can be recognized and incorporated into research and practice. Studies and interventions both need flexibility built in, so that the cultural frames of those being studied will be respected, and knowledge of them will be effectively used toward culturally relevant work. We believe that approaching caregivers of all backgrounds from within their contexts (social, cultural, familial) and, thus, from their frames of reference, is more effective than trying to move them to ours.

Resources on Alzheimer's Disease for African American Families

African American Communities: www.alz.org/Resources/Diversity/BlackAfricanAmerican.asp

National Alzheimer's Association, General Resources: www.alz.org/Resources/Diversity/general.asp

Planning Ahead for Long-Term Care: www.thirdage.com/healthgate/files/20650.html

Third Age: Support and Assistance for Caregivers: www.thirdage.com/healthgate/files/20648.html

24-hr Nationwide Contact Center Helpline: 1-800-272-3900

University of North Carolina Institute on Aging, Bibliography: www.aging.unc.edu/cad/bibliography/index.html

References

Adams, B., Aranda, M. P., Kemp, B., & Takagi, K. (2002). Ethnic and gender differences in distress among Anglo American, African American, Japanese American, and Mexican American spousal caregivers of persons with dementia. *Journal of Clinical Geropsychology, 8*(4), 279–301.

Administration on Aging. (2003). *A profile of older Americans: 2003.* Retrieved February 2, 2005, from www.aoa.gov/prof/Statistics/profile/2003/4_pf.asp

Ajrouch, K. J., Antonucci, T. C., & Janevic, M. R. (2001). Social networks among Blacks and Whites: The interaction between race and age. *Journal of Gerontology: Social Sciences, 56B*(2), S112–S118.

Alzheimer's Association. (2003). *African-Americans and Alzheimer's disease: The silent epidemic.* Retrieved August 24, 2005, from www.alz.org/Resources/Diversity/downloads/AA_EDU-SilentEpidemic.pdf

Aneshensel, C. S., Pearlin, L. I., & Schuler, R. (1993). Stress, role captivity, and the cessation of caregiving. *Journal of Health and Social Behavior, 34,* 54–70.

Aranda, M. P., & Knight, B. G. (1997). The influence of ethnicity and culture on the caregiver stress and coping process: A socio-cultural review and analysis. *The Gerontologist, 37,* 342–354.

Barnes, L. L., Mendes de Leon, C. F., Bienias, J. L., & Evans, D. A. (2004). A longitudinal study of Black–White differences in social resources. *Journal of Gerontology: Social Sciences, 59B*(3), S146–S153.

Bourgeois, M. S., Beach, S. R., Schulz, R., & Burgio, L. D. (1996). When primary and secondary caregivers disagree: Predictors and psychosocial consequences. *Psychology and Aging, 11,* 527–537.

Burton, L. M., & Dilworth-Anderson, P. (1991). The intergenerational roles of aged Black Americans. *Marriage and Family Review, 16,* 311–322.

Center on an Aging Society. (2005). *A Decade of Informal Caregiving.* Retrieved February 2, 2005, from http://ihcrp.georgetown.edu/agingsociety/pdfs/caregivers1-E.pdf

Dilworth-Anderson, P., & Boswell, G. (in press). Spiritual and religious coping values and beliefs among African American caregivers: A qualitative study.

Dilworth-Anderson, P., Brummett, B. H., Goodwin, P., Williams, S. W., Williams, R. B., & Siegler, I. C. (2005). Effect of race on cultural justifications for caregiving. *Journal of Gerontology: Social Sciences, 60B,* 257–262.

Dilworth-Anderson, P., & Burton, L. (1999). Critical issues in understanding family support and older minorities. In T. Miles (Ed.), *Full-color aging: Facts, goals, and recommendations for America's diverse elders* (pp. 93–105). Washington, DC: The Gerontological Society of America.

Dilworth-Anderson, P., & Gibson, B. E. (2002). The cultural influence of values, norms, meanings, and perceptions in understanding dementia in ethnic minorities. *Alzheimer Disease and Associated Disorders, 16*(2), S56–S63.

Dilworth-Anderson, P., Goodwin, P. Y., & Williams, S. W. (2004). Can culture help explain the physical health effects of caregiving over time among African American caregivers? *Journal of Gerontology: Social Sciences, 59B*(3), S138–S145.

Dilworth-Anderson, P., Williams, S. W., & Cooper, T. (1999). Family caregiving to elderly African Americans: Caregiver types and structures. *Journal of Gerontology: Social Sciences, 54,* S237–S241.

Dilworth-Anderson, P., Williams, I. C., & Gibson, B. E. (2002). Issues of race, ethnicity, and culture in caregiving research: A twenty-year review. *The Gerontologist, 42,* 237–272.

Farran, C. J., Miller, B., Kaufman, J. E., & Davis, L. (1997). Race, finding meaning, and caregiver distress. *Journal of Aging and Health, 9,* 316–333.

Foley, K. L., Tung, H. J., & Mutran, E. J. (2002). Self-gain and self-loss among African-American and White caregivers. *Journal of Gerontology: Social Sciences, 57B,* S14–S22.

Franklin, D. (1997). *Ensuring inequality: The structural transformation of the African-American family.* New York: Oxford University Press.

Gallagher-Thompson, D., Arean, P., Coon, D., Menendez, A., Takagi, K., Haley, W. E. et al. (2000). Development and implementation of intervention strategies for culturally diverse caregiving populations. In R. Schulz (Ed.), *Handbook of dementia caregiving: Evidence-based interventions for family caregivers* (pp. 151–185). New York: Springer.

Goodenough, W. H. (1999). Outline of a framework for a theory of cultural evolution. *Cross-Cultural Research*, 33, 84–107.

Haley, W. E., Gitlin, L. N., Wisniewski, S. R., Mahoney, D. F., Coon, D. W., Winter, L. et al. (2004). Well-being, appraisal, and coping in African American and Caucasian dementia caregivers: Findings from the REACH study. *Aging & Mental Health*, 8(4) 316–329.

Haley, W. E., Roth, D. L., Coleton, M. I., Ford, G. R., West, C. A., Collins, R. P. et al. (1996). Appraisal, coping, and social support as mediators of wellbeing in black and white family caregivers of patients with Alzheimer's disease. *Journal of Consulting and Clinical Psychology*, 64, 121–129.

Haley, W. E., West, C. A., Wadley, V. G., Ford, G. R., White, F. A., Barrett, J. J. et al. (1995). Psychological, social, and health impact of caregiving: A comparison of Black and White dementia family caregivers and noncaregivers. *Psychology and Aging*, 10, 540–552.

Henderson, J. N., & Gutierrez-Mayka, M. (1992). Ethnocultural themes in caregiving to Alzheimer's patients in Hispanic families. *Clinical Gerontologist*, 11, 59–74.

James, S. A., Hartnett, S. A., & Kalsbeek, W. D. (1983). John Henryism and blood pressure differences among Black men. *Journal of Behavioral Medicine*, 6, 259–278.

Jarrett, R. L., & Burton, L. M. (1999). Dynamic dimensions of family structure in low-income African American families: Emergent themes in qualitative research. *Journal of Comparative Family Studies*, 30, 177–187.

Jolicoeur, P. M., & Madden, T. (2002). The good daughters: Acculturation and caregiving among Mexican-American women. *Journal of Aging Studies*, 16, 107–120.

Katz, M. B. (1993). *The "underclass" debate: Views from history.* Princeton, NJ: Princeton University Press.

Keith, C. (1995). Family caregiving systems: Models, resources, and values. *Journal of Marriage and the Family*, 57, 179–190.

Klonoff, E., & Landrine, H. (1994). Culture and gender diversity in commonsense beliefs about the causes of six illnesses. *Journal of Behavioral Medicine*, 17, 407–418.

Lawton, M. P., Rajagopal, D., Brody, E., & Kleban, M. H. (1992). The dynamics of caregiving for demented elders among Black and White families. *Journal of Gerontology: Social Sciences*, 47, S156–S164.

Luckey, I. (1994). African American elders: The support network of generational kin. *Families in Society: The Journal of Contemporary Human Services*, 75, 82–89.

Mausbach, B. T., Coon, D. W., Depp, C., Rabinowitz, Y. G., Wilson-Arias, E., & Kraemer, H. C. (2004). Ethnicity and time to institutionalization of dementia patients: A comparison of Latina and Caucasian female family caregivers. *Journal of the American Geriatric Society*, 52, 1077–1084.

McDonald, K., & Armstrong, E. (2001). De-romanticizing Black intergenerational support: The questionable expectation of welfare reform. *Journal of Marriage and the Family*, 63, 213–223.

Miller, B., & Guo, S. (2000). Social support for spouse caregivers of persons with dementia. *Journal of Gerontology: Social Sciences, 55B,* S163–S172.

National Academy on an Aging Society. (2000, May). *Caregiving: Helping the elderly with activity limitations.* Number 7. Retrieved February 2, 2005, from www.agingsociety.org/agingsociety/pdf/Caregiving.pdf

National Alliance for Caregiving and The American Association of Retired Persons. (1997). *Family caregiving in the U.S.: Findings from a national survey.* Washington, DC: The Gerontological Society of America.

National Center for Health Statistics. (2002). *The second longitudinal study of aging (LSOA II).* Retrieved August 24, 2005, from www.cdc.gov/nchs/lsoa.htm

Nelson, K., Geiger, A. M., & Mangione, C. M. (2002). Effect of health beliefs on delays in care for abnormal cervical cytology in a multi-ethnic population. *Journal of General Internal Medicine, 17,* 709–716.

Nkongo, N. O., & Archbold, P. G. (1995). Reasons for caregiving in African American families. *Journal of Cultural Diversity, 2*(4), 116–123.

Noonan, A. E., Tennstedt, S. L., & Rebelsky, S. G. (1996). Making the best of it: Themes of meaning among informal caregivers to the elderly. *Journal of Aging Studies, 10*(4), 313–327.

Picot, S. J., Debanne, S. M., Namazi, K. H., & Wykle, M. L. (1997). Religiosity and perceived rewards of Black and White caregivers. *The Gerontologist, 37*(1), 89–101.

Piercy, K. W. (1998). Theorizing about family caregiving: The role of responsibility. *Journal of Marriage and the Family, 60,* 109–118.

Population Reference Bureau. (2003). *The aging of the United States, 1999 to 2025.* Retrieved July 23, 2003, from www.prb.org/Content/NavigationMenu/Ameristat/Topics1/Estimates_Projections/The_Aging_of_the_United_States,_1999_to_2025.htm

Pyke, K. D., & Bengtson, V. L. (1996). Caring more or less: Individualistic and collectivist systems of family eldercare. *Journal of Marriage and the Family, 58*(2), 379–392.

Roberts, J. S., Akinleye, D., Hipps, Y. G., & Green, R. C. (2005). Beliefs about prevention and treatment of Alzheimer's disease among African Americans. *News Release, Alzheimer's Association International Conference on Prevention of Dementia, June 18–21, 2005, Washington, DC.* Retrieved July 18, 2005, from www.alz.org/preventionconference/pc2005/061905newresearch.asp

Roff, L. L., Burgio, L. D., Gitlin, L., Nichols, L. Chaplin, W., & Hardin, J. M. (2004). Positive aspects of Alzheimer's caregiving: The role of race. *Journal of Gerontology: Psychological Sciences, 59B*(4), 185–190.

Roschelle, A. R. (1997). *No more kin: Exploring race, class, and gender in family networks.* Thousand Oaks, CA: Sage.

Roth, D. L., Haley, W. E., Owen, J. E., Clay, O. J., & Goode, K. T. (2001). Latent growth models of the longitudinal effects of dementia caregiving; a comparison of African American and white family caregivers. *Psychology and Aging, 16,* 426–436.

Skaff, M. M., & Pearlin, L. I. (1992). Caregiving: Role engulfment and the loss of self. *Gerontologist, 32,* 656–664.

Sterritt, P., & Pokorny, M. (1998). African American caregiving for relatives with Alzheimer's disease. *Geriatric Nursing, 19,* 127–134.

Taylor, J. T., & Chatters, L. M. (1986). Patterns of informal support to elderly black adults: family, friends, and church members. *Social Work, 31,* 432–438.

Taylor, R. J., & Chatters, L. M. (1991). Extended family networks of older Black adults. *Journal of Gerontology: Social Sciences, 46,* S210–S217.

Tennestedt, S. L., Chang, B., & Delgado, M. (1999). Patterns of long-term care: A comparison of Puerto Rican, African-American, and Non-Latino White elders. *Journal of Gerontological Social Work, 30*(1/2), 179–199.

Tennstedt, S., McKinlay, J., & Sullivan, L. M. (1989). Informal care for frail older persons: The role of secondary caregivers. *The Gerontologist, 29,* 677–683.

White, T. M., Townsend, A. L., & Stephens, M. A. P. (2000). Comparisons of African American and White women in the parent care role. *The Gerontologist, 40*(6), 718–728.

Young, R. F., & Kahana, E. (1995). The context of caregiving and well-being outcomes among African and Caucasian Americans. *The Gerontologist, 35,* 225–232.

Zollar, A. C. (1985). *A member of the family: Strategies for Black family continuity.* Chicago: Nelson-Hall.

Working with American Indian Families

CHAPTER 10

Working with American Indian Families

Collaboration with Families for the Care of Older American Indians with Memory Loss

LEVANNE R. HENDRIX AND FR. HANK SWIFT CLOUD-LEBEAU

Many older American Indian[1] people are teachers for all Americans in lessons of survival, endurance, and adaptability. They may be the conscience of America.

Historical Perspectives

For non-Indian health-care providers, some measure of understanding of American Indian history and Indian ways needs to take place before the possibility of a productive clinical interaction can take place (Hennessy & John, 1996).

It is important to keep in mind that American Indian (AI) elders and families have different issues than other ethnic groups in that immigration from another place did not happen. American Indian people were here first and were colonized; they were invaded, not discovered. It has been estimated that there were between five and ten million indigenous peoples living in what is now the United States at the time of first European contact (1492), and that "no spot of earth was unknown" to Indian people (Waldman, 1985).

147

The history of Native American Nations or First Peoples Nations over the last 500 years has been one of conflict, oppression, loss of land, and decimation of population by infectious disease (influenza, pneumonia, meningitis, whooping cough, tuberculosis, smallpox, syphilis, measles, typhus, cholera, chicken pox), introduced by White people. The AI population declined by 10% from Indian–White conflict, and by 25–50% by infectious disease to 237,000 by 1900, according to a special census performed by the federal government (Dorris, 1994; Waldman, 1985). By comparison, of the 250,000 emigrants who crossed the plains between 1840 and 1860, only 362 died by conflict with Indians (Calloway, 1999). For those AIs who remained, this period of Native American history was one of survivorship against extreme adversity.

The period 1880–1934 is considered by historians as an era of Indian suppression and repression of Native American cultures. In 1883 it became a federal offense to openly practice "Indian Religion," which set the stage for the misrepresentation of the "ghost dance" by the U.S. military as a hostile uprising by reservation-bound Indians in South Dakota. The law was not repealed until 1934, when John Collier, Commissioner of the Bureau of Indian Affairs, reversed laws banning ceremonies and spiritual practices as part of the Wheeler-Howard Act, also known as the Indian Reorganization Act (Deloria & Lytle, 1983). Complete religious freedom, including the return of artifacts from graves, was not gained until the passage of the American Indian Freedom of Religion Act of 1978.

One outcome of religious and military repression in the late 1800s was the Wounded Knee Massacre, December 29, 1890, which has come to be representative of the injustices to Indians during the reservation era of Native American history (Trafzer, 2000). Approximately 350 unarmed men, women, and children were killed by Hotchkiss mounted guns as the Lakota band, led by Big Foot, came in to the Red Cloud agency under a white flag of surrender (personal family history, Fr. Hank LeBeau; Hill, 1999). Black Elk, the Oglala spiritual leader, witnessed the carnage and stated, "I wished that I had died too, but I was not sorry for the women and children. It was better for them to be happy in the other world, and I wanted to be there too" (Trafzer, 2000, p. 321). Wounded Knee is one example of many genocidal actions taken by the U.S. government against Indian Nations, and most Tribes have similar historical events that color the lives of their peoples today.

Boarding Schools

In the late 1800s and early 1900s, missionary groups were given responsibility for the education and "civilization" of Indian children. These groups assigned themselves geographic areas in Indian Country, accounting for the wide variety of Christian religious affiliations in present-day AI communities (Deloria, 1988). Indian children were forced to attend Christian boarding schools, many times long distances from their homes, where Indian language and cultural traditions were suppressed. (Fr. LeBeau remembers hearing about how his mother, as a young child, was forced to stand on a dormitory chair all night for speaking her Lakota language.) While in the boarding schools many Indian children were lost to tuberculosis, meningitis, pneumonia, and whooping cough, due to crowded conditions and lack of natural immunity to disease, as attested to by the boarding school graveyards and published first-hand accounts (see Calloway, 1999). However, the boarding school experience also taught many of today's elders to read, write, and speak English, as well as mathematics. Most of the early training at boarding schools was for vocational or domestic work, with skilled trades added later.

Upon return to the reservations from years at boarding schools, many AIs found that they no longer fit in with tribal culture, and they were not accepted in the White man's society. Cultural confusion and alienation combined with historical grief and anger left many Indian people in identity crisis. One example of this overwhelming confusion is the story of Plenty Horses.

Plenty Horses (Oglala Lakota) arrived at the Pine Ridge Indian Reservation, after five years at Carlisle Indian School in Pennsylvania, in 1890, and witnessed the Massacre at Wounded Knee in December. On January 7, 1891, Plenty Horses shot and killed Army Lieutenant Edward W. Casey. At his trial, Plenty Horses explained: "Five years I attended Carlisle and was educated in the ways of the White man. When I returned to my people, I was an outcast among them. I was no longer an Indian. I was not a White man. I was lonely. I shot the lieutenant so I might make a place for myself among my people. I am now one of them. I shall be hung, and the Indians will bury me as a warrior." However, Plenty Horses was not convicted of murder, as the judge ruled that "a state of war" existed at the time of the killing. Plenty Horses' lawyers had argued that if a state of war did not exist, then all of the victims of Wounded Knee were murdered, and all of the soldiers would have to be tried as murderers. Instead, 20 Congressional Medals of Honor were awarded to the soldiers of the Seventh Cavalry who took part in the "Battle" of Wounded Knee, as this event remains designated in the military documents. These medals are still being contested by the Lakota Nation today, as "Medals of Dishonor," which should be rescinded. Plenty Horses was set free and sent home to the Rosebud reservation, where family members still reside (Calloway, 1999, pp. 413–414; Hill, 1999).

During the late 19th century and early 20th century, many American Indian children were removed from Indian families and adopted out to White families, resulting in social and cultural alienation. This practice was not stopped until 1978, with the passage of the Indian Child Welfare Act (ICWA; Waldman, 1985). There are older Americans today who are discovering their Indian heritage for the very first time, having been adopted out and "raised White."

Martin Wakazoo (Oglala Lakota), Executive Director of the Native American Health Center in Oakland, CA, for over 20 years, believes that many urban Indians consider themselves refugees from "America's covert war on American Indian culture." He blames the federal government policies of boarding school educations, adoption by non-Indians, sterilizations without consent,[2] and relocation to cities (Magagnini, 1997, p. 3).

In the old days, core values of bravery, individual freedom, generosity and sharing, getting along with one another and with nature, and the Indian wisdom imparted by the elders provided a measure of security and protection from anxiety (Bryde, 1971; personal family history, Fr. LeBeau). However, Indians who moved to urban areas as a result of federal relocation programs experienced "racism, humiliation, and the need to conform to survive" in the urban world (Fr. LeBeau, 1997, unpublished interview). Many aging AI carry the responsibility of survivorship of the Indian Holocaust. Batts (1996) postulates that internalized oppression and long-term racism may result in the survival strategies of "system beating" (manipulating the system or others by using racial guilt, acting out anger, or "being invisible"), "blaming the system," "anti-White attitude" (avoidance of contact, distrust of all Whites), or complete denial of Indian heritage. These strategies may be reactive behaviors to a dysfunctional Eurocentric society, and the perception of a hostile environment, including the health-care system. Eduardo Duran, based on his 15 years experience of providing psychotherapeutic services to AI, and his own experience of being Native American, writes that depression, alcoholism, violence, and anxiety may be functional reactions to the real experiences of genocide, oppression, racism, and cultural alienation, and should be considered as cultural post-traumatic stress disorder (PTSD; Duran & Duran, 1995).

Al Cross, an Indian elder sociologist, writes that the urbanization of American Indians was the result of involvement in the World War II effort as soldiers and as defense workers and of the federal relocation programs of the 1950s and 1960s. President Eisenhower authorized a program of "Relocation and Termination" to move AI from reservations, providing job training, jobs, and housing, to such urban areas as Chicago, Denver, Albuquerque, Los Angeles, San Francisco, Oakland, and San Jose, partially accounting for California having the largest Native American population of any state. "Termination" was aimed at terminating the "trust" relationship between the federal government and those Tribes/Nations deemed to be economically self-sufficient at that time. The impact of relocation was the large mass movement of Indians from reservations to urban environments, and was the largest migration since the mass movement of Indians under the Indian Removal Act of 1830, which removed all Indians east of the Mississippi to the western Indian Territory (Cross, 1996, p. 183).

Health Care

Older AIs have a unique relationship with the federal government in that health care, social programs, and education were negotiated, promised, and paid for by treaty with ceded land with the U.S. Federal Government. The health-care system, in particular, has evolved into an extremely complex structure for the older AI to negotiate. An AI may be eligible for health-care benefits from Medicare/Medicaid, the Indian Health Service (which may also contract with local health-care providers), Tribal health services, the Veteran's Administration, or other third-party payors (John & Baldridge, 1996; John, Hennessey, Roy, & Salvini, 1996; Pevar, 1992). Indian Health Service (IHS) and Tribal health care services are primarily available to those AI elderly who live on or near reservation lands, with benefits ceasing after 180 days residence off-reservation. Benefits may be reinstated after residency is resumed (Kramer, 1996).

Urban-dwelling AIs rely on Medicare/Medicaid, Veterans benefits, third-party payors from employment, and a small amount of IHS funding for community clinics. Several urban studies have indicated that at least one third of urban-dwelling AI families have no health insurance coverage. No health-care services were designated for relocated older urban Indians who may have moved to urban areas for housing, jobs, training, and educational opportunities during the federal relocation programs of the 1950s and 1960s, and then stayed to raise their families. Many of these urban Indians are choosing to age in place in metropolitan areas, with frequent trips "home" to Tribal or reserved lands. Currently, there are 28 nongovernmental and non-Tribal programs that provide direct clinical services for urban-dwelling AI, most of which offer a sliding-scale fee and some no-cost services for the uninsured. However, this complex health-care delivery system has many gaps in service, especially in long-term care services for AI elderly with chronic illness, cognitive loss, or functional disability (Hendrix & Fee, 2004).

The building of "trust" with aging Indian health-care recipients and their families requires a willingness by the health-care provider to work collaboratively, and this aspect of care cannot be overemphasized. The building of a successful relationship takes time and should be based upon an attitude of humility and respect. The individual older AI is a unique product of his or her reality of Tribal, familial, and spiritual history, and the degree to which that individual has been exposed to and has integrated (or rejected) dominant Western culture (Hendrix, 2003).

The historical context in working with AI families cannot be overstated as an influence in the trust-building process. Non-Indian health-care providers need to keep in mind that they are always regarded as "non-Indian" and, therefore, are kept at a cultural distance. As more AIs are educated as health-care providers and other professionals, there is more of an expectation from the AI community to be cared for by Indian staff. It should also be noted that superficial use of cultural concepts by non-Indians may reinforce stereotypes and result in alienation rather than in culturally competent care (Yeo, 1996). Stereotypical expectations of Indian behavior by non-Indians become a barrier to the effectiveness of the health-care relationship.

Many AIs consider an "illness" to be the result of an imbalance between the physical, emotional, mental, and spiritual aspects of a person's life. Some AIs may consider illness to be the result of a person's misdeeds or the influence of supernatural forces. "White man's medicine" may be used for "White man's diseases" (diabetes, gallbladder disease, heart disease, hypertension) and Indian medicine used to treat all other problems (family problems, emotional problems, behavioral problems, healing of the spirit; Alvord & Van Pelt, 2000; Hendrix, 2003). A survivalist attitude described by Strong (1984) as "passive forbearance" utilized as a coping skill, tends to influence Indian help seeking, and many conditions are considered a natural part of aging and, therefore, do not need treatment or heroics.

American Indian culture is extremely diverse, and there is no single cultural tradition that affects health beliefs and health care. For example, in a Southwest Indian Nation, thought and language have the power to shape reality, and negative thought forms can bring those thoughts to fruition. Discussion of possible disease complications or adverse reactions may not be advisable. Tribal tradition prohibits the mention of "death" and the touching of dead people (Bennahum, 1998). Members of another group of Pueblo Indians, in the same general geographic area, are taught that each person is put on the earth for a specific purpose, and when the purpose is accomplished, the person is ready to leave this world for the next. Death is spoken of openly, and the people desire all medical information in order to make a decision (Correa & Furakawa, 1998). Many AI people are more comfortable with the subject of death and dying than are Western health-care providers, as death is often taught as a natural part of life—a continuum, rather than an ending (Hendrix, 2003). Specific Tribal or Clan rituals, ceremonies, or traditions that may be appropriate in caring for individual older AIs with cognitive impairment should be explored with an AI family early in the relationship.

AI Families and the Older AI with Memory Loss

Many AI families value the interdependence of family and community as much as the autonomy of the individual. Focus on the present, acceptance of life as it comes, and normalization of physical and cognitive decline as part of aging may be common factors found in working with families caring for AIs with cognitive impairment (Hendrix, 2001; Miller, 2002; Ogrocki, Welsh-Bohmer, & Allen, 1997).

Mental illness carries a stigma in some Indian cultures, and the term *dementia* may be mistaken for *mental illness*. In one survey of 73 Pueblo caregivers of older AIs with cognitive impairment, bathing and transferring were the daily activities that gave the elders the most difficulty, and only a few could perform any of the instrumental activities without assistance. None of the care recipients with memory loss could negotiate with outside agencies or arrange for services. The most frequently occurring behavior difficulties were understanding instructions, recognizing people they know, finding their way around the house, and remembering words. Only approximately one third of the elders exhibited restlessness and agitation all of the time, and the least common behaviors were "wandering or getting lost" and engaging in behaviors that might be dangerous to themselves or others (John et al., 1996).

Interviews with four urban AI key informants (AI health or social service providers for 15+ years) support the previous findings. Informants revealed that the term *dementia* is "not known" and "not used." There was very little known about dementia in general, but there was a large community focus on diabetes. The informants did not claim knowledge of any relationship between diabetes and memory loss. Cognitive loss was reported as not being recognized by AI families until elders become "confused," "forget important events," "do not recognize relatives," or "forget medications." These informants further reported that older AIs are not likely to talk to others about their feelings, especially a young person, as this is not currently a cultural value. Older AIs with memory loss were consistently described as expressing feelings of "fearfulness" and "loneliness" and as not likely to express their fears verbally. Many AI families would respond to the elder by "becoming more watchful, helpful, and patient," and they may address the cognitive impairment issues by asking, "Is there something bothering you?" (Hendrix & Fee, 2004, pp. 29–30).

Additionally, Fr. LeBeau stresses that AI families need to be taught ways of "being with" the older AI with cognitive impairment. That is, they should be taught specific techniques of interacting and communicating with the person with advancing dementia, as there is a tendency to withdraw from oral communication as the dementia progresses.

Dementia may be perceived as normal aging, or that "Grandma's getting glimpses of the other side," "getting ready to leave," or "time to go home," in which case, death is not viewed as negative but as the next stage of life (Hendrix & Fee, 2004). In preliminary findings among Oklahoma Choctaw people, Henderson (1994) suggests that the cultural meaning of dementia varies across Native American Tribes "in accordance with individually held health beliefs that are part of larger cultural systems." He describes three general belief systems for dementias: (a) a combination of biomedical and lay models, (b) a belief that dementia is part of normal aging, and (c) the belief that behaviors are a means of communication during transition to the next world (Henderson, 1994, in John et al., 1996, p. 190).

Communication Style

Older Indian people often use a communication style that is metaphoric, indirect, and reflective of the oral history tradition. Stories about Tribes, families, or clans are often given in response to a direct question about themselves asked by a non-Indian health-care provider. If the provider can be patient and is able to listen carefully, the sought-after information is often contained in the story. In the old days, a slow way of talking was used to slow AI people down, and the stories were used by elders to teach the young people ways of behaving (Fr. LeBeau, 1997, unpublished interview; Hendrix, 2001).

Family Structure and Roles

Some studies report that well over one half of older AIs age in place and live within 5 miles of relatives who assist with shopping, transportation, and other daily living needs. However, there have been profound changes in the social support system and family systems that have forced some AI caregivers to reduce their elder-care roles (Pollaca, 2001). Fictive kin may play a role in elder-care, and it is common to find a nonblood relation "keeping" (providing housing and care for) an older AI. Decision makers in the family may or may not be the elders. Caregivers are usually female relatives, and although the concept of "caregiver burden" was found to be offensive among Pueblo caregivers, caregiver stress was acutely felt (Hennessy & John, 1995). Interactions with older AIs often involve the whole family, including children and babies (Hendrix, 2001).

Historically, older Indians held a special place in the Tribe/Nation as the teachers of children and keepers of wisdom, and in many traditions, they were Tribal leaders with positions of authority in the household. The Indian meaning of *elder* is different than its meaning for other groups, in that *elders* are chosen by the AI community for their wisdom, leadership, experience, and dedication. Therefore, *elders* are usually older Indians, but not all old Indians are *elders*. It has been said that the older AIs are responsible for the *tribal data bank*, remembering who is related to whom, past and present, as well as for the accumulated knowledge of the Tribe (Pollaca, 2001). There are both matriarchal and patriarchal lineage patterns in AI culture, and the knowledge of kinship was an essential function of the elders, especially in view of the decimation of whole villages and social structures by recurring infectious disease epidemics, and the increasing frequency of intertribal marriage due to boarding schools and relocation.

A Healing Approach

A healing of the spirit has been found to be helpful by many AI families in dealing with the effects of intergenerational grief and anger. The additional stress felt by families caring for an older AI with cognitive impairment can exacerbate these feelings, as the keeper of wisdom and family history slowly forgets. If the family relationship has been turbulent, there can be additional stress. Fr. LeBeau (Lakota), Episcopal priest, and substance abuse and spiritual counselor for over 25 years (on-reservation in South Dakota and in the urban San Francisco Bay Area), utilizes a medicine wheel approach to visually explain "The Red Road Philosophy" (promulgated by Gene Thin Elk) to establish a connection between "balance" and "imbalance" with AI families in a traditional way. The circle is the most important element, reestablishing the interconnectedness of all things, with the spiritual source in the center (God, Creator, Great Spirit).

In counseling American Indian families, and from his own experience of being a First Nations person, Fr. LeBeau has developed an approach to spiritual healing based on 12 Virtues contained within the Lakota tradition and described by Joseph Marshall (2001) as follows:

1. Humility—"to be humble, modest, unpretentious" (Marshall)—not putting oneself forward, the first and most difficult of the virtues, enables one to hear what is being said by others, to try to accept your brother and your sister, to gain acceptance of what is (LeBeau).

2. Perseverance—"to persist, to strive in spite of difficulties" (Marshall)—giving more back to fellow man, we are all in that circle with the spiritual source in the center (LeBeau).
3. Respect—"to be considerate, to hold in high esteem" (Marshall)—recognition of the sacred in all beings and in all things (LeBeau).
4. Honor—"to have integrity, to have an upright and honest character" (Marshall)—behaving with honor despite racism and injustice (for example, refusal of the Lakota people to sell the Black Hills, despite continuing reservation poverty) (LeBeau).
5. Love—"to place and hold in one's heart" (Marshall)—to place another person's heart in your heart (LeBeau).
6. Sacrifice—"to give of oneself, an offering" (Marshall)—giving up the material, pleasure-run life where it is all about "me" and "my" (especially in alcohol recovery), when you give back, you sacrifice for the greater good, the sacred hoop gets stronger with each sacrifice, and suffering is therefore not necessarily a negative thing (LeBeau).
7. Truth—"that which is real, the way the world is" (Marshall)—acceptance, do the best that you can with the world as it is (LeBeau).
8. Compassion—"to care or to sympathize"—"The ability to feel compassion is to understand need. When need is not recognized and alleviated, our spirits sink into darkness" (Marshall, 2001, p. 133).
9. Bravery—"having or showing courage" (Marshall)—the courage to change and to accept what is, is as important as the courage to battle in the warrior society (LeBeau).
10. Fortitude—"strength of heart and mind" (Marshall)—the strength of your mind and your heart, in there you find peace, within there you find yourself (LeBeau).
11. Generosity—"to give, to share, to have a heart" (Marshall)—to give and share from your heart, no strings attached, unconditional (LeBeau).
12. Wisdom—"to understand what is right and true, to use knowledge wisely" (Marshall)—to understand and accept that we are who we are because the Creator made us that way for a reason, happiness is what we make it (LeBeau).

Long-Term Care Issues and Medicaid

Most older AIs with cognitive impairment will not present to the health-care provider complaining of "memory loss" (Hendrix, 1999; Hendrix & Fee, 2004), but they are more likely to come to the attention of the health-care system in seeking care for chronic conditions such as diabetes, hypertension, heart disease, or arthritis. In addition, cognitive impairment is likely to cause difficulties in chronic illness management and in performing instrumental activities of daily living (IADLs), such as using the telephone, paying bills, preparing meals, and managing medications. In one survey of older urban AI, only the number of IADLs was predictive of service need, and respondents were more likely to report needing services as the number of reported IADL limitations increased (The Urban Indian Health Institute, 2004). Wallace, Satter, and Zubiate (2003) reported that nationally, between 14% and 44% of AI/AN would benefit from Medicaid in-home service programs, based on the following: (a) The 2000 Census reported that among all AI/AN nationally, of those 65 years and older, 14% reported self-care difficulties with activities of daily living (ADLs), and (b) The National Resource Center on Native American Aging, utilized mostly on-or-near reservation data to determine that about 40% of older AIs had one or more difficulties with ADLs, and that 22% had two or more difficulties out of a list of six (Wallace et al., 2003).

As the number of older AIs increases, the incidence of dementia is also projected to increase, straining a health-care system that was designed to mainly provide acute care. Several studies have shown that nursing home care is not desired by most older AIs, and that they prefer to remain in their own or a relative's home, with home care assistance (Chapleski, 1997; Urban Indian Health Institute, 2004). In one long-term care needs assessment conducted by the Seattle Indian Health Board, "a majority" of the older AI respondents preferred having care services provided by persons of their own culture but made it clear that "quality care" was most important.

State Medicaid is one source of funding for home- and community-based long-term care services on reservations and urban programs, and it is less costly than institutional care for elders and for Tribes. The UCLA Center for Health Policy Research in partnership with the Indian Health Service published a series of "Tool Kits" for developing new programs utilizing existing Medicaid funding for home care and Tribal health services. The "Tool Kits" can be downloaded from the Internet (see Resources at the end of this chapter). As health-care needs change in the AI communities from infectious disease to chronic illness, in-home long-term care assistance allows a majority of older AIs with functional disabilities or dementia to remain in familiar environments. Services that can be provided in the home and are described in the Medicaid regulations include personal care services (assists with eating, dressing, bathing, toileting, transfer, walking independently [ADLs]); homemaker services (assists with cleaning, cooking, paying bills, shopping, managing medications [IADLs]); chore services (heavy household chores); respite care (short-term relief for caregivers); and home health care (requires state licensing and physician prescription for skilled intermittent nursing care, diagnosis specific). As of 1998, 529,304 American Indians were enrolled in the Medicaid program in the United States, which is 1.3% of Medicaid enrollees (Wallace, Satter, & Zubiate, 2003). Surveys conducted in Indian Country and urban centers have consistently indicated that older AIs need help in accessing services that may be available and have asked for case management services (Hendrix, 1999; John, 1995; Kramer, 1992, 1996; Urban Indian Health Institute, 2004).

Elder Abuse Issues

Research has shown that older persons with cognitive impairment are at greater risk for situations of elder abuse. Carol Hand identified a continuing public policy issue for Native Americans, in that elder abuse laws and protective services are the result of "public policy created for collectivities of strangers" being applied to Indian "communities of relatedness." Cultural heterogeneity plays a continuing role in the Tribal definitions of "abuse" and "neglect" (Carson & Hand, 1998). There is an inclination toward a nonpunitive approach toward the abuser, combined with effort toward "healing" and restitution, rather than legal proceedings and incarceration (Hudson, Armachain, Beasley, & Carlson, 1998). While neglect is the type of abuse most often reported in Indian Country (Clouse, La Counte, Eagle Sheild, & Barber, 1998), financial abuse may not be recognized as abuse, often taking the culturally appropriate form of younger family members moving in with aging relatives to be able to share Social Security benefits and housing (especially when substance abuse problems are present). Urban Indian families are particularly vulnerable to the stresses of acculturation, multigenerational households, and multigenerational caregiving. Anecdotally, older urban AIs with dementia may be referred to the health-care system via Adult Protective Services after a wandering incident. Such an incident would not necessarily be handled in the same manner on Tribal land, and may put further hardship on urban-dwelling AI families required to pay for custodial care.

Recommendations

Culturally appropriate caregiver training, respite care, and family support programs become increasingly important resources for development by health-care systems as the American Indian populations age. Cognitive impairment may present differently in older AIs due to different cultural values and different traditional activities. With these factors in mind, the following recommendations are made:

1. The first resources that AI people are likely to go to for help are other family members and other Indians (Hendrix & Fee, 2004). Therefore, community-based and AI peer-led education becomes critical in informing AI families and caregivers about memory loss and cognitive impairment.

2. Denial may be used as a prevalent coping strategy, but the health-care provider should take special care to distinguish between denial and unwanted intervention.

3. Faith in God, spiritual practice, and religious faith are strong influences in the lives of many AIs. Clergy and spiritual leaders may be valuable partners in helping AIs access the health-care system and in providing spiritual support for families and caregivers.

4. AI traditional healers should be integrated with medical model care whenever possible, in accordance with the AI elder and family wishes.

5. Health-care providers are advised to use a "non-fear-based" approach and to start a discussion about memory loss with indirect approaches (for example, talking about specific behaviors, to draw out and educate). Small groups are suggested, and education and care planning should include the entire family (Hendrix & Fee, 2004).

6. It is strongly recommended by AI communities that AI educators or peer counselors teach AI people.

Notes

1. The term *American Indian* is used to refer to indigenous peoples, Native Americans, or First Nations Peoples in the lower 48 states, rather than the *American Indian/Alaska Native* (AI/AN) designation, because current study indicates that there are significant cultural and epidemiological differences between the Alaska Native groups and American Indians.

2. A General Accounting Office investigation of "involuntary sterilization" practices by the Indian Health Service (IHS) examined the years 1973–1976 at four IHS facilities. Results showed that 3,406 involuntary sterilizations were performed during the 3-year period. As a result of strong activism by American Indian women and others, the IHS was transferred to the Department of Health and Human Services in 1978 (Jaimes, 1992, p. 326).

Resources

Indian Health Service, Eldercare Initiative: www.his.gov/MedicalPrograms/elderCare/index.asp

Indian Health Service Program Statistics Team: www.his.gov/NonMedicalPrograms/HIS-Stats/index.asp

National Congress of American Indians: Washington, DC; phone: (202) 466-7767; www.ncai.org

National Indian Council on Aging, Inc.: 10501 Montgomery Blvd., Suite 210, Albuquerque, NM 87111; phone: (505) 292-2001; fax: (505) 292-1922; www.nicoa.org

Native Elder Research Center, University of Colorado Health Science Center, Resource Center for Minority Aging Research: www.uchsc.edu/sm/nerc

Native Health Research Database—University of New Mexico Health Sciences Center Library and the Indian Health Service: http://hsc.unm.edu.nhrd

Native Web: www.nativeweb.org

References

Alvord, L. A., & Van Pelt, E. (2000). *The scalpel and the silver bear: The first Navajo woman surgeon combines Western medicine and traditional healing*. New York: Bantam Books.

Batts, V. A. (1996). *Modern racism: New melody for the same old tunes*. Unpublished essay in Multicultural aging resource kit (1998), American Society on Aging, San Francisco, CA.

Bennahum, D. (1998, February). Navajo beliefs and end-of-life issues. *Indian Elder Caregiver*. Albuquerque: New Mexico Geriatric Education Center.

Bryde, J. F. (1971). *Modern Indian psychology* (Rev. ed.). Vermillion: Institute of Indian Studies, University of South Dakota.

Calloway, C. G. (1999). *First peoples: A documentary survey of American Indian history*. Dartmouth College, NY: Bedford/St. Martin's.

Carson, D., & Hand, C. (1998). Dilemmas surrounding elder abuse and neglect within Native American communities. In *Understanding and combating elder abuse in minority communities conference proceedings* (pp. 87–96). Long Beach, CA: Archstone Foundation.

Chapleski, E. E. (1997). Long-term care among American Indians: A broad lens perspecive on service preference and use. In K. S. Markides & M. R. Miranda (Eds.), *Minorities, aging, and health* (pp. 68–75). Thousand Oaks, CA: Sage.

Clouse, J., La Counte, C., Eagle Sheild, J., & Barber, R. (1998). Elder abuse in Indian Country—Where are we? In Archstone Foundation (Eds.), *Understanding and combating elder abuse in minority communities* (pp. P31–P56). Long Beach, CA: The Archstone Foundation.

Correa, J. K., & Furakawa, C. (1998, February). Isleta beliefs and end-of-life issues. *Indian Elder Caregiver*. Albuquerque: New Mexico Geriatric Education Center.

Cross, A. (1996). Working with American Indian elders in the city: Reflections of an American Indian social worker. In G. Yeo & D. Gallaher-Thompson (Eds.), *Ethnicity and the dementias*. Washington, DC: Taylor & Francis.

Deloria, V., Jr. (1988). *Custer died for your sins: An Indian manifesto*. Norman: University of Oklahoma Press.

Deloria, V., Jr., & Lytle, C. M. (1983). *American Indians, American justice*. Austin: University of Texas Press.

Dorris, M. (1994). *Paper trail*. New York: HarperCollins.

Duran, E., & Duran, B. (1995). *Native American postcolonial psychology*. Albany: State University of New York Press.

Henderson, J. N. (1994). *Dementing disease in North American indigenous populations*. Paper presented at the annual meeting of the American Public Health Association, Washington, DC.

Hendrix, L. R. (1999). Cultural support in health care: The older urban American Indian of the San Francisco Bay area. (Dissertation, The Union Institute and University, 1999). *Dissertation*.UMI No. 9939832).

Hendrix, L. R. (2001). Health and health care of American Indian and Alaska Native elders. In G. Yeo (Ed.), *Ethnic specific modules of the core curriculum in ethnogeriatrics*. Rockville, MD: Bureau of Health Professions, U.S. Department of Health and Human Services. ww.stanford.edu/group/ethnoger/index.html

Hendrix, L. R. (2003). *Revisiting sacred ways: Spiritual support and Native American theologies for the health care provider*. (SGEC Working Paper No. 16). Palo Alto, CA: Stanford Geriatric Education Center.

Hendrix, L. R., & Fee, C. (2004). American Indian. In G. Yeo (Ed.), *Mental health aspects of diabetes in elders from diverse ethnic backgrounds* (pp. 18–29). Palo Alto, CA: Stanford Geriatric Education Center.

Hennessey, C. R., & John, R. (1995). The interpretation of burden among Pueblo Indian caregivers. *Journal of Aging Studies, 9*, 215–229.

Hennessey, C., & John, R. (1996). American Indian family caregivers' perceptions of burden and needed support services. *Journal of Applied Gerontology, 15*(3), 275–293.

Hill, R. W., Sr. (1999). *Wounded Knee, a wound that won't heal: Did the Army attempt to cover up the massacre of prisoners of war?* Unpublished essay.

Hudson, M., Armachain, W. D., Beasley, C., & Carlson, J. R. (1998). Elder abuse: Two Native American views. *The Gerontologist, 38*(5), 538–548.

Jaimes, A. M. (Ed.). (1992). *The state of Native America: Genocide, colonization, and resistance*. Boston, MA: South End Press.

John, R. (1995). *American Indian and Alaska Native elders: An assessment of their current status and provision of services*. Rockville, MD: Indian Health Service.

John, R., & Baldridge, D. (1996). *The NICOA report: Health and long-term care for Indian elders*. [A report by the National Indian Council on Aging for the National Indian Policy Center.] Washington, DC: National Indian Policy Center.

John, R., Hennessey, C. H., Roy, L. C., & Salvini, M. L. (1996). Caring for cognitively impaired American Indian elders: Difficult situations, few options. In G. Yeo & D. Gallagher-Thompson (Eds.). *Ethnicity and the dementias*. Washington, DC: Taylor & Francis.

Kramer, B. J. (1992). Health and aging of urban American Indians. *Western Journal of Medicine, 157*, 281–285.

Kramer, B. J. (1996). Dementia and American Indian populations. In G. Yeo & D. Gallagher-Thompson (Eds.), *Ethnicity and the dementias* (pp. 175–182). Washington, DC: Taylor & Francis.

Magagnini, S. (1997, June 30). Long-suffering urban Indians find roots in ancient rituals. *The Sacramento Bee*, p. 3. Retrieved March 8, 2006, from http://www.

sacbee.com/static/archive/news/projects/native/day2_main.html.

Marshall, J. M., III. (2001). *The Lakota way: Stories and lessons for living.* New York: Viking Compass.

Miller, R. (2002). Cultural and social considerations in applying standardized assessment tools to AI/AN populations. In *A guide to comprehensive geriatric assessment in Indian Country* (pp. 34–44). Albuquerque: New Mexico Geriatric Education Center and the Indian Health Service Elder Care Initiative.

Ogrocki, P., Welsh-Bohmer, K., & Allen, F. (1997). Poster presentation—30th annual meeting, Gerontological Society of America, San Francisco; Bryan Alzheimer's Disease Research Center; Duke University Medical Center, Durham, NC.

Pevar, S. L. (199f2). *The rights of Indians and tribes* (2nd ed.). Carbondale: Southern Illinois University Press [American Civil Liberties Union Handbook].

Pollaca, M. (2001). American Indian and Alaska Native elderly. In L. K. Olson (Ed.), *Age through ethnic lenses: Caring for the elderly in a multicultural society.* Boulder, CO: Rowman & Littlefield.

Strong, C. (1984). Stress and caring for elderly relatives: Interpretations and coping strategies in an American Indian and White sample. *The Gerontologist, 24*(3), 251–256.

Trafzer, C. E. (2000). *As long as the grass shall grow and the rivers flow: A history of Native Americans.* Orlando, FL: Harcourt College.

Urban Indian Health Institute. (2004). *Urban American Indian/Alaska Native long-term care needs assessment: Final report.* Seattle, WA: Seattle Indian Health Board.

Waldman, C. (1985). *Atlas of the north American Indian.* New York: Facts on File.

Wallace, S. P., Satter, D., & Zubiate, A. (2003). *Medicaid home care and Tribal health services for Washington: A tool kit for developing new programs.* Los Angeles, CA: UCLA Center for Health Policy Research, University of California. Retrieved December 5, 2004, from www.healthpolicy.ucla.edu

Yeo, G. (1996). Geriatric education: Cross-cutting issues, accomplishable tasks. In S. M. Klein (Ed.), *A National agenda for geriatric education: Forum report* (pp. 59–61). Rockville, MD: Bureau of Health Professions, Department of Health and Human Services.

Working with Asian American Families

CHAPTER 11

Working with Asian Indian American Families

VYJEYANTHI S. PERIYAKOIL

Background

According to the 2000 census, there are over 1.6 million people of Asian Indian origin in the United States, accounting for about 0.6% of the total U.S. population. Asian Indians make up the third largest subgroup of Asian Americans. Small numbers of Asian Indians came to the United States as traders in the 18th century. Since that time, Asian Indians have immigrated to the United States in waves, though the pace of the immigration has been regulated by various changes in the immigration rules. In fact, in 1917, their immigration was outlawed, and they were denied citizenship, ownership of land, and the right to marry Caucasians until 1946 (Asia Society, The, 1996; Jensen, 1988; Periyakoil, 2004). In the decades since 1985, large numbers of young and highly educated Asian Indians have immigrated to the United States to work in the high-technology industry. Asian Indians cohorts can be found in every state of the United States; concentrations of over 60,000 can be found in California, Texas, New York, New Jersey, and Illinois, followed by the Washington D.C. area. In addition to vast differences in acculturation levels, Asian Indians in the United States speak many different Indian dialects (Bengali, Gujarati,

Hindi, Kannada, Malayalam, Marathi, Tamil, Telugu, and more) and practice different religions (Buddhism, Christianity, Hinduism, Islam, Jainism, Sikhism, and Zorastrianism). This diversity has resulted in tremendous heterogeneity in the Asian Indian population in the United States.

Due to family reunification laws, the numbers of Asian Indian elders who followed their offspring to this country has risen. Thus, we currently have several different cohorts of elders of Asian Indian origin: (a) those who immigrated to the United States in the first half of the 20th century, (b) baby boomers who immigrated in the 1960s and 1970s and who are now retired or approaching retirement, (c) elderly Asian Indians who have lived in India all their lives and who have immigrated recently to be reunited with their children, and (d) the second-generation Asian Indian Americans who were born in the United States and who are aging. In the 2000 Census, over 66,000 Asian Indians age 65 and over were reported to live in the United States. Although 89% were born outside the United States, only 12% were linguistically isolated, the smallest percentage of any of the 10 largest Asian subpopulations. Nine percent were in poverty; 31% reported having less than 9 years of education, and 32% had a bachelor's degree or more (Yeo & Hikoyeda, in press).

The Traditional Family System

Asian Indians in India traditionally have large extended families and a strong family support system. In contrast, Asian Indian Americans living in the United States often have a nuclear family system. However, aging parents who immigrate to live with their children are often financially and socially dependent on their children. The lack of a well-integrated public transport infrastructure in the United States enforces social isolation on these elders, as many of them lack the ability and the resources to maintain and drive their own cars. Thus, many of these elders are often home bound.

Traditionally, the Asian Indian society has been stereotyped as being a male-dominant society, with women assuming a submissive role. Decisions are thought to be male driven, and women are thought to play a passive role. In the modern era, the role of the Asian Indian woman is rapidly evolving. While some Asian Indian families may still be somewhat male dominated, women play active roles in decision-making processes, although men may continue to serve as spokespersons of the family unit. Thus, clinicians are cautioned to avoid stereotypical generalizations and are advised to use open-ended questions to explore the values and decision-making styles of individual families.

Traditional Health Beliefs

Providers may need to understand some of the traditional beliefs relating to health and healing in order to work most effectively with elders with dementia and their families, although there is great variation in the degree to which Asian Indian families practice them. *Ayurveda* has been practiced for almost 5,000 years in India as a science of healing. *Ayurveda* describes three fundamental universal energies that regulate all natural processes on both the macrocosmic and microcosmic levels. These three energy systems are known as the *tridosha* and consist of *pitha* (bile), *vatha* (wind, air), and *kapha* (phlegm). In a healthy person, these three driving forces are perfectly balanced, and any disequilibrium between them manifests as a symptom of disease. Ayurvedic principles have been in practice for so long that they have been absorbed into everyday thought and practice, so that they may be followed unconsciously. Some common beliefs based on these principles include the conviction that milk and bananas should not be eaten together, and that drinking warm water promotes health, and drinking cold water makes the body vulnerable to illness. Asian Indian patients may also be taking Ayurvedic herbs and alternative medicines while on allopathic treatment, so clinicians are advised to routinely inquire about them. Some Asian Indian elders, especially those who come from rural areas, may believe that certain diseases are caused by evil spirits and so practice rituals to cleanse the possessed individual (Periyakoil, 2004).

Many who practice Hinduism or Sikhism believe in reincarnation, meaning that every living being has multiple lives and goes through the cycle of birth and death multiple times. Many also believe in *karma*, which can be understood to denote the fruit of one's actions, including those during previous lives, which are thought to influence events of current and future lives. Asian Indian elders and families, therefore, may believe that dementia is the result of bad *karma* from past lives and so may feel that any interventions are powerless in the face of *karma*. Also, the belief in reincarnation may strongly influence the way they perceive and find meaning in their life and death. Asian Indian families who practice Islam may also believe that illness is the result of bad actions (not necessarily from past lives), and that the illness washes away the sins (Periyakoil, 2004).

Health-care providers may encounter religious paraphernalia worn by many elders from India, such as special clothing (*tupi*, a religious cap worn by Moslems), sacred ornaments (*mangalsutra*, a necklace worn by married Hindu women), sacred threads around the body (worn by Hindu males), or amulets (*kara*, a steel bracelet worn by Sikh men who have undergone the Amrit ceremony or baptism). These are considered sacred and should never be removed or cut without the consent of the patient or a family member (Periyakoil, 2004).

Risk Factors for Dementia

With the recent advances in biomedicine, life expectancies have increased, resulting in a rapidly aging population. Dementia is a geriatric degenerative neurological disorder with its prevalence increasing with increasing age. As the life expectancies of Asian Indian elders are increasing, it is anticipated that the prevalence of dementia will increase. Apolipoprotein E4 allele (apo E4) on a gene on chromosome 19 is a risk factor for the commonly occurring late-onset Alzheimer's disease, the most common form of dementia. Luthra and colleagues found that the apo E3/E3 and apo E2/E3 combinations of the apo E genotypes were found to be protective in a cohort of Asian Indians, and the apo E4 genotype increased the risk of developing Alzheimer's disease and vascular dementia (Luthra et al., 2004). Other researchers showed that there was a very low prevalence of Alzheimer's disease (AD) in a cohort in Ballabgarh, India, but the association of apo E4 with AD was similar in strength in Indian and U.S. samples (Chandra, et al., 2001; Ganguli et al., 2000).

Diabetes and Dementia

Many Asian Indian elders have type II diabetes mellitus, usually associated with hyperinsulinemia and significant insulin resistance. These patients are at very high risk for coronary vascular disease and stroke. Severe cerebral small vessel disease and multiple small strokes can often result in vascular dementia. Type II diabetes is thought to be associated with an increased risk of both Alzheimer's disease and vascular dementia. The following factors are thought to be operative: (a) Type II diabetes is closely related to the "metabolic syndrome," a cluster of metabolic and vascular risk factors (e.g., dyslipidemia and hypertension); (b) hyperglycemia and secondary "toxic" glucose metabolites may damage neurons and the vasculature of the brain; and (c) insulin can directly modulate synaptic plasticity and learning and memory, and disturbances in insulin signaling pathways in the periphery and in the brain were recently implicated in Alzheimer's disease and brain aging. Insulin also regulates the metabolism of β-amyloid and tau, the building blocks of amyloid plaques and neurofibrillary tangles (Biessels & Kappelle, 2005; Messier 2005).

Hypertension, Dyslipidemia, and Dementia

Hypertension is a risk factor for stroke, ischemic white-matter lesions, cardiovascular disorders, and vascular dementia (Vicario, Martinez, Baretto, Diaz Casale, & Nicolosi, 2005). The risk increases with increasing blood pressure. Hypertension has also been related to the neuropathological manifestations of AD (Skoog, 2003). A high cholesterol level in mid-life is also thought to be a risk for AD, and cholesterol-lowering drugs (specifically statins) are thought to reduce this risk (Sjogren & Blennow, 2005). Both hypertension and dyslipidemia are common in Asian Indian elders. In fact, Asian Indian Americans are known to have a higher prevalence of hypertension and hypercholesterolemia, compared to the general U.S. population (Ivey et al., 2004). The Asian Indian diet is often rich in saturated fats, such as ghee (clarified butter), palmolein, margarine, peanut oil, and cotton oil, and high in salt (pickled vegetables, etc.). Educating elders about the risks associated with dyslipidemia and hypertension and advising dietary modifications is helpful in promoting wellness.

Lower Prevalence of Dementia in Asian Indians

In contrast to the overall prevalence of dementia reported in developed countries of 5–10% after age 60 or 65 (Biswas, Chakraborty, Dutt, & Roy, 2005), the reported prevalence of dementia in Indian elders is much lower (Shaji, Bose, & Verghese, 2005). Lower life expectancies, underdiagnosis, and false negatives in assessments are thought to be contributing reasons. However, it cannot be denied that the decreased prevalence could also be due to decreased genetic risks and, possibly, dietary and environmental factors.

Curcumin and the Asian Indian Diet

Recent research has focused on the possible protective effects of curcumin, an active ingredient of the herb turmeric, in dementia. Turmeric or *haldi* powder is obtained from the root of the plant *Curcuma longa*. Curcuma is a member of the ginger family and is a perennial plant that grows to a height of about 1 m. Turmeric, a yellow powder, is extracted from the Curcuma root and widely used in Asian Indian cooking both as a natural coloring agent (yellow color) and as a flavoring agent. Curcumin (a diferuloylmethane), the active ingredient found in turmeric, is a key ingredient in Indian curry. Curcumin has anti-inflammatory and antioxidative properties and is thought to suppress oxidative damage, inflammation, cognitive deficits, and amyloid accumulation in the aging brain, thus serving as a protective factor in dementia (Yang et al., 2005).

Assessment and Management of Dementia

Culturally sensitive interviews of the patient and family members and clinical assessment are the most important diagnostic tools for dementia. A comprehensive history and physical examination with special attention to the onset and rate of progress of cognitive problems, a laboratory evaluation to rule out hypothyroidism (TSH), syphilis (VDRL), and vitamin B_{12} deficiency are recommended. Brain imaging studies should be considered in patients if (a) dementia onset occurs before age 65, (b) focal neurologic deficits are present, or (c) the clinical picture suggests normal-pressure hydrocephalus (triad of onset has occurred within 1 year, gait disorder, and unexplained incontinence). Systematically translated versions of the commonly used dementia screen, the Mini-Mental State Examination (MMSE), are available in Hindi, Gujarati, Marathi, Kannada, Telugu, and Malayalam Indian dialects. These are available on the Internet (www.minimental.com).

Disclosure of Diagnosis

Once the health-care professional has made the diagnosis of dementia, it is of critical importance to disclose the news about the diagnosis in a culturally competent and compassionate manner. As in many other Eastern cultures, the autonomy unit of an Asian Indian family may consist of the patient and one or more key family members. Acculturated elders who have embraced (American) mainstream values may prefer to make their own decisions. Others may still defer to key family members to make all health-care decisions for them. In certain cases, families may request that the patient not be told of the diagnosis of dementia. In such cases, the health professional should first check in with the patient and ascertain his or her wishes. For example, saying, *"Mrs. Reddy, I understand that you would prefer that I not discuss your illness with you and that you would prefer to have your husband/son/daughter make health care decisions for you. Is this true? ... OK, I will have further discussions with your husband/son/daughter. But if you ever need any information about your health status or have any questions, please feel free to ask me."*

At present, there is no curative therapy for dementia. See chapter 7 of this text for information on treatment options. Establishing a therapeutic alliance with both the patient and the family fosters an ongoing trusting relationship and facilitates management. Proactive education of the patient (in the early stages of dementia) and caregiver is helpful.

Caregiver Stress

Caregivers of those with dementia are often subject to enormous and cumulative stresses. In fact, 80% of caregivers for those with dementia report stress and about 50% report depression (Small et al., 1997). Health professionals caring for patients with dementia should also monitor the patient's caregivers for signs of caregiver stress and make appropriate referrals to caregiver support groups, as these have been shown to effectively alleviate stress. Consider offering support and respite services, such as respite care and adult day care for those with dementia, as these interventions reduce caregiver stress, offer meaningful social stimulation to the patient, and may possibly help postpone patient institutionalization. While some Asian Indian caregivers may be open and vocal about the stresses experienced, others (especially elderly wives) may feel reluctant to voice their stresses, because they may feel that such expressions are demonstrative of a lack of loyalty to their loved ones. Gentle and explorative questions will likely elicit the true state of affairs. Normalizing their experience might be helpful: *"Mrs. Patel, often caregivers of dementia patients become very stressed. This will likely result in health problems in the future. There are some simple things we can do to help with caregiver stress. Can you please tell me how you are feeling?"*

Conclusion

Initial data have indicated that there is a lower prevalence of dementia in Asian Indians compared to their Western counterparts. This could be due to false negatives in assessment, underreporting, under-diagnosis, and lack of culturally appropriate diagnostic tools. This could also be due to a truly low prevalence of dementia due to food habits and lifestyles of Asian Indians. More research is required to clarify the former issues and to possibly learn from the latter issues.

References

Asia Society, The. (1996). *Linking past to present: Asian Americans then and now.* Retrieved November 24, 2005, from www.askasia.org/frclasrm/readings/r000192.htm

Biessels, G. J., & Kappelle, L. J. (2005). Increased risk of Alzheimer's disease in Type II diabetes: Insulin resistance of the brain or insulin-induced amyloid pathology? *Biochemical Society Transactions, 33*(Pt. 5), 1041–1044.

Biswas, A., Chakraborty, D., Dutt, A., & Roy, T. (2005) Dementia in India—A critical appraisal. *Journal of Indian Medical Association, 103*(3), 154–158.

Chandra, V., Pandav, R., Dodge, H. H., Johnston, J. M., Belle, S. H., DeKosky, S. T. et al. (2001). Incidence of Alzheimer's disease in a rural community in India: The Indo–U.S. study. *Neurology, 54*, 985–989.

Ganguli, M., Chandra, V., Kamboh, M. I., Johnston, J. M., Dodge, H. H., Thelma, B. K. et al. (2000). Apolipoprotein E polymorphism and Alzheimer disease: The Indo–U.S. Cross-National Dementia Study. *Archives of Neurology, 57*(6), 824–830.

Ivey, S. L., Patel, S., Kalra, P., Greenlund, K., Srinivasan, S., & Grewal, D. (2004). Cardiovascular health among Asian Indians (CHAI): A community research project. *Journal of Interprofessional Care, 18*(4), 391–402.

Jensen, J. M. (1988). *Passage from India: Asian Indian immigrants in North America*. New Haven, CT: Yale University Press.

Luthra, K., Tripathi, M., Grover, R., Dwivedi, M., Kumar, A., & Dey, A. B. (2004). Apolipoprotein E gene polymorphism in Indian patients with Alzheimer's disease and vascular dementia. *Dementia & Geriatric Cognitive Disorders, 17*(3), 132–135.

Messier, C. (2005). Impact of impaired glucose tolerance and type 2 diabetes on cognitive aging. *Neurobiology of Aging, 26*(Suppl 1),

Newman, A. B., Fitzpatrick, A. L., Lopez, O., Jackson, S., Lyketsos, C., Jagust, W. et al. (2005). Dementia and Alzheimer's disease incidence in relationship to cardiovascular disease in the Cardiovascular Health Study cohort. *Journal of the American Geriatrics Society, 53*(7), 1101–1107.

Periyakoil, V. (2004). Older Asian Indian Americans. In R. Adler & H. Kamel (Eds.), *Doorway thoughts: Cross cultural care for older adults*. Sudbury, MA: Jones & Bartlett/American Geriatrics Society.

Shaji, S., Bose, S., & Verghese, A. (2005). Prevalence of dementia in an urban population in Kerala, India. *British Journal of Psychiatry, 186*, 136–140.

Sjogren, M., & Blennow, K. (2005). The link between cholesterol and Alzheimer's disease. *World Journal of Biological Psychiatry, 6*(2), 85–97.

Skoog, I. (2003). Hypertension and cognition. *International Psychogeriatrics, 15*(Supp. 1), 139–146.

Small, G. W., Rabins, P. V., Barry, P. P., Buckholtz, N. S., DeKosky, S. T., Ferris, S. H. et al. (1997). Diagnosis and treatment of Alzheimer disease and related disorders. Consensus statement of the American Association for Geriatric Psychiatry, the Alzheimer's Association, and the American Geriatrics Society. *Journal of the American Medical Association, 278*, 1363–1371.

Vicario, A., Martinez, C. D., Baretto, D., Diaz Casale, A., & Nicolosi, L. (2005). Hypertension and cognitive decline: Impact on executive function. *Journal of Clinical Hypertension* (Greenwich), 7(10), 598–604.

Yang, F., Lim, G. P., Begum, A. N., Ubeda, O. J., Simmons, M. R., Ambegaokar, S. S. et al. (2005). Curcumin inhibits formation of amyloid beta oligomers and fibrils, binds plaques, and reduces amyloid *in vivo*. *Journal of Biological Chemistry, 280*(7), 5892–5901.

Yeo, G., & Hikoyeda, N. (in press). Asian and Pacific Island elders. In G. Maddox (Ed.), *Encyclopedia of aging* (4th ed.). New York: Springer.

CHAPTER 12

Working with Chinese American Families

PENG-CHIH WANG, HUI-QI TONG, WEILING LIU,
SUSAN LONG, LAURIE Y.L. LEUNG, EDIE YAU,
AND DOLORES GALLAGHER-THOMPSON

Background

The Chinese population over 65 years of age currently represents about 10% of all Chinese Americans. According to 2000 U.S. Census figures, Chinese Americans, numbering more than 2.4 million, were found to be the largest subgroup of Asian Pacific Islander Americans, comprising approximately 24% of this group (U.S. Bureau of the Census, 2002). Between 1990 and 2000, the Chinese American population increased by approximately one million due to Mainland China's open door policy, and many students and professionals chose to stay in the United States. Another group of immigrants, who came from Hong Kong, worried about the 1997 transfer of British sovereignty to China. The recent political climate in Taiwan (independence vs. reunification with Mainland China) and the desire to seek higher education for their children also created an impetus for many Chinese to come to this country. Another recent phenomenon is the so-called *astronaut families*. An astronaut family is an arrangement whereby some of the migrant family members return to their countries of origin to work, while the remaining family members, usually the women and children, continue to reside in the host country (Ho, Bedford, & Goodwin, 1997).

Finally, many of the refugees from Vietnam, Laos, and Cambodia were ethnic Chinese. They constituted the second "wave" of Southeast Asian refugees. A significant number of them were survivors of rape, incarceration, forced migration, and torture (Lee, 1996). There are also *overseas Chinese* from countries such as Japan, Korea, Singapore, and Thailand, and other countries. In summary, this new influx of immigrants has emerged as one of the most diverse Asian American groups in terms of generation status, language spoken, and economic and educational backgrounds.

The true prevalence of dementia is unknown, because there are currently no large-scale prospective population-based studies examining the prevalence of Alzheimer's disease and related disorders among Chinese Americans. Previous research at Shanghai demonstrated that 4.6% of those over age 65 had dementia, and 24.3% of those over 85 had dementia (Zhang et al., 1990). In addition, Lin et al.'s (1998) study of Chinese in Taiwan demonstrated that the prevalence rate of dementia was 3.7%, increasing from 1.3% in people 65–69 years old and 16.5% of those over 85 years and older. By contrast, in the United States, 3–11% of persons older than 65 years of age and 25–47% of those older than 85 years of age have dementia (Evans et al., 1989, 1991). Recently, Huang et al. (2003) published the first systematic report of the sociodemographic characteristics of newly admitted older Chinese to an urban nursing home in the United States. Using the Minimum Data Set database, 258 newly admitted residents (125 Chinese, 57 White, 53 Hispanics, and 23 African Americans) over age 60 were compared. The majority of Chinese Americans included first-generation immigrants who primarily spoke Cantonese or Mandarin Chinese. Compared with Whites, they were more likely to be married, less likely to have lived alone, more likely to be using Medicaid, less likely to make medical decisions alone, and more likely to depend on family members for decision making. Nearly 75% of this group demonstrated significant cognitive impairment.

Assessment for Dementia in Chinese Populations

Performance on objective tests is one of the most important pieces of data considered in the clinical diagnosis of dementia (American Psychiatric Association, 1994). As indicated in chapter 4 of this text, cultural factors are important to keep in mind when assessing for memory deficits in Chinese individuals. Certain variables, such as age and education, are common factors contributing to level of performance on cognitive screens, while variables such as language and ecological validity are equally important, though less widely studied. Level of education is an especially salient challenge for many older Chinese American individuals who may have little or no formal schooling. Another factor to consider when assessing for dementia is language. The linguistic challenges are much different for individuals who immigrated during the past few decades; most of those making up this cohort are monolingual and non-English speaking (Yeo & Gallagher-Thompson, 1996). Ecological relevance of test items is also important; researchers who develop screening tests from academia or the mainstream culture may reflect the researchers' life experiences or life-styles. By contrast, a Chinese grandmother from a rural area might be good at cooking, growing vegetables, and caring for children, actions that in her culture reflect good cognitive abilities, but she may be likely to score in the "impaired" range due to the inapplicability of the screening test (Teng, 2002). Researchers have addressed this issue by attempting ecologically valid translations of existing cognitive screens, whereby the translated versions may not retain the exact wording of the original but are contextually and ecologically relevant for the target population. For example, Teng and colleagues (1994) created the CASI (Cognitive Abilities Screening Instrument) for studies in the United States and Japan, and subsequently translated it into Chinese for use in China and Taiwan. In an unpublished doctoral dissertation, Leung (2004) found that the CASI may have utility with the Chinese population in an urban U.S. area (San Francisco Bay Area). An informal qualitative analysis conducted at the item level revealed interesting culturally relevant information. For example, several Taiwanese participants informed the interviewers that the months for the different seasons fall on different months than are designated in the United States, where spring traditionally falls between March and June; for the Taiwanese participants, spring falls between January and March. Scores on the CASI were adjusted in the study to reflect such cultural differences.

When conducting cognitive assessments with Chinese individuals, it may be helpful to consider the following:

1. What is the first language of the individual? Be aware that there are a variety of different Chinese dialects, each different from another in either subtle or major ways. Even perfected translated versions of instruments may not capture these differences very well. When in doubt, it is best to conduct a short interview to gain further understanding after conducting the assessment in the standardized format.
2. It is best to conduct the assessment in the first language of the person, if necessary, using a bilingual, bicultural examiner, if possible.

3. Even when using well-established English-language instruments, remember that certain items may lack ecological validity.
4. If at all possible, use more than one instrument for cross-validity. No single instrument can adequately diagnose a person 100% of the time.

For a more comprehensive discussion of assessment in Asian populations, see chapter 4.

Culturally Based Views of Dementia

Researchers working with Chinese Americans in California found that definitions of dementia are variable (Braun & Browne, 1998; Elliott, Di Minno, Lam, & Tu, 1996; Takamura, 1991). Chinese Americans may view dementia as a form of normal aging, a form of mental illness, a source of shame, the result of fate, retribution for the sins of the family or of one's ancestors, or imbalance between the body complementary forms of energy (*yin* and *yang*).

The most common response to memory loss of older Chinese individuals is to consider it as a normal consequence of growing old. Chinese people use "*Lao hu tu*" to describe older people who have dementia and associated disorders, which translates into English as "senile stupidity" or "senile silly" (Zhan, 2004). Many Chinese who hold this traditional view might not seek dementia services until the disease is advanced. Elliott et al. (1996) stated that stigmatization of Alzheimer's disease (AD) and dementia not only inhibits Chinese American families from seeking diagnosis and assistance but also makes it difficult for researchers to recruit Chinese family caregivers to participate in dementia studies (Gallagher-Thompson et al., under review).

Traditional Chinese Family Structure

In this chapter, the commonly held belief that there is one "type" or "prototype" of Chinese family is challenged. Different family members come to the United States at different times and show varying degrees of acculturation, which is defined as individual changes as a result of contact and interaction with another distinct culture (Berry, Trimble, & Olmedo, 1986). They exhibit a wide range of cultural values from traditional to "Americanized" (Lee, 1997; Sue & Sue, 1999). In terms of the more traditional Chinese family, there are many unique characteristics of which to become aware. For example, the traditional family system is heavily influenced by Confucianism, Buddhism, and Daoism, which all emphasize harmonious interpersonal relationship and interdependence (Bowman & Singer, 2001). Family interaction/communication is governed by assigned roles defined by family hierarchy, obligation, and family duties. Western ideals of independence and free expression of emotions are seen as disruptive to family rule and harmony. Males in the family, especially the father and oldest son, have dominant roles. Throughout history, Chinese mothers have been portrayed as self-sacrificing and overinvolved with their children. Traditionally, in accordance with the custom of "thrice obeying," women were expected to comply with their fathers or elder brothers in youth and with their husbands in adulthood. As wives, their value was judged by their ability to produce a son and to serve their in-laws (Lee, 1996).

Filial Piety and Caregiving in Chinese American Families

Filial piety is an integral part of Chinese culture and is, therefore, embraced by three of China's major philosophies: Confucianism, Buddhism, and Daoism. Among the three, Confucianism, with its well-documented social hierarchy, supported the ideals of filial piety the most. Many other regions in East Asia, such as Japan, Korea, Singapore, and Vietnam, are heavily influenced by Confucianism and filial piety as well.

In Confucian thought, *xiao* (filial piety), love and respect for one's parents and ancestors, is a virtue to be cultivated. While parents rear children into adulthood, children provide for their parents' comfort in their old age to show gratitude in return. Filial piety involves many different duties, including taking care of one's own health so as not to make the parents worry, not traveling far without purpose while parents are still alive, taking care of the parents, burying them properly after death, bringing honor to the family, and having a male heir to carry on the family name.

The practice of filial piety is deeply ingrained in the Chinese family value system, and caring for elders is traditionally viewed as a moral and social responsibility. Filial piety is such a cornerstone of Chinese family values that it remains deeply ingrained in most Chinese American families, regardless of levels of acculturation. In traditional Chinese culture, family membership, inheritance of property, and distribution of authority are defined through the main axis of father and son; sons, especially the oldest one, assume the responsibility of caring for aged parents. As one Chinese proverb goes, "To raise a son (is) to protect yourself at old ages *(yang er fang lao)*" (Lan, 2002). A daughter is "married out," considered "spilled water," given away to the family into which she married, headed by her husband's father.

In a traditional family, in which three generations usually cohabitate, the son provides economic support for his parents; his wife, as the serving agent for her husband, provides personal care, such as cooking and doing laundry. When her husband's parents are ill, she becomes the de facto caregiver, but it is still up to the son(s) to make major decisions regarding aspects of caregiving, such as how to split the duties among siblings and whether to institutionalize an ill parent.

This cultural belief and practice have major implications for basic research and intervention research with patients with AD and their families. For example, even if the daughter-in-law provides the most care for the older relative, obtaining consent from her to participate in any form of research will generally entail consulting her husband, though ultimately she is the one who signs the paperwork. In situations in which a daughter is caring for her parents, she may even call up an uncle and consult with him before making a decision. Thus, the consenting process with Chinese families can take longer and usually involves the whole family. Flexibility in adapting the consent process to the particular family dynamic at hand is essential for researchers to consider (Hinton & Levkoff, 1999).

In the context of caregiving for those with dementia, respect for the older person (Elliott et al., 1996; Jones, 1995) and acceptance of age-related cognitive changes and dependency (Yu, Kim, Liu, & Wong., 1993) are believed to contribute to positive caring attitudes. Chinese families taking care of family members with dementia tend to rely heavily on the extended family and not to seek external help until all the resources within the family system have been exhausted. A caregiver once said: "We usually handle problems ourselves, but if the problem is serious, we can ask a professional, preferably one bilingual and bicultural" (Pang et al., 2002). Nevertheless, Chinese families are growing geographically and emotionally further apart, and a growing number of studies show that filial obligation is related to increased caregiver burden and distress among Chinese caregivers (Chou, LaMontagne, & Hepworth, 1999; Fuh, Wang, Liu, Liu, & Wang, 1999), which in turn are associated with eventual institutionalization of the elder (Gaugler, Kane, Kane, Clay, & Newcomer, 2003).

With immigration and acculturation, the status of elders and the ways of practicing filial piety are being modified among ethnic Chinese families as well as among other ethnic groups from East Asia, such as Japanese and Koreans. For example, in the San Francisco Bay Area in Northern California, researchers studied the phenomena of "subcontracting filial piety" in dual-income families in which caring for the older person was carried out by someone employed by the family or contracted through the In-Home Supportive Service (IHSS) or a combination of both, based on factors such as economic status of the caring children (Lan, 2002).

Research shows that institutionalization of older people around the globe is not widespread. In Chinese American families in which adult children care for a parent with dementia, placement in a nursing home is still often stigmatized as a failure of filial piety. It is usually a final resort when all other resources have been exhausted and the condition of the older person is so advanced that professional intervention becomes absolutely necessary. As Lan put it, "The cultural norms of filial piety and parental authority, which have traditionally governed intergenerational relationships in ethnic Chinese societies, are modified and transformed after immigrant families resettle in the United States" (p. 833). Nonetheless, filial piety remains a principal influence of caregiving in Chinese American families (Yick & Gupta, 2002).

According to Lee (1996), there are several distinct shifts in the contemporary Chinese American family:

1. The traditional Chinese extended family has gradually yielded to a more nuclear family, in which functional relations apply instead of actual household structure.
2. Favoritism of sons has slowly decreased, because daughters now attain comparable education and careers and can be counted on to take care of aged parents.
3. Successful child rearing is now measured mostly by the children's academic and career achievements.

Service Needs and Barriers to Help Seeking

In Zhan's (2004) study, Chinese American caregivers identify barriers that impeded their access to AD services and to gaining support from the Chinese American community. These barriers include not knowing about AD at the early stage of the disease, strong stigma attached to AD, lack of family and community support, and negative interactions with health professionals and service providers. In addition, based on empirical qualitative data, Hinton, Guo, Hillygus, and Levkoff (2000) cited three main themes that emerged when recruiting Chinese caregivers of those with dementia into a research program:

1. Chinese communities often view cognitive decline and behavioral problems as a normal part of aging.
2. Research is regarded as potentially harmful, as it might stress out their loved ones.

3. Labeling the older relative as suffering from AD or dementia carries a negative connotation for the older relative and stigmatizes the whole family.

Feelings of discrimination may also be a barrier to getting help. A caregiver stated the following in Hinton's study: "They (health-care providers at a local clinic) will be nice to Americans (non-Chinese). They don't like (those) especially from Mainland China. I also think that income is another reason. Mostly, they treat different people differently" (Hinton, Franz, & Friend, 2004, p. 141).

Before their loved one had an AD diagnosis, Chinese American caregivers indicated that they were out of the dementia information loop. They had very little knowledge about dementia or AD. This fact may contribute to caregivers' delayed response and primary care providers having a difficult time breaking the bad news to the Chinese family (Zhan, 2004).

The culturally based stigma regarding AD might also prevent Chinese American caregivers from seeking help earlier. For example, a caregiver from Zhan's study reported: "Some of my dad's friends suggested we relocate our house and they thought my mom's 'craziness' was caused by bad feng shui" (2004, p. 24).

Help-seeking patterns among Chinese American families can be complex and may lead to intergenerational conflicts in a family (Pang, Jordan-Marsh, Silverstein, & Cody, 2003). Regardless of who the primary caregiver for the patient with AD is, children are usually the family's "cultural broker," but parents or parents-in-law need to face the role reversal, the caregiver burden, and the high risk of physical illness.

Furthermore, families can hinder elders from getting appropriate health care. Because the adult children do not live with their older parents and are perceived as being busy, it is common for the elders to try not to bother them. This statement is especially true for those who come to the United States to join adult children who have thrived in American society. These elders live separately from their children, because they do not want to bother their children; they might choose to live in Chinese senior apartments instead. They can have a more similar age group to interact with, and most importantly, they can accompany each other to health care and other functions. In Pang et al.'s study, researchers presented the following quotes to illustrate the views Chinese elders have of their relationships with their children: "I will not bother my family if I can take care of the problem myself. (My children) have their own work to worry about. Only when I have some serious disease will I think about bothering them. Our children will definitely be involved when something serious happens to us" (2003, p. 867). Researchers in this study concluded that some older Chinese people started moving away from traditional expectations regarding the type of help they expect from their sons and daughters. They use more neighborhoods (i.e., Chinese senior apartments) and friends as social support networks instead of their own children for seeking medical service and other types of help.

In addition to the traditional cultural stigma associated with AD, the Chinese elders also faced various structural barriers to accessing formal health-care services. Major concerns for these Chinese elders included lacking English proficiency to communicate with care providers and having restricted mobility. Furthermore, some elders found the U.S. health-care system to be confusing and intimidating. The Chinese elders may prefer not to use their Medicare or Medicaid benefits, because they do not fully understand the policies and what treatments and medications are covered. In addition, inability to predict the costs of doctor's visits is a frightening proposition and discourages some elders from using the medical service for their or their loved one's treatments (Pang et al., 2003).

Intervention Programs for Chinese American Caregivers

Despite the difficulty in accessing this population, some literature has reported programs that show potential for alleviating stresses and burdens associated with long-term caregiving. Hinton and Levkoff (1999) used a narrative approach to interview Chinese American family members who provide care to older relatives who have dementia. The results were that the Chinese Americans in Boston tended to use the split caregiver model for reasons of family hierarchy. The senior male makes all the care decisions, even if he is in California, and a daughter living near her ill parent provides all the care. The researchers found that Chinese American caregivers did not use support groups for emotional support. The reason is that available Alzheimer's support groups were largely composed of English-speaking Whites, whose language and behavior were strange and discomforting to the Chinese Americans (Hinton & Levkoff, 1999).

An example of a support service for family members with AD or related dementias in California is the Asian American Dementia Care Network. The goal of the program is to provide bilingual, bicultural social and support services for Chinese and Vietnamese families. It is a collaboration of the Alzheimer's Association, John XXIII Multi-Services Center in San Jose, and Self-Help for the Elderly in the San Francisco Bay Area. The process is as follows: Once eligibility is established, the care advocate makes a home visit to meet the person with dementia and the family to assess the needs of the caregiver and to capture a broader picture of the situation. If the person with dementia has not been diagnosed, the care advocate provides assistance in obtaining a diagnosis either through the primary-care physician or by identifying another clinic to make an appropriate diagnosis. For those with dementia, the network provides a monthly caregiver support group in each community facilitated in their respective language (Cantonese, Mandarin, or Vietnamese). Education is a crucial component of the program, because many families have unanswered questions about the disease and how to care for their elders. At the end of one year, a reassessment is completed. In most cases, the family has greater support and no longer needs care management. In some cases, the family has greater needs and benefits from ongoing care management.

In a study performed at the Older Adult and Family Center called the "Chinese Caregiver Assistance Program" (Tang et al., in press), 51 Chinese American caregivers were randomly assigned to the Home-Based Behavioral Management Program (HBMP) or to a telephone support program. HBMP is derived from the cognitive theories of Beck, Rush, Shaw, and Emery (1979) and the behavioral theories of depression by Lewinsohn, Munoz, Yougren, and Zeiss (1986), which define the role of negative cognitions, behavioral avoidance, and lack of self-generated positive reinforcement in determining affective states. Overall, this program taught a limited number of cognitive–behavioral mood management skills, including hands-on skills to manage care recipients' behavioral problems; effective communication skills to better relate with care recipients, primary-care physicians, and other family members; and strategies to help caregivers get in and keep positive moods, including doing more small everyday pleasant activities. In the telephone support group, participants received phone calls from research staff at the Older Adult and Family Center every other week. All the interventionists were bilingual or bicultural Chinese Americans. In addition, staff members came from different regions of China, including Taiwan, mainland China, and Hong Kong, so the interventions could be delivered in Mandarin, Cantonese, and English. Results were strongly supportive of the efficacy of the HBMP over the phone support program; these caregivers exhibited the greatest reduction in depressive symptoms and caregiver-related burden as well as positive changes on related measures of caregivers' quality of life.

A new project funded by the Alzheimer's Association is being carried out at the Older Adult and Family Center in collaboration with a variety of community-based agencies serving Chinese elders. The goal of this project is to create a series of videotapes/DVDs illustrating successful cognitive behavioral techniques used in the previously described caregiver project and to make this information more readily available to Chinese families.

The accompanying notebook will be written in both Mandarin and Cantonese dialects.

Conclusion and Future Research Directions

Studies show that ethnicity is a key factor in successful help, regardless of social or economic status (Braun & Browne, 1998). When working with Chinese American families, providers need to be aware that culture influences caregiving decisions. Helpful recommendations for those working with Chinese American families in general are as follows:

- Respect should be shown to patients, clients, and family members by addressing them by their last names and appropriate titles. Particular respect should be shown to elders.
- Encouraging family involvement is the key issue for building rapport with Chinese American caregivers.
- Health-care providers need to take an active role in finding solutions and confirming decisions; the approach most acceptable to Chinese American families is one that is kind and supportive but directive and parent-like.
- Because many Chinese families coming for treatment expect concrete help, providers are advised to focus on problem solving rather than on insight into their problems, as is typically done in cognitive behavioral intervention programs.
- New solutions to problems need to be action oriented and behaviorally based rather than focused on expression and discussion of feelings. For Chinese Americans, solving problems means taking effective action to handle problems.
- It is important that mental health professionals assume case management functions for the family, connecting them to resources in the community at large. Some of the social services needs may include financial assistance, child care, legal assistance, and immigration and citizenship issues.

Specifically for those who work with Chinese caregivers, it is recommended that they follow the above guidelines as well as involve all relevant family members (not just the primary caregivers) in the process. Although only a few examples of successful intervention programs have been developed and implemented for Chinese American caregivers, the future for this field is promising. More research is needed to develop culturally appropriate programs as well as effective outreach methods to recruit program participants. Gallagher-Thompson et al. (under review) suggest using professional and media referrals to bring attention to these programs for people in need. New intervention programs need to be integrated with the local community for advice and support; for example, to facilitate focus groups in order to gather information on the needs of Chinese American caregivers. Overall, there have been great efforts to provide more culturally appropriate services for the Chinese American population, but there is much room for improvement in the current services provided, as well as the need for more bilingual, bicultural researchers and service providers.

References

American Psychiatric Association. (1994). *Diagnostic and statistical manual of mental disorders* (4th ed.). Washington, DC: Author.

Beck, A. T., Rush, A. T., Shaw, B. F., & Emery, G. (1979). *Cognitive Therapy of Depression*. New York: Guilford Press.

Berry, J., Trimble, J. E., & Olmedo, E. L. (1986). Assessment of acculturation. In W. J. Lonner & J. W. Berry (Eds.), *Field methods in cross-cultural research* (pp. 291–324). Beverly Hills, CA: Sage.

Bowman, K. W., & Singer, P. A. (2001). Chinese seniors' perspectives on end-of-life decisions. *Social Science & Medicine, 53*(4), 455–464.

Braun, K. L., & Browne, C. (1998). Cultural values and caring patterns among Asian Pacific Islander Americans. In D. R. R. McNamara (Ed.), *Social gerontology* (pp. 155–182). New York: Greenwood Press.

Chou, K. R., LaMontagne, L. L., & Hepworth, J. T. (1999). Burden experienced by caregivers of relatives with dementia in Taiwan. *Nursing Research, 48*(4), 206–214.

Elliott, K. S., Di Minno, M., Lam, D., & Tu, A. M. (1996). Working with Chinese families in the context of dementia. In G. Yeo & D. Gallagher-Thompson (Eds.), *Ethnicity and the dementia* (pp. 89–100). Philadelphia, PA: Taylor & Francis.

Evans, D. A., Funkenstein, H. H., Albert, M. S., Scherr, P. A., Cook, N. R., Chown, M. J. et al. (1989). Prevalence of Alzheimer's disease in a community population of older persons. Higher than previously reported. *Journal of the American Medical Association, 262*(18), 2551–2556.

Evans, D. D. A., Smith, L. L. A., Scherr, P. P. A., Albert, M. M. S., Funkenstein, H. H. H., & Hebert, L. L. E. (1991). Risk of death from Alzheimer's disease in a community population of older persons. *American Journal of Epidemiology, 134*(4), 403–412.

Fuh, J. L., Wang, S. J., Liu, H. C., Liu, C. Y., & Wang, H. C. (1999). Predictors of depression among Chinese family caregivers of Alzheimer disease patients. *Alzheimer Disease & Associated Disorders, 13*(3), 171–175.

Gallagher-Thompson, D., Rabinowitz, Y., Tang, P., Tse, C., Kwo, E., Hsu, S. et al. (under review). Recruiting Chinese Americans for dementia caregiver intervention research. *American Journal of Geriatric Psychiatry*.

Gaugler, J. E., Kane, R. L., Kane, R. A., Clay, T., & Newcomer, R. (2003). Caregiving and institutionalization of cognitively impaired older people: Utilizing dynamic predictors of change. *Gerontologist, 43*(2), 219–229.

Hinton, L., Franz, C., & Friend, J. (2004). Pathways to dementia diagnosis: Evidence for cross-ethnic differences. *Alzheimer Disease & Associated Disorders, 18*(3), 134–144.

Hinton, L., Guo, Z., Hillygus, J., & Levkoff, S. (2000). Working with culture: A qualitative analysis of barriers to the recruitment of Chinese American family caregivers for dementia research. *Journal of Cross-Cultural Gerontology, 15*(2), 119–137.

Hinton, L., & Levkoff, S. (1999). Constructing Alzheimer's: Narratives of lost identities, confusion and loneliness in old age. *Culture, Medicine and Psychiatry, 23*, 453–475.

Ho, E. S., Bedford, R., & Goodwin, J. (1997). "Astronaut" families: A contemporary migration phenomenon. In W. Friesen, M. Ip. E. Ho, R. Bedford, & J. Goodwin (Eds.), *East Asian New Zealanders: Research on new migrants* (pp. 20–39). Auckland: Department of Sociology, Massey University.

Huang, Z. B., Neufeld, R. R., Likourezos, A., Breuer, B., Khaski, A., Milano, E. et al. (2003). Sociodemographic and health characteristics of older Chinese on admission to a nursing home: A cross-racial/ethnic study. *Journal of the American Geriatrics Society, 51*(3), 404–409.

Jones, P. S. (1995). Paying respect: Care of elderly parents by Chinese and Filipino American women. *Health Care for Women International, 16*, 385–398.

Lan, P. C. (2002). Subcontracting filial piety: Elder care in ethnic Chinese immigrant families in California. *Journal of Transcultural Nursing, 13*(3), 202–209.

Lee, E. (1996). Chinese families. In M. McGoldrick, J. Giordano, & K. K. Pearce (Eds.), *Ethnicity and family therapy* (2nd ed.) (pp. 249–267). New York: Guilford Press.

Lee, E. (1997). Chinese American families. In E. Lee (Ed.), *Working with Asian Americans: A guide for clinicians* (pp. 46–78). New York: Guilford.

Leung, L. (2004). *Validation of the cognitive abilities screening instrument (CASI) with cognitively intact and cognitively impaired Chinese elderly.* Unpublished doctoral dissertation, Pacific Graduate School of Psychology, Palo Alto, CA.

Lewinsohn, P. M., Munoz, R. F., Yougren, M. A., & Zeiss, A. M. (1986). *Control your depression.* New York: Prentice Hall.

Lin, R. -T., Lai, C. -L., Tai, C. -T., Liu, C. -K., Yen, Y. -Y., & Howng, S. -L. (1998). Prevalence and subtypes of dementia in southern Taiwan: Impact of age, sex, education, and urbanization. *Journal of the Neurological Sciences, 160*(1), 67–75.

Pang, E. C., Jordan-Marsh, M., Silverstein, M., & Cody, M. (2003). Health-seeking behaviors of elderly Chinese Americans: Shifts in expectations. *The Gerontologist, 43*(6), 864–874.

Pang, F. C., Chow, T. W., Cummings, J. L., Leung, V. P., Chiu, H. F., Lam, L. C. et al. (2002). Effects of neuropsychiatric symptoms of Alzheimer's disease on

Chinese and American caregivers. *International Journal of Geriatric Psychiatry, 17*(1), 29–34.

Sue, D. W., & Sue, D. (1999). Counseling Asian Americans. In D. W. Sue & D. Sue (Eds.), *Counseling the culturally different: Theory and practice* (3rd ed.) (pp. 255–271). New York: John Wiley & Sons.

Takamura, J. C. (1991). Asian and Pacific Islander elderly. In N. Mokuau (Ed.), *Handbook of social services for Asian and Pacific Islander Americans* (pp. 185–202). New York: Greenwood Press.

Tang, P. C. Y., Tse, C., Hsu, S., Leung, L. Y. L., Wang, P. -C., Kwo, E. et al. (in press). Coping with caregiving program for Chinese dementia caregivers. *The Gerontologist: Practice Concepts Section.*

Teng, E. L. (2002). Cultural and educational factors in the diagnosis of dementia. *Alzheimer's Disease and Associated Disorders, 16*(Supp. 2), 77–79.

Teng, E. L., Hasegawa, K., Homma, A., Imai, Y., Larson, E., Graves, A. et al. (1994). The cognitive abilities screening instrument (CASI): A practical test for cross-cultural epidemiological studies of dementia. *International Psychogeriatrics, 6,* 45–56.

U.S. Bureau of the Census. (2002). The Asian population: 2000. *Census 2000 Brief.* Washington, DC: U.S. Department of Commerce.

Yeo, G., & Gallagher-Thompson, D. (1996). *Ethnicity and the dementias.* Philadelphia, PA: Taylor & Francis.

Yick, A. G., & Gupta, R. (2002). Chinese cultural dimensions of death, dying and bereavement: Focus group findings. *Journal of Cultural Diversity, 9*(2), 32–43.

Yu, E. S., Kim, K., Liu, W. T., & Wong, S. C. (1993). Functional abilities of Chinese and Korean elders in congregate housing. In D. Barresi & D. Stull (Eds.), *Ethnic elderly and long term care* (pp. 87–100). New York: Springer.

Yu, E. S., Liu, W. T., Levy, P., Zhang, M. Y., Katzman, R., Lung, C. T. et al. (1989). Cognitive impairment among elderly adults in Shanghai, China. *The Journal of Gerontology, 44*(3), 97–106.

Zhan, L. (2004). Caring for family members with Alzheimer's Disease: Perspectives from Chinese American Caregivers. *Journal of Gerontological Nursing, 30*(8), 19–29.

Zhang, M. Y., Katzman, R., Salmon, D., Jin, H., Gai, G. J., Wang, Z. Y. et al. (1990). The prevalence of dementia and Alzheimer's disease in Shanghai, China: Impact of age, gender, and education. *Annals of Neurology, 27,* 428–437.

Appendix

The following is a list of national and international resources for the Chinese population.

International

Alzheimer's Disease Association

Blk 157, Toa Payoh Lorong 1, #01-1195, Singapore 310157
phone: +65 353 8734; fax: +65 353 8518
e-mail: alzheimers.tp@pacific.net.sg
Web site: www.alzheimers.org.sg)

The Catholic Foundation of Alzheimer's disease and related dementia

Web site: www.cfad.org.tw)

This foundation, located in Taiwan, provides information about educational services and adult day care centers.

Tzu Chi Foundation

USA Main Office, 206 E. Palm Ave., Monrovia, CA 91016
phone: 626-305-1188; fax: 626-305-1185

Tzu Chi provides food, clothing, material necessities, medical care, and spiritual consolation for victims of disasters, the sick, and older people. Tzu Chi's medical care network includes two hospitals in Taiwan and a system of free mobile clinics around the world. What is unique about Tzu Chi's medical service is the attitude of the personnel. Tzu Chi doctors and nurses treat patients as they would their own kin, and with the intent to heal patients in both body and mind. Tzu Chi not only aims to treat the symptoms of a disease, but also to address how a patient's illness affects daily life and family. Tzu Chi has established the world's third largest marrow donor registry, which has handled over one hundred marrow transplants both in Taiwan and abroad. (Information retrieved from www. tzuchi.org/)

National

Alzheimer's Association

225 N. Michigan Ave., Fl. 17, Chicago, IL, 606001-7633
phone: 1-800-272-3900
Web site: www.alz.org

The Alzheimer's Association is the first and largest voluntary health organization dedicated to finding prevention methods, treatments, and eventual cure for Alzheimer's disease.

Alzheimer's Association Diversity Toolbox
Web site: www.alz.org/Resources/Diversity/Chinese.asp

This Web site includes Chinese-language educational information about Alzheimer's disease and dementia care, as well as information about dementia-related issues in Chinese American communities. For example, fact sheets can be found in both English and Chinese about steps to enhance communication, interact with persons with Alzheimer's disease, understand challenging behaviors, and respond to persons with Alzheimer's disease.

Alzheimer's Disease Education & Referral Center (ADEAR)
Web site: www.alzheimers.org/

This Web site includes answers to specific questions about Alzheimer's disease; free publications about Alzheimer's disease symptoms, diagnosis, related disorders, risk factors, treatment, caregiving tips, home safety tips, and research; referrals to local supportive services and Alzheimer's disease centers that specialize in research and diagnosis; literature database searches for further research and reading; and training materials, guidelines, and a newsletter for health-care and caregiving professionals.

Catholic Charities USA
Web site: www.catholiccharitiesusa.org/

Catholic Charities USA is the membership association of one of the nation's largest social service networks. Catholic Charities agencies and institutions nationwide provide vital social services to people in need, regardless of their religious, social, or economic backgrounds. Catholic Charities USA supports and enhances the work of its membership by providing networking opportunities, national advocacy and media efforts, program development, training and technical assistance, and financial support.

CHAPTER 13

Working with Filipino American Families

MELEN R. MCBRIDE

This chapter focuses on cultural values and practices of Filipino Americans associated with caregiving for their elders. Patterns of family help seeking and shared caregiving are discussed as elements of Filipino American families' holistic approach to the complex process of caring for an aging family member. Selected resources, suggestions for providers, and vignettes are included to highlight concepts, help increase cultural awareness, and contribute to skill building when working with Filipino Americans. Demographic and historical perspectives are included as background information on the Filipino population in the United States.

General Description of the Population

The Filipino American community is a culturally eclectic group. Their ancestral heritage has been influenced by many cultures. From pre-colonial times to the present, parts of the Malayan, Chinese, Euro-Spanish, American, Muslim, and Judeo-Christian traditions (in particular, Catholicism) have found their way into the Filipino culture as it is known today. Its multiculturalism has also been influenced by geographic boundaries defined by 7,200 islands, of which only 1,000 are habitable. Thus, the art of blending and infusing cultural traits and values has become a dynamic feature of the Filipino personality.

Based on Census 2000 data for older Asian Americans only, Filipinos are the second largest population aged 55 and over (21.2%) and 65 and over (20.6%). Of the latter age group, 90.5% are foreign born, 17% are linguistically isolated, 29.4% had less than a ninth grade education, and 8.4% live in poverty (Yeo & Hikoyeda, 2006). This includes World War II veterans who came to the United States after Section 260 of the U.S. Immigration and Naturalization Act was passed in 1990, granting immediate citizenship to an estimated 175,000 eligible Filipino veterans, many of whom lived in the Philippines. In 2003, the Veterans Administration estimated there were 29,350 remaining veterans, and about 7,000 are in the United States (Lachica, 2005; Ramos, 2005). Many of them continue to face economic challenges, have no stable support network, are at risk for health crises, and are ineligible for the usual veteran's benefits (Chin, 1993; Federal Council on Aging, 1994; Lachica, 2005; McBride, 1993). It is projected that the flow of aging Filipino immigrants could continue into the next century.

Of the 2.4 million Filipinos in the United States in 2000, 78.2% reported only one race. Many Filipino households are multigenerational, with a mean household size of 3.41 persons. Married couples (61.7%) and nonfamily (20%) comprise the bulk of Filipino households. Only 29.3% of households speak English only and 24.1% speak English "less well." While 50% of all Asians reside in three states—California, New York, and Hawaii—49.3% of the Filipino-only subgroup live in one state—California. Sixty-five percent of Filipino females, 16 years of age and older, are in the labor force—a rate that exceeds that for all Asians (56.4%) and for the total population (57.5%). Although the median income for Filipino males is $35,560 and $31,450 for females, they earn less than Asian males ($40,650) and the total working population ($37,057) (Reeves & Bennett, 2004). This demographic profile suggests that a frail immigrant Filipino elder who lives with other adults may be in a setting where caregivers would need affordable and culturally and linguistically appropriate resources. With a high proportion of Filipino women in the labor force, home-based care, including respite care, may be a critical need in these households.

Truly monolingual elders may be difficult to find among Filipino elders, yet the preference to communicate in a Filipino language is strong. There are an estimated 80 or more languages in the Philippines. However, eight major distinct languages are spoken (Lamzon, 1978). These languages, Pilipino or Tagalog (the national Filipino language), Cebuano, Ilocano, Illongo, Bikolano, Waray, Kapampangan, and Pangasinanes, are well represented in the Filipino American community (Bautista, 1993; Peterson, 1978; Valencia-Go, 1989). For many Filipino immigrants, English-speaking skills are much more developed than are comprehension skills. However, verbal skills are strongly influenced by the indigenous language they speak.

Immigration History

The year 1763 marked the arrival of the first Filipino immigrants in the United States. They were the first Asian immigrants, settling in Louisiana to escape forced labor and enslavement in Spanish ships involved in the Spanish–Mexican galleon trade (1565–1815) carrying cargos from the Philippines. These *Manilamen* and their descendants, the Filipino Cajuns, introduced wine making from coconut (*tuba*[1]) and initiated the shrimp sun-drying process as an industry. From 1763 to 1906, mariners, adventurers, and domestic helpers arrived in southeastern Louisiana. Some moved on to California, and others went to Hawaii, Washington, and Alaska, seeking employment in the whaling or fishing industry (Espina, 1974; Tompar-Tiu & Sustento-Seneriches, 1995).

The second period (1906–1934) of Filipino immigration consisted of three subgroups. The *sakadas* were less-educated rural laborers who were recruited to replace Japanese labor on Hawaiian plantations. They intended to return home and had little inclination to be a part of American society. Those who stayed and remained single are referred to as *manongs* (older brothers) or *old-timers*. The *pensionadas*, a group of Filipino scholars with limited government subsidies, returned home after completing their education, while the unsuccessful ones stayed behind. Later immigrants, the *pinoys*, came to seek economic prosperity and join their families. Many worked on the farmlands of California (San Joaquin valley, Sacramento, and Salinas) and Washington, in the Alaska fisheries and canning factories, and in service industries as domestics, busboys, and janitors. Considered an economic and social threat, the *pinoys* experienced blatant discrimination and violence that eventually led to changes in the immigration laws and expansion of the antimiscegenation laws in California and other states to include Filipinos (Tompar-Tiu & Sustento-Seneriches, 1995; Yeo et al., 1998). Many remained unmarried, relegated to low social status and low-paying jobs. Many of the oldest-old Filipino elders today may have been part of this group, or the old-old might have been children in that period.

The third period (1935–1965) of Filipino immigration included more women and families. It consisted of World War II veterans, military staff and their families, students, and professionals and their families. Although this period began the "brain drain" in the Philippines, the contribution of Filipinos to American society was significant despite the economic exploitation and racism they experienced (Tompar-Tiu & Sustento-Seneriches, 1995; Yeo et al., 1998).

From 1965 to the present, more diversity occurred in the Filipino American community. The fourth period of immigration included highly educated, predominantly female professionals; participants in the 1965 Family Reunification Program, especially the older "followers of children"; aging World War II veterans; refugees of the Marcos regime; and short-stay visitors (students, businesspeople, and tourists). The Filipinos with short-term visas, called *overseas contract workers* (OCW) by the Philippine government, developed into a labor pool for low-paying or unpopular jobs, such as those in long-term care facilities, the home-care industry, and others with undesirable working conditions. Most Filipinos who are now caregivers to elders in their families may have been child immigrants (first generation) during the third and fourth periods of Filipino immigration or are native born (second-generation) children of earlier immigrants. Some immigrants have grown old "in place." They expect to be cared for by their children or other members of the extended family in various ways, including through formal resources. Such expectations come from the traditional Filipino values of filial responsibility and respect for elders, the effects of acculturation, and their experience with the health-care system.

A new period of Filipino immigration is evolving at the turn of the 21st century due to the severe nursing shortage in the United States. New arrivals known as *overseas Filipino workers* (OFW) consist of professional nurses contracted by health-care institutions for two years, physicians who retrained in nursing, physical therapists, or other health professionals who have family members in the United States (Kimura, 2005; Peterson, 2002; Santos, 2005; Stephenson, 2005).

Traditional Family System and Values

The Filipino family has been described as a most able social service system in which respect and love for parents are taught and expected of children (National Media Production Center, 1974). Traditional Filipino American families pass on this value to the new generation. In Philippine society, it is acceptable for several generations of families to share one household. Thus, caring for aging family members is integrated over time into the family dynamics. Putting the family welfare before the self, loyalty, and interdependence are traits deeply imbedded in the Filipino culture (Almirol, 1982; Medina, 1991). Family is the major source of emotional, moral, and economic support.

Filipino men are expected to be heads of households and providers of the family's economic security and safety. However, the traditional family tends to be matriarchal. The women raise the children, nurture the family, and manage home finances. It is common practice for women to be primary decision makers while being respectful of the men's role, making every effort to preserve it (McBride, Nora, & Periyakoil, 2005; Medina, 1991; Miranda, McBride, & Spangler, 1998). A highly acculturated, bicultural older woman may adapt shared decision making with her spouse. In a multigenerational family in which acculturation levels vary across generations, eldercare is woven into the complex dynamics of the household. Often, the Filipino woman keeps the family functional. Because employment and career opportunities are attractive options to them, particularly the baby boom generation, we can anticipate an increase in the number of families accessing formal home-care services for their elders.

A traditional family consists of the nuclear family, bilateral (father's and mother's) extended family, and kin (cousins, in-laws, godparents, townmates, or friends), who keep close emotional, moral, spiritual, and economic ties (Medina, 1991). It is an open system, absorbing new members not only by marriage but also through kinship, compassionate friendships, or *utang na loob* (feelings of indebtedness). Shared responsibilities and recognition of kin relations are considered essential elements of the extended family (Castillo, Weisblat, & Villareal, 1968).

Studies of Filipino indigenous personality theory describe an emphasis on shared identity interacting as coequals, or *kapwa* (Enriquez, 1990), as the foundation of Filipino values. These values—interacting with others on an equal basis, sensitivity to and regard for others, respect and concern, helping out, understanding and making up for others' limitations, rapport, and acceptance—stress the importance of sensitivity and close attention to other people and relationships. The social function of smooth interpersonal relationship may have evolved out of the survival needs of ancestral tribes, living in an agricultural archipelago of 7,200 islands where natural calamities are common occurrences (Enriquez, 1990; Tompar-Tiu & Sustento-Seneriches, 1995). As major historical events and sociopolitical conditions occurred, including integration into new cultures, these factors may have strengthened. It may be advantageous to Filipino elders that these values are preserved to ensure a caregiving system free of bureaucracy.

Levels of Interactions

In everyday interactions, eight interrelated levels of relationships have been identified in two major categories: *Ibang-Tao* (the external or "outsider") with five levels and *Hindi Ibang-Tao* (the internal or "one of us") with three levels. These modes of interaction range from *Pakikitungo* (civility, Level 1) to *Pakikiisa* (oneness or full trust, Level 8). At *Pakikisalamuha* (Level 2), one may superficially choose to interact with others, whereas *Pakikilahok* (joining or participating, Level 3) has a degree of commitment. *Pakikibagay* (conforming, Level 4) and *Pakikisama* (adjusting, Level 5) may include some behavioral or attitudinal change. When a relationship reaches *Pakikipagpalagayang-loob* (mutual trust, Level 6) and *Pakikisangkot* (active involvement, Level 7), the chances of important breakthroughs can occur. To achieve *Pakikiisa* (full trust, Level 8) requires long-term commitment and sincere desire to nurture the relationship (Enriquez, 1979; Pe-Pua, 1990; Santiago, 1982). Health-care providers may find these stages helpful when working with the family to plan care for the elder.

Respect for Elders

Language and nonverbal behaviors are used by the Filipino family to teach and show respect. Children are taught at an early age to be respectful to persons older than they, even when the age difference is small (Blust & Scheidt, 1988; Ishisaka & Tagaki, 1982). Family members are accorded special titles of respect and reverence. They are as follows: *Lolo* (grandfather), *Lola* (grandmother), *Tatay* (father), *Nanay* (mother), *Kuya* (older brother), *Ate* (older sister), *Tito* (uncle), *Tita* (aunt), *Manong* (man older than you), and *Manang* (woman older than you). To address the person with respect, one uses the title before the first name (e.g., *Lola* Maria). Respectful and polite verbal responses to elders or strangers must include the word *po* for emphasis. For example, "Thank you, grandfather" translates to "*Salamat po, Lolo*" (Lamzon, 1978; Wolff, 1988). With permission from the elder, a provider may use these titles to help build a trust relationship. A respectful gesture consists of a young person taking an elder's hand and touching his or her forehead with the back of the elder's hand. This is accompanied by a gently spoken verbal request: "*Mano po, Lolo?*" (conceptual translation, "May I greet you with respect, please?").

Thus, the oldest family members are the most respected persons in the household (Eggan, 1968; Medina, 1991), and highly traditional parents impart this value to their children. Competing expectations and highly individualistic social norms in American society tend to lessen the impact of this tradition in younger Filipino Americans. Some tensions in intergenerational or multicultural households may be associated with these changes. However, filial piety remains strong in Filipino American families (Superio, 1993), and Filipino researchers assert that caring for the elder as a family obligation is still well rooted in the mores of Philippine society (Enriquez, 1992; Medina, 1991).

Perspectives on Dementia in the Filipino Community

There is little information for Filipino American elders on disability rates associated with aging and major chronic health problems, including dementia (McBride, Morioka-Douglas, & Yeo, 1996). In the absence of epidemiologic data, the prevalence of dementia or Alzheimer's disease is poorly understood in older Filipinos. Among cases seen during the first eight years of nine California Alzheimer's Disease and Diagnostic Centers, Filipinos comprised 0.7% of the total number of individuals who came for evaluation, compared to approximately 2% of the population of older Californians (Yeo & Lieberman, 1993, unpublished data). Studies of risk factors for various types of dementia in Filipinos are unavailable, although the high prevalence of coronary heart disease and uncontrolled hypertension among those 50 years of age and older (Angel, Armstrong, & Klatsky, 1989; Garde, Spangler, & Miranda, 1994; Klatsky & Armstrong, 1991; Liu & Yu, 1985; National Heart Lung and Blood Institute [NIMH], 2000a, 2000b; Nora & McBride, 1996; Ryan et al., 2000; Stavig, Igra, & Leonard, 1988) strongly suggests the possibility of vascular-type dementia for the group. Vascular complications of diabetes may be another risk factor for dementia. Fujimoto (1995) found that Filipinos in Hawaii had the highest prevalence rate of diabetes among all Asians and Pacific Islanders (21.8%). Zhang, Anderson, Lavine, & Mantel (1990) reported cases in Guam of Filipinos with Parkinson's disease and amyotrophic lateral sclerosis who also had changes in mental function.

Precise information on the degree to which strokes, Alzheimer's disease, vascular dementia, diabetes, and neurological conditions may be taking their toll on Filipino elders and their families is limited, and culturally appropriate interventions have yet to be designed to assist family caregivers. The multilinguality of Filipino elders has important implications in the differential diagnosis of cognitive impairments. Screening tools to evaluate memory function have not been developed and tested on older Filipinos. Scores from the Mini-Mental Status Examination (MMSE) may be influenced by literacy level, language comprehension, and computational skills (McBride, Morioka-Douglas, & Yeo, 1996).

According to key informants in the Filipino community, memory loss is associated with growing old and is not necessarily related to certain health problems, such as diabetes or hypertension. The term *dementia* is rarely used in casual conversation, although *Alzheimer's* or *senility* is commonly used to talk about cognitive changes. Behaviors such as forgetfulness, being "picky," and wandering are considered signs of memory loss. In some situations, these behaviors may be explained by "too much going on in the brain" or side effects of medications (McBride, Fee, & Yeo,

2005). The belief that Alzheimer's disease can be passed on could delay early diagnosis. Families are protective of the children's future, and indications of a genetic predisposition to a disease would be a source of *hiya* (shame) or embarrassment. When the disease is suspected or a diagnosis is confirmed, the elder or family may initially discuss concerns with a trusted family member, friend, or a minister (McBride, Morioka-Douglas, & Yeo, 1996; Tompar-Tiu & Sustento-Seneriches, 1995).

Caregiving in Filipino Families

Caring for elders is a strong Filipino value. The tendency for Filipino American families to accept caregiving responsibility by keeping elders at home may create stressful and difficult situations. Conversely, when the family is able to act on its value system, a sense of harmony, satisfaction, and inner peace are the potential rewards. Health beliefs of the elder and the family may significantly influence their caregiving approach and their willingness to access resources (Bautista, 1993; Orque, 1983).

Older Filipino men who are caregivers of spouses may relegate many of the physical aspects of caregiving to adult children and retain responsibility for managing the household. However, when the husband is a care recipient, the family supports the spouse who would be the primary caregiver, if she is able. Healthy older Filipino Americans who are acculturated and have adapted Western values may prefer to make their own healthcare decisions (McBride, Nora, & Periyakoil, 2005). They may consult family members during the process or simply choose to inform the family of their decision.

Decisions about elder care may be influenced by socio-economic factors, especially when an affluent family member is providing significant resources. In a power imbalance, the family might defer the final resolution of issues to this person after a series of discussions and information exchange. Regardless of sex, an elder in a traditional family may expect the firstborn adult child to have the primary role of decision maker. If the person lives outside the United States, telephone and Internet services are used extensively, and a family visit is arranged, if feasible. On other occasions, the family may delegate the decision making to a family member or a kin who is a health professional or employed in health care. They would expect the decision maker to use his or her knowledge about health to educate the family and the elder and to advocate for their needs (McBride, Nora, & Periyakoil, 2005).

In a pilot study, 10 family caregivers for three frail elders were interviewed to describe caregiving roles and functions. All participants had college educations; 80% were professionals and 20% had home-based businesses. Four primary caregivers indicated that their role evolved by family consensus (50%), self-assignment (25%), and default (25%). Six family members functioned as secondary caregivers. Their responsibilities included assessing family resources, linking family to community resources, providing caregiving information, teaching home-care skills, and providing psychosocial support (McBride & Parreno, 1992).

The primary caregivers' tasks consisted of physical care, health maintenance, financial management, leisure and recreation, spiritual care, transportation, and supply inventory. Respite care was available through the secondary caregivers. Debriefings, family meetings, music sessions, family events, pastoral visits, telephone conferences, and networking were strategies used to share caregiving functions. Seven caregivers lived within a 15–75 mile radius of the elder's home—a factor that enabled families to share activities and offer emotional support to each other. Short-term, formal home-care services were carefully screened before they were utilized.

With the increasing demands and pressures on many Filipino American families, their help-seeking behaviors are often described by service providers and leaders in the Filipino community during consultations and training activities. At the Stanford Geriatric Education Center, Melen McBride summarized these behaviors in six modes of help-seeking patterns using indigenous terms from the community:

1. *Kayahin na natin* (rely on ourselves): This may involve a conscious decision to alter family priorities: a woman may work less hours or quit her job, family tasks may be redistributed, and young family members are expected to rearrange their priorities (e.g., a socially active, 24-year-old, U.S.-born daughter was asked to care for a frail, 83-year-old family friend three times a week while going to graduate school and maintaining two part-time jobs and outside interests).

2. *Maghanap ng paraan* (search for a strategy): Outside resources may be cautiously accessed to protect the family's privacy. Fear of stigma and concerns over genetic links to a disease could limit optimum use of services (Anderson, 1983; Tompar-Tiu & Sustento-Seneriches, 1995).

3. *Tingnan natin* (let's see how it goes): Services are used, but conclusions about the effectiveness of services are delayed. The availability of a culturally compatible provider is critical to utilization, particularly when the elder has had minimal social contact outside the family system before the impairment.

4. *Magbisitahan* (visit family): Family visits across the United States might be arranged for respite care, redistribution of financial burden,

closure on unfinished family matters, reciprocation for past indebtedness (*utang na loob*), and other mutually acceptable reasons. For
the elder with undiagnosed dementia, an unstable environment may
lead to unintended problems.

5. *Magkuha ng bantay* (get a trusted companion): Providing a companion (*bantay*) who is often brought over from the Philippines may
have a more positive outcome. However, many families would not be
able to arrange this option.

6. *Iuwi na* (take elder home): Taking the elder back to the Philippines
has its advantages and disadvantages.

The last three patterns require a strong and effective extended family network
in the United States and in the Philippines. Some of these patterns appear to
be adapted for other issues as well, such as childrearing and parenting.

For traditional families, the presence of an elder in the home, even one
who is frail, can be a source of comfort and validation of the family's identity and cultural values. How and when the decision is made and eventually
implemented could tie up the family's time and resources. Those without
extended families or close ties with kin would not have this option. For
many Filipino Americans, resolving complex caregiving issues may be their
first experience with a family crisis in the United States. Caregivers may
deny feeling stressed, especially in situations when family relationships are
involved. Brown (1982) found catecholamine excretion level to be a more
accurate measure of stress over self-report of stress for Filipino Americans.

In some instances, the Filipino community takes on caregiving
responsibilities, as an extended family, for elders who do not have biological ties in the United States. In the San Francisco Bay area, a group
formed to assist newly naturalized World War II Filipino veterans who
were frail and at risk of elder abuse because of their social and living conditions (Chin, 1993; McBride, 1993). Basic needs were assessed, and formal
and informal resources were mobilized. For the few elders who opted to
return to the Philippines after social service interventions, the community supported their decision with donations to a travel fund. The Filipino
value of helping out and concern for the other person (Enriquez, 1990),
as demonstrated in this situation, is also known as *bayanihan*. The older
Filipino's natural religiosity can be a vital force for coping with stressors,
accepting suffering as a spiritual offering, explaining causes and remedies
for illnesses, and being passive and patient by accepting one's fate.

As traditional families become acculturated, and generations of Filipino Americans adopt more American values, filial piety and respect for
aging parents may be expressed in new ways. Superio (1993) interviewed

Filipino Americans to ascertain their beliefs about filial responsibility and compared these beliefs across age groups. Ninety percent of the participants believed that the duty to care for aging parents should be taught to the children. When the issue of caring for elders in the children's home was raised, 57% of the young native-born, 54% of the young foreign-born, and 50% of the older foreign-born participants believed that children should care for them in their homes. Seventy-four percent of the middle-aged, foreign-born participants preferred that their children "give support" and "make other arrangements," but decidedly "not a nursing home." Perhaps at the time of the study, the middle-aged group may actually have been involved in caregiving. A hands-on caregiving experience as one of the "sandwich generation" may explain this group's responses.

It appears that Filipino Americans still hold strong beliefs that children should care for their aging parents. The doctrines of the Catholic Church tend to reinforce these beliefs, and many turn to the church community for moral, emotional, and spiritual support. Family caregivers may also seek assistance from indigenous faith healers, a community resource originating from animism in ancestral times (Andres, 1987). Although a traditional family caregiver may use both these opposing systems, Bulatao (1964) explained that this "split-level Christianity" seldom creates guilt or moral dilemma and may be due to profound faith in God and God's mercy. Care giving may also represent the "sacrificing-self" that embodies a tribute to the elder, stress, adversity, commitment, triumph, and satisfaction in an enduring family relationship (Galang, 1995). The continuous flow of Filipino immigrants to the United States may keep this value alive for generations.

Assessing the family's knowledge and skills to care for a frail elder is an important aspect of the plan of care. Supporting family caregivers and preparing for gradual shifts in future caregiving practices are necessary elements for cross-cultural caregiving programs. An intervention model could be considered that contains community-based, family-centered programs providing culturally accurate information, infused with humor and tailored to participants' literacy level; emphasis on realistic coping strategies; and use of electronic media (CD-ROM, I-Pod, etc.; National Heart, Lung, and Blood Institute, 2003). Research on the effectiveness of support groups for Filipino family caregivers of elders is yet to be developed; however, models implemented in Asian groups with bicultural, bilingual facilitators could be adapted.

Resources for Filipino Families and Service Providers

The following nonprofit community agencies may be contacted for health education and social service programs:

The *Alzheimer's Disease Association of the Philippines* (ADAP) is a recently formed organization. For more information, phone 632-723-1039 or e-mail to secretariat@alzphilippines.com.

The *Family Caregiver Alliance* offers programs to support and sustain families and friends who provide long-term care at home. The alliance is located at 180 Montgomery St., Ste 1100, San Francisco, CA 94104; phone: 800-445-8106; fax: 415-434-3388; e-mail: info@caregive.org; Web site: www.caregiver.org/caregiver/jsp/home.jsp

The *Filipino American Service Group, Inc.* (FASGI) provides social services to low-income and homeless Asian Pacific Islanders individuals, with the language and cultural capacity, in Los Angeles County, 135 N. Park View Street, Loa Angeles, CA 90026; phone: 213-487-9804; fax: 213-487-9805; e-mail: FASGI@fasgi.org; Web site: www.fasgi.org

International Community Health Services has outreach services for the Filipino community to increase access to services. It offers in-language materials, brochures, assistance in scheduling appointments, and other services to the community. Contact the Community Health Education Department at 206-788-3676 or visit the Web site (www.ichs.com/clinicalservices/healtheducation/communityoutreach).

The *Kalusugan Wellness Center* has health education programs for primary prevention and health promotion to Filipino seniors, adults, and youth. The Fil-Am Wellness Center is located at 1419 E. 8th Street, National City, CA 91950. Visit the Web site (www.webkalusugan.org) for more information.

The *National Alliance to Nurture the Aged and the Youth* (NANAY) provides psychological, social, health, and emotional support for youth and elders through intergenerational activities. It is located in Florida (South Dade and Palm Beach), California (San Francisco/Bay Area), Arkansas (Little Rock), and Michigan. Visit the Web site (www.nanay.com/) for more information or call 305-981-3232 or 305-981-4000 (health center).

Suggestions for Working with Filipino American Families

Because of the diversity among Filipino Americans, the following strategies may not work with every Filipino family. Awareness of how acculturation reshapes values and beliefs helps in modifying the approaches for the best culturally sensitive care of Filipino elders with dementia.

Family and Cultural Assessment

1. Identify beliefs about health and aging that the family uses to explain the cause and prognosis of memory impairment or disability. Family stories provide important information. Allow time for building rapport.
2. Ascertain how the family makes decisions, who makes major decisions, and who the "expert consultants" in the family are. These experts are the family's informal resource, who may be health professionals.
3. Encourage the decision makers, family experts, and caregivers to describe help-seeking options that are being considered.
4. Create an extended-family genogram that represents the various caregiving roles and resources for the elder. These may include individuals who live outside the United States.
5. Identify aspects of the immigration history of the family, the caregiver, and the elder that may be useful for planning treatment and management of dementia.

Communication and Building Trust

1. Attend to physical symptoms first at the initial visit to reassure the elder that complaints are taken seriously.
2. Write clearly on a prescription pad all medical recommendations, not just medications. Handwritten recommendations to take home are preferable over standard impersonal form letters. This helps with adherence to a treatment plan and for discussing the plan with family and friends.
3. Utilize a bilingual, bicultural health-care provider to make the first and follow-up contacts until the plan of care has been agreed upon. This person can be designated as the "culture expert" who can be called upon for consultation for as long as service is provided.
4. Create a pool of "cultural experts" who are active in the Filipino community with appropriate training for those who are interested. Keep in mind that not every Filipino is an expert in his or her culture.
5. Develop a list of words (Tagalog and English) that are used often by the caregiver, family, and elder to talk about dementia and other issues. Incorporate them into the service provider's vocabulary when interacting with the elder and the family.

6. Be prepared to answer personal questions, such as "Are you married?" or "Do you have children?" Although it may not relate to provider's goal, the exchange enables most Filipino families to translate the interaction into human terms. These icebreakers may move you sooner to higher levels of interactions.

Issues Related to Advance Directives or Guardianship

An advance directive is a person's written declaration of treatment preferences and of a designated decision maker in the event of serious incapacitating or terminal illness that renders the person unable to make decisions.

1. Clarify who is the designated decision maker. Traditional elders usually prefer to pass on the responsibility to firstborns. Gender is less of an issue than birth order.
2. Determine what an advance directive means to the elder and the family. Currently, this concept is beginning to be discussed in households when acculturated members bring up the subject. Faith-based educational programs may contribute to a gradual awareness of the topic. Some may feel superstitious, and others may harbor guilt feelings from unexpressed or unexplored moral and ethical conflicts. Many traditional Filipino Catholics learned their values in a highly authoritative environment.
3. Provide enough time for consultation, decision making, and getting consents and signatures.

Vignettes

The following actual cases highlight some points discussed in this chapter. They were slightly altered to protect the families' privacy.

All Children Are Responsible

Mr. H., an 84-year-old widower, was admitted to a skilled nursing facility for short-term rehabilitation after a mild stroke. He was considered cognitively intact, although the staff noted occasional memory deficit. Family members were asked about signing an advance directive. Mr. H.'s three daughters had discussed this issue with him at different times before his illness. However, he had not expressed his preference at that time. The family indicated that they would again discuss the issue with their father before the social worker's interview. After several sessions with the social worker, Mr. H. felt ready and listed the names of his three daughters in birth order as being legally responsible for his welfare.

Although the family was not consulted by Mr. H., the siblings accepted the arrangement. Mr. H. felt confident that his daughters, who were all professionals, could handle issues that might come up. The daughters requested that in an emergency, they should be contacted by birth order.

A Family Health Team

Mr. and Mrs. T., an aging couple, immigrated to the United States to join their firstborn adult daughter. They left behind a son and his family, and an unmarried son and daughter who were also scheduled to immigrate to the United States in a few months. When they were reunited, they lived together and shared resources. The oldest daughter, who continued to live on her own, facilitated the adjustment period. Because of her previous work experience as a public health nurse, she was able to guide the family in accessing health and community resources. Visits with extended family members residing in the East served to rekindle kinships from the past. Years later, when the father died, the household had stabilized. All the siblings who lived in the United States remained single. When Mrs. T. had her first stroke, the oldest daughter (the public health nurse) negotiated with Mrs. T.'s physician to treat the episode in the home. In 3 days, Mrs. T. pulled out of the crisis with slight hemiplegia, apraxia, and mild dementia. A home rehabilitation program was instituted with the assistance of a home-care agency. The son learned ambulation techniques, and the other daughter took over personal care training. Treatment continued to be arranged through the oldest daughter. Full physical recovery was not expected, but the family managed the post-stroke residuals. Mrs. T. feels she is receiving the best care any mother could get from her children.

The vignettes underscore the importance of cross-cultural awareness and communication. Creating a culturally competent health-care system has many challenges. The first step is to become aware of one's cultural values to understand how they might facilitate or hinder constructive patient–provider interactions.

Note

1. Non-English terms used in the chapter are in Pilipino or Tagalog, the national language in the Philippines.

References

Almirol, E. (1982). Rights and obligations in Filipino-American families. *Journal of Comparative Studies, 13*(3), 291–305.

Anderson, J. (1983). Health and illness in the Pilipino immigrants. *Western Journal of Medicine, 139*(6), 811–819.

Andres, T. D. (1987). *Understanding the Filipino.* Quezon City, Philippines: New Day.

Angel, A., Armstrong, M. A., & Klatsky, A. L. (1989). Blood pressure among Asian Americans living in Northern California. *American Journal of Cardiology, 64,* 237–240

Bautista, M. (1993). *Social service utilization between noninstitutionalized frail Pilipino and White elders.* Unpublished master's thesis, San Francisco State University, San Francisco, CA.

Blust, E., & Scheidt, R. (1988). Perceptions of filial responsibility by elderly Filipino widows and their primary caregivers. *International Journal on Aging and Human Development, 26*(2), 91–106.

Brown, D. E. (1982). Physiological stress and culture in a group of Filipino Americans: A preliminary investigation.. *Annals of Human Biology, 9*(6), 55–63.

Bulatao, J. (1964). Hiya. *Philippine Studies, 12,* 424–438.

Castillo, G., Weisblat, A., & Villareal, F. (1968). The concepts of nuclear and extended family: An exploration of empirical referents. *International Journal of Comparative Sociology, 9*(1), 1–4.

Chin, S. (1993, December 20). Filipino veterans poor in land they fought for. *San Francisco Examiner,* p. A-5.

Eggan, F. (1968). Philippine social structure. In G. Guthrie (Ed.), *Six perspectives in the Philippines* (pp. 1–48). Manila, Philippines: Bookmark.

Enriquez, V. (1979). Towards cross-cultural knowledge through cross-indigenous methods and perspective. *Philippine Journal of Psychology, 12,* 9–15.

Enriquez, V. (1990). *Hellside in paradise: The Honolulu gangs* (Report for the Community Affairs Committee, Center for Philippine Studies). Honolulu: University of Hawaii.

Enriquez, V. (1992). *From colonial to liberation psychology: The Philippine experience.* Quezon City: University of the Philippine Press.

Espina, M. (1974). Filipinos in New Orleans. *The Proceedings of the Louisiana Academy of Sciencess, 37,* 117–121.

Federal Council on Aging. (1994). *Annual report to the President.* Washington, DC: Author.

Fujimoto, W. (1995). Diabetes in Asian and Pacific Islander Americans. *Diabetes in America.* Washington, DC: National Institute of Health, National Institute of Diabetes, Digestive, and Kidney Diseases.

Galang, C. (1995). *Care of aging parents: The experiences of middle-aged Filipino women.* Doctoral dissertation, University of San Diego. (UMI Dissertation No. 9532648).

Garde, P., Spangler, Z., & Miranda, B. (1994). *Filipino Americans in New Jersey: A health study.* Final report of the Philippine Nurses Association of America to the State of New Jersey Department of Health, Office of Minority Health.

Ishisaka, H., & Tagaki, C. (1982). Social work with Asian and Pacific Americans. In J. Green (Ed.), *Cultural awareness in the human services* (pp. 122–156). Englewood Cliffs, NJ: Prentice Hall.

Kimura, A. (2005, October 22). Asia: Philippines in shock from heavy loss of doctors and nurses. *The Asahi Shimbun.* Retrieved October 25, 2005, from www.asahi.com/english/Herald-asahi/TKY200510220131.html

Klatsky, A. L., & Armstrong, M. A. (1991). Cardiovascular risk factors among Asian Americans living in Northern California. *American Journal of Public Health, 81,* 1423–1428.

Lachica, E. (2005). *VA Fact Sheet: VA Benefits for Filipino Veterans,* American Coalition for Filipino Veterans, Inc.

Lamzon, T. (1978). *Handbook of Philippine language groups.* Quezon City, Philippines: Manila University Press.

Liu, W., & Yu, E. (1985). Asian Pacific American elderly: Mortality differentials, health status, and use of services. *Journal of Applied Gerontology, 4*(1), 35–64.

McBride, M. (1993, March). *Health status of recently naturalized Filipino WWII veterans.* Paper presented at the annual conference of the American Society on Aging, Chicago.

McBride, M., Fee, C., & Yeo, G. (2005). Filipino Americans. In G. Yeo (Ed.), *Mental health aspects of diabetes in elders from diverse ethnic backgrounds.* Stanford, CA: Geriatric Education Center.

McBride, M., Marioka-Douglas, N., & Yeo, G. (1996). *Aging and health: Asian/Pacific Island American elders* (Working Paper Series No. 3, 2nd ed.). Stanford, CA: Stanford Geriatric Education Center.

McBride, M., Nora, R., & Periyakoil, V. J. (2005). Filipino Americans. *Doorway thoughts: Cross-cultural health care for older adults* (Vol. II). Sudbury, MA: Jones & Bartlett.

McBride, M., & Parreno, H. (1992). Generativity and caregiving: Functions at midlife of women in Filipino families. *The Gerontologist, 33,* 268.

Medina, B. (1991). *The Filipino family.* Diliman, Quezon City: University of the Philippines Press.

Miranda, B., McBride, M., & Spangler, Z. (1998). Filipino Americans. In L. D. Purnell & B. J. Paulanka (Eds.), *Transcultural health care: A culturally competent approach* (pp. 245–272). Philadelphia, PA: F.A. Davis.

National Heart, Lung, and Blood Institute. (2000a). *Addressing cardiovascular health in Asian Americans and Pacific Islanders: A background report* (NIH Publication No. 00-3647). Bethesda, MD: Author.

National Heart, Lung, and Blood Institute. (2000b). *Asian Americans and Pacific Islander Workshops: Summary report on cardiovascular health* (NIH Publication No. 00-3793). Bethesda, MD: Author.

National Heart, Lung, and Blood Institute. (2003). *Cardiovascular risk in the Filipino community: Formative research from Daly City and San Francisco, California.* U.S. Department of Health and Human Services, NIH, NHLBI: Author.

National Media Production Center. (1974). The Filipino family: Most able social welfare agency. *New Philippines*, p. 23.

Nora, R., & McBride, M. R. (1996). Health needs of Filipino Americans [Special Issue]. *Asian American Pacific Islander Journal of Health, 4*(1–3), 138–139.

Orque, M. (1983). Nursing care of Filipino American patients. In M. Orque et al. (Eds.), *Ethnic nursing care: A multicultural approach* (pp. 149–181). St. Louis, MO: C.V. Mosby.

Pe-Pua, R. (1990). Pagtatanung-tanong: A method for cross cultural research. In V. Enriquez (Ed.), *Indigenous psychology: A book of readings* (pp. 213–249). Quezon City: Philippine Psychology Research and Training House.

Peterson, N. (2002). Mentoring Filipino nurses. *Arizona Nurse.* Retrieved October 25, 2005, from www.findarticles.com/p/articles/mi_qa3928/is_200203/ai_n9072539

Peterson, R. (1978). *The elder Filipino* (Research Monograph, Center for Aging, San Diego State University). San Diego, CA: Campanille Press.

Ramos, E. (n.d.). The Filipino Veterans Equity Act. Retrieved October 19, 2005, from www.pinoynation.com/naffaa/ww2veterans.htm

Reeves, T. J., & Bennett, C. (2004). *We the people: Asians in the United States, Census 2000 Special Report, CENSR-17.* U.S. Census 2000. Washington, DC: U.S. Department of Commerce, Economics and Statistics Administration, U.S. Census Bureau.

Ryan, C., Shaw, R., Pliam, M., Zapolinski, A. J., Murphy, M., Valle, H. V. et al. (2000). Coronary heart disease in Filipino and Filipino-American patients: Prevalence of risk factors and outcomes of treatment. *Journal of Invasive Cardiology, 12,* 134–139.

Santiago, C. (1982). Pakapa-kapa: Paglilinaw ng isang konsepto sa nayon [Pakapa-kapa as a method for clarifying an indigenous concept in the barrio]. In R. Pe-Pua (Ed.), *Filipino psychology: Theory, method and application* (pp. 161–170). Quezon City: Philippine Psychology Research and Training House.

Santos, J. (2005, September 12). *6000 Pinoy doctors want to become nurses to get jobs abroad.* Retrieved October 25, 2005, from www.pinoyprofessionals.com/Pinoy/Doctors/6000-Pinoy-Doctor-Want-To-Become-Nurses-To-Get-Jobs-Abroad

Stavig, G. R., Igra, A., & Leonard, A. R. (1988). Hypertension and related health issues among Asians and Pacific Islanders in California. *Public Health Reports, 103,* 28–37.

Stephenson, F. E. (2005, February 3). *Incentives matter: Doctors and nurses edition.* Retrieved October 25, 2005, from http://divisionoflabour.com/archives/000632.php

Superio, E. (1993). *Beliefs held by Pilipinos regarding filial responsibility.* Unpublished master's thesis, San Jose State University, San Jose, CA.

Tompar-Tiu, A., & Sustento-Seneriches, J. (1995). *Depression and other mental health issues: The Filipino American experience.* San Francisco: Jossey-Bass.

Valencia-Go, G. (1989). *Integrative aging in widowed immigrant Filipinos: A grounded theory study.* Unpublished doctoral dissertation, Adelphi University, New York. (UMI No. 8923910).

Wolff, J. (1988). *Pilipino phrasebook.* Oakland, CA: Lonely Planet.

Yeo, G., & Hikoyeda, N. (2006). Asian and Pacific Island Elders. In G. Maddox (Ed.), *Encyclopedia of aging* (4th ed.). New York: Springer.

Yeo, G., Hikoyeda, N., McBride, M., Chin, S.-Y., Edmonds, M., & Hendrix, L. (1998). *Cohort analysis as a tool in ethnogeriatrics: Historical profiles of elders from eight ethnic populations in the United States* (SGEC Working Paper No. 12). Stanford, CA: Stanford Geriatric Education Center.

Yeo, G., & Lieberman, M. (1993). *Cases in the California ADDTC data bank by ethnicity.* Unpublished data.

Zhang, Z. X., Anderson, D. W., Lavine, L., & Mantel, N. (1990). Patterns of acquiring parkinsonism-dementia complex on Guam from 1944 through 1985. *Archives of Neurology, 47*(9), 1019–1024.

CHAPTER 14

Working with Hmong American Families

LINDA A. GERDNER, XA XAVIER XIONG, AND DEU YANG

Background and History

The word *Hmong*[1] literally means being *free* and can be used as a singular or plural. Throughout history, despite geographic location, Hmong people have struggled to maintain their unique culture with a commitment to remain *free* despite pressure from dominant cultures. The Hmong are an ethnic minority from Southeast Asia. Documentation shows the Hmong living in China since ancient times. During the 19th century, they migrated in large numbers to Laos, Vietnam, Burma, and Thailand. During the Vietnam War, the Hmong living in Laos were widely recruited to the American effort by the U.S. Central Intelligence Agency (CIA). The alliances of the Hmong were divided during the Secret CIA War. Some followed the communist Pathet Lao under the Hmong leadership of Lo Faydang. Others joined the anticommunists under Hmong general Vang Pao and moved to Long Cheng, the secret CIA base. Those who served the U.S. cause monitored the Ho Chi Ming Trail (the route used by the North Vietnamese soldiers to transport ammunition to invade South Vietnam), gathered intelligence information for the CIA, and rescued U.S. air pilots whose aircraft had been shot down. As many as 20,000 Hmong were killed while serving the United States and they died at a rate 10 times that of the

U.S. soldiers. This had a devastating impact on the Hmong family and clan structure (Hamilton-Merritt, 1993; Quincy, 1995).

Following the communist takeover of Laos in 1975, the U.S. military withdrew its troops, forcing the Hmong who had served as U.S. allies to flee their homeland or suffer persecution or death by the communist Pathet Lao. Many escaped by crossing the treacherous Mekong River and fled to refugee camps in Thailand until conditions in Laos improved or until resettlement opportunities became available in other countries, such as the United States, Canada, France, and Australia (Cooper, 1998; Hamilton-Merritt, 1993). The Hmong began arriving in the United States in the mid-1970s and constitute a growing sector of the population.

Because of the covert nature of the U.S. operations in Laos, the heroics and sacrifices made by the Hmong were long unrecognized by the U.S. government. In 2000, the U.S. government provided formal recognition of this special status and compensation by passing the Hmong Veteran's Naturalization Act waiving the English-language test and residency requirement for attainment of U.S. citizenship to Hmong veterans and their spouses (U.S. Department of Justice, 2001).

The 2000 census reports 186,310 Hmong living in the United States, a 97% increase in one decade (1990 to 2000). States with the highest populations are California (95,000), Minnesota (70,000), Wisconsin (50,000), North Carolina (20,000), and Michigan (15,000). Hmong leaders believe these statistics are a 50–60% underrepresentation, primarily due to the language barrier confronting the Hmong when completing the census report (Doyle, 2001; Pfeifer, 2001). Of the total Hmong census in 2000, 55.6% were foreign born, 45.3% had no formal education, 34.8% were linguistically isolated, 38.4% were at or below the poverty level, and 2.8% were 65 years or older. Of these elders, 64.1% were unable to speak English (Lee et al., 2003).

In December 2003, the U.S. State Department announced a resettlement program for surviving Hmong refugees living at Wat Tham Krabok, the sole remaining refugee settlement in Thailand (Nelson, 2003). By July 2005, approximately 13,000 of these refugees had resettled in the United States (Avenido, 2005).

When compared to other refugee or immigrant groups in U.S. history, the federal Office of Refugee Resettlement has identified the Hmong as having the greatest difficulty adjusting to life in America (Hunn, n.d.). This is particularly true for the Hmong elders. By the time of their arrival in the United States, elder Hmong had endured numerous losses (lifestyle, key relationships, role identity) and threats to their cultural heritage (Parker, 1996). For many, this is compounded by language barriers, low socioeconomic status, lack of formal education, insufficient means of transportation, and social isolation (Thao, 2002; Parker, 1996). These are factors that have been linked to individuals who are at high risk for health disparities (Kue, Redo, & Yang, 1995), yet health issues of elder Hmong (such as dementia) remain a neglected area of research.

Importantly, Hmong elders do not fit the chronological ages that have traditionally been established in the United States for defining elders (Smith, 1995). This is attributed to several factors. For example, in Laos, it was not unusual for Hmong couples to begin having children at age 15 and, subsequently, become grandparents by 30 to 40 years of age. In addition, the harsh living conditions in Laos during the war and the refugee camps in Thailand have resulted in trauma and stress likely to have accelerated the aging process.

Family/Clan Structure

The family and clan structure are critical to the environmental domain of the Hmong elders. Clans provide the basic form of social organization and structural unity for the Hmong community. In the United States the Hmong are organized into an 18 patrilineal clan structure. Clan names include the following: Chang, Cheng, Chue, Fang, Hang, Her, Khang, Kong, Kue, Lee, Lor, Moua, Pha, Thao, Vang, Vue, Xiong, and Yang. To support this clan structure, the Hmong are concentrated in enclaves throughout the country, with the largest being in the St. Paul/Minneapolis area of Minnesota.

Membership in a clan is achieved by birth. Hmong practice exogamy, meaning that marriage partners must be from outside of one's own clan. Upon marriage, a woman leaves her clan and joins the clan of her husband. Polygyny, in which males can marry more than one wife, was permissible for Hmong men in Laos (Faderman, 1998). This practice arose as a means of social welfare for unattached women, as was the case in many parts of the world including the Middle East and Africa. The degree to which this tradition continues in the United States is unknown but believed to be much less frequent primarily because of the legal implications.

Traditionally, the Hmong have strong family bonds that are based on interdependence rather than independence. This places the individual within the context of the greater whole. Consequently, individuals are not defined in isolation but in relationship to the family.

Elders within the family are highly respected and sought after for wisdom acquired over a long life. They are cherished for the continuity they represent with the past and the investment they have made in the present (Gerdner, Xiong, & Cha, 2006). The eldest male takes on the leadership role within the family. It is recognized that any life event or decision that affects one family member will systemically have a direct or indirect impact on all of its members. Therefore, decisions are made as a group under the leadership of the eldest male. The clan leader is consulted when there is an unresolved dispute. Health-care providers must be cognizant of the decision-making structure preferred by the elder and his or her family.

By tradition, the eldest married son has the primary responsibility for the care of his aging parents, with his wife providing the actual hands-on care. Gerdner (2003) is currently conducting an in-depth exploration of the informal family/clan care structure for elders with chronic conditions such as dementia.

Heterogeneity

Hmong are a heterogeneous group impacted by a variety of factors, such as country of birth, level of education, spirituality, ability to speak and read English, and degree of acculturation (Barrett et al., 1998). It is important for health-care providers to honor the individual expression of culture and accommodate the associated variation of needs. An individual needs assessment is imperative to this process.

Spirituality

Traditionally, the Hmong practice a combination of animism and ancestor worship. This belief system has important implications for perceptions of health and illness. The Hmong traditionally believe that each human has multiple souls. It is generally believed that there are three primary souls, but the exact number may vary by informant (Cooper, 1998; Rice, 2000). Although only distantly related to the concept of *soul* from a Christian perspective, both view these spiritual entities as the core of the individual (Lemoine, 1996). Traditionally, the Hmong believe that these souls must remain in harmony to sustain health and wellness. Spiritual illness occurs when one or more of these souls separate from the physical body. The seriousness of the illness is determined by the number of souls that are lost, the length of absence from the body, and the exact circumstances surrounding soul loss. Spiritual illness is treated by traditional healers such as a *txiv neeb* (shaman) or a *khawv koob* (practitioner of magic healing). Within this belief system, there is an acknowledgment that some illnesses may have a physiological cause. Physiological illness is traditionally treated with herbs or other organic remedies as prescribed by a Hmong herbal medicine expert.

Importantly, the Hmong have also been influenced by the religious beliefs of the dominant cultures in Laos, Thailand, and the United States. Although no statistics are available on the number of Hmong who have converted to Christianity, their presence is evident by the number of churches established in areas that are densely populated by the Hmong (e.g., First Hmong Independent Baptist Church, First Hmong Lutheran Church, Hmong Community United Methodist Church). Importantly, some Hmong who self-identify as Christian may retain varying degrees of beliefs regarding the impact of spirits on their lives and health. The person's spiritual status may also change over time. For example, some were raised with animistic beliefs, then converted to Christianity, and later (possibly during a time of crisis) reverted back to their original animistic beliefs (Plotnikoff, Numrich, Wu, Yang, & Xiong, 2002). A smaller number of Hmong have been influenced by Buddhism.

Language

The ability to speak, read, and write the language of the dominant culture largely impacts the person's willingness and ability to acculturate. As previously stated, 64.1% of the elder Hmong living in the United States are unable to speak English. Hmong originated as an oral culture. In fact, a written Hmong language was not developed until 1956. Many Hmong elders living in the United States have maintained this oral tradition and are unable to read or write Hmong. The Hmong language is multitonal and has two dialects: *Hmoob Dawb* (White Hmong) and *Hmoob Ntsuab* or *Hmoob Leeg* (Green Hmong). Those who speak the more complex Green Hmong dialect are usually able to understand the more simplistic White Hmong dialect, but generally, the reverse is not true. The tone for the Green Hmong dialect is softer as compared to the White Hmong.

Acculturation

There are varying degrees of acculturation within the Hmong population. An extensive literature search revealed three instruments with established psychometric properties to measure acculturation in the Hmong American community. The Hmong Acculturation Questionnaire (Bosher, 1995) is comprised of 120 items based on a Likert scale. The Berry–Peters Acculturation Scale (Berry, Kim, Power, Young, & Bujaki, 1989) was adapted specifically for use with Hmong refugees (Fang, 1998). This adapted version is comprised of 168 items that address demographic information, language, and levels of acculturation (assimilation, integration, separation, and marginalization). The length of the instruments (although appropriate for research purposes) may preclude the feasibility for use by clinicians.

A viable option is the Suinn–Lew Asian Self Identity Acculturation Scale (SL-ASIA scale; Suinn, Ahua, & Khoo, 1992). The scale is comprised of 21 items that address language (four questions), identity (four questions), friendship choice (four questions), behaviors (five questions), generation/ geographic history (three questions), and attitudes (one question). Scores range from 1 (low acculturation) to 5 (high acculturation). Psychometric properties are well established within the Asian population (Suinn, Rickard-Figueroa, Lew, & Vigil, 1987). This instrument has been adapted for use with Hmong Americans and is currently being tested as part of a larger ethnographic study conducted by Gerdner (2003) that involves interviews with family caregivers, traditional healers, and community liaisons.

Perceptions and Care of Persons with Dementia

The Hmong do not have a word that directly translates to the meaning of dementia. *Tem toob* is the Hmong word that is used to describe an elder with severe memory impairment and chronic confusion. *Tem toob* is not a new concept to the Hmong. They have an ancient proverb that addresses this concept, which was told to us by May Lo (December 14, 2004): *Ntoo laus ntoo to qhov, neeg laus neeg hnem hnov. Ntoo laus ntoo khoob, neeg laus neeg tem toob.* The English translation is, "As a tree ages, it has holes. A person who ages becomes forgetful. An old tree is hollow. An old person has memory loss or impairment." Gerdner, Xiong, and Cha (2006) discuss the traditional treatment of *tem toob* by Hmong persons living in Laos.

There are no statistics on the estimated prevalence of dementia in the Hmong American population. Gerdner and Tripp-Reimer (2001) are completing qualitative data analysis from a focused ethnographic study to explore the prevalence, perception, and care of elder Hmong Americans with chronic confusion (i.e., dementia). Participants include family caregivers, traditional healers, and community liaisons living in select areas of Minnesota and Wisconsin. The majority of interviews were conducted in the Hmong language with the assistance of an interpreter. Preliminary findings indicate that chronic confusion in elder Hmong Americans is an important but neglected issue. Unfortunately, some members of the Hmong American community associate a negative stigma with elders who have chronic confusion and memory impairment (i.e., dementia). This stigma may extend beyond the elder to the entire family. Consequently, in an effort to maintain the elder's dignity and respect within the community, family members may postpone or avoid seeking help from persons outside of the family (Tempo & Saito, 1996).

Western Medicine

Researchers have found that the majority of Hmong Americans do not see the value of seeking Western medicine for the treatment of elders with chronic confusion and memory impairment (Gerdner & Tripp-Reimer, 2001; Olson, 1999). Overall, elder Hmong Americans usually limit their use of medical care to emergency situations. This has led to the lack of available information regarding the prevalence of dementia within the Hmong American community. This is compounded by a lack of available assessment tools that are linguistically and culturally appropriate for the assessment of cognitive impairment in Hmong elders. Currently, Xa Xiong, MD, and Fred Coleman, MD, are in the process of testing an adapted version of the Mini-Mental State Examination (Folstein, Folstein, & McHugh, 1975) in a community mental health program in Madison, Wisconsin.

There are multiple causes and risk factors associated with dementia. Vascular dementia is seen in about 20% of persons with dementia, and hypertension is the primary risk factor for vascular dementia (Boyd, Garand, Gerdner, Wakefield, & Buckwalter, 2005). There are few statistics pertaining to the overall health status of Hmong elders, but hypertension appears to be a problem of sizable proportion (Culhane-Pera & Xiong, 2003), placing these individuals at risk for vascular dementia.

Without proper assessment and diagnosis, there is always risk that disturbances in memory and cognition may be due to other factors, such as depression (Fischer, 1996). There is a high rate of depression among Hmong elders due to earlier loss, trauma, and difficulties in adapting to life in America. There is no word in the Hmong language that directly translates to the diagnostic term for depression. The word with the closest meaning is *nyuaj siab* and is considered to be a normal response to an adverse "life event" requiring no medical or psychological intervention. Most of the Hmong still believe that once the event has passed and a person has a healing ceremony, *nyuaj siab* will no longer exist. Mental health treatment is somewhat new to the Hmong. An individual is at risk of being labeled "crazy" by some members of the Hmong community if treatment is sought for a "mental dysfunction," such as depression. These misconceptions have brought much resistance to seeking medical or psychological intervention.

The language barrier is another reason that depression may be overlooked and left untreated among the Hmong. The person may somatize the mental distress through physical complaints of headaches, fatigue, abdominal distress, and neck and low back pain. This hinders recognition of the psychological nature of the complaint and may lead to misdiagnosis or mistreatment. Consequently, there is need to enhance awareness through education programs in Hmong American communities in an effort to promote early detection and treatment. Education and treatment programs need to be conducted in a linguistically and culturally sensitive manner. This can be facilitated through the use of a professional medical interpreter and a cultural broker who provides mediation and serves as a bridge between Western healthcare providers, the elder, and his or her family..

Spiritual Healers

Some Hmong believe that *tem toob* (memory impairment) has a spiritual cause. Under these circumstances, a shaman may be called upon to perform a *ua neeb kho* (traditional healing ceremony). During this ceremony, the shaman enters a trance enabling him or her to travel to "the other world" to negotiate for the return of the afflicted person's lost or abducted soul. The negotiation process involves burning incenses and spirit money and usually an animal sacrifice (i.e., chickens, pig, cow). At the completion of the ceremony, the shaman will loosely tie a red or red and white entwined string around the neck, wrist, or ankle of the afflicted person. The purpose of this string is to protect the soul from evil spirits and secure the soul to the body. To emphasize the importance of this string, the first author was told the story of an elderly woman who the family believed was having an extraordinarily prolonged and painful death. They could not understand what was preventing the inevitable and had difficulty watching her suffer. Finally, a family member suggested that the red string tied to her wrist was preventing her soul from leaving her physical body. A family decision was made to cut the string, and the elder woman died "within an hour" of the string being cut. It is important that health-care professionals understand the spiritual significance of this string. It is critical that this string be left intact during daily care and medical procedures.

Also during a healing ceremony a shaman may request that a *moj zeej*, or image of a human figure, be cut from cloth (usually red) and appliquéd to the back of the afflicted person's shirt as another means of protection from malevolent spirits (Shaman Chia Fong Yang, personal communication, September 9, 2005). Appliquéd shirts may be worn under a jacket or may be layered under another shirt so that it is less obvious to non-Hmong or Christian Hmong scrutiny. Health-care professionals should remain open minded and nonjudgmental about traditional Hmong belief systems.

Herbalists

The majority of Hmong American elders grow medicinal herbs in their backyards. During the winter months, the plants are repotted and placed indoors. The Hmong herbal medicine expert, who sells *tshuaj ntsuab* (fresh herbs), *tshuaj qhuav* (dried roots), and other organic substances (dried animal parts, rhinoceros bones/skin/dried blood, etc.) for healing purposes, is a common sight at Hmong American festivals, weekend flea markets, and homes. Gerdner, Xiong, and Cha (2006) encountered a number of herbalists in the open-air markets of Laos and Thailand who sold remedies that they claimed were effective in the treatment of chronic confusion in elders. However, interviews with Hmong American family caregivers of persons with dementia and traditional healers found that while there was a widespread use of herbal and organic remedies for a variety of conditions believed to have a physiological cause (i.e., hypertension), there were no remedies available in the United States for elders with chronic confusion (Gerdner & Tripp-Reimer, 2001). Health-care providers are advised to query the elder and the family on the use of herbal and organic remedies.

Other Traditional Treatment Modalities

While living in Laos, Hmong persons used a variety of treatment modalities for their health concerns. Although none of these treatments are used specifically for chronic confusion, a basic understanding of some of the more common treatments is important, because they continue to be preferred by many elder Hmong Americans with comorbid conditions. Many of these treatments cause bruising of the skin and may be misinterpreted as dependent adult abuse. Some of the more common treatments include *txhuav* (cupping), *zaws hno* (vigorous massage with needle pricking), *dia kav* (silver spoon rubbing), *baws* (pinching), and *zuaj* (massage).

Txhuav (cupping) refers to the application of a bamboo jar, a glass cup, or an animal horn to the skin to cause local congestion through a negative pressure created by heat. Sometimes it is used in combination with bloodletting. Typically, cupping is used to alleviate swelling and pain (i.e., back pain, headaches, and leg pain), promote blood circulation, and remove stasis.

Zaws hno (vigorous massaging of the stomach followed by needle pricking of the fingers) is used to treat an upset stomach due to rapid food ingestion. Neng Xiong, who is a traditional Hmong healer, said that this technique is used to inhibit the chemical that causes irritation to the stomach lining and promotes peristalsis, relieving the upset stomach.

Dia kav (rubbing the skin with a silver spoon) is a method that may be used to treat a variety of febrile illnesses as well as stress-related symptoms (i.e., headaches, muscle aches, pain). In advance of this treatment, oil or Tiger Balm is applied to sooth the skin and increase peripheral circulation. Residual marks (i.e., linear petechiae and ecchymosis lesions) may appear on the skin surface where the rubbing occurred (back, neck, temporal areas, nasal bridge, and chest). These usually resolve within several days.

Baws (pinching) refers to vigorous pinching of the nasal bridge by using the thumb and the index finger. It is performed to relieve headaches. This technique produces a vertical ecchymosis mark on the nasal bridge. Again, this should not be confused with dependent adult abuse. In addition, *zuaj ib ce* (massage therapy) is used in the treatment of stress-related symptoms, such as headaches, muscle aches, and pain.

Providing Culturally Appropriate Services for Hmong Elders and Families

Verbal and Nonverbal Communication

Because the majority of Hmong elders do not speak English, professional health-care interpreters are essential when working with this population (Allen, Matthew, & Boland, 2004). The dialect of the interpreter should match the dialect of the elder and family. It is optimal to have an interpreter who is of the same sex as the person who is the focus of communication. In his or her work, the interpreter is faced with numerous challenges. The Hmong language does not include words that are directly translatable to medical terms used by health-care professionals (Johnson, 2002). Consequently, an extensive explanation may be required to convey these concepts. This becomes even more complicated when there is a lack of basic understanding in human anatomy and physiology as encountered with many elder Hmong. The National Council on Interpreting in Health Care (NCIHS) developed a Web site (www.ncihc.org) to explore this topic further. Enslein, Tripp-Reimer, Kelley, Choi, and McCarty (2001) also developed an evidence-based protocol to facilitate the effective use of language interpretation services in health-care settings for persons with limited English.

Nonverbal communication is critical, especially during interactions between a non-Hmong-speaking person and a non-English-speaking Hmong individual. When a person is unable to understand the spoken words, body language and tone of voice become the focus. Therefore, it is important to use a soft, gentle voice (Vawter, Culhane-Pera, Babbitt, Xiong, & Solberg, 2003) and to convey a sense of patience. Direct eye contact is generally considered to be disrespectful within the Hmong culture. Hmong persons customarily look down toward the floor as an indication that they are listening intently to the person (Vawter et al., 2003). Coauthor Xiong noted that in the Hmong culture, it is considered inappropriate and disrespectful for a woman, stranger, or younger person to rub or place

Table 14.1   Working with Hmong Elders with Dementia

---

1. Avoid discussing important topics (e.g. care issues) with the patient alone.

2. Identify a family member and/or a clan leader of the patient.

3. Organize a family conference that includes an invitation to the clan leader.

4. Discuss the important topics (e.g., pathological process of the disease, prognosis, and treatment plans) in a culturally and linguistically sensitive manner. Be forthright and avoid using dogmatic statements when discussing the prognosis.

5. Offer to include the clan leader in the decision-making process.

6. Be supportive of the family / clan leader wishes.

---

their hand on the top of a man's head. Permission to examine the head of a Hmong patient should be requested in advance.

Establishing Rapport and Trust

To establish a trusting relationship, it is imperative to maintain a sincere, open-minded, nonjudgmental attitude. Words must be consistent with actions. Members of the Hmong community (i.e., elders, traditional healers) must be treated with respect and dignity. Traditional beliefs should be accommodated whenever possible as a means of supplementing Western medicine. Even though you may not be able to speak the Hmong language, it may be helpful to learn a few simple phrases, such as *nyob zoo* ("hello"), *ua ntsaug* ("thank you"), and *sib tshiv dua* ("see you later"). Coauthor Xiong's recommendations for working with Hmong elders with dementia are listed in Table 14.1.

Working with Families

Despite an extensive search, we were unable to locate any educational materials specifically developed for Hmong Americans on the topic of dementia. There is a critical need to provide culturally and linguistically appropriate information (Allen et al., 2004) to the Hmong on this topic. Many elders have retained the oral tradition of communication. This is evidenced by the number of elder Hmong who remain in contact with family members back in Laos and Thailand by sending audiotaped messages in lieu of written letters. The audio and video method of communication has been transferred to health education. Healtheast in the Minneapolis/St. Paul area of Minnesota with support from the Hmong Health Care Coalition developed educational audiotapes on a variety of health-care topics for Hmong elders. Sample titles include *What Happens When You Go to* the Hospital?, Overcoming Depression: Hope for a Better Life, and Caring for Your Heart and Blood Pressure.

However, it has been suggested that the Hmong prefer individualized face-to-face health education training programs (Allen et al., 2004). Shadick (1993) identified the need to acknowledge that both the educator and Hmong learner have specific areas of expertise. For example, the educator is knowledgeable about the disease process and various approaches to care that have been effective with others. Family members have expertise regarding the historical background of the individual and his or her personal likes and dislikes.

Family teaching should be conducted from a positive reference point. For example, rather than stating, "an environment that is over stimulating may cause the person to be anxious and agitated," it is better to state, "a low stimulus environment will be more calming and less stressful to the elder." Emphasizing the negative is viewed as predicting an adverse event.

Cha (2003) stated that Hmong "rely heavily on both kin and clan leaders for support and information" and advised that outreach efforts include these authority figures. Clan leaders should be consulted on the development of family training programs. Programs that are endorsed by clan leaders have better chance of succeeding.

When developing a training program, it is important to remember that grandparents often live in the home of a married son who has children of his own. Children may have difficulty adjusting to a grandparent who has cognitive impairment, particularly if the grandparent is no longer able to recognize the child (Gerdner & Tripp-Reimer, 2001). Consequently, Sarah Langford, Linda Gerdner, and Shoua Xiong are in the process of completing an illustrated children's book to assist Hmong children with this phenomenon. The book will be published by Hmongland publishing company (accessible through www.hmongabc.com).

Activities to Promote Reminiscence

The Hmong story cloth, *paj ntaub dab neeg*, became a popular form of artistic expression during the confinement of Hmong refugees who sought shelter in Thailand following the communist takeover of Laos in 1975 (MacDowell, 1989). Story cloths are created by drawing representations of daily life, community celebrations, or Hmong folktales onto a piece of fabric. These images are then embroidered using multicolored thread. Usually the cloth is finished with a border of triangles (MacDowell, 1989). Story cloths may be used as the basis for a reminiscence intervention. For example, the health-care provider could point to scenes on the cloth that depict daily life (harvesting rice, grinding corn) in Laos to elicit personal stories of the elder's life.

Community Services

The Hmong have strong family, clan, and community bonds. Dunnigan (1986) observed that experiences throughout history taught the Hmong that "security depends on solidarity." He explains that reliance on persons outside of the Hmong community threaten this unity. It is expected that such views would impact the use of community services highlighting the need for services that are culturally responsive.

An adult day service has been established in St. Paul, Minnesota, that provides a culturally responsive environment for frail and cognitively impaired Hmong elders during the day when families are at work or are otherwise unavailable. The elders were opposed to referring to this service as day care (which they associated with child care). The name *Tsev Laus Kaj Siab* refers to a place for elders where there is freedom from tension and worry. Noon meals and snacks are catered from a local Hmong restaurant. At the time of this writing, 70 Hmong elders used the services of this organization, with 10 having chronic confusion and memory impairment. A low stimulus room is available as needed for these individuals. Walls are decorated with elaborately embroidered story clothes depicting village life in Laos. Craft activities are based on Hmong culture and include weaving with a *paj ntaub* (traditional hand loom), watching Hmong videos (e.g, folktales such as *Nuj Nplhaib & Ntxawm*), and listening to traditional music and the Free Asian Radio broadcast in Hmong from Washington, DC.

Overall, Hmong are opposed to placing elders in a nursing home. One long-term care facility located near a Hmong enclave in St. Paul, Minnesota, has a unit dedicated to Southeastern Asians (Hmong, Vietnamese, Cambodian, and Thai). At the time of this writing, approximately 60% of the 39 residents were Hmong. It serves Hmong elders living not only in Minnesota but has also had admissions from Wisconsin, California, and Michigan. The facility has a full-time Hmong liaison who serves as an interpreter and cultural broker. Unit staffing includes Hmong American nurses, certified nursing assistants (CNAs), therapy aides, and other support staff. The goal is to have at least one Hmong American on staff at all times. The facility has a financial incentive program for Hmong American CNAs who would like to advance their education and become a professional nurse (LPN, RN).

The unit is integrated, serving both frail and cognitively impaired elders. Family members generally delay admission until justified by a serious safety issue. For example, an elder Hmong man may have hallucinations and delusions that the communist Patho Lao are trying to kill him.

Hallways are decorated with Hmong story clothes. The unit houses a diverse Hmong video library including videos of traditional village life in Laos. A special radio was purchased, allowing residents to listen to Hmong Minnesota radio. This station provides traditional music and news (reported in the Hmong language) from around the world. Each November, staff members organize a formal Hmong New Year celebration.

Meals are culturally appropriate and include rice dishes that elders find especially appealing, such as *zaub tsuag* (bland vegetable soup). When an elder self-identifies as being "sick," traditional Hmong protocol mandates a special diet of rice and boiled fowl (i.e., chicken). Although the authors have encountered discrepancies within the Hmong community on the appropriateness of serving boiled vegetables during times of illness, we have consistently been informed that onions are prohibited. Family members often bring food from home as an expression of love. A few family members have purchased a dorm-sized refrigerator that is placed in the resident's room to accommodate storage of and easy access to these extra food items.

Occasionally, care issues related to gender arise. For example, a male resident may resist the advice or directives given by a female health-care provider. On one occasion, a male resident demanded that his wife stay at his side 24 hr per day, regardless of her responsibilities at home. These situations have warranted intervention by staff. *Family night* council meetings are conducted on a quarterly basis to promote rapport and communication between staff and family. These meetings include a catered meal from a local Asian restaurant.

Staff members are dedicated to providing an environment that supports the cultural needs of the individual. The facility has a written policy that includes a signed agreement enabling the resident/family to utilize alternative treatment modalities. Although it is not possible to conduct shamanic healing ceremonies at the facility because of the animal sacrifice and noise level from chanting and use of *nruas neeb* (brass drum), *tswb neeb* (finger bells), and *txiab neeb* (shaman scissors); residents are permitted to leave the facility with family so as to participate in these ceremonies in the home. When death is approaching, staff members are responsive and supportive to the rituals associated with the dying process of the resident and the grieving process of the family.

Case Example

The following case example reflects the challenges encountered by one family in providing care and community services for an 86-year-old Hmong man. The elder was born in Laos and fled to Thailand in 1975 following the Communist takeover. He lived in a refugee camp in Thailand for five years until he and his wife were given permission to come to the United States in 1981. After his wife died in 2002, he moved in with his son and daughter-in-law, who lived in North Carolina. During this time, he began exhibiting signs of cognitive and functional impairment. These behaviors were misinterpreted as an unwillingness to cooperate. The elder's inappropriate verbal response to questions was mistakenly attributed to impaired hearing. His belligerence and uncooperativeness were misinterpreted as willful personality traits. When the Hmong elder began experiencing urinary incontinence, the son decided other living arrangements were warranted.

The elder was relocated to a culturally diverse city on the East Coast to live with his grandson, wife, and their three young children. He continued to be incontinent of bowel and bladder and required assistance with bathing. The elder was able to put on his own clothing but needed assistance with buttons and zippers. The grandson took on the responsibility for these duties, due to their personal nature, rather than have his young wife (age 18) provide this care. The elder continued to be uncooperative and often responded inappropriately to verbal stimuli. Again, these behaviors were attributed to willful intension. The family did not become seriously alarmed until the elder began wandering outside during the cold, snowy winter weather.

The elder was examined by a male Hmong physician and diagnosed with dementia and uncontrolled diabetes. The grandson consulted his uncle about his grandfather's care. The young grandson was concerned about his abilities to manage his grandfather's diet and insulin injections. In addition, there were safety issues associated with his grandfather's wandering. Consequently, it was decided that his grandfather would be admitted to a long-term care facility (LTCF) where other elders from Southeast Asia also resided. This unit integrated frail elders with those who were cognitively impaired. Staff members were successful in managing the elder's diabetes, but his behaviors became increasingly problematic. Staff members were alerted when he wandered into another resident's room, confusing the elder Hmong woman with his wife. The cultural broker and interpreter, a young female, attempted to intervene by reasoning with the elder man. The elder had been raised in a patriarchal society and found no value in words spoken from a young Hmong female whom he viewed as attempting to dictate his behaviors. Five months after his admission, it was decided that he should be transferred to an Alzheimer's Special Care Unit (SCU) housed in another LTCF.

The elder male was the only Hmong in the SCU, and there were no Hmong-speaking staff. Living in an environment that was not culturally supportive exacerbated his cognitive impairment. He managed to escape the unit in "the middle of the night" and found his way to his grandson's home. The grandson called the assigned nurse case manager who arranged community services that would facilitate the elder's care at home. Before going to work, during the week, the grandson assisted his grandfather with morning care. This included bathing, dressing, and preparing breakfast for his grandfather. A van then transported the grandfather to a local adult day center that served the Hmong community. The elder remained at the adult day center from 9 A.M. to 3 P.M., while his grandson was at work. The elder returned by van to his grandson's home by mid-afternoon, where family provided care and supervision. This arrangement worked nicely until the grandson's employment required him to work weekends, during a time when the adult day center was not available. The elder continued to live with his grandson but remained alone much of the time on the weekends. He caused alarm on two occasions when he wandered out of the house during the cold of winter. On the first occasion, he was found and returned home by his great grandchildren. On the second occasion, he was found "wandering the streets" by the police and was returned to his family.

The elder was subsequently admitted to a LTCF where he is currently the only Hmong, thus causing emotional isolation. The elder is reportedly "unhappy" in this culturally deprived unit, but his behaviors are no longer viewed as problematic to the other residents. The case manager has contacted the clan leader and attempted to organize a family meeting. However, it is reported that there is really nothing that the clan leader can do, because family members are not receptive to a group meeting. The case manager is trying to find placement in an adult foster care facility that is dedicated to Hmong elders. In the meantime, in an effort to relieve some of the social isolation, the case manager has purchased a shortwave radio (SCA/SCMO) that airs a Hmong Radio Station 24 hr per day, which broadcasts music and world news in the Hmong language.

Traditional Care in Dying and Death

By tradition, the Hmong believe that each person is given a "visa" that determines their *txoj hmoo* (mandate of life) or length of time they will reside on earth during this lifetime. If a person is seriously ill, the family may consult a shaman. The shaman will perform a *ua neeb saib* (diagnostic ceremony) to determine if it is appropriate to perform *ntxiv ntaww*, a ceremony to extend the "mandate of life." This ceremony can only be performed three times during the life of an adult. If the person's condition advances to a terminal stage, the shaman may perform a ceremony known as *fiv yeem* (request) in an effort to extend the life force by calling on the "God of the sky" for this purpose. In appreciation, an animal sacrifice is made to the "God of the sky" (Shaman Chia Fong Yang, personal communication, September 9, 2005).

Traditionally, it is believed that discussing or making plans in advance of a family member's death will "unlock the gate of the evil spirits" causing the person to die prematurely. When it becomes apparent that death is imminent, it is important to approach the patient, family, and clan in a culturally and linguistically sensitive manner, similar to that presented in Table 14.1. It is critical to facilitate the traditional protocol for the dying person who retains the traditional animist/ancestor belief system.

To prevent spiritual harm from befalling the family, it is generally preferred that the dying elder be in his or her own home or the home of an immediate family member at the time of death (Bliatout, 1993). Immediate and extended family gather for a constant vigil at the bedside (Culhane-Pera, 2003). The purpose is not only to support one another, but it is also believed that the dying person will impart "wisdom and blessings" to those who listen (Bliatout, 1993; Culhane-Pera, 2003). As death approaches, the family may dress the elder in the *khaub ncaws laus* (traditional ceremonial attire). There are distinct differences between the ceremonial attire of the White Hmong and the Green Hmong. The attire of the White Hmong includes a black loose-fitting robe with needlework at the hem, cuffs, and collar. This attire is symbolic of the transformation that will occur when the elder dies and travels to the land of his or her ancestors (Culhane-Pera, 2003). Following death, cloth shoes may be placed on the feet. Next, *maaj* (hemp) fiber is used to hand-weave protective soles to the bottom of the shoes. It is believed that this foot covering will protect the feet of the deceased throughout their travels to the other world.

In addition, it is customary for the family to groom the body of the deceased person. In the traditional animist/ancestor belief system, the body must be left in its purest, most natural form to facilitate reincarnation. Consequently, autopsy is generally forbidden. This value system has been retained by many Hmong who have converted to Christianity. It is believed that cutting or dismembering the body will delay reincarnation and will result in negative consequences to the spirit in the next life (Culhane-Pera & Xiong, 2003). Similarly, it is believed that the body should be free of metal pieces following death and prior to burial (Vawter & Babbitt,

1997). This includes silver fillings, metal staples, and metal prosthetic devices such as that found in a hip replacement. Culhane-Pera and colleagues (2003) compiled a series of case studies to assist the health-care provider in the complexities and recommendations to achieve culturally responsive end-of-life care for Hmong persons.

Conclusions

Proper diagnosis and care of Hmong elders with dementia is an important and timely issue. This is evidenced by an event that occurred during the summer of 2005 in which an elder Hmong man with "memory problems" wandered away from his home in Wisconsin. After 21 days of intensive searching, the man was found 2 miles from his home. The elder had spent the majority of time in a wooded area, where he covered himself with leaves and branches at night "for protection." He went without food for the 21-day period but found a discarded plastic bottle that he used to collect drinking water from a creek. After losing the bottle, he was found crawling on his hands and knees in high grass searching for another plastic container. The elder was transferred to the hospital, where he was treated for dehydration. Even though he was found with $41 in his pocket, his inability to speak English and operate a phone prevented him from seeking help (Moua, 2005).

The issue of chronic confusion and memory impairment (i.e., dementia) in the Hmong American community has not received the attention that it deserves. Too often, health-care providers erroneously assume that minimal use or an absence in the use of formal care services by minority groups is due to a preference for informal care structures or that family caregivers are receiving sufficient support from their existing networks (Burton et al., 1995). It is important to remember that Hmong American elders are a heterogeneous group when identifying possible barriers that may impact their access and utilization of community resources. Table 14.2 provides a summary of potential barriers as discussed in this chapter.

Acknowledgments

The effort in writing this chapter was funded in part by a grant from the National Institute of Health/National Institute of Nursing Research (NIH/NINR) KO1 NR008433 (PI: Linda Gerdner). The authors would like to thank Fred Coleman, MD, for his review and comments on an earlier version of this chapter.

Table 14.2 Barriers for Hmong American Elders Who Use Community Resources

Barrier	Description
Language	64.1% of Hmong American elders are unable to speak English. Many Hmong American elders have retained the oral tradition of Hmong language and are thus unable to read or write the Hmong language. Health education materials must be culturally and linguistically appropriate. For example, audio and video materials may be more appropriate than written information. The Hmong language does not include words that are directly translatable to medical terms such as dementia.
Health beliefs	Confusion and memory problems may be considered a normal aspect of aging. May be viewed as having a spiritual cause that requires mediation from a shaman.
Lack of formal education	45.3% of all Hmong Americans have no formal education. This is likely to include a lack of understanding of basic human anatomy and physiology that would be essential to understanding malfunctions of the body and the disease process.
Stigma	Negative stigma associated with elder confusion and memory problems may impede help-seeking behaviors.
Lack of cultural responsiveness	Community health-care services may lack responsiveness to the needs of the elder and his or her family.
Mistrust	Misconceptions leading to mistrust of Western medicine.
Lack of financial resources	38.4% of the total Hmong American population is below the poverty level.

Note

1. All Hmong words are written in the White Hmong dialect.

References

Allen, M., Matthew, S., & Boland, M. J. (2004). Working with immigrant and refugee populations: Issues and Hmong case study. *Library Trends, 53*(2), 301–328.

Avenido, G. (2005, July 25). Refugee State Coordinator, Minnesota Department of Human Services.

Barrett, B., Shadick, K., Schilling, R., Spencer, L., del Rosario, S., Moua, K. et al. (1998). Hmong/medicine interactions: Improving cross-cultural health care. *Family Medicine, 30*(3), 179–184.

Berry, J. W., Kim, U., Power, S., Young, M., & Bujaki, M. (1989). Acculturation attitudes in plural societies. *Applied Psychology: An Internatioinal Review*, *38*(2), 185–206.

Bliatout, B. (1993). Hmong death customs: Traditional and acculturated. In D. K. Irish, K. F. Lundquist, & V. J. Nelson (Eds.), *Ethnic variations in dying, death and grief: Diversity in universality* (pp. 79–100). Washington, DC: Taylor & Francis.

Bosher, S. D. (1995). *Acculturation, ethnicity, and second language acquisition: A study of Hmong students at the post-secondary level.* Doctoral dissertation. Minneapolis: University of Minnesota.

Boyd, M. A., Garand, L., Gerdner, L. A., Wakefield, B. J., & Buckwalter, K. C. (2005). Delirium, dementias, and related disorders. In M.A. Boyd (Ed.), *Psychiatric nursing: Contemporary practice* (3rd ed., pp. 671–708). Philadelphia: Lippincott, Williams & Wilkins.

Burton, L., Kasper, J., Shore, A., Cagney, K., LaVeist, T., Cubbin, C. et al. (1995). The structure of informal care: Are there differences by race? *The Gerontologist, 35,* 744–752.

Cha, D. (2003). *Hmong American concepts of health, healing, and conventional medicine.* New York: Routledge.

Cooper, R. (Ed.). (1998). *The Hmong: A guide to traditional lifestyles.* Selangor Darul Ehsan, Malaysia: Times Edition Pte.

Culhane-Pera, K. A. (2003). Cultural complications in end-of-life care for a Hmong woman with gallbladder cancer. In K. A. Culhane-Pera, D. E. Vawter, P. Xiong, B. Babbitt, & M. M. Solberg (Eds.), *Healing by heart: Clinical and ethical case stories of Hmong families and Western providers* (pp. 258–264). Nashville, TN: Vanderbilt University Press.

Culhane-Pera, K. A., Vawter, D. E., Xiong, P., Babbitt, B., & Solberg, M. M. (Eds.). (2003). *Healing by heart: Clinical and ethical case stories of Hmong families and Western providers.* Nashville, TN: Vanderbilt University Press.

Culhane-Pera, K. A., & Xiong, P. (2003). Hmong culture: Tradition and change. In K. A. Culhane-Pera, D. E. Vawter, P. Xiong, B. Babbitt, & M. M. Solberg (Eds.), *Healing by heart: Clinical and ethical case stories of Hmong families and Western providers* (pp. 11–68). Nashville, TN: Vanderbilt University Press.

Doyle, M. (2001, August 16). Census 2000: The missing Hmong? *Hmong Times*, p. 1.

Dunnigan, T. (1986). Processes of identity maintenance in Hmong society. In G. L. Hendricks, B.T. Downing, & A.S. Deinard (Eds.), *The Hmong in transition* (pp. 41–53). New York: Center for Migration Studies.

Enslein, J., Tripp-Reimer, T., Kelley, L. S., Choi, E., & McCarty, L. (2001). Evidence-based protocol: Interpreter facilitation for persons with limited-English proficiency. In M. Titler (Series Ed.), *Series on evidence-based practice for older adults.* Iowa City: The University of Iowa College of Nursing Gerontological Nursing Interventions Research Center, Research Dissemination Core.

Faderman, L. (1998). *The Hmong and the American immigrant experience: I begin my life all over.* Boston, MA: Beacon Hill.

Fang, K. B. (1998). *Acculturation as a predictor of attitudes toward seeking professional psychological help in the Hmong community.* Fresno: California School of Professional Psychology.

Fischer, P. (1996). The spectrum of depressive pseudo-dementia. *Journal of Neural Transmission, 47*(Supp), 193–203.

Folstein, M. G., Folstein, S. E., & McHugh, P. R. (1975). "Mini mental state" a practical method for grading the cognitive state of patients for the clinician. *Journal of Psychiatric Research, 12*, 189–198.

Gerdner, L. A. (2003). *Ethnogeriatric cultural competence: Chronic confusion* (Grant No. K01 NR008433-01). Bethesda, MA: National Institute of Health/ National Institute of Nursing Research.

Gerdner, L. A., & Tripp-Reimer, T. (2001). Hmong illness beliefs, behaviors, and care structures. Grant funded by the University of Minnesota.

Gerdner, L. A., Xiong, S. V., & Cha, D. (2006). Traditional treatment of chronic confusion and memory impairment in elder Hmong. *Journal of Gerontological Nursing, 32*(3), 23–30.

Hamilton-Merritt, J. (1993). *Tragic mountains: The Hmong, the Americans, and the secret wars for Laos, 1942–1992.* Bloomington, IN: Indiana University Press.

Hunn, D. (n.d.). The lost generation: Elder Hmong immigrants struggle with life in America. Retrieved June 20, 2003, from http://clovisindependent.com/ projects/Hmong/hmongstory1.html

Johnson, S. K. (2002). Hmong health beliefs and experiences in the western health care system. *Journal of Transcultural Nursing, 13*(2), 126–132.

Kue, Y., Redo, C., & Yang, X. S. (1995). *Barriers to accessing health care. Blending cultures: Health care for Hmong elderly.* Milwaukee: Wisconsin Geriatric Education Center.

Lee, S., Pfeiffer, M. E., Seying, K., Todd, R. M., Grover, M., Vang, H. et al. (2003). *Hmong 2000 Census Publication: Data and Analysis.* Washington, DC: Hmong National Development Inc.

Lemoine, J. (1996). The constitution of a Hmong shaman's powers of healing and folk culture. *Shaman, 4*(1–2), 144–165.

MacDowell, M. (1989). *Stories in thread Hmong pictorial embroidery.* East Lansing: Michigan Traditional Arts Program Folk Arts Division, Michigan State University Publications.

Moua, W. (2005, August 11). Man is found after 21 days. *Hmong Today, 2*(16), pp. 1, 14–15.

Nelson, T. (2003, December 19). New day for exiled Hmong. *Pioneer Press,* pp. 1A, 14A.

Olson, M. C. (1999). The heart still beat, but the brain doesn't answer. *Theoretical Medicine, 20*, 85–95.

Parker, M. K. (1996). *Loss in the lives of Southeast Asian elders.* Doctoral dissertation. Minneapolis: University of Minnesota.

Pfeifer, M. (2001). *U.S. Census 2000: Trends in Hmong population distribution across the regions of the United States.* St. Paul, MN: Hmong Cultural Center.

Plotnikoff, G. A., Numrich, C., Wu, C., Yang, D., & Xiong, P. (2002). Hmong shamanism: Animist spiritual healing in Minnesota. *Minnesota Medicine, 85*(6), 29–34.

Quincy, K. (1995). *Hmong: History of a people. Chency* (2nd ed.). Washington: Eastern Washington University Press.

Rice, P. L. (2000). *Hmong women and reproduction.* Westport, CT: Bergin & Garvey.

Shadick, K. M. (1993). Development of a transcultural health education program for the Hmong. *Clinical Nurse Specialist, 7*(2), 48–53.

Smith, G. (1995). *Medical management of the Hmong elderly. Blending cultures: Health care for Hmong elderly.* Milwaukee: Wisconsin Geriatric Education Center.

Suinn, R. M., Ahua, C., & Khoo, G. (1992). The Suinn–Lew Asian Self-Identity Acculturation Scale: Concurrent and factorial. *Educational and Psychological Measurement, 52*(4), 1041–1046.

Suinn, R. M., Rickard-Figueroa, K., Lew, S., & Vigil, P. (1987). The Suinn–Lew Asian self-identity acculturation scale: An initial report. *Educational and Psychological Measurement, 47,* 401–407.

Tempo, P., & Saito, A. (1996). Techniques of working with Japanese American families. In G. Yeo & Gallagher-Thompson (Eds.), *Ethnicity and the dementias* (pp. 109–122). Washington, DC: Taylor & Francis.

Thao, Y. J. (2002). *The voices of Mong elders: Living, knowing, teaching, and learning with an oral tradition.* Doctoral dissertation. Claremont, CA: Claremont Graduate University.

U.S. Department of Justice. (2001). Bureau of citizenship and immigration services. Hmong veteran's naturalization act of 2000. Retrieved May 2, 2005.

Vawter, D. E., & Babbitt, B. (1997). Hospice care for terminally ill Hmong patients: A good cultural fit? *Minnesota Medicine, 80,* 42–44.

Vawter, D. E., Culhane-Pera, K. A., Babbitt, B., Xiong, P., & Solberg, M. M. (2003). A model of culturally responsive health care. In K. A. Culhane-Pera, D. E., Vawter, P. Xiong, B. Babbitt, & M. M. Solberg (Eds.), *Healing by heart: Clinical and ethical case stories of Hmong families and Western providers* (pp. 297–356). Nashville, TN: Vanderbilt University Press.

CHAPTER 15

Working with Japanese American Families

NANCY HIKOYEDA, WESLEY K. MUKOYAMA, LAN-
JOUN (DORA) LIOU, AND BARBARA MASTERSON

This chapter addresses the need for culturally appropriate dementia and Alzheimer's disease (AD) services and interventions for Japanese American (JA) elders and their caregivers. Appropriate services and public policies will play an increasingly important role in enhancing quality of life for JA elders, because the risks of AD and vascular dementia increase with age and assimilation in this population (Graves et al., 1996; Larson, 1993).

Background

According to the 2000 U.S. Census, there were 240,527 Japanese Americans in the United States 55 years of age and older. Of these, nearly 20% were foreign born (U.S. Census Bureau, 2004). Older JAs are the most acculturated of all the Asian/Pacific Islander elders due to the length of time they have been in the United States (since the 1860s) and the decline in immigration from Japan in recent years (Young & Gu, 1995).

Japanese Immigration

Japanese Americans (JAs) have a long history in the United States, and their story spans four distinct historical periods (Kitano, 1993). During the Immigration Period (1890–1924), the first Japanese arrived on the U.S.

mainland and in Hawaii as contract laborers. These early pioneers worked on the railroads, in mines, on farms, and on plantations. Many of these early immigrants fully intended to return to Japan after making their fortunes but never did. In the prewar era (1924–1941), increasing hostility and racial discrimination directed toward JAs was witnessed. The wartime evacuation period (1941–1945) included the uprooting and internment of all people of Japanese descent from the U.S. west coast into 10 relocation centers. During the postwar period (1945–present), JAs have been resettling throughout the United States. It is ironic that more recently, JAs have been labeled a "model minority" because of their "successful" assimilation into American society (Daniels, 1990; Kitano, 1993).

Geographic Concentration

With the exception of Hawaii, the majority of JAs reside on the west coast of the U.S. mainland; however, JAs may be found throughout the country in both urban and rural areas. Early in their history, Japanese communities, called *Nihonmachis* (Japantowns), were formed to meet the needs of JA immigrants. Japantowns provided cultural brokers (bilingual/bicultural community liaisons), housing, medical services, schools, Japanese dry goods/food stores, restaurants, hotels, newspapers, Christian churches, and Buddhist temples as well as other resources and services for Japanese families. Only three Japantowns remain today, all in California (Los Angeles, San Francisco, and San Jose). *Nihonmachis* provided Japanese families with a stable ethnic community life, protection from an unfriendly environment, and needed resources (Glenn, 1986; Ichioka, 1988; Kitano, 1993). Today, all three *Nihonmachis* are increasingly more ethnically diverse but continue to serve as social, cultural, and religious centers.

Regionally, although JAs share many common values and traditions, within-group differences exist. For example, JAs living in Hawaii have been found to have some characteristics that are different from JAs living on the U.S. mainland (e.g., more aggressive/assertive, social), primarily because Hawaiian JAs have been the majority ethnic group rather than a minority. Additionally, they were not interned during World War II, and their life experiences have differed in many other respects from their mainland counterparts (Fugita & O'Brien, 1991).

Generations and Identity

The early Japanese settlers believed that intergenerational relationships were so important to JA identity that each generation was given a distinct Japanese name. Understanding the JA individual's generational identification within the family and community can be helpful in assessing personal attitudes, beliefs, preferences, and behaviors.

The first generation of JA pioneers was the *Issei*. Although the first Japanese immigrants came in the 1860s, the majority of *Issei* males arrived between 1909 and 1924 followed by Japanese females (Glenn, 1986). Frequently, marriages were arranged by parents or marriage brokers, and many *Issei* men were married by proxy in Japan to "picture brides" (Ichioka, 1988). When the picture brides arrived in the United States, many of them met their husbands for the first time, and some discovered that their husbands had not been entirely honest about their lives in America. Divorce was not an option in Japanese culture (Glenn, 1986; Ichioka, 1988; Kitano, 1993). While caring for their growing families, the *Issei* women worked beside their husbands on the farms, businesses, or in low-wage domestic service occupations (Glenn, 1986). Most of the *Issei* are now gone; however, the cultural values and norms by which they were raised were passed down to subsequent generations. The *Issei* endured many hardships doing hard labor, living in substandard housing in a foreign land with an unfamiliar language and customs. As parents, the *Issei* sacrificed throughout their lives so their children could become successful in American society.

The children of the *Issei* are the *Nisei*, who were born from 1918 to 1940, and who are the JA elders of today. *Nisei* were raised in an environment that promoted an ethic of hard work and an emphasis on education as the means to a better life. Before World War II, *Issei* parents encouraged their *Nisei* offspring to maintain the Japanese language and culture by attending "Japanese school" in addition to public schools (Kitano, 1988). *Nisei* children were encouraged to study and work hard and become good U.S. citizens.

The third generation is called the *Sansei*, a large and heterogeneous cohort born shortly before, during, or after World War II. Even though the majority of *Sansei* did not have the camp experience, they suffered the aftermath of the wartime discrimination, economic loss and recovery, and reestablishment of the JA identity. Due to anti-Japanese sentiment and evolving family dynamics, they were not pushed to learn the Japanese language, and consequently, most *Sansei* do not speak or understand Japanese (Fugita & O'Brien, 1991). The *Sansei* are currently the primary caregivers for their elderly *Nisei* parents.

Yonsei are fourth-generation and *Gosei* are fifth-generation JAs. These descendants of the *Issei* are the most acculturated and assimilated, which is most evident in their out-marriage rate exceeding 50% (Kitano, 1993). It is not known how strongly ingrained the Japanese cultural values such as filial piety are in these generations or the extent of their commitment to helping JA elders age in place. *Sansei* and *Gosei* preferences for long-term care are also not known, although there is evidence they would consider options other than family care (Young, McCormick, & Vitaliano, 2002).

In recent years, a contemporary term, *Nikkei*, has been used to refer to JAs as a whole. *Nikkei* has been used to unify the JA community into one common intergenerational identity.

Three additional JA subgroups exist whose members will impact elder-care in the future. *Kibei* are *Nisei* who were sent to Japan for their education when young and later returned to the United States. Japanese is frequently their language of choice, and they identify closely with Japanese traditions and culture (Kitano, 1993). The number of *Kibei* is not known. The second group consists of Japanese women, known as "war brides," who immigrated to the United States after World War II following marriages to American servicemen (Daniels, 1990; Glenn, 1986). It is estimated that as many as 46,000 war brides came to the United States at this time (Daniels, 1990; Simpson, 1998). Many of these older women are believed to live alone, either as widows or divorcees, outcasts in their Japanese homeland and uncomfortable in mainstream U.S. society. For the most part, these women prefer Japanese as their language of choice. The most recent immigrants are the *Shin Issei* (newcomers), primarily Japanese businessmen and their families. While *Shin Issei* may not be older adults themselves, those who stay in the United States eventually bring their older parents (Kitano, 1993). All three of these subgroups will benefit from culturally sensitive dementia/AD services in the future.

Discrimination

JAs have faced decades of institutionalized racism in America (Kitano, 1969, 1993). For example, from 1870 to 1952, the Naturalization Act denied citizenship to Asians. In 1906, JA public school students in San Francisco were segregated, and intermarriage was forbidden in California. The 1908 Gentleman's Agreement limited the immigration of laborers from Japan. The 1913 California Alien Land Law barred noncitizens from owning land, and there was increasing housing and employment discrimination. The 1924–1952 Immigration Exclusion Act prohibited further Japanese immigration. Finally, in 1942, Executive Order No. 9066 authorized the evacuation and internment of all JAs on the west coast of the United States without cause, even though the majority of internees were U.S. citizens.

The evacuation and internment of 120,000 JAs into 10 relocation centers (known as "camps") was the most significant event in the history of *Isseis* and *Niseis*, and the experience has been a common unifying thread in west coast JA communities. With two days notice, each family was forced to dispose of all their possessions and property, as they were allowed to pack and take only what they could carry. The relocation centers were located in isolated inland deserts surrounded by guard towers, armed guards, and barbed wire fences. Each family was assigned a single room in hastily constructed barracks. Privacy was ignored as internees were forced to use open communal toilets and showers and have meals in mess halls. These demeaning conditions drastically altered JA family structure, relationships, and roles (Kitano, 1969). However, in spite of the harsh camp conditions, schools, churches, athletic activities, dances, and social events were initiated to give the younger JAs the semblance of a normal life.

The Japanese spirit was further revealed when, in spite of their incarceration, 1,500 young *Nisei* males from the camps and 3,000 from Hawaii volunteered to serve in the European front in the 442nd Regimental Combat Team and the 100th Infantry Battalion. In combat, these units sustained an enormous number of casualties and became the most highly decorated military units in U.S. history (Kitano, 1993).

The early postwar era, a time of resettlement, was also traumatic for JA families. After leaving the camps, some families discovered that their homes and personal property, left for safekeeping, had been destroyed. Others were discouraged from returning to their hometowns due to violent anti-Japanese demonstrations. Over time, however, JA families reestablished family relationships and Japantowns as well as their educational, cultural, social, and religious organizations (Glenn, 1986). Fifty years after the relocation, during the administration of President Ronald Reagan, redress and reparations were granted by the U.S. Congress. The order included a formal apology from the U.S. government, funds for curriculum development and dissemination of educational materials about the injustice, and token monetary reparations to surviving internees.

Japanese American Family Values and Norms

Traditional JA family values and norms originated during the *Meiji* era (named after Japanese Emperor *Meiji*), which existed in Japan when the *Issei* left their homeland. These values originated from Buddhist, Shinto, and Confucian teachings and served as guidelines for individual behavior as well as social norms in JA society (Kitano, 1993). Knowledge of these norms helps to explain attitudes, beliefs, and behaviors toward dementia/AD, caregiving, and service utilization.

Japanese terms define expectations for individual behavior in traditional Japanese families. *Oyakoko* is filial piety, which is the familial obligation and duty to care for parents and grandparents to reciprocate for past care. Because Japanese family hierarchy is patriarchal and traditional, JA elders believe in primogeniture, in which the oldest son is generally considered the decision maker with primary responsibility for parental care. (The actual caregiving responsibilities usually fall upon the daughter-in-law.) *Enryo* means to hesitate or refuse something initially (e.g., assistance or food) so as not to appear aggressive or greedy. Thus, JA elders will frequently refuse assistance at first, even if it is needed or desired. *Shikataganai* is a sense of fatalism or a belief that "nothing can be done"—an acceptance of life events. Caregivers may feel that dementia/AD is normal and that stress is an accepted part of caregiving. *Gaman* mandates that people be stoic in adverse circumstances, even if experiencing pain or discomfort. Thus, adversity is believed to make a person better and stronger. *Haji* is a sense of shame felt by an individual and reflected on the family unit. The entire family can "lose face" if one member does something embarrassing or bad such that the presence of an individual with dementia/AD may be felt to stigmatize a family (Kitano, 1993).

Other traditional Japanese values may be directly opposed to expected "American" attitudes and behaviors. For example, while Americans are encouraged to be autonomous and independent, traditional JAs are taught to value collectivism and to place the family's needs before those of the individual. Therefore, one must avoid situations that are burdensome to the family. JAs are taught to show deference to authority and to avoid confrontations and maintain harmony, which prohibits questioning or disagreeing with a physician or others in a position of authority. In interpersonal encounters, traditional JAs prefer indirect communication rather than assertive or aggressive interactions. Family members are taught to keep troubles and problems within the family circle—both for privacy and to save face (Kendis, 1989; Kinoshita & Gallagher-Thompson, 2004). In this context, a social stigma may be associated with seeking an assessment or treatment for dementia or participation in a support group with other JAs.

Perspectives of Dementia and Alzheimer's Disease among Japanese American Families

There has been very little research among JAs to determine their perceptions of dementia/AD, and most of the existing data tend to be from Hawaiian rather than U.S. mainland populations. In the available studies, many JA elders perceived that dementia/AD was expected in normal aging (Ross et al., 1997). An interesting gender difference was observed in Hawaii that interfered with early diagnosis. Dementia/AD in JA men escaped early detection because they avoided going to the doctor, and the typical daily activities of JA males tended to mask cognitive deficits, which are more obvious in women who must perform a wider range of daily tasks (Ross et al., 1997).

Perceived causes of dementia/AD varied. Dementia/AD was attributed to genetics, bad karma (for past behavior), or family upbringing (Ross et al., 1997). Others believed that those with dementia/AD were insane or senile (Braun & Brown, 1998).

In the caregiving literature, Adams, Aranda, Kemp, and Takagi (2002) compared distress management among Anglo, African, Japanese, and Mexican American spousal caregivers of individuals with dementia. They measured stress and coping strategies, appraisal processes, coping styles, and coping resources for the first time in a JA population. Overall, the JA caregivers differed in very few measures from the other groups. However, they scored higher on pessimistic appraisal than Anglos and African Americans due to passive fatalism (*shikataganai*) and perseverance (*gaman*), which helped the mostly female JA caregivers accept and adapt to their caregiving. JA women also scored higher on depression and distress outcomes than males and were second only to Mexican Americans.

Based on the scant research and knowledge about the cultural mandates of JA elders, dementia/AD may be a silent epidemic among JA families, because individuals fail to recognize early cognitive and behavioral changes (Ross et al., 1997) and wait until a crisis occurs to seek help (Braun & Brown, 1998). Ross et al. (1997) interviewed family informants of 191 noninstitutionalized JA men with dementia between the ages of 71 and 93. In 60% of the cases of identified dementia, family members did not recognize a memory problem, or the subjects had no assessment done. Overall, 28 had severe dementia, and 32% had no previous evaluation; 97 had problems with memory and thinking, and 51% had not received testing; and among 7 men with very mild dementia, none had seen a physician.

Furthermore, among the caregivers, Japanese family values are changing, and shifts in family expectations, attributed to changes in women's roles, and increased acceptance of outside services, have been observed (Young, McCormick, & Vitaliano, 2002). Assimilation is also a factor, because *Sanseis* tend to prefer blended rather than ethnic-specific services and seem to be influenced by changing attitudes toward institutionalization (Young, McCormick, & Vitaliano, 2002).

Strategies to Support Japanese American Family Caregivers

One solution to improve the quality of care for JA elders and support their caregivers was inspired by, and for, the *Issei*—the commitment to provide Japanese-specific community-based services and programs (Hikoyeda & Wallace, 2001). As the needs of older *Issei* increased, larger JA communities developed their own ethnic-specific social services network and long-term care continuum. The most comprehensive services may be found in Seattle, Los Angeles, the San Francisco Bay area, and Chicago. These include a wide array of JA-specific senior services/programs: senior centers, nutrition programs, transportation services, case managers, support groups, adult day care, intergenerational day care, residential housing for independent living, home care, assisted living, board and care homes, intermediate care, dementia care, and skilled nursing facilities. However, not all services or levels are offered in all locations.

The Japanese-specific services are believed to provide a familiar and comfortable environment for older JAs (Hikoyeda & Wallace, 2001). However, they were not to replace family care but to provide an extension of family care (Young, McCormick, & Vitaliano, 2002). Sustainability of these ethnic-specific community-based services presents an enormous challenge as federal, state, and local assistance continues to decrease (Young, McCormick, & Vitaliano, 2002).

Case Study

The following case study introduces a multigenerational, multiracial JA family caring for parents with dementia/AD. This case highlights cultural issues, family values, and dynamics, as well as other factors that influence JA family care.

DS is the mother of two children and caregiver for her JA mother-in-law who has Alzheimer's disease and father-in-law who is also showing signs of dementia. DS is a second-generation Chinese American woman whose parents were born in China and immigrated to the United States. Her 85-year-old father-in-law, *Jiichan* (which means Grandfather), is an English-speaking *Kibei Nisei*, and her 83-year-old mother-in-law, *Baachan* (Grandmother), was born and raised in Japan and understands some English. DS's husband, RS, was born in America and is the youngest of three sons.

A year ago, DS's in-laws moved in from another city, where they lived with their older son and his wife, who is from Japan. Jiichan and Baachan moved primarily because Jiichan could not get along with his son's wife. There was also an incident during which RS felt that his parents were not being cared for adequately by his brother's family. At the time of the move, the grandparents were warmly welcomed into DS and RS's home.

DS and RS agreed to care for Baachan, because Jiichan admitted that he could no longer do so. DS quit her job as a teacher to care for her in-laws. In return, Jiichan agreed to provide financial assistance to build another bedroom and add an extension to the home. However, Jiichan, described as a traditional, stubborn, patriarchal Japanese male, was very critical of DS. DS also notices conflicting cultural differences (e.g., Chinese families speak out and communicate with each other, whereas JA families withhold their feelings).

DS brought Baachan to the JA senior center. The social worker at the center noticed that DS was distressed and recommended that she join the caregiver support group. When interviewed for the support group, DS was sad and tearful and admitted that she was not sleeping well. She said that Jiichan was constantly interfering with family matters, complaining, critical, and abusive to her, saying that she did not care for her children properly.

DS felt that Jiichan was critical of her because she was not Japanese and not suitable for his son. DS stated that she wanted this arrangement to work, because her religious faith encouraged extended families. However, she felt inadequate in her efforts to please her in-laws. DS also felt that her husband was not supportive, because he did not understand how much Jiichan's constant criticism affected her and how his father's remarks were abusive. It became evident that in the 7 months the in-laws were living with them, DS's family was being split apart due to clash of cultures and personalities.

In addition to the support group, DS started individual counseling, and soon after, her husband followed. During counseling, RS admitted that he sensed the tension between his wife and father but felt helpless in trying to mediate. RS had talked to his father but was not sure his father listened. The joint sessions bonded RS and DS together, and they were ready to have Jiichan join them in family counseling.

Subsequent counseling sessions included the entire family, including a 15-year-old daughter and a 12-year-old son. Baachan was eventually assigned to a Japanese-speaking case manager/counselor. It became clear that there were many factors involved in the family's conflicts. These included Jiichan's borderline personality disorder with narcissistic features, probably due to issues with his mother (whom he stated abandoned him in Japan). He also had increasing symptoms of paranoia caused by his apparent dementia and stress of caring for Baachan. The cultural differences in attitude between Jiichan and his Chinese American daughter-in-law, the relationship between Jiichan and Baachan that was attributed to an arranged marriage, and the generational differences between Jiichan and RS had made the living arrangements almost unbearable.

The counseling strategy was first to strengthen the relationship and support between DS and RS. They were encouraged to respect Jiichan's pride while recognizing his losses of memory and independence and his worsening dementia. After a few sessions, RS stated "I realize that my father will not change and I will have to learn to cope with that." This was a profound and insightful statement, as RS recognized and respected his father's plight and the responsibility RS had accepted to care for his mother with the hope of giving his children the experience of living in an extended family. DS has grown to respect her husband's support as well as his determination to care for his mother and father. This filial obligation is clearly a Japanese cultural value that RS has either consciously or unconsciously accepted.

RS has become more involved with the internal issues of his family, communicating more with his father, helping his wife, and interacting with his children. RS has made appointments for his parents to be evaluated for dementia and Alzheimer's disease. Meanwhile, counseling with DS will continue along with her participation in the caregiver support group. Family counseling will continue after Jiichan and Baachan are evaluated.

Implications, Recommendations, and Conclusions

Implications

Several trends have been noted among JA families that will impact dementia/AD services in the United States. First, JA cohorts are living longer, indicating anticipated growth in dementia/AD cases, needed services, education, and outreach. Second, available family care will be limited due to increasing employment demands on younger caregivers. Third, increasing assimilation and intermarriage may dilute traditional Japanese values or expectations for family care so that JAs may wish to provide family care, but may be unable to do so. Fourth, because younger JA cohorts are expected to be more amenable to outside assistance, the demand for services/programs is expected to grow. Finally, all JA elders do not live near large Japanese communities, so those in rural or suburban areas will need culturally sensitive dementia services.

Recommendations for Services

Increased outreach and education in the JA community about dementia/AD and the benefits of early diagnosis and treatment are needed. It should be emphasized that early detection may lead to treatment for a potentially reversible condition, stabilization of existing dementia symptoms, or time to plan for cognitive decline (Ross et al., 1997).

Interventions for JA elders with dementia require consideration of cultural issues. First, providers must acknowledge the diversity within the JA population and avoid stereotyping (Braun & Brown, 1998). Second, providers need to understand that JA attitudes, behaviors, and perceptions are influenced by cohort history, degree of acculturation/assimilation, cultural values and norms, length of time in the United States, discrimination, generation, gender, geography, socioeconomic status, family dynamics, traditional caregiving practices, as well as other factors. When working with JA family caregivers, dementia care depends on the special needs of the elders and the caregiver's capacity and desire to provide the necessary assistance. Furthermore, many JA family caregivers are in the "sandwich generation," caring for their children as well as their parents.

Culturally appropriate services must be provided for JA elders and their caregivers. The services should include training about the importance of establishing rapport and trust, explanatory models of disease, an assessment of the language used to discuss dementia (Braun & Brown, 1998; Dilworth-Anderson & Gibson, 2002), determination of family decision makers, religious beliefs, and the elder/caregiver's sense of internal and external control (Braun & Brown, 1998).

JA caregivers should be given increased access to information about supportive dementia/AD services. They also need information about depression, screening for depression, treatment, and coping skills. Support groups, either mainstream or ethnic specific (depending on the JA caregiver's preference), should be encouraged and made available (Adams et al., 2002).

Consideration should also be given toward educating caregivers about the financial and legal issues affecting dementia/AD care. Despite the existence of legal services providers within the JA community, there is little outreach encompassing the rights and expectations of those for whom care is provided and the responsibilities and alternatives available for JA care providers.

Recommendations for Public Policy

JA caregivers of individuals with dementia/AD can benefit from information and referral services, training, financial and hands-on assistance, respite, and other resources. Furthermore, increased culturally sensitive mental-health services can reduce the stress among JA caregivers if available. These include increased resources for outreach regarding depression and the importance of early diagnosis and treatment. Culturally appropriate educational materials on dementia/AD, in English and Japanese, should be available in different formats (e.g., books, videos, fact sheets).

JAs have suffered from the labeling of the population as a "model minority." Resource allocations have been minimal because of the belief that JA families "take care of their own." However, it is unrealistic to expect that JA community-based organizations can successfully meet all the needs and preferences of JA families as they struggle with sustainability in this era of dwindling local, state, and national resources. Furthermore, policy makers must not neglect this subgroup based on stereotypes and misinformation.

Recommendations for Future Research

The research agenda for JAs suffering from dementia/AD should include the development of culturally relevant assessments, examinations of help-seeking behaviors, examinations of the influence of traditional Japanese values and norms on physical and emotional health, and evaluations of existing interventions. Studies on JA caregiver stress and coping, appraisal processes, coping styles, and coping resources were noticeably absent in the literature and should be pursued further (Adams et al., 2002). Younger JA cohorts should be surveyed to plan for future needs and preferences.

Conclusion

While JAs are considered the most assimilated of the Asian populations in the United States, many JA elders and their caregivers maintain traditional Japanese language, customs, beliefs, and values. These and other factors must be considered to enhance the quality of life and care of JA elders with dementia/AD.

Acknowledgment

The authors would like to thank Dr. Kellie Takagi for her assistance with the manuscript.

Resources for Japanese American Family Caregivers

Information on Japanese Americans and dementia/AD is available in English and Japanese from the following sources:

The Alzheimer's Association, Northern California and Northern Nevada, 2065 W. El Camino Real, Suite C, Mountain View, CA 94040; phone: 800-272-3900; Web site: www.alznorcal.org

Ethnic Elders Care Network: Web site: www.ethnicelderscare.net

Family Caregiver Alliance (FCA), 180 Montgomery Street, Suite 1100, San Francisco, CA 94104; phone: 800-445-8106; Web site: www.caregiver.org

References

Adams, B., Aranda, M. P., Kemp, B., & Takagi, K. (2002). Ethnic and gender differences in distress among Anglo American, African American, Japanese American, and Mexican American spousal caregivers of persons with dementia. *Journal of Clinical Geropsychology, 8*(4), 279–301.

Braun, K. L., & Brown, C. V. (1998). Perceptions of dementia, caregiving and help seeking among Asian and Pacific Islander Americans. *Health and Social Work, 23*(4), 262–274.

Daniels, R. (1990). *Coming to America: A history of immigration and ethnicity in American life.* Princeton: Harper Collins.

Dilworth-Anderson, P., & Gibson, B. E. (2002). The cultural influence of values, norms, meanings, and perceptions in understanding dementia in ethnic minorities. *Alzheimer Disease & Associated Disorders, 16*(Supp. 2), S56–S63.

Fugita, S. S., & O'Brien, D. J. (1991). *Japanese American ethnicity: The persistence of community.* Seattle: University of Washington Press.

Glenn, E. N. (1986). *Issei, Nisei, War Bride: Three generations of Japanese American women in domestic service.* Philadelphia, PA: Temple University Press.

Graves, A. B., Larson, E. B., Edland, S. D., Bowen, J. D., McCormick, W.C., McCurry, S. M. et al. (1996). Prevalence of dementia and its subtypes in the Japanese American population of King County, Washington state. The Kame Project. *American Journal of Epidemiology, 144*(8), 760–771.

Hikoyeda, N., & Wallace, S. P. (2001). Do ethnic-specific long term care facilities improve resident quality of life? Findings from the Japanese American community. *Journal of Gerontological Social Work, 36*(1/2), 83–106.

Ichioka, Y. (1988). *The Issei: The world of the first generation Japanese immigrants 1885–1924.* New York: The Free Press.

Kendis, R. J. (1989). *An attitude of gratitude: The adaptation to aging of the elderly Japanese in America.* New York: AMS Press.

Kinoshita, L. M., & Gallagher-Thompson, D. (2004). Japanese American caregivers of individuals with dementia: An examination of Japanese cultural values and dementia caregiving. *Clinical Gerontologist, 27*(1/2), 87–101.

Kitano, H. H. L. (1969). *Japanese Americans: The evolution of a subculture.* Englewood Cliffs, NJ: Prentice Hall.

Kitano, H. H. L. (1993). *Generations and identity: The Japanese American.* Needham Heights, MA: Ginn Press.

Larson, E. B. (1993). Illnesses causing dementia in the very elderly. *The New England Journal of Medicine, 328*(3), 203–205.

Ross, G. W., Abbott, R. D., Petrovich, H., Masaki, K. H., Murdaugh, C., Trockman, C. et al. (1997). Frequency and characteristics of silent dementia among elderly Japanese-American men: The Honolulu-Asia Aging study. *The Journal of the American Medical Association, 277*(10), 800–805.

Simpson, C. C. (1998). Out of an obscure place: Japanese war brides and cultural pluralism in the 1950s. *Journal of Feminist Cultural Studies, 10*(3), 47–67.

U.S. Census Bureau. (2004). *American FactFinder datasets.* Retrieved February 19, 2004, from http://factfinder.census.gov/servlet/datasetmainpaageservle t?)program-DEC&_langu-eng&.ts

Young, H. M., McCormick, W. M., & Vitaliano, P. P. (2002). Evolving values in community-based long-term care services for Japanese Americans. *Advances in Nursing Science, 25*(2), 40–56.

Young, J. J., & Gu, N. (1995). *Demographic and socioeconomic characteristics of elderly Asian and Pacific Island Americans.* Seattle, WA: National Asian Pacific Center on Aging.

CHAPTER 16

Working with Korean American Families

AILEE MOON

In late July of 2005, a tragic story of a Korean immigrant family shocked the Korean American community. An elderly woman with dementia who was living with her son's family had become increasingly violent, hitting and throwing things at family members, and breaking windows on several occasions in her attempts to leave the house. Her daughter-in-law, the primary caregiver, was also caring for her father, who had come to live with the family a few months before the incident after he became physically impaired following a stroke. On the tragic day, the caregiver daughter had to go somewhere for a few hours and asked her father to care for her mother-in-law while she was gone. When she returned, the two elderly relatives were dead. Allegedly, her father killed the demented woman and then took his own life. The family and authorities speculated that he committed the homicide in order to free his daughter and the family from all the heavy burdens associated with the increasingly difficult caregiving situation.

In a less tragic, more common situation, we find caregivers facing difficult decisions and then trying to live with their decisions. Mrs. Kim's father came to Seattle, Washington, to live near his daughter, his only child, soon after his wife died. Her father was living in an apartment by himself, because he insisted that he wanted to be independent and did not wish to burden his daughter's family. One day, Mrs. Kim received a call from the police department. Apparently, her father was wandering in a neighborhood far from his apartment and did not know how he got there or how to get home. Mrs. Kim thought he was just confused as he was getting older and did not think it was anything serious to worry about. A few months later, she received a call from the apartment manager who told her that her father could no longer live in the apartment because he had done some "strange" things to other tenants. He had gotten lost trying to find his way home on several occasions, and he had asked people to call another Korean tenant, not his daughter, to pick him up; he threatened to kill people who became involved if they told his daughter about the incidents. Mrs. Kim brought him home and took him to a doctor; he was diagnosed as being in a moderate stage of Alzheimer's disease. Although Mrs. Kim tried to care for him, it became too difficult for the family, physically and emotionally. Her father repeatedly told her that he wanted to go home, meaning he wanted to return to Korea. A year later, Mrs. Kim took him to Korea and placed him in a nursing home for elders with dementia, where he could speak and interact with other Koreans and have Korean meals. Since making that decision, Mrs. Kim's life has never been the same: She has felt much guilt and shame, and she blames herself for "abandoning" her father who had given her so much.

Were there any alternative care arrangements or support systems available to the family caregivers in both of these cases? Were all available resources explored and exploited, as needed? Were there any special circumstances and needs that limited their ability to use alternative care arrangements and existing services? What could have been done to prevent the death of the two elder parents? While answers to these questions, as well as many issues and challenges faced by elders with dementia and their families, may have more commonalities than differences across all ethnic and racial groups, this chapter attempts to address the questions in the context of Korean immigrant families, focusing on the issues that are more specific to the Korean ethnic immigrant, and the Korean cultural group.

Immigration and Socioeconomic Background

It was only after the passage of the Immigration and Naturalization Act of 1965 that Koreans immigrated to the United States in substantial numbers. The Korean population in the United States has increased more than 15-fold during the past three decades, from about 70,000 in 1970 to 1.08 million (Korean alone) or 1.23 million (Korean alone plus Korean in combination with others) in 2000 (U.S. Census Bureau, 2002; Yu, Choe, & Han, 2002). Using the "Korean alone" data, two-thirds of the Korean American population live in seven states: California (32.1%), New York (11.1%), New Jersey (6.1%), Illinois (4.8%), Washington (4.4%), Texas (4.2%), and Virginia

(4.2%). Compared to other Asian American groups, Korean Americans are underrepresented in the West and overrepresented in the South: For example, 21% of Korean Americans live in Southern states, compared to 10% of Japanese, 13% of Filipinos, and 14% of Chinese (Yu et al., 2002).

The population of older Koreans in the United States during the past three decades has grown at an even faster rate, increasing 20-fold, from 3,270 in 1970 to 66,254 in 2000 (Min & Moon, in press). In addition to a substantial increase in the immigration of elderly Koreans during the past two decades, the aging of younger Korean immigrants admitted to this county in the 1960s and 1970s has contributed to the overall growth of the population of older Koreans. In 2000, the proportion of the age group 65 years and older constituted 6.8% of the Korean American population, but it is the fastest-growing age group, increasing from only 2.4% in 1980, to 4.3% in 1990, and to 6.8% in 2000.

While the Korean American population has a relatively short history of immigration to the United States, the 2000 Census suggests that the population has become more diverse. The proportion of Koreans born in foreign countries decreased from 73% in 1990 to 65% in 2000; the proportion of those who do not speak English well dropped from 52% in 1990 to 28%, although over three-quarters of Korean Americans continue to speak a language other than English, mostly Korean, at home (82% in 1990 and 78% in 2000) (Moon, 1998; U.S. Census Bureau, 1992, 2000, 2002). However, these foreign-born and limited English proficiency percentages remain very high for the 65 and older age group—94% and 77%, respectively, in 2000 (Min & Moon, in press).

Korean Americans show one of the highest levels of educational achievement; in 2000, 49% had at least a bachelor's degree, far higher than the national figure of 27%. Korean American elders, however, exhibit significantly lower educational attainment: 45% did not graduate from high school, while 23% completed high school education, and the remaining 32% had at least some college education (Center for Korean American and Korean Studies, 2002; Yu et al., 2002).

The overall income picture of Korean Americans, however, does not seem to correlate highly with their overall educational levels. In 2000, their average individual income for the age group between 25 and 64 ($32,807) was lower than the national average of $35,017 (Center for Korean American and Korean Studies, 2002). In addition, foreign-born Korean Americans exhibit significantly lower incomes than U.S.-born Korean Americans and the general population: For example, the median individual income of foreign-born Korean Americans in 2000 was $20,000, compared to $32,080 for the U.S.-born Korean Americans and the national median income of $26,000. The lower incomes of foreign-born Korean Americans could be attributed to issues and difficulties associated with immigration and adjustment in a new country, especially among relatively recent immigrants educated in Korea who experience limited economic and employment opportunities due to language and cultural differences.

Family System and Values in Transition

With the increasing diversity among Korean Americans and the lack of a representative national study on the values and practices concerning family life and elder care in the population, it is difficult to generalize about the family system and values in the Korean American family. However, there is increasing evidence to suggest that many Korean Americans have gradually moved away from the traditional Korean family norms and belief systems, which were strongly rooted in Confucianism. Instead, whether acculturated or adjusting to the social and economic environment of a host country, they have been more accepting of the Western or American values and ways of life, especially in gender roles, child–parent relations, and family care for their elders (Min, 2001; Moon & Hoang, 1997; Youn, Knight, Jeong, & Benton, 1999).

In a study of Korean immigrant parents and their adolescent children in 190 families, the majority of both groups challenged the traditional hierarchical and patriarchal norms of Korean family (Moon & Hoang, 1997). For example, 56% of the parents and 60% of the children disagreed that the eldest person should have the most authority in making important family decisions; 73% of the parents and 50% of the children rejected that the eldest son should be responsible for taking care of older parents.

Findings from a recent study of 29 Korean American social and health-care providers who work directly with Korean American elders in Los Angeles are striking in that almost all of them did not believe in the traditional norm and practice of filial piety: Over 90% expressed disbelief on having to live together with their older parents at their parents' wish; on having older parents make the final decision on important family matters; on having to obey the decisions of parents; and on daughters-in-law having more responsibilities than married sons for care of their parents (Moon, 2004). In addition, 78% of them disagreed with the statement, "it is wrong to place an elderly parent in a nursing home."

Similarly, the majority of Korean immigrant elders do not seem to hold the traditional beliefs about proper living arrangement and elder care, perhaps in reaction to the realities of changing familial values and attitudes toward elder care among their adult children, combined with the availability of public income and other support programs (e.g., Supplemental

Security Income and subsidized housing) and community-based health and social services (e.g., adult day health care centers), which enable independent living. In fact, a study of 153 first-generation Korean immigrant elders found that about three-quarters (74%) of them supported an adult child's decision to place an impaired parent in a nursing home, and about two-thirds disagreed that children should live together with their parents when the parents are physically and functionally able (62%) or when they have functional limitations and require extensive assistance with their personal care (64%) (Min, 2001).

Youn et al. (1999) found that Korean American family caregivers of elders with dementia exhibited lower levels of familism than Korean caregivers living in Korea but higher levels than White Americans. They also found that Korean and Korean American caregivers experienced higher levels of burden, depression, and anxiety than did White Americans.

These findings seem to suggest that most Korean Americans are no longer willing to practice filial piety in the traditional sense, nor do most of their parents expect their children to do so. Thus, one can argue that filial piety in practice has rapidly become an "abandoned old fashion" in many Korean American families (Kim, Moon, & Shin, 1997). It can also be argued that researchers and practitioners who tend to stress or overstate the practice of filial piety in today's Korean American families based on yesterday's tradition of family life could overlook the elders' desire and need for independent living. In this regard, the notion that Asian Americans take care of their aging parents could be an overgeneralized assumption that is subject to verification within each Asian American community.

The extended family system, the most defining traditional family unit in most Asian countries, including Korea, where the eldest son and his wife live with and care for their aging parents, has not only been weakened but has also undergone a major shift in its meaning and purpose in Korean American families. Today, the majority of Korean American elders live alone or with a spouse only. Among those who live with adult children and grandchildren, many seem to be caregivers rather than care recipients, caring for their grandchildren and performing housekeeping roles while their adult children work outside the home. As found in a study of immigrant elders and their living arrangements (Kritz, Gurak, & Chen, 2000), demand for the elder's assistance with domestic work, limited economic resources, lack of acculturation, and shorter durations of residence in the United States (perhaps the adjustment period) seem to significantly influence the likelihood of Korean American elders living with children. Therefore, practitioners should not assume that a multigenerational living arrangement is a sign of the practice of filial responsibility for care of aging parents or relatives (Moon & Rhee, in press).

At the same time, living alone or with a spouse only may not necessarily mean isolation or a lack of family contact or support. Geographic proximity to the Korean ethnic community and availability of health, social, recreational, and other services in the Korean language seem to influence and enable establishment of independent living among Korean American elders, especially monolingual Korean immigrant elders. Studies have shown that regardless of whether Korean American elders live alone or with children, their perceived good relationships and frequent contacts with children remain significant factors for morale and life satisfaction for most Korean American elders (Moon, 1996; Moon, White, & Lee, 2005).

Prevalence of Dementia

At present, no national data on the prevalence of dementia or Alzheimer's disease among Korean Americans are available. In Korea, several prevalence studies estimated 8.0–11.5% of Koreans 65 years of age or older as having dementia, with 50–66% of them diagnosed as having Alzheimer's disease, 20–30% having vascular dementia, and the remaining having other conditions, such as Parkinson's disease, Huntington's disease, and head injuries (Kwon, 2001; Lee et al., 2002; Park, Ko, Park, & Jung, 1994; Suh, Kim, & Cho, 2003; Yoon et al., 2002).

Some researchers believe the age-specific prevalence of dementia among Asian American populations to be similar to that of the U.S. population as a whole (Braun, Takamura, Forman, Sasaki, & Meininger, 1995). However, Watari and Gatz (2004) indicated that dementia may be a greater problem for Korean Americans than other Asian American groups. This is based on the findings from a comparative study that the lifetime prevalence rate of cognitive deficits, measured by a mental screening test, is higher among Korean American elders in Los Angeles (3%) than among other Asian American groups (Yamamoto, Rhee, & Chang, 1994). In 2000, only 6.8% of Korean American elders, compared to 11.9% of the total elderly population 65 years of age or older, belonged to the age group of 85 years and older, an age group with the highest prevalence rate of dementia. However, considering that Korean Americans are expected to live longer than ever before, joining the oldest old age group of 85 years or older at a faster rate than other age groups, combined with continuous immigration of Korean elders and the aging of younger Korean immigrants who came to the United States in the 1970s and the 1980s, it is reasonable to predict that the number of Korean American elders and families affected by dementia will grow significantly in the next two decades.

Perceptions About the Causes, Symptoms, and Treatment of Dementia

Dementia (*chi-mae* in Korean) and Alzheimer's disease are relatively new words but are frequently used by Koreans and Korean Americans to refer to what had previously been labeled as senility, insanity, or crazy mental illness. Strongly influenced by the Chinese, most Koreans in the past believed dementia was a consequence of "bad blood," sins committed by the person with dementia or the family or their ancestors, an act of evil spirits, improper alignment of a house or the grave of an ancestor, or lack of respect for ancestors or care of their graves (Elliot, Minno, Lam, & Tu, 1996). However, recent focus groups and survey findings suggest that most Korean Americans no longer share these beliefs, perhaps because they have increasingly been exposed to biomedical explanations of dementia and because of a strong hold of Christian religion among approximately 70–80% of Korean Americans, which tends to denounce such beliefs as superstitious and non-Christian.

In a study of 109 Korean Americans at two Korean Christian churches in Los Angeles, Watari and Gatz (2004) found that only 7% identified "old age" as the cause of Alzheimer's disease, 6% attributed it to "failure to keep mentally active," 10% to "senility," while 45% correctly indicated the cause as "unknown." Another recent survey of 78 Korean immigrants in Los Angeles showed only 4% related one's dementia to the improper alignment of a house or the grave of an ancestor, and 8% thought it could be retribution for sins of ancestors or family misdeeds; two-thirds of the study participants were 60 years of age or older, and 19 were practitioners working with Korean American elders (Moon, 2005).

The same survey conducted by Moon (2005), however, suggests that persons with dementia are still stigmatized. The nature and source of stigma have shifted from traditional superstitious and supernatural beliefs around the family and family history to the individual's personality (being passive, stubborn, or quiet) and one's life history of hardship and stress. Specifically, over three-quarters of survey participants believed that the likelihood of developing dementia would be higher for those individuals who had experienced much hardship and stress in their lifetimes or had unresolved personal issues or family problems (77%), for those with reserved or passive personality (76%), and for those who experienced serious cultural shocks or adjustment problems as consequences of immigration to the United States (74%). In contrast, 49% thought that having a parent or sibling with dementia would increase the likelihood of developing dementia, and 36% believed that older men were more likely to develop dementia than women of the same age.

Like many other groups (Braun & Browne, 1998; Braun et al., 1995; Connell & Gibson, 1997; Connell, Kole, Avey, Benedict, & Gilman, 1996; Dilworth-Anderson & Gibson, 2002; Yeo & Gallagher-Thompson, 1996), a common misunderstanding about dementia among Korean Americans is that memory loss and associated behavioral changes are part of the normal aging process (Braun et al., 1995; Moon, 2005). A comparative study of Filipino, Korean, Vietnamese, and Native Hawaiian adults in Hawaii found that 61% of Korean Americans, the highest among the groups, believed that Alzheimer's disease was a natural part of the aging process and that only 25% were able to recognize symptoms of Alzheimer's disease (Braun et al., 1995). In Moon's (2005) Los Angeles survey, 83% of respondents thought memory loss and associated behavior were normal consequences of growing old.

The tendency to perceive dementia as being a result of having a less desirable personality or a difficult and stressful life history with unresolved personal or family problems could lead the person with dementia and his or her family members to deny or conceal suspected symptoms of dementia and thereby delay seeking medical diagnosis and treatment and supportive services outside the family. Early detection, diagnosis, treatment, and use of supportive services may be further hindered by the association of memory loss with natural aging processes, and a lack of knowledge about warning symptoms of dementia.

In addition, for most Korean Americans, Alzheimer's disease is just another name for dementia rather than being one of many causes of dementia. Not knowing that other conditions (such as depression and vitamin B_{12} deficiency) or even medications for other illnesses can cause dementia, combined with the common belief that there is no medical cure for dementia, has meant that treatable and reversible cases of dementia have gone undiagnosed, and the symptoms have gone untreated (Steckenrider, 1993).

Many Korean Americans seem to view practice of religious faith as an effective avenue for prevention and cure or alleviation of dementia. Eighty-five percent of survey respondents believed that people with religious faith would be less likely to develop dementia than those with no religion; 82% reported that religious faith could alleviate symptoms and slow progression of the disease; 43% thought that faith could cure it; while 33% reported that acupuncture, herbal medicine, and natural food diet could alleviate the disease (Moon, 2005). Although religion and spirituality could play an important role in coping with stress and illness, such beliefs in the power of religion related to prevention and cure of dementia should be addressed with sensitivity, emphasizing the importance of seeking medical and other supportive services that could contribute to alleviating symptoms and progression of dementia.

Knowledge and Utilization of Dementia-Related and Long-Term Care Services

The tragic deaths of two beloved elders and sending a father with Alzheimer's disease to Korea for residential care could probably have been avoided had there been a residential care facility for dementia patients with a "Korean program" in terms of language and other cultural aspects of services, including serving Korean food, having staff members who spoke Korean, and other Korean residents for companionship. A lack of financial ability to pay for such residential care, a lack of knowledge about the disease, a lack of information about various supportive programs for dementia patients and their family caregivers, as well as little or no knowledge about how to care for dementia patients with behavioral and other problems might also have contributed to the outcomes for the two families.

The question of availability, knowledge, accessibility, and use of dementia-related services is the most critical issue surrounding dementia that needs to be addressed in the Korean American community. Most participants in the Los Angeles survey (Moon, 2005), including 19 health and social service providers, mostly social workers at adult day health-care centers, reported having no or little knowledge about services available to dementia patients (89%) or services and programs designed to help their family caregivers (90%). An earlier study (Moon, Lubben, & Villa, 1998) also found that Korean immigrant elders in Los Angeles have very low levels of awareness and utilization of 15 community long-term care services in both absolute and relative terms compared to non-Hispanic White Americans.

Data from nine California Alzheimer's Disease Diagnostic and Treatment Centers (ADDTCs) revealed that in comparison to their population sizes within the nine counties served, Asians and Pacific Islanders under-enrolled by approximately 50% at centers specializing in Alzheimer's disease assessment and care (Chow, Ross, Fox, Cummings, & Lin, 2000). When reviewing data from Los Angeles's St. Barnabas ADDTC, it was further concluded that both Korean American and non-Korean-American elders underutilized community services designed to help people with cognitive decline and memory loss, such as support groups and case management (Watari & Gatz, 2004). It was also found that an average of 3 or 4 years elapsed from the appearance of initial symptoms until assessment. This average time lag is substantially longer than the median lag time of 1.5 years from first symptom appearance to initial physician visit found in a study of 1,480 caregivers of Alzheimer's disease patients (Knopman, Donohue, & Gutterman, 2000).

Equally evident, however, is that if available services were known to them and if services were also accessible and acceptable to them, in terms of location, language, and culture, Korean Americans would use such services. For example, Moon et al. (1998) indicated that when only those elderly respondents who were aware of community services were examined, the service utilization rate was significantly higher for Korean immigrant elders than for White elders with respect to transportation and visiting nurse services. In addition, as of June 2005, nearly one third of clients at the St. Barnabas Alzheimer's Adult Day Care Center in Los Angeles were Korean Americans (personal communication, June 15, 2005). At the same time, the author identified at least 20 adult day heath-care centers in Los Angeles and Orange counties serving approximately 1,800 Korean American elders, representing 9% of the 21,145 Korean elders the 2000 Census counted in the two counties. Despite the common assumption that Asian Americans do not place their aging relatives in nursing homes, the author identified 910 Korean American elder residents living in 12 selected nursing homes in the areas where the population of Korean Americans was concentrated in the two counties, constituting over 4% of the population in the counties. This number could have been higher if all the nursing homes in the two counties had been contacted. Nonetheless, none of these nursing facilities serving primarily Korean Americans is equipped to admit dementia patients with serious cognitive impairment or behavioral problems.

It must be emphasized that the findings on the availability and use of day care programs and residential care facilities in Los Angeles and Orange counties in California, with the highest concentration of health and social service providers specializing in serving the Korean American population, should not mask the reality of many Korean Americans, especially those living in locations with low numbers of Korean Americans, who may not be able to use needed services due to a lack of information, and language, cultural, and transportation barriers. In addition, ineligibility for Medicare or Medicaid health insurances, due to noncitizenship, short duration of U.S. residence, or other immigration status, and the low income status of some Korean immigrant elders and their families create additional barriers to accessing needed health and social services.

Strategies for Meeting the Needs of Dementia Patients and Family Caregivers

A correct understanding of disease is a prerequisite for the correct interpretation of warning signs and appropriate help-seeking behaviors (Werner,

2003). The strategies for meeting the needs of dementia patients and their family caregivers in the Korean American community must begin with public education to increase knowledge about dementia, its known and unknown causes, the symptoms, the importance of early detection and accurate diagnosis, and the potential benefits of medical assessment and treatment. In this effort, stigmatizing perceptions of the persons with dementia (e.g., stress, personality, hardship in lifetime, unresolved problems) must be addressed and recognition of dementia as a medical condition, not a normal part of the aging process, must be increased. Specific symptoms of dementia in various stages of progression must also be included for practical help with early detection. The information that medications to alleviate the symptoms and supportive services are available is also important to encourage aggressive help seeking. It is equally important to understand that praying, acupuncture and herbal medicines, and healthy lifestyles (good diet, exercise, and reducing stress) may neither protect nor cure dementia; no combination of these alternative treatments can substitute for medical treatment.

Second, information about where to go for diagnosis of dementia, with a possibility that memory loss could be caused by reversible disorders, as well as information about available supportive services for dementia patients and family caregivers within and outside the Korean American community, such as Alzheimer's day care centers, the Alzheimer's Association, caregiver resource centers, caregiver support groups, and residential care facilities for dementia patients, should become widely available. As found in the recent Los Angeles survey, most Korean Americans have little or no such information, which is critical for improving quality of life for people with dementia and their family caregivers.

Free public information, in the form of printed materials and videos in the Korean language, on dementia and available services must be widely available. In fact, a study demonstrated that videos and brochures developed in native languages that incorporated culturally specific perceptions of dementia, caregiving, and help seeking significantly increased awareness of Alzheimer's disease and sources of help among Korean American participants, as well as other Asian and Pacific Islanders in Hawaii (Braun et al., 1995).

In addition, Korean ethnic media, churches and temples, social clubs, doctors and nurses, adult day care centers, nursing homes, and general social and health service agencies within and outside the Korean American community who have direct contact with Korean Americans need to actively engage in the dissemination of appropriate and practical information to the public and their clients. Practical information should include telephone numbers and other contact information for local services for those affected by dementia, including service centers or specialists and supportive services, and Web page addresses for information on relevant dementia diseases, particularly those available in Korean, such as the Alzheimer's Association's Web page.

Because most first-generation Korean Americans rely on Korean ethnic media, particularly national and local newspapers, for news and information, and attend Korean ethnic churches or temples, they could be most effective in reaching a large number of Koreans in most parts of the country. For example, a Korean media campaign on dementia could have a tremendous impact on increasing public awareness of dementia and related services nationally and locally.

Considering that most Korean Americans, especially elders, contact Korean ethnic service organizations in local areas for a variety of information and service needs and Korean-speaking doctors for their medical care, general social and health service organizations and Korean-speaking physicians and nurses serving Korean Americans could and should play a special role in detecting dementia and providing information and referral about dementia and related services available locally for both patients and their families. For this reason, there is a special need for training these professionals in order to increase their sensitivity and knowledge about dementia and related locally available services, as well as addressing their own biases and misperceptions about dementia. Also, because many Korean American elders and some of their adult children have language barriers, these service organizations should be willing to provide or have information about obtaining needed interpretation services, in addition to general information and referral services.

Third, caregivers caring for relatives with dementia urgently need to be able, as needed, to increase their knowledge about dementia and caregiving and use of available supportive services, such as the Alzheimer's Association's safe return bracelet, Alzheimer's day care centers, respite care, case management, and support groups. Family caregivers must be informed about not only the range of available services, but also how to access them, and how the services can benefit themselves and care recipients directly and indirectly.

In fact, a study revealed that among Korean American Alzheimer's disease patients, those living with family generally exhibited more severe symptoms and more severe dementia-related problems than those who lived alone at the initial assessment, suggesting that family members were not able to detect the disease until patients had serious behavioral problems (Watari & Gatz, 2004). The study also found that use of case management services and Alzheimer's day care resource centers was significantly lower among Korean Americans than non-Korean-American groups. Recent studies of caregivers further indicated that participation in combined different strategies and services (e.g., skill training, family counseling, case management, behavior-management strategies, and environmental modification) of high intensity (frequency and duration) produced a significant improvement in knowledge and ability to care, caregiver burden, depression, subjective well-being, and perceived caregiver satisfaction (Schulz & Martire, 2004). Among various programs designed to enhance family caregiving for Alzheimer's disease, the programs that emphasized behavioral-skills training were found to show the greatest impact in reducing caregiver burden (Gitlin et al., 2003; Schulz & Martire, 2004).

Therefore, concentrated efforts within and outside the Korean American community to provide directly, or link to, practical and intensive intervention or training programs for family caregivers, such as skill training, case management, and family counseling, as well as respite care and other supportive services, would be critical for enhancing the well-being of Korean American dementia patients and their family caregivers. Again, a special consideration for caregivers with limited English skills should be taken into consideration when referring them to such programs and services, either by offering them in Korean or by providing a Korean translation service.

Finally, the most serious service gap exists in day care programs and Alzheimer-specialized nursing homes for Korean American Alzheimer's patients who have limited English skills or strong cultural preferences or need. Cultural and language barriers to access existing adult day care centers and residential nursing facilities mean that these centers are, in essence, nonentities to many Korean American dementia patients.

In this regard, there must be a special policy and program development initiative, with financial and other incentives, to promote the establishment of a unit within existing adult day care centers and nursing homes to make it possible for Korean American dementia patients or other ethnic groups with special cultural and language needs to access such critical services. In localities with low numbers of Korean American elders, one such center and nursing home in the area can be negotiated and designated for creation of such a unit or for infusion of a "Korean program" by hiring one Korean-speaking staff member and providing Korean meals. The Korean American community leaders, including religious leaders, social and health service providers, and elders and family caregivers, should also be actively engaged in this effort of searching for practical solutions to the problem of disconnection in the continuum of care for the growing number of Korean American dementia patients and family caregivers for now and for the future.

Resources

Alzheimer's Association, Web site (in Korean): www.alz.org/resources/diversity/korean.asp. The Alzheimer's Association has education and service information in Korean, such as warning signs of Alzheimer's disease, assessment tools, getting a diagnosis, and available resources and services.

Department of Aging, City of Los Angeles, 3580 Wilshere Blvd., Suite 300, Los Angeles, CA 90010; phone: 800-834-4777, 213-252-4030; Web site (in Korean): www.cityofla.org/DOA/pdf/SeniorFoc_Kor.pdf. The City of Los Angeles Department of Aging has information in Korean on a variety of services available to residents of Los Angeles, including a Family Care Support Program and an adult day care center for patients with Alzheimer's disease and their family caregivers.

St. Barnabas Senior Services, 675 S. Carondelet Street, Los Angeles, CA 90057; phone: 213-388-4444; fax: 213-738-9467; Web site (In Korean): www.la4seniors.com/korean_st_barnabas.htm. St. Barnabas Senior Services currently has four Korean-speaking social workers, including an Alzheimer specialist. It also houses an Alzheimer's disease diagnosis and treatment center and Alzheimer's day care resource center (www.saintb-la.org/main/adc.html).

References

Braun, K. L., & Browne, C. V. (1998). Perceptions of dementia, caregiving, and help seeking among Asian and Pacific Islander Americans. *Health & Social Work, 23,* 262–274.

Braun, K. L., Takamura, J. C., Forman, S. M., Sasaki, P. A., & Meininger, L. (1995). Developing and testing outreach materials on Alzheimer's disease for Asian and Pacific Islander Americans. *The Gerontologist, 35,* 122.

Center for Korean American and Korean Studies. (2002). Census Information, Retrieved May 10, 2005, from www.calstatela.edu/centers/ckaks/census/data_7803.html

Chow, T. W., Ross, L., Fox, P., Cummings, J. L., & Lin, K. (2000). Utilization of Alzheimer's disease community resources by Asian-Americans in California. *International Journal of Geriatric Psychiatry, 15,* 838–847.

Connell, C. M., & Gibson, G. D. (1997). Racial, ethnic, and cultural differences in dementia caregiving: Review and analysis. *The Gerontologist, 37,* 355–364.

Connell, C. M., Kole, S. L., Avey, H., Benedict, C. J., & Gilman, S. (1996). Attitudes about Alzheimer's disease and the dementia service delivery network among family caregivers and service providers in rural Michigan. *American Journal of Alzheimer's Disease,* May/June, 15–25.

Dilworth-Anderson, P., & Gibson, B. (2002). The cultural influence of values, norms, meanings, and perceptions in understanding dementia in ethnic minorities. *Alzheimer's Disease and Associated Disorders*, 16(Supp. 2), S56–S63.

Elliott, K., Minno, M., Lam, D., & Tu, A. (1996). Working with Chinese families in the context of dementia. In G. Yeo & D. Gallagher-Thompson (Eds.), *Ethnicity and the dementias* (pp. 89–108). Washington, DC: Taylor & Francis.

Gitlin, L., Belle S. H., Burgio, L., Czaja, S., Mahoney, D., Gallagher-Thompson, D. et al. (2003). Effects of multicomponent intervention on caregiver burden and depression: The REACH multisite initiative at 6-month follow-up. *Psychological Aging*, 18, 361–374.

Kim, J., Moon, A., & Shin, H. (1997). Elderly Korean American women living in two cultures. In Y. Song & A. Moon (Eds.), *Korean American women living in two cultures*. Los Angeles, CA: Academia Koreana, Keimyung-Baylo University Press.

Knopman, D., Donohue, J. A., & Gutterman, E. M. (2000). Patterns of care in the early stages of Alzheimer's disease: Impediments to timely diagnosis. *Journal of American Geriatric Society*, 48(3), 300–304.

Kritz, M., Gurak, D., & Chen, L. (2000). Elderly immigrants: Their composition and living arrangements. *Journal of Sociology and Social Welfare*, 27(1), 85–114.

Kwon, S. M. (2001). Characteristics and symptoms of dementia. *Journal of Counseling and Guidance*, Winter, 6–18.

Lee, D. Y., Lee, J. H., Ju, Y. S., Lee, K. U., Kim, K. W., Jhoo, J. H. et al. (2002). The prevalence of dementia in older people in the urban population of Korea: The Seoul Study. *Journal of the American Geriatrics Society*, 50, 1233–1239.

Min, J. W. (2001). *The process and outcomes of long-term care decision-making among Korean American elders*. Doctoral dissertation, Department of Social Welfare, University of California, Los Angeles.

Min, J. W., & Moon, A. (in press). Social work practice with Asian American elders. In B. Berkman (Ed.), *Handbook on Aging*. Oxford: Oxford University Press.

Moon, A. (1996). Predictors of morale among Korean immigrant elderly in the USA. *Journal of Cross-Cultural Gerontology*, 11(4), 351–367.

Moon, A. (1998). Demographic and socioeconomic characteristics of Korean American women and men. In Y. Song & A. Moon (Eds.), *Korean American women from tradition to modern feminism* (pp. 37–44). Westport, CT: Greenwood.

Moon, A. (2004). [Cultural and non-cultural factors in elder abuse assessment and intervention among Korean and non-Hispanic White American service providers]. Unpublished data.

Moon, A. (2005). [Perception and knowledge about dementia and related services: A survey of Korean Americans]. Unpublished data.

Moon, A., & Hoang, T. (1997). Korean immigrant families: Value orientation and adolescents' attitudes toward parents. In Y. Song & A. Moon (Eds.), *Korean American women living in two cultures* (pp. 44–66). Los Angeles, CA: Academia Koreana, Keimyung-Baylo University Press.

Moon, A., Lubben, J., & Villa, V. (1998). Awareness and utilization of community long-term care services by elderly Koreans and Non-Hispanic White Americans. *The Gerontologist*, 38(3), 309–316.

Moon, A., & Rhee, S. (in press). Social work practice with immigrant and refugee elders. In B. Berkman (Ed.), *Handbook on aging.* Oxford: Oxford University Press.

Moon, A., White, W., & Lee, Y. (2005). [Factors contributing to life satisfaction among Korean immigrant and White elders]. Unpublished data.

Park, J., Ko, H. J., Park, Y. N., & Jung, C. H. (1994). Dementia among the elderly in a rural Korean community. *British Journal of Psychiatry, 164,* 796–801.

Schulz, R., & Martire, L. M. (2004). Family caregiving of persons with dementia: Prevalence, health effects, and support strategies. *American Journal of Geriatric Psychiatry, 12*(3), 240–249.

Shadlen, M. F., & Larson, E. B. (1999). Unique features of Alzheimer's disease in ethnic minority populations. In T. P. Miles (Ed.), *Full-color aging: Facts, goals, and recommendations for America's diverse elders* (pp. 33–51). Washington, DC: The Gerontological Society of America.

Steckenrider, J. S. (1993). What people know about Alzheimer's disease: A study of public knowledge. *The American Journal of Alzheimer's Care and Related Disorders & Research, 8*(1), 6–14.

Suh, G. H., Kim, J. K., & Cho, M. J. (2003). Community study of dementia in the older Korean rural population. *Australian and New Zealand Journal of Psychiatry, 37,* 606–612.

U.S. Census Bureau. (1992). Census of the population, 1990 (U.S.) General population characteristics (CP-1-1). Washington DC: U.S. Department of Commerce, Bureau of the Census.

U.S. Census Bureau. (2000). Supplementary survey PUMS data set. Retrieved from www.census.gov/c2ss/www/Products/PUMS.htm

U.S. Census Bureau. (2002). The Asian population: 2000. [Census 2000 Brief]. Retrieved April 21, 2005, from www.census.gov/prod/2002pubs/c2kbr 01-16.pdf

Watari, K. F., & Gatz, M. (2004). Pathways to care for Alzheimer's disease among Korean Americans. *Cultural Diversity and Ethnic Minority Psychology, 10*(1), 23–38.

Werner, P. (2003). Knowledge about symptoms of Alzheimer's disease: Correlates and relationship to help-seeking behavior. *International Journal of Geriatric Psychiatry, 18,* 1029–1036.

Yamamoto, J., Rhee, S., & Chang, D. (1994). Psychiatric disorders among elderly Koreans in the United States. *Community Mental Health Journal, 30,* 17–27. [In Korean]

Yeo, G., & Gallagher-Thompson, D. (Eds.). (1996). *Ethnicity and the dementias.* Washington, DC: Taylor & Francis.

Yoon, S., Lee, Y., Son, T. Y., Oh, H. J., Han, G. S., & Kim, K. H. (2002). Factors associated with dementia and depressive symptoms in older persons living in the community. *Journal of the Korean Gerontological Society, 21*(3), 59–73.

Youn, G., Knight, B. G., Jeong, H., & Benton, D. (1999). Differences in familism values and caregiving outcomes among Korean, Korean American, and White American dementia caregivers. *Psychology and Aging, 14,* 355–364.

Yu, E., Choe, P., & Han, S. I. (2002). Korean population in the United States, 2000: Demographic characteristics and socio-economic status. *International Journal of Korean Studies*, Spring/Summer, 71–107.

CHAPTER 17

Working with Vietnamese American Families

JANE NHA UYEN TRAN, CAROLEE GIAO UYEN TRAN,
AND LADSON HINTON

Vietnamese Migration and Acculturation

The Vietnamese population in the United States is over 1,100,000 people, comprising 10.9% of the U.S. Asian American population (U.S. Census Bureau, 2001). Only 5% of Vietnamese are age 65 and above, compared to 12.4% of the overall population (U.S. Census Bureau, 2001). As this population ages, there will be considerable growth in the number of Vietnamese elders, including those with Alzheimer's and other dementias. California has the largest population of Vietnamese. Most Vietnamese Americans are refugees and displaced immigrants who arrived at the end of the Vietnam War. In 1975, nearly 125,000 Vietnamese refugees came to the United States (U.S. Committee for Refugees, 1976–1990). This initial wave included many South Vietnamese military officers, government officials, professionals, and business leaders, who, along with their families, were evacuated by air or boat from South Vietnam during the Communist takeover. This group was predominantly ethnic Vietnamese, more educated, and had more prior exposure to Western culture than those who migrated later.

A second major wave of migration began in 1977. This migration wave coincided with increasing economic reorganization and political repression in South Vietnam, as well as with the outbreak of hostilities between Vietnam and China. The refugees who fled Vietnam at this time included ethnic Vietnamese, as well as many ethnic Chinese, the latter fleeing persecution within Vietnam due to the Communist government's attempts to rid the country of Sino influence. Many in this second wave were members of business or merchant-class families whose only route of escape was by small boats—thus, the name "boat people"—or overland through Cambodia and Thailand. Tragically, many of these refugees experienced pirate attacks, starvation, and other traumas as they made their way to various refugee camps in Thailand, Hong Kong, the Philippines, Indonesia, and Singapore. After arriving, many spent years at overcrowded refugee camps with unsanitary conditions while waiting to be sponsored to the United States or other countries. This is in stark contrast to the much briefer stays in refugee camps for members of the first wave. Malnutrition was common among the refugee camp population, and schools were unavailable for children and adults.

Another distinct wave of migration began in 1979, when official programs sponsored by the United Nations, in concert with the U.S. and Vietnamese governments, permitted certain Vietnamese groups to migrate to the United States. The first of these programs, the Orderly Departure Program, allowed Vietnamese to be reunited with relatives already in the United States. By the mid-1980s, substantial numbers of Vietnamese were leaving the country via this program. Subsequent programs permitted South Vietnamese reeducation camp survivors, Amerasian offspring, and persecuted ethnic minorities (e.g., Montagnards) to leave Vietnam. Because many reeducation camp survivors were imprisoned in the extremely harsh and deplorable conditions of jungle camps for months to years prior to coming to the United States (Freeman, 1989), they are an older Vietnamese subgroup at higher risk for clinical depression and other mental health conditions (D. E. Hinton et al., in press; L. Hinton et al., 1993).

The range of acculturation among older Vietnamese Americans is broad, with the single best indicator of acculturation being the elder's English-language abilities. Most Vietnamese elders currently living in North America were born in Vietnam and migrated to the United States as adults during one of the aforementioned migration waves. Vietnamese who came in the later waves often have less ability with English. Vietnam is distinctly divided linguistically, culturally, and socially into three separate regions: Bac (North), Trung (Central), and Nam (South). The primary language for all three regions is Vietnamese, but there are regional differences in pronunciation, intonation, and idiomatic expressions. It is common for older Vietnamese to speak French or, particularly among ethnic Chinese-Vietnamese, one of the Chinese dialects. Those who immigrated between 1975 and 1977 are more likely to speak English, particularly those who worked for the U.S. military, government, or businesses. Most Vietnamese elders speak Vietnamese as their first language and have varying levels of English-language proficiency. According to Census 2000 data, nearly two thirds of all Vietnamese surveyed reported preferring to speak Vietnamese at home, and rated their English-speaking abilities as "less than very well."

Some Vietnamese elders remain dependent on younger family members when outside of the Vietnamese American community, particularly in medical settings. Vietnamese vary in their exposure to the medical community both here in the United States, as well as back in Vietnam. Some older Vietnamese who migrated after 1975 may view the U.S. health-care system with suspicion as a result of their experiences with the health-care system in Vietnam, which was perceived as ineffective and, as a government-sponsored program, as having close ties to the Communist regime. This sentiment was expressed by a Vietnamese caregiver interviewed as part of a qualitative study on the experiences of Vietnamese caregivers for people with dementia: "In Vietnam, after the Communist took over, the good doctors also left, just like the boat people. There were 'so so' doctors at the hospital, and we did not trust them."[1]

Caregiving in the Context of Vietnamese Family Systems and Cultural Values

There are fundamental differences between Vietnamese and Anglo European-American culture that may help the reader understand Vietnamese family dynamics. The following brief review is general, and substantial diversity in the commitment to core Vietnamese cultural values should be expected based on characteristics such as gender, nativity, acculturation, age or generation, and socioeconomic status (Hinton, Fox, & Levkoff, 1999; Hinton & Kleinman, 1997).

In contrast to Anglo European-American culture, Vietnamese culture is oriented toward the family and the group, rather than the individual, and emphasizes interdependence (Timberlake & Cook, 1984). This reflects the strong influence of Confucian teaching throughout Asia, which emphasizes close family ties, hierarchy, and order in interpersonal relationships, rather than individual autonomy (Jamieson, 1993; Shon & Ja, 1982). The family and individual are viewed as continuous and interdependent. That is, the individual is the product of all the generations from the beginning of time; therefore, a person's behavior and situation reflect not only one's self and family, but also ancestors and future generations. There is the expectation that each member of the family adhere to specified hierarchical roles, and there is a strong emphasis on the Confucian concept of filial piety and order. The family unit works under the tenet that there is unquestioned respect and love for parents, grandparents, and other elders. This concept looms especially large when caregivers and families are faced with difficult decisions, such as whether to pursue institutionalized care for the person with dementia, as discussed later in this chapter.

In many respects, the traditional role of the Vietnamese elders within the family differs from that of their Anglo counterpart. For instance, Anglo elders strive to maintain independent living and avoid being a "burden" on their children. The sense of purpose and self-esteem an Anglo elder has may even be linked to his or her ability to live without assistance from others. On the contrary, traditional Vietnamese elders may value independence, but they also expect that they will be taken care of in old age by their children, as a just reward for having demonstrated filial piety toward their own parents, and for having raised their own children well. As Vietnamese elders become frail, their families are expected to care for and house them. Vietnamese children often grow into adulthood with constant cues and reminders that they are expected to look after their aging parents and kin. Nursing home and other custodial placement continue to be viewed with low regard by the Vietnamese community, and can be potentially stigmatizing, because this violates the norms of filial duty and may be further interpreted as a sign of intergenerational conflict.

Likewise, traditionally oriented Vietnamese families will view the Western "burden" as an honor, a way in which parents and ancestors can be "repaid" and filial piety demonstrated. In explaining her motivation for persevering in the difficult care of her mother with dementia, one Vietnamese woman declared: "It is better that we respect our parents when they are still alive to make them happy. If they are sad, that is not respectful. When they are old, they don't need money. That's why I do whatever I can to make my mother happy." This predominant perspective has great impact on the care of the elder with dementia, and the real or perceived societal and cultural expectations of caregiving placed upon the Vietnamese family.

In the Vietnamese culture, where the individual represents the family as a whole, the concepts of shame and guilt assume a different meaning than in North American culture. The Vietnamese concept of "loss of face" implies that the entire nuclear, as well as the extended family, loses respect and status in the community when there is an unfortunate event.

Behaviors that sometimes accompany the mid-to-late stages of dementing illness—continence issues, loss of social cues, and physical aggression, among others—can cause embarrassment and loss of face for the family. Some Vietnamese families are thus reluctant to report symptoms. It is not uncommon that these families delay seeking help from the medical community until the behaviors become unsafe, or all other measures have been exhausted. To the extent that these behaviors are understood as "craziness" (or the product of moral failure on the part of the elder or family), psychoeducation emphasizing their brain-based etiology has the potential to reduce stigma and lessen family burden.

Traditional Vietnamese society is strongly kinship based and largely patriarchal, with much importance placed on being "male." Decision making is deferred to the eldest male, who may or may not decide important family actions in conference with the rest of his family. The eldest son is also charged with the responsibility for making sure his parents are taken care of in old age. However, it is usually the eldest son's wife, or other female family members, especially those who are unmarried, to whom the actual activities of caregiving fall. This can mean that even though the wife and daughters of the person with dementia are the primary caregivers, important decisions pertaining to the elder's health care may involve the eldest male relative if there are no sons.

The kinship system theoretically provides a support net that aids some families' ability to avoid custodial placement of demented elders. This is a profound consideration, given the Vietnamese community's general taboo against children not caring for their elders. Kibria's (1993) ethnographic study of Vietnamese women and their supportive networks points to the crucial role extended family members, and even non-kin, have in alleviating burdens of caregiving in families. Large extended families have the advantage of assistance from many female family members for basic tasks, such as feeding, hygiene care, and daily activities, required by elders with dementia.

Vietnamese Cultural Views and Explanations of Dementia

In Vietnamese, the term for Alzheimer's dementia and similar conditions is *lẫn trí*, which is often translated as "confused mind." Persons with dementia are described as *mất trí nhớ*, a Vietnamese term meaning having "loss of memory." Alternatively, dementia may be labeled and understood in terms of Alzheimer's disease, brain shrinkage, strokes, and vascular risk factors such as hypertension. Even past the point of formal diagnosis, it is common for Vietnamese American caregivers (and caregivers more generally) to combine biomedical labels and understandings with traditional views of aging, and health, that fall outside mainstream Western biomedical views (Hinton et al., 2005; Yeo et al., 2001).

Within Vietnamese culture, it is expected that some old people will exhibit mental deterioration. In the Vietnamese language, the term *lẫn* is often used to refer to persons who exhibit forgetfulness and other cognitive symptoms. *Lẫn* can be translated as "confusion" or "not being right in the mind." There are a number of additional terms that have roughly the same meaning, including *lầm lẫn*, *lầm lộn*, or *lẫn lộn*, which all essentially equate to a state of confusion. Vietnamese have generally associated being *lẫn* with the normal process of aging, rather than a disease. The following common Vietnamese expression reflects this sentiment and bears strong similarities to views of aging in Chinese culture (Hinton & Levkoff, 1999): "A human being is like a machine, it is normal that it wears out when it is old."

Among Vietnamese, the tendency to normalize symptoms of dementia may also be due to lack of familiarity with the term *Alzheimer's disease*, particularly among those who have recently arrived or have little access to English-language media. Routine information and resources provided by hospital and community social workers have helped expand awareness of demential illness within the Vietnamese community. It should also be noted that Alzheimer's is receiving more attention in Vietnam, in the Vietnamese-language publications within the United States, and through outreach to the Vietnamese community in the United States by the Alzheimer's Association and other organizations.

Eastern medicine is another very important aspect of Vietnamese culture that may influence how dementia-related symptoms are interpreted. While a comprehensive review of Eastern medicine is beyond the scope of this chapter, the following major and interrelated concepts are relevant to how Vietnamese interpret dementia symptoms. Western philosophy and healing traditions view the mind and body in a dualistic way, but Eastern medicine envisions the mind and body as unified, as an integrated system with reciprocal effects. As a result, the mind and thought processes reflect the body's ailments, and vice versa. Also fundamental to Eastern medicine is the notion that conservation and flow of the mind and body's vital energy, or *Qi*, is essential for health. It is not coincidental that the direct translation of the Vietnamese term for health, *sức khỏe*, is "health force." The body's *Qi* is thought to be stored in five fundamental organ systems: heart, liver, spleen, lungs, and kidneys. Taxing the body via an indulgent lifestyle, such as overeating, overworking, and even excessive sexual activity, are all thought to lead to damage of the fundamental organs and depletion of *Qi*, causing diseases (Schipper, 1982). Within this paradigm, dementia may be attributed to the person's premorbid lifestyle.

Another important and related theory of Eastern medicine is that of *yin* and *yang* (also described as "hot and cold"). In this context, hot and cold do not refer to temperature, but rather to properties of bodily organs, internal states, and dietary substances. To maintain health, one must maintain a balance of "hot" and "cold" by regulating inner states (e.g., emotions, desires, thinking). This can be done, for example, through exercising self-control in emotion, thought, and behavior, as well as by regulating material substances that are ingested, such as diet and medications (Schipper, 1982). Failure to do so can lead to imbalance and disease, the result of excess "hot" or "cold."

This has important implications for how Vietnamese may interpret and respond to dementia-related symptoms. For example, one male caregiver we interviewed attributed his wife's dementia to "taking too many Western medicines" that "made her nature and mind hot." Another interpreted his wife's aggression and agitation as caused by excess "heat." In the context of these cultural explanations, effectively treating the symptoms of dementia might involve dietary changes, herbal medicine, and reducing the use of "hot" Western medicines to bring the body back into balance.

The tropes of balance and excess also help us to understand the cultural basis for a tendency among many Vietnamese to believe that dementia is caused by emotional stress and life trauma. For example, dementias and accompanying decline in memory and other cognitive abilities are commonly attributed to "thinking too much" and *bị áp lực* (being stressed). Excessive thinking or stress reflects an unbalanced inner state that may lead to damage to the "nerves" and brain disease (i.e., dementia) if corrective actions are not taken. Thus, Vietnamese may connect the onset of dementia or confusion to antecedent stressful or traumatic life events that eventually cause *Đầu óc căng thẳng* (the brain or nerves to be stretched tight/thin).

The following Vietnamese caregiver linked traumatic events early in life with damage to the nerves and confusion in old age: "I think it is the result of how you live when you were young. They have to cope with the war, financial problems. They don't have a disease, but because they worry too much, they die young. It affects their nerves." Another caregiver with a parent with dementia, as well as two extended relatives with dementia, observed: "It only happens to people who do not know how to take care of their minds. If we let ourselves worry all the time, or become sad to the point that we cannot sleep, our mind will be overworked, and when we get old, it will surely give you problems." This quotation illustrates how the person with dementia may, to some extent, be viewed as responsible for his or her illness because of a perceived failure to exert sufficient self-control and discipline in their mental activity. Moral responsibility for dementia may also have roots in Confucianism (Hinton, Guo, Hillygus, & Levkoff, 2000).

In addition to mind and body interconnectedness, Eastern medicine also views the person as more permeable to environmental influences, such as wind and spirits, which have the potential to cause imbalances in the mind and body, creating physical or mental illness (Phan & Silove, 1999). Therefore, some common illnesses such as the cold or flu may be attributed to *trung gío* ("catching wind"), rather like "catching a cold," or the wind being *gío độc* ("poisonous"). Wind illness has also been linked to anxiety symptoms among Vietnamese (Hinton et al., in press) and is a plausible causal attribution for dementia-related symptoms of which clinicians should be aware. Wind illness is often treated by cupping (burning a candle in a glass cup, or warming the cup via water, and placing the cup rim down on skin). Coining is also used, in which a coin is used to rub aromatic oils on the chest or back in parallel lines, in order to release the "poisonous" wind. As both methods produce considerable bruising and superficial marks, clinicians across the health-care continuum, including social workers and mental health workers, should clarify any questions that arise during assessments to avoid mistaking the marks for signs of abuse.

Spiritual and religious views may also influence how Vietnamese understand dementia. In her review of what she refers to as the "Vietnamese religious complex," Hue-Tam Ho Tai notes the importance of folk religion, Confucianism, Buddhism, and Taoism, and, more recently, Catholicism (Ho Tai, 1985). Ho Tai refers to these as a complex because Vietnamese religion has historically been an amalgamation of the above-mentioned traditions. Consequently, Vietnamese today may draw upon several of these traditions in their everyday lives. Clinicians should thus not be surprised if a Vietnamese-Catholic also endorses Buddhist concepts, as well as practices ancestor worship. Such Buddhist concepts as fate, perseverance, and enduring suffering may all play important roles in shaping the Vietnamese caregiving experience and response to illness. Acceptance of fate, including illness, is positively valued and may lead to the view that one should not challenge one's life situations. Vietnamese caregivers and elders may therefore approach dementia and caregiving in a more fatalistic way, as a situation to be endured without resort to formal assistance. Developing dementia may be regarded as one's "Karma."

Within the religious complex, illness may also be viewed as resulting from spirit possession. Among Vietnamese, the idea that spirit possession can be a cause of illness has roots in folk religion, ancestor worship, and Taoism. Discontented spirits may "take over" the mind and body of the elder, causing the dementia to manifest. The spirits are sometimes thought to be those of ancestors and deceased offspring who are not "at rest" but can also be the spirits of unknown strangers. In such cases, families will seek Catholic or Taoist exorcisms and use spiritual mediums in attempts to cure the elder with dementia of symptoms. We documented one case of a Vietnamese man who believed his wife's dementia was caused in part by spirit possession (Yeo et al., 2001).

Tailoring Assessment and Treatment Strategies for Vietnamese Families

Assessment

Recognizing dementia in Vietnamese elders may be more challenging for a number of reasons. Linguistic barriers may arise when older Vietnamese prefer to use their native language but are being treated by non-Vietnamese-speaking clinicians. In such situations, clinicians will need to use interpreters and work effectively with them (McPhee, 2002). As mentioned earlier, Vietnamese may often attribute cognitive deterioration and functional decline to "old age" and thus not bring them to the attention of clinicians. Vietnamese elderly with clinical depression rather than dementia may present with cognitive symptoms such as forgetfulness or confusion.

Noncognitive symptoms, such as sadness, excessive worry, or loneliness may also be the presenting symptoms of dementia. Particularly when the initial symptoms of dementia are of a psychiatric or behavioral nature, Vietnamese elders and their families may be more hesitant to disclose symptoms to clinicians due to perceived shame, embarrassment, or concerns about "loss of face." As mentioned earlier, the Vietnamese concept of "loss of face" implies that the entire nuclear and extended family loses respect and status in the community when family members act out in inappropriate ways. Socially inappropriate or disinhibited behavior, personality change, continence issues, and physical aggression among others may trigger family embarrassment and shame.

Most Vietnamese family members will expect that elders be shown respect because of the prestige traditionally reserved for elders in Vietnamese society. This knowledge can be crucial in being able to conduct a successful assessment with the elder and his or her family members. As a general rule of conduct, respect can be shown in the following manner: refer to the elder by using specific titles in accordance with their place in the family hierarchy, use both hands when giving or receiving something, keep one's arms crossed or hands folded in front, make a concerted effort to greet the elder when entering and leaving, and avoid direct eye contact with elders and persons of higher status, which may include health-care providers. Many older Vietnamese persons, especially those who are less acculturated or have more recently arrived, may be unfamiliar with the practice of shaking hands and avoid it. Shaking hands with a woman may be considered inappropriate unless she offers her hand first. Interpersonal space in conversation with a Vietnamese person may be slightly more distant or closer than is common in North America. Raising one's voice, pointing, or openly expressing emotion may be considered disrespectful or in bad taste, depending on the region from which the older person originated in Vietnam. As with language pattern, each of the three geographical regions of Vietnam is said to have its own style of social interaction. Northern and Central Vietnamese are known for being more formal and reserved, while Southerners have a reputation for being less so, although many Vietnamese deviate from these general descriptions.

Involving family members to provide collateral history is vital in the assessment process, because dementia may undermine the ability of the person with dementia to accurately recall or recognize relevant symptoms. Family members may be less likely to reveal more distressing symptoms or behaviors in the presence of the elder, or to fully disclose their own felt burden, so interviewing them separately may be important. As discussed elsewhere in this volume, formal cognitive assessment is a critical part of assessment, although there are limited data on the use of standard instruments (e.g., Mini-Mental State Examination [MMSE] or Cognitive Abilities Screening Instrument [CASI]) for assessment of older Vietnamese. Also essential is assessment of basic activities of daily living, such as feeding, bathing, dressing, mobility, toileting, and continence, as well as more complex tasks including managing finances, cooking, using appliances, and organizing/taking medications (items that are part of standard activities of daily living scales). Because in many of the more traditional Vietnamese families, it is viewed as "normal" and even desirable (as a sign of respect or filial piety) for elders to depend on others, the clinician's challenge becomes discerning the elder's ability to perform tasks independently and, for dementia diagnosis, whether this represents a change related to cognitive, as opposed to physical, causes.

Disclosure of diagnosis by practitioners and education of the family by social workers or other clinicians should be informed by appreciation for the family's preferences and beliefs. Studies of Asians, including Vietnamese, have found that patients and families may prefer limited disclosure of a serious medical diagnosis, such as cancer, to the afflicted person (Mitchell, 1998). These issues should be addressed early on with both the patient and family, so disclosure of diagnosis can be done in a way that respects the patient's wishes. Eliciting and working with the elder's and the family's conceptions of dementia can also be an important strategy to build rapport and promote open flow of information in a clinical encounter. It can also be important to support the family's caregiving and help-seeking efforts explicitly (e.g., "As an expert in this matter, I think that you and the family have done an extraordinary job caring for your parent. Many families would not have done so much. And I think that it shows what a good son/daughter you are that you are now enlisting the help of your doctor"). Family psychoeducation is essential and may be time consuming because Vietnamese families may be less familiar with the biomedical model of dementia (Ayalon & Arean, 2004).

In addition to cognitive symptoms and functional change, noncognitive behavioral and psychiatric symptoms, such as agitation, depression, and psychosis, should be routinely assessed. These symptoms are extremely common during the course of dementia, and studies have found them to be strongly associated with caregiver burden and increased care-recipient disability in other populations (e.g., Hinton, 2002; Schulz, O'Brien, Bookwala, & Fleissner, 1995). Failure to educate families about the noncognitive aspects of dementia may impede symptom disclosure in future clinical visits, as families may attribute these to causes other than dementia. Standard instruments such as the Neuropsychiatric Inventory (Cummings, Mega, Gray, Rosenberg-Thompson, & Gornbein, 1994) can be used to evaluate behavioral symptoms, although Vietnamese versions and norms are not currently available.

The potential interaction of cognition with other medical conditions should also be evaluated (Maslow, 2004). Vascular diseases (e.g., diabetes) are common among Vietnamese, and their management may be complicated by cognitive dysfunction or behavioral changes, such as aggression and resistance to care. Engaging family in the management of these medical conditions and the coordination of medical and dementia care is critical because progression of vascular disease may hasten the progression of cognitive decline. A recent study found that Vietnamese frequently use traditional Asian health practices and want to discuss these with their clinicians, but they often perceive significant barriers to doing so (Ngo-Metzger et al., 2003). Clinicians should routinely assess this aspect and strive to maintain a pragmatic and nonjudgmental stance.

Given that the majority of Vietnamese patients with dementia live with relatives or a caregiver, it is also highly valuable to assess the family system in which the patient resides. This can be done with a simple genogram identifying key members of the family in relationship to the elder with dementia. Areas of particular interest include the characteristics of the primary caregiver, the adequacy of the support system, the decision-making process within the family, and varying levels of acculturation among key family members. Assessing clinicians would do well to avoid assuming that the primary caregiver is also the primary decision maker, as these two roles may reside with different members of the family. In multigenerational Vietnamese families, the "division of labor" within the family may be complex, as sons or daughters who are not primary caregivers or decision makers may be designated to interact with the health-care system on the part of the elder with dementia. Despite the importance of elders within Vietnamese families, social and cultural shifts brought about by migration to the United States may have caused traditional roles to change. In families that have experienced great upheavals, the responsibility for major health-care decisions may rest with the younger generation, who are often more fully bicultural, fluent in English, and comfortable navigating the health-care system.

In addition to assessing the elder's level of functioning and family dynamics, it would be useful to assess the migration history and level of acculturation of the individual and family members. The level of acculturation and degree of premigration stress and trauma may influence their openness to the biomedical model of dementia and engagement in the treatment process. Particularly in refugee families, it is important for the clinician to be aware that older Vietnamese and their family members may have suffered multiple trauma and losses of family members prior to or during migration. Some common traumatic experiences reported by Vietnamese Americans include trauma associated with chaotic evacuations during the fall of Sai Gon; starvation, piracy, and violence (including rapes and witnessing atrocities) during the escape from Vietnam; months or years in overcrowded refugee camps; harsh treatment under Communist rule after 1975; and loss of homeland, family, and community.

It is also helpful to ascertain areas of strength and resources for the elder and family members. This will be informative in clarifying areas and levels of treatment needed, as well as resources for the family. For example, knowing that a patient is premorbidly highly educated, verbal, and active enables providers to incorporate these elements into the behavioral modification portion of the treatment plan to encourage optimal functioning. Ascertaining the family's social support systems, such as priests, nuns, monks, churches, temples, extended family members, and various Vietnamese community agencies, will also help inform providers of possible sources of support for the patient and family, especially at the later stages of the dementia. Moreover, being aware of various Vietnamese community agencies may provide families and clinicians with resources to manage the language barrier, the complicated health-care and mental health-care systems, and misunderstandings that may arise from having a cross-cultural working relationship. Many Vietnamese caregivers may not be aware of the resources available to them, including local chapters of the Alzheimer's Association and the Area Agencies on Aging.[2] Thus, assessing the family's resources will inform providers of the elder's access to appropriate medical, mental health care, and other community resources, as well as Medicaid, if custodial placement is needed.

Last, providers must also assess the physical and emotional health of the primary caregivers of the individual with dementia. Studies have documented that caregivers suffer adverse mental and physical health compared with noncaregivers (Schulz et al., 1995). Because caregivers play a critical role in the lives of persons with dementia, prompt assessment and treatment of caregiver physical and mental health issues can minimize patient–caregiver stress and defer institutionalization of the individual with dementia. There are several Vietnamese-language screening tools— the Hopkins Symptom Checklist and the Vietnamese Depression Scale— that have been shown to accurately identify depression in adult Vietnamese (Hinton et al., 1994). The Geriatric Depression Scale also accurately identifies depressed older Vietnamese (Mui, Kang, Chen, & Domanski, 2003).

Treatment

In treating the Vietnamese patient with dementia, it is important to discuss the diagnosis, treatment, and progression of the dementia with the patient and family in a manner consistent with Vietnamese culture. For example, given that Vietnamese families tend to be patriarchal and value closeness, it is important to inquire which family members play a key role in the caregiving and decision-making process, and to include them in the discussions.

Prompt and ongoing treatment of comorbid medical conditions, such as hypertension, congestive heart failure, chronic obstructive pulmonary disease, diabetes, and hypothyroidism, can reduce disability and maximize functioning. Medication treatment with cholinesterase inhibitors should be considered, as they may slow the rate of cognitive decline. Maximizing treatment of vascular risk factors may also slow cognitive decline. Given that the Vietnamese diet often consists of high glucose starches, such as white rice and noodles, and high sodium ingredients, such as *nuoc mam* (fish sauce), which tends to worsen conditions such as diabetes and hypertension, it is important to include dietary counseling and consider referral to a nutritionist.

Problematic behavioral symptoms, such as agitation, disinhibition, and wandering, and associated caregiver distress can be helped through psychoeducation, behavioral approaches, and judicious use of pharmacologic interventions. In clinical interventions with families, it will be less stigmatizing and shaming to the elder and family members if the problematic behavioral symptoms can be reframed as part of the disease process, rather than any "weakness" or "misbehavior" on the part of the patient. Furthermore, it will be helpful to refer the patient and family to organizations that can provide educational materials on community resources, support groups, legal and financial issues, respite care, and future care needs and options. Hospital social workers, patient care coordinators, and other clinicians can lay much groundwork during the early stages and, thus, help prepare and educate families regarding the progressive and terminal nature of Alzheimer's. Additionally, it is important to discuss the patient's need to have advance directives and to identify surrogates for medical/legal decision making.

Given the obvious fact that involvement from family members and the primary caregiver is necessary and critical to the success of any treatment plan, it is important for the treatment planning process to be both collaborative and respectful. For example, caregivers and family members can play a valuable role in ensuring that medications are taken and other treatment activities are accomplished correctly. Additionally, potential problems can be identified earlier if the caregiver and family members are instructed to watch for behavioral changes that may indicate adverse treatment effects or declining medical or cognitive functioning.

As previously mentioned, while many Vietnamese Americans hold health beliefs that resemble the mainstream Western biomedical model, they may also integrate Eastern methods, such as using an herbalist. Therefore, a Vietnamese patient and family may have gone to many traditional Chinese herbalists prior to seeing a Western clinician. They may even be combining the two types of treatment without disclosing doing so to either practitioner. Yet, other Vietnamese caregivers and patients may turn to the Eastern practices more familiar to them due to disappointment or frustration with Western medicine. It is necessary for clinicians to be aware that Vietnamese may interpret medication side effects as evidence that the medications are causing the body to become "too hot" or "too cold." This may lead to use of diet/herbal remedies as compensation, or to decreased compliance with prescribed medications. Clinicians who assess compliance nonjudgmentally and routinely will be aware of the behavior and better positioned to address this important issue.

Keeping in mind our earlier discussion of the importance of concepts such as perseverance, endurance of suffering, fate, and "loss of face" within Vietnamese culture, it is important for providers to be mindful of these values and incorporate them into the treatment planning process whenever appropriate. For example, being able to understand the significance of these concepts to the Vietnamese families will enable providers to better understand why some Vietnamese caregivers and families may be reluctant to seek assistance and endure difficult caregiving situations even though help may be available. Of note, culturally, Vietnamese hold utmost reverence toward their elders; therefore, realize that elders should be treated with respect regardless of their health status. This means that the elder should be allowed to be in control of the treatment process to the extent possible, particularly in the earlier stages of dementia.

Furthermore, whenever indicated, the treatment plan should include utilizing Vietnamese community resources, such as Vietnamese priests, nuns, monks, churches, temples, or any healing folk rituals that may help the patient and family cope with the illness. Vietnamese-specific senior services now exist in some communities and may be an extremely valuable support to elders with dementia and their families. Showing that providers have knowledge of and respect for the Vietnamese patient's cultural values will enhance the likelihood that the patient and his or her family will be open to and responsive to the treatment recommendations offered by the providers. Thus, it is very important for the provider to show openness toward and respect for the patient and his or her family belief system as it relates to their understanding of the disease and preferences for treatment.

In summary, it will be useful to develop and implement an ongoing treatment plan with goals that include the following: (a) medication use if clinically indicated; (b) referral for culturally and linguistically appropriate support services and activities such as exercise, recreation, and adult day care; (c) maximization of treatment of coexisting vascular and other medical conditions; (d) assessment and management of behavioral problems, including using behavioral techniques, such as environmental modification and task simplification, and using written instructions and reminders to help the patient complete cognitively appropriate tasks; (e) support and, if necessary, mental health referral for caregivers; and (f) integration of Vietnamese health beliefs and practices with Western treatment.

Out-of-Home Care and the Vietnamese Dementia Patient

The social and practical support usually provided within kinship-based communities normally allows families to provide adequate care in the home. Practical care responsibilities are dispersed among nuclear and extended family members. Families might designate one primary caregiver or rotate caregiving duties based on various work schedules and out-of-home commitments. In such situations, families would be greatly helped by being provided with resources regarding transportation, meal deliveries, and subsidized in-home care. Hospital programs, such as home health nursing to provide medication checks, physical therapy, and the like, are also important supports for Vietnamese elders and their families.

In order to help families with placement issues, social workers and other clinicians can assess the appropriate level of care needed by the elder and present these observations to families within their cultural framework. As during the initial phases of diagnosis, clinicians should be inquiring about changes in the elder's continence issues, behavioral manifestations, medication intake, ability to ambulate, skin breakdown if bed or chair bound, and the family's ability to adequately and safely address these and other challenges that arise. Because most families and caregivers are likely to resist custodial or institutional placements, even when providing care becomes too arduous, it would be helpful for clinicians to be prepared to offer the caregiver realistic and sustainable options aside from placement, if at all possible.

At this juncture, medical social workers and discharge planners can be especially helpful in ensuring that families are aware of financial benefits such as Medicaid, subsidized in-home care, and different placement options, in order to help them decide the most realistic course of action. Clinicians can work with families to draw out preferences regarding location, food, appropriate levels of care, and the like, to ensure that a particular placement is appropriate to the elder's needs, budget, and cultural persuasion. Considerations such as a family's preference for Vietnamese-speaking staff at the placement, or the facility's willingness to provide a culturally appropriate diet and milieu, can be addressed by social workers to provide options among the different available facilities. A united message from the elder's clinicians regarding the need for a higher level of care will also help family members reframe custodial care and mitigate family shame and felt stigma.

Cultural adherence to Confucian tenets of filial piety and respect for parents and elders complicates the difficult processes involved in finding appropriate care for elders with dementia. The explicit expectation that children care for their parents until death is a real hardship, because many Vietnamese feel they have little choice, even when the demands of caregiving become overwhelming. Despite the fact that respecting and caring for one's elder with dementia does not make providing and maintaining in-home round-the-clock care a less-challenging task, many Vietnamese have expressed views similar to those of the following caregiver: "If we put our mother in a nursing home, it is like neglecting her. ... Our parents raise us, but when they get old, we do not take care of them. We put them in there [nursing homes] so we can wash off our responsibility. If we take care of them, it means that we love them, and if we do not take care of them, it means that we do not love them." To have strangers taking care of one's elders is still considered an ungrateful act and lacking in respect toward one's parents and ancestors. Another caregiver describes her mother's reaction to being institutionalized: "Her children always showed filial piety. That's why she will never think of somebody wanting to harm her. She only thinks that now that she is old and sick, that her children do not care for her anymore because they have put her in a nursing home."

Realize that caregivers and family members may feel ashamed for placing their elders outside the home, because it may cause them to feel that they have failed in fulfilling their filial duties. In providing supportive psychotherapy or clinical services to these family members, it may be helpful for providers to acknowledge the sense of shame and sadness that family members feel in institutionalizing the patient with dementia, while reframing the courageous act of making such a difficult decision as being loving and filial toward the elder.

Families that ultimately decide to place their elders in custodial or institutional care often rely on validation and support from within their families, as well as the extended community. At such time, some families may consult spiritual guides, seek advice from a church community, or ask the opinion of friends within the community. In the face of difficult decisions, such as placing an elder in a nursing facility, some Vietnamese draw strength from their religion, as illustrated in the following quotation: "At that time, I discussed with my church, asked them to pray on my problem. If Jesus agrees to put my mother in the nursing home, then the hospital will accept her. If they accept her, my brother will agree to sign the admission papers. If the hospital does not accept her, that means Jesus does not want her there. Or if the hospital accepts her and my brother refuses to sign the papers, it means Jesus does not want it and I will gladly keep my mother."

Understanding the Vietnamese Perception of Death and Dying

While the course of Alzheimer's disease and related dementias varies considerably from person to person, these are progressive and ultimately fatal conditions. Particularly in the later stages of dementia, issues related to death and dying come to the fore, and most families (Vietnamese or not) usually have a difficult time viewing dementia as a progressively terminal illness. As with other aspects of the Vietnamese culture, attitudes toward end-of-life issues are diverse, given the previously outlined variations in beliefs and explanations of illness.

There are a number of cultural beliefs that are likely to affect decisions at the end of life for Vietnamese elders and their families. These include an aversion to dying in the hospital because of the belief that souls of those who die outside the home wander with no place to rest, an avoidance of death and dying in the home for fear opening up one's home to bad spirits, the perception that consenting to end-of-life support for a terminally ill parent contributes to her death and is an insult to one's ancestors and parent, and Buddhist beliefs in karma that interpret difficult deaths as punishment for bad deeds in former lives by the dying person or another family member.

Many Vietnamese people see death as a natural phase of the life cycle. This attitude toward death may be influenced by the fact that elders are highly respected in Vietnamese culture, and therefore, aging and death may not conjure up as many negative connotations as within Western cultures. Further, Vietnamese immigrants in the United States are influenced by spiritual beliefs linked not only to Catholicism or Buddhism, but also to Taoism, animism, and Confucianism. For example, reverence for ancestors and the use of home altars, where homage is paid to family ancestors, are common even among Vietnamese Christians. These religious and cultural/societal norms influence Vietnamese views of death, allowing them to reframe the process and the event. For instance, concepts of reincarnation prevalent among Buddhists, ancestor worship, and the belief of going to heaven after death, may cause death to be viewed as something fortunate, and fitting with life's natural cycle. In addition, many Vietnamese people have lived through wars, witnessing deaths and suffering as results of such wars. This fact, as well as historically higher mortality rates among infants and adults in Vietnam, can make the Vietnamese view death more as a normal part of life.

While general discussions about death and dying may be viewed as inauspicious and in poor taste to the Vietnamese family, it is a common practice among Vietnamese elders to make concrete preparations for death. These preparations include setting aside money to pay for the burial, choosing a burial site with a favorable orientation in accordance with the laws of *feng shui*, buying a coffin, and even buying or having burial clothes made long before they are actually needed. In a study conducted in Hawaii by Braun and Nichols (1996), both Christian and Buddhist Vietnamese participants said that preparations for death included praying and preparing wills for distribution of property. The act of making concrete preparations for one's own death is seen as a common responsibility that elders carry out for themselves as well as their children. Even though Vietnamese elders may prepare for the rituals of death, active end-of-life care planning is a foreign and unfamiliar undertaking for most Vietnamese families. It was reported in this study that few Vietnamese elders were aware of their options with regard to advance directives. Issues related to "Do Not Resuscitate" orders or removal of feeding tubes were usually not considered (Braun & Nichols, 1996). This is perhaps multifactorial, attributable to most elder's reliance on their children for interpretation and the possibility that their children may be uncomfortable with the subject matter.

Some Vietnamese families may also prefer that the diagnosis of a serious or terminal illness not be disclosed directly to an older family member to prevent additional stress for the elder, making informed consent and decisions regarding code status awkward. Whatever the intent, know that families may not be forthcoming with reasons. So the clinician may need to specifically inquire of the patient about presenting information and discuss the family's preference for what information they feel the elder may want to have. Again, because there is such variation in acculturation and beliefs among Vietnamese, clinicians and providers should remain attuned to these variations.

Notes

1. Here and throughout this chapter, we use quotations from Vietnamese caregivers that are based on a qualitative study of Vietnamese American family caregivers of persons with dementia conducted in the San Francisco Bay Area by the authors. The methods and findings of this study are described elsewhere (see Hinton, Franz, Yeo, & Levkoff, 2005; Yeo, Tran, Hikoyeda, & Hinton, 2001).

2. Information on Vietnamese families can be found through (a) Administration on Aging (phone: 202-619-7501 or 800-677-1116; Web site: www.aoa.dhhs.gov), (b) National Alzheimer's Association (phone: 800-272-3900; Web site: www.alz.org), (c) local Alzheimer's Association chapters, (d) Alzheimer's Disease Education and Referral Center (phone: 800-483-4380; Web site: www.alzheimers.org/adear), (e) Family Caregiver Alliance (phone: 800-445-8106; Web site: www.caregiver.org), and (f) National Association of Area Agencies on Aging (phone: 202-296-8130; Web site: www.n4a.org).

References

Ayalon, L., & Arean, P. A. (2004). Knowledge of Alzheimer's disease in four ethnic groups of older adults. *International Journal of Geriatric Psychiatry, 19,* 51–57.

Braun, K. L., & Nichols, R. (1996). Cultural issues in death and dying. *Hawaii Medicine Journal, 55,* 260–264.

Cummings, J. L., Mega, M., Gray, K., Rosenberg-Thompson, S., & Gornbein, T. (1994). The Neuropsychiatric Inventory: Comprehensive assessment of psychopathology in dementia. *Neurology, 44,* 2308–2314.

Freeman, J. (1989). *Hearts of sorrow: Vietnamese American lives.* Stanford, CA: Stanford University Press.

Hinton, D. E., Hinton, L., Tran, M., Nguyen, L., Hsia, C., & Pollack, M. H. (in press). Orthostatically induced panic attacks among Vietnamese refugees: Associated flashbacks, catastrophic cognitions, and psychopathology. *Transcultural Psychiatry*.

Hinton, L. (2002). Improving care for ethnic minority elderly and their family caregivers across the spectrum of dementia severity. *Alzheimer Disease and Associated Disorders, 16*(Supp. 2), S50–S55.

Hinton, L., Chen, J., Du, N., Tran, C. G., Lu, F., Miranda, J., & Faust, S. (1993). DSM-III-R disorders in Vietnamese Refugees: Prevalence and correlates. *Journal of Nervous and Mental Disease, 181,* 113–122.

Hinton, L., Du, N., Chen, J., Tran, C. G., Newman, T. B., & Lu, F. (1994). Screening for major depression in Vietnamese refugees: A comparison of two instruments. *Journal of General Internal Medicine, 9,* 202–206.

Hinton, L., Fox, K., & Levkoff, S. (1999). Exploring the relationships among aging ethnicity, and dementing illness. *Culture, Medicine and Psychiatry, 23,* 403–413.

Hinton, L., Franz, C., Yeo, G., & Levkoff, S. (2005). Conceptions of dementia in a multi-ethnic sample of family caregivers. *Journal of the American Geriatric Society, 53,* 1405–1410.

Hinton, L., Guo, Z., Hillygus, J., & Levkoff, S. E. (2000). Working with culture: A qualitative analysis of barriers to recruitment of Chinese-American family caregivers for dementia research. *Journal of Cross-Cultural Gerontology, 15,* 119–137.

Hinton, L., & Kleinman, A. (1997). Cultural issues in primary care medicine. In *Primary Care Medicine CD-ROM*. St. Louis, MO: Mosby Yearbook.

Hinton, L., & Levkoff, S. E. (1999). Constructing Alzheimer's: Narratives of lost identities, confusion, and loneliness in old age. *Culture, Medicine and Psychiatry, 23,* 453–475.

Ho Tai, H. (1985). Religion in Vietnam: A world of gods and spirits. In *Vietnam: Essays on history, culture, and society, 1985* (pp. 22–39). New York: The Asia Society.

Jamieson, N. (1993). *Understanding Vietnam*. Berkeley: University of California Press.

Kibria, N. (1993). *Family tightrope: The changing lives of Vietnamese Americans*. Princeton, NJ: Princeton University Press.

Maslow, K. (2004). Dementia and serious coexisting medical conditions: A double whammy. *Nursing Clinics of North America, 39,* 561–579.

McPhee, S. J. (2002). Caring for a 70-year-old Vietnamese woman. *Journal of the American Medical Association, 287,* 495–503.

Mitchell, J. L. (1998). Cross cultural issues in the disclosure of cancer. *Cancer Practice, 6,* 153–160.

Mui, A. C., Kang, S. Y., Chen, L. M., & Domanski, M. D. (2003). Reliability of the Geriatric Depression Scale for use among elderly Asian immigrants in the USA. *International Psychogeriatrics, 15*(3), 253–271.

Ngo-Metzger, Q., Massagli, M. P., Clarridge, B. R., Manocchia, M., Davis, R. B., Iezzoni, L. I. et al. (2003). Linguistic and cultural barriers to care:

Perspectives of Chinese and Vietnamese immigrants. *Journal of General Internal Medicine, 18*, 44–52.

Phan, T., & Silove, D. (1999). An overview of indigenous descriptions of mental phenomena and the range of traditional healing practices amongst the Vietnamese. *Transcultural Psychiatry, 36*(1), 79–94.

Schipper, K. (1982). *The Taoist body.* Berkeley: University of California Press.

Schulz, R., O'Brien, A. T., Bookwala, J., & Fleissner, K. (1995). Psychiatric and physical morbidity effects of dementia caregiving: Prevalence, correlates, and causes. *Gerontologist, 35*, 771–791.

Shon, S., & Ja, D. (1982). Asian families. In M. McGoldrick, J. Pearce, & J. Giordano (Eds.), *Ethnicity and family therapy* (pp. 208–228). New York: Guilford Press.

Timberlake, E. M., & Cook, K. O. (1984). Social work and the Vietnamese refugee. *Social Work, 29*(2), 108–112.

U.S. Census Bureau. (2001). Retrieved April 13, 2005, from www.census.gov

U.S. Committee for Refugees. (1976–1990). *World refugee survey.* New York: American Council for Nationalities Service.

Yeo, G., Tran, J. N. U., Hikoyeda, N., & Hinton, L. (2001). Concepts of dementia among Vietnamese American caregivers. *Journal of Gerontological Social Work, 36*(1/2), 131–152.

Working with Latino/Hispanic American Families

CHAPTER 18

Working with Hispanic/Latino American Families with Focus on Puerto Ricans

JULIÁN MONTORO-RODRÍGUEZ, JEFF A. SMALL,
AND T. J. MCCALLUM

La familia es un sistema de relaciones interdependientes donde los padres no se entienden sin referencia a los hijos, los abuelos a los nietos, los primos a los tíos, los que reciben asistencia sin sus cuidadores. This definition of the family as a system of interdependent relationships has strong support among researchers and practitioners in the field of health and human services (Schultz, Gallagher-Thompson, Haley, & Czaja, 2000). However, there is still a need to recognize the significant role of specific contextual factors and environmental conditions among ethnocultural family and group systems. The conceptual consensus about the family system has to include diversity as a central feature; furthermore, it has to be translated into specific interventions aimed to support family care for culturally diverse older adults with dementia. For example, if you were unable to understand the meaning and concepts expressed in the opening statement, then our first recommendation would be to consider learning and providing services in Spanish as an initial step in understanding how to deliver much-needed assistance to dementia-impacted ethnocultural Latinos and Hispanics. Bicultural and bilingual skills relative to Hispanics are part of the basic training of any intercultural competency model (Valle, 1998). In this chapter, we identify strategies to help community organizations' staff, managers, and leaders to promote and create multicultural engagements and dementia interventions directed to ethnically diverse populations, in particular, ethnocultural Hispanics such as Puerto Ricans.

Dementia and Latin and Hispanic Families: Significance and Background

Prevalence of Dementia among Latinos and Hispanics

The Alzheimer's Association's latest report (2004b) indicates that Alzheimer's disease and related dementias are projected to increase more than sixfold among Hispanics in the United States by 2050. This increase means that 1.3 million Hispanics will have Alzheimer's disease by 2050, compared to fewer than 200,000 currently living with the disease. This growth together with the increasing life expectancy among Hispanics (87 years by the middle of the 21st century) underscores the need to consider the impact of Alzheimer's disease among Latin and Hispanic families in the United States. Even more, the projection of this prevalence is conservative, given other contextual factors, such as the earlier age of onset of the first symptoms of Alzheimer's disease for Latinos, the association of Alzheimer's disease with old age, poor education, higher vascular disease risk factors (including diabetes), and barriers to health utilization (such as lack of language proficiency, knowledge about Alzheimer's disease, information, medical insurance, lack of diagnostic tools, and understanding of diversity and cultural factors by providers).

Hispanic Demographic Changes

Latinos in the United States are a very heterogeneous group comprised of people born on the mainland and those migrating from different countries with unique historical and cultural traditions. During the last few decades, the population of Latin and Hispanic people in the United States has escalated due to increased immigration and higher-than-average birth rates. They are actually expected to contribute about 44% of the population growth on the mainland between 2000 and 2020, and about 62% from there to the middle of the century (U.S. Department of Commerce, 1997). An interesting demographic change is that they are now the largest minority in the United States (U.S. Department of Commerce, 2003). Among Latinos and Hispanics, the largest subgroup is of Mexican origin (about 68%), with Puerto Ricans being the second largest group (about 9%) from a single place, and the rest coming from Cuba (about 4%), other Central and South American countries (about 15%), and other Latin origins (about 4%). The rapidly changing demographics require taking seriously the cultural diversity that Latin and Hispanic families bring with them and exhibit daily in their interactions with health and human service professionals. Researchers and clinicians are challenged to find strategies to work effectively with these families, so that the meeting of cultures represents an opportunity to better address the needs of their members, in particular, those affected by dementia.

Hispanic Puerto Ricans in the United States

The relationship between the United States and Puerto Rico is as complex and unique as Puerto Rican history and immigration over the past two hundred years. A mix of indigenous peoples, Spanish colonialists, and African slaves, Puerto Rican islanders have historically drawn from all three heritages in terms of religious beliefs and cultural practices (U.S. Census Bureau, 2000). Many people of Puerto Rican descent living in the continental United States describe themselves as Puerto Rican rather than American. It is also common for Puerto Ricans to describe themselves as *Bouricuas*, in reference to how the indigenous peoples (the Taino) referred to the island before Spanish colonization (Cauce & Domenech-Rodríguez, 2002). Despite the fact that Puerto Rico has not been granted statehood, islanders relocating to the continental United States are not considered immigrants (U.S. Library of Congress, 2004). Such moves are considered *internal migration*, even though language barriers and cultural conflicts experienced by Puerto Ricans moving to the United States often parallel the experiences of immigrants to the United States. However, Puerto Rican migration has traditionally been unique because of its circularity. Many Puerto Ricans remain connected to the island through family and friends who remain or return. Migration patterns since the 1950s suggest that when the economic conditions are better on the mainland than in Puerto Rico, migration to the mainland increases (Alicea, 1990). During economic downturns, many people return to the island. This type of circular migration is possible because of the geographic proximity of the island to the mainland and the lack of legal barriers to mainland reentry.

Puerto Rican migration began as a result of the Spanish–American War. At the conclusion of the war in 1898, Puerto Rico shifted from being a Spanish colony to being a U.S. commonwealth. In 1917, Puerto Ricans became U.S. citizens, but this resulted in little internal migration. It is estimated that there were only about 2,000 Puerto Rican-born people living in the continental United States at that time (U.S. Library of Congress, 2004). The majority of these people relocated to New York City. By 1930, there were only about 40,000 Puerto Rican-born people who had made the internal migration. It was the end of World War II that heralded mass migration to the continental United States. From 1945 to 1955, approximately 25,000 Puerto Ricans migrated west each year. By 1955, it is estimated that 700,000 Puerto Ricans called the mainland their home, and the numbers reached about a million by the 1960s (U.S. Library of Congress, 2004). Two of the main reasons for this steady flow of internal migrants to the continental United States were that returning veterans were relocating near their military training bases and there was an increase in factory jobs throughout the country (Cuadrado & Lieberman, 2002). Another crucial factor was the advent of affordable air travel.

In the year 2000, there were 3.4 million Puerto Ricans living in the continental United States, only slightly less than the 3.8 million people living in Puerto Rico (U.S. Census Bureau, 2000). Though the majority of mainland Puerto Ricans live in the northeast (New York City, Boston, and New Jersey), there is a marked increase in the number of Puerto Ricans relocating to Florida in the last decade (Cuadrado & Lieberman, 2002). About 5% of the Puerto Rican population is over the age of 65, similar to other Latino groups. However, fewer Puerto Rican elders live alone than other Latinos, Anglo-Americans, or African Americans (Seigel, 1999). Approximately half of all older Puerto Ricans live with a spouse, and another 32% live with others (most often other family members). Those Puerto Rican elders who live alone have the highest rates of poverty among all ethnic groups. The fact that Puerto Rican elders rarely live alone, coupled with the high poverty rate for those who do, presents unique caregiving challenges in this community.

Caregiving for Those with Dementia: Theory, Research, and Interventions

Caregiving Research Findings

Considerable research confirms that family caregivers of those with dementia are at increased risk for experiencing psychological distress and negative health outcomes, such as anxiety, depressive symptoms, physical morbidity, and a number of illnesses (Schulz, O'Brien, Bookwala, & Fleissner, 1995). Much of the literature also demonstrates that racial, ethnic, and cultural variations in the nature and effects of the experience of acting as caregiver of those with dementia are central to improving the theoretical understanding of this family experience by distinguishing its universal elements from those mediated by the representations and experiences of specific cultural groups (Patterson et al., 1998). Recent reviews of published research on cross-cultural caregiving (Aranda & Knight, 1997; Connell & Gibson, 1997; Dilworth-Anderson, Williams & Gibson,

2002; Janevic & Connell, 2001; Pinquart & Sorensen, 2005) indicate that there are cross-cultural differences in the nature and effects of caregiving to those with dementia. In particular, differences are related to social support, stress and coping processes, psychological outcomes, and the use of formal services. A consensus exists among social gerontologists about the need to better understand the origin of these differences and to develop theoretical models that specify cultural conditions influencing these caregivers' outcomes among ethnocultural groups.

Ethnocultural Factors and Dementia Caregiving

Research has supported that ethnicity and culture may help to predict burden and psychological distress among ethnic groups. For example, Valle, Cook-Gait, and Tazbaz (1993) reported significant differences between Mexican and Anglo-American caregivers to dementia-affected older adults in their reactivity to the caregiving role, with Latino caregivers feeling more bothered with the overall caregiving situation and specific tasks. Research also shows that Latinos perceive their caregiving responsibilities to be a greater burden when compared to African American caregivers (Cox & Monk, 1990, 1993). Empirical findings also suggest that Latino caregivers in comparison to Anglo Americans experience poorer health, but the evidence is equivocal for differences in psychological distress (Aranda & Knight, 1997; Connell & Gibson, 1997; Coon et al., 2004; Knight & McCallum, 1998). Based on the existing research, it can be hypothesized that Latino caregivers experience at least similar and possibly higher levels of burden and depression as compared to Anglo-American caregivers, and higher levels of burden and distress when compared to African American caregivers.

The origins of these significant ethnocultural differences just mentioned, however, are unclear, because most research does not identify specific cultural factors (Janevic & Connell, 2001). There is a need to examine the role of the race/ethnicity variable and its effects on caregivers' health and well-being in the presence of cultural perceptions and meanings among caregivers of people with dementia. Cultural representations about stress and illness are organized experiences that have behavioral and coping implications with regards to health outcomes (Moss-Morris et al., 2002; Petrie & Weinman, 1997; Schiaffino, Shawaryn, & Blum, 1998; Skelton & Croyle, 1991). Most of the research examines the impact of these dimensions in studies of illness adaptation for patients experiencing diverse chronic conditions (heart disease, arthritis, cancer, hypertension, diabetes, etc.). It has also been suggested that illness beliefs and literacy have important implications for those who care for relatives experiencing a chronic illness. Accordingly, caregivers' representations about the illness may regulate their responses. There is some evidence of this for those who care for family members with schizophrenia, spouses and caregivers of individuals with chronic health problems, and, more recently, first-degree relatives of people with Alzheimer's disease (Roberts & Connell, 2000; Roberts et al., 2003). However, there has been no systematic cross-cultural examination of illness perceptions and beliefs among caregivers of people with dementia, and no research studies have investigated the association between cultural illness/stress representations and health behavior and well-being among Latin and Hispanic family caregivers.

Recent research on cultural values and attitudes toward Alzheimer's disease care has examined factors such as the caregiver's mastery of, and cultural reasons and justification for, caring, knowledge and information about Alzheimer's disease, respect for older adults, perceived cultural barriers to social and medical service use, acculturation, family orientation and support, religious values and involvement, stigma or punishment from God, and attitudes toward caregiving. Latin caregivers share similar cross-cultural patterns with respect to cultural factors, such as the reported endorsement of stronger views on filial support (Cox & Monk, 1990) and a lower level of knowledge about Alzheimer's disease (Ayalon & Arean, 2004). Research has also focused on specific cultural aspects influencing the caregiving experience among Latinos. In particular, attention has been directed to values such as respect for the elderly, perceiving adults as depositaries of tradition and experience and taking on a central role within the family support system (Beyene, Becker, & Mayen, 2002), the importance of family relations and family orientation with extended family support (Montoro-Rodríguez, & Kosloski, 1998), the process of acculturation (Chun, Balls Organista, & Marin, 2003), and the social stigma or shame associated with Alzheimer's disease and other dementias (Gallagher-Thompson, Solano, Coon, & Arean, 2003). There is also evidence pointing to the critical role of cultural factors in the use of community services, such as respite (Kosloski, Schaefer, Allwardt, Montgomery, & Karner, 2002). The main recognized barriers include language limitations, attractiveness, attitudes, information, and bureaucratic complexity (Montoro-Rodríguez, Kosloski, & Montgomery, 2003).

Dementia Interventions for Ethnocultural Groups

The influence of culture is also evident from reports indicating higher service use by Latino caregivers participating in specific, coordinated, ethnic-sensitive services such as the "El Portal Latino Alzheimer's Project" in Los Angeles (Aranda, Villa, Trejo, Ramirez, & Ranney, 2003) and the Palo Alto Veterans Administration (VA)/Stanford project, part of the

Resources for Enhancing Alzheimer Caregiver's Health (REACH) National Collaborative Study (Gallagher-Thompson et al., 2003b). (See chapter 20 for more details.) From these innovative programs, we learn that just providing respite services is not enough, and that successful promotion and partnership with community leaders are essential to service use. As they indicate, "significant community education about dementia and staff education about cultural norms were essential to successful service delivery in ethno-cultural groups" (Starns, Karner, & Montgomery, 2002, p. 172).

Puerto Rican Characteristics, Hispanic Culture, and Caregiving

The influence of Puerto Rican ethnocultural factors on family caregiving must be considered while accounting for several important aspects associated with Puerto Rican families. Among them, and perhaps the most influential and noted in the literature, is *socioeconomic status* (as indicated by education, income, and occupational prestige). Latin and Hispanic families attain lower levels of socioeconomic status when compared to White counterparts; however, Puerto Rican families report even lower median income levels in comparison to Mexicans and Cubans (Sanchez-Ayendez, 1998). Likewise, almost two thirds of Puerto Ricans in the United States have not completed high school (U.S. Department of Commerce, 2003), and among Latin older adults, Puerto Ricans have lower levels of formal education than Mexicans and Cubans (Krause & Goldenhar, 1992). Puerto Ricans' low level of income might derive in part from their low educational achievement, which is likely associated with limited access to prestigious occupations and professional career paths. These characteristics certainly have an impact on the caregivers' ability to access formal care, on their level of information and knowledge about the symptoms and treatments of Alzheimer's disease, and on their own physical and psychological health. In fact, results from research including intervention strategies indicate that Latin caregivers show poorer self-rated health and higher rates of depressive symptoms (Aranda et al., 2003), and Puerto Rican elders are more likely to report any disability, and report even greater disability, than either African or White American elders (Tennstedt, Chang, & Delgado, 1998).

The economic needs and low socioeconomic status of Puerto Ricans have resulted in important changes within the family structure, particularly for women, over the past 30 years. More Puerto Rican women are working to support their families, are less likely to be married, are more likely to head their families on their own, and are more likely to have children at younger ages and prior to marriage (Ortiz, 1995). Clearly, these are conditions that challenge the ability of Puerto Rican families to function as the main informal support system for relatives with dementia, and those conditions impose additional strains for women to assume their expected role as caregivers.

The *acculturation experience* of Puerto Ricans is another important dimension that assists researchers and service providers in understanding the needs of family caregiving of relatives with dementia. The influential role of acculturation among Puerto Ricans is connected with their experience of internal migration and resettlement, socioeconomic hardships, discrimination, and minority status, among other contextual factors. As Cortes (2003) indicated, acculturation is a multidimensional construct that encompasses specific ways to fully capture the unique and often stressful adjustment experiences that may lead to distress for Puerto Ricans. In his study (2003) of Puerto Ricans in New York, in addition to measures of acculturation such as place of birth, number of years residing in the (mainland) United States, and involvement with Puerto Rican and American culture, Cortes also used the concepts of anger, disillusionment, and nostalgia about life in Puerto Rico as alternative measures. Calderon-Rosado and colleagues found that length of residence in the (continental) United States, but not language acculturation, was related to the use of formal services among disabled Puerto Rican elders and their caregivers (Calderon-Rosado, Morrill, Chang, & Tennstedt, 2002). Their findings also suggest that the most commonly used measure of acculturation, language, may be less relevant in a population with a history of circular migration. Therefore, in designing dementia interventions for Puerto Rican caregivers, clinicians and researchers need to postulate bilingual and, even more importantly, bicultural programs to reduce potential barriers to access community-based services among this population.

The main ethnocultural characteristics of Puerto Rican families consist of an integrated system of learned patterns of beliefs, customs, and behaviors. These ethnocultural aspects are relevant in the role they assume in mediating or moderating the response to the emergence of a crisis, such as Alzheimer's disease within the family. The key cultural factors associated with Latin and Hispanic families, and by inclusion, with Puerto Ricans, resemble a distinct way of understanding reality in comparison to Anglo-Americans. They have distinct worldviews with regard to general assumptions about reality and values (see Ponton, 2001, for a review). Research on Puerto Rican culture has identified *familism* as the central cultural value. It refers to a strong commitment to the family as a system of support, learning, socialization, and assistance (Sanchez-Ayendez, 1998; Zayas & Palleja, 1988). As an illustration, Puerto Rican mothers participating in a focus group study expressed that family closeness and respect for authority were of greater importance than independence and assertiveness (Gonzales Ramos, Zayas, & Cohen 1998). The centrality of the family comes with associated values and behaviors based, for the most part, on religious teachings, such as *personalismo*, which indicates the idea that every individual has an absolute value as a person and ought to be treated with dignity; *respeto*, which attributes authority to seniority, parents, and deference in general to adults; *marianismo*, which assigns specific roles and attitudes for women as reflected by the Virgin Mary; *machismo*, which indicates a gender/sexual identity and distribution of labor within the household; and *fatalism*, which refers to the idea of a higher purpose, yet unknown, that explains actual personal events or situations.

These key cultural values are shared by all Latin and Hispanic groups (see Cauce & Domenech- Rodríguez, 2002; Gallagher-Thompson et al., 2003b; Ponton, 2001), and they need to be considered when planning and implementing interventions, especially when the goal is to engage in interpersonal interactions and maintain continuous communication. For example, we find that values such as *personalismo* and its religious and sociopolitical ideas as proclaimed by Enmanuel Mounier (1954) are explicitly mentioned in the mission and rationale for action in many Latin movements and charitable organizations, such as the Catholic Worker movement "Casa de San Diego" (2005) in Houston, Texas. One of the main principles is to "enable every individual to live as a person, that is, to exercise a maximum of initiative, responsibility, and spiritual life." The values of *personalismo*, family solidarity, and family reciprocity describe a collective rather than individualistic and competitive cultural worldview. For Puerto Ricans, family relations are further reinforced with the family practice of *compadrazo*, which places added responsibility on non-kin to care for family members (Cauce & Domenech-Rodríguez, 2002). As Gallagher-Thompson and colleagues (2000a) indicated, cultural caregiving interventions need to focus on interpersonal relations and social interactions. We are also confident that a focus on personal interactions would reflect the broader cultural idea of the person as an absolute value, that is, of the precedence of a person over any other material or societal reality.

Research has also indicated that the level of familism might decline as Hispanics embrace Anglo-American culture (Sabogal, Marin, & Otero-Sabogal, 1987). In a study of highly acculturated Puerto Ricans in Ohio, however, this negative association was not replicated. Feelings of mutual obligations, reciprocity, and solidarity toward one's family members did not decline with increased acculturation, measured as language proficiency and number of years in the (continental) United States (Montoro-Rodríguez & Kosloski, 1998). Because participants were members of a local Catholic parish, it may be that membership in a religious organization factored into the results. Therefore, whether the relationship between acculturation and familism may be moderated by ethnicity or other factors (such as membership in religious organizations) remains an interesting possibility. It is a challenge for community organization's staff, managers, and leaders to identify under what conditions Puerto Rican families can resort to, incorporate, and benefit from these contextual factors and cultural values, to respond and adjust efficiently to the challenging experience of caring for relatives with dementia. Interventions for Puerto Ricans, as indicated by Delgado (1995), need to reinforce their cultural heritage by providing opportunities to maintain their cultural identity, resorting from traditional roles (such as folk healers) to social clubs, community centers, and organizations.

Finally, another contextual factor that has been identified as central to the Latin caregiving experience is associated with health representations about dementia and dementia care (e.g., knowledge about Alzheimer's, expectations about care, social stigma, and other aspects associated with the condition). Research among older adults indicates that there is a need for accurate information about Alzheimer's disease and community services for older adults, in particular, among families with low socioeconomic status (Edwards, Cherry, & Peterson, 2000). Although cross-ethnocultural research on illness representations and knowledge about Alzheimer's disease is limited and based on small samples and qualitative data, it is assumed that minorities have a different set of representations about dementia and also a higher level of misconceptions about Alzheimer's disease (Ayalon & Arean, 2004; Dilworth-Anderson & Gibson, 2002; Hinton, Franz, Yeo, & Levkoff, 2005; Roberts et al., 2003). Among Puerto Ricans participating in a focus group study, culturally influenced beliefs contributed to their personal experiences as caregivers, such as declaring their strong commitment to family–home care. On the other hand, the lack of knowledge about dementia was the main barrier to recognition of initial symptoms and understanding of the disease (Neary & Mahoney, 2005). Puerto Ricans also seem to use mixed models (biomedical and folk understanding of dementia) in their narratives about their relatives' condition, as they attribute Alzheimer's disease not only to an abnormal brain disorder but also to normal aging or family tragedies, migration, and psychological distress (Hinton & Levkoff, 1999). There is, therefore, a pressing need to address these culturally based conceptions and to create mechanisms to reach out to the Hispanic and Puerto Rican caregiving population to provide education and raise community awareness. As an illustration, evidence from the Alzheimer's disease educational intervention (AHORA) indicated that training staff members by increasing their level of knowledge about Alzheimer's and about common Hispanic beliefs resulted in positive changes in self-reported patient-care behaviors (Gallagher-Thompson, Haynie, Takagi, Valverde, & Thompson, 2000).

Family Roles, Acculturation, and Communication

Research on Puerto Rican family caregiving and cultural factors has been scanty and for the most part qualitative or exploratory. It has also been subsumed under larger studies including other Latin and Hispanic groups. Based on the limited available data and with no intention of being exhaustive, we now identify strategies for culturally competent models for Hispanic and Puerto Rican family caregivers. We conclude by suggesting specific intervention strategies that may assist families in providing better care to relatives with Alzheimer's disease.

The importance of family identity and process in Puerto Rican caregiving presents obvious benefits and challenges as well. Regarding the latter, intergenerational differences in opinion and degrees of acculturation to American culture can create tension and conflict between family members (Neary & Mahoney, 2005). Because most minority and nonminority caregivers of those with dementia in the United States are adult children (Alzheimer's Association, 2004a; Sanchez-Ayendez, 1998), the potential for intergenerational role conflict is considerable. Adult Puerto Rican children are likely to be more proficient in English than their parents, and thus, often become the "social brokers" for parents in identifying community services and health-care providers (Kanellos, 1994). The dependence on adult children for such services may be unsettling for parents, especially those who migrated from Puerto Rico as adults. Perhaps this explains why many older adults who migrated in the 1980s and 1990s (when they were 55 years of age or older) have returned to Puerto Rico (Sanchez-Ayendez, 1998). The change in roles can also be a challenge for adult children (Morycz, 1994). Brewer (2005) eloquently portrays the precarious juggling of family roles by adult children, who one moment find themselves as the submissive offspring, but the next moment have to provide "parental" direction and nurturing to their parent or grandparent with dementia. Role reversals are not, of course, unique to intergenerational relationships. Spouses often find themselves having to take on the responsibilities of the other when dementia is present (e.g., financial transactions, homemaking). Whether one is a spouse or adult child, knowing when it is acceptable and propitious to switch roles is something that caregivers must gradually learn by trial and error (Morycz, 1994).

Intergenerational conflict can be heightened when there are different degrees of acculturation by caregivers and the family member with dementia (Janevic & Connell, 2001). Younger adult caregivers are likely to identify more with the dominant culture (Neary & Mahoney, 2005; Sanchez-Ayendez, 1998), striving toward upward educational and employment mobility. As a result, they may place less value on maintaining family unity by keeping the family member with dementia at home. In support of this, Mausbach et al. (2004) found that Latina caregivers who showed greater acculturation reported less positive views of caregiving and were more likely to place their family member with dementia in a facility.

On the other hand, an important benefit of strong family ties is that primary caregivers may be more likely to turn to other family members for support in their caregiving endeavors, which could ease the burden on any one individual (though see Levkoff, Levy, & Weitzman, 1999, and Sanchez-Ayendez, 1998, for evidence suggesting that caregiving responsibilities still fall primarily on the shoulders of the adult daughter or other female family member). The value placed on interdependence in the family unit (*familismo*) also seems to promote "aging in place," as reflected in Latino families being more likely than Caucasians to care for persons with dementia at home for a longer period of time (Levkoff et al., 1999; Mausbach et al., 2004; Neary & Mahoney, 2005; Sanchez-Ayendez, 1998; Yaffe et al., 2002). As noted by one Puerto Rican caregiver: "the Puerto Rican is raised in a family that is always united. Rarely are there those that put [their elderly] in a nursing home in Puerto Rico, there are not many cases...we are like this. And the children also remain in the home, you see, because this is not like the American. The American quickly throws the child out so that it leaves and becomes independent. I do not find anything good with this. ... No, us Puerto Ricans want that all the world live together" (Levkoff et al., 1999, p. 350).

One challenge, however, in caring for persons with dementia at home for longer periods of time is related to managing the increasing dementia-related behaviors as the disease progresses (Calderon & Tennstedt, 1998; Sink, Covinsky, Newcomer, & Yaffe, 2004). As the abilities of the person with dementia to carry out activities of daily living (ADL) decline, caregivers are called upon to shoulder more and more of the care for their family member (Neary & Mahoney, 2005). Over time, the increased caregiving responsibilities exact a toll, which may explain, in part, why Latino caregivers appear to have higher rates of depression compared to nonminority caregivers (Cox & Monk, 1993).

One domain strongly associated with ADL functioning and caregiver burden is the quality of communication between persons with dementia and their caregivers. It is well established that language and communication impairments are among the most prevalent and disabling symptoms of dementia (Small, Geldart, & Gutman, 2000; Sink et al., 2004). In fact, caregivers have reported more difficulty coping with language and communication problems than with memory or behavioral disturbances (Murray, Schneider, Banerjee, & Mann, 1999). In a study that conducted focus groups with caregivers of persons with dementia, researchers found that increases in communication problems were related to decreases in the persons' abilities to function in ADLs/IADLs (Small et al., 2000). Based on this relationship, the authors argued that interventions that seek to improve communication may enable the caregiver to more successfully support the person's abilities in ADLs, thereby reducing caregiver burden.

Although communication is central to culture in that it is both a means of transmitting culture and of representing culture, there appear to be no published studies that focus on communication patterns between Puerto Rican caregivers and family members with dementia. This is a significant gap in the literature, because the styles and functions of communication vary both across and within cultures. For example, one culture may rely more on what is not said than on what is spoken (Hall, 1976). Similarly, within a culture, individuals typically identify with a reference group based on categories such as geographical location, ethnicity, religion, or age. As a result, our communication behaviors and preferences become molded by the reference group and serve to distinguish "us" from "them."

An illustration of this in relation to intergenerational caregiving contexts is that of age-based stereotypes and the influence these have on communication. For example, in Anglo-American culture, aging is often cast in a negative light by emphasizing the increasing physical and cognitive declines associated with getting older, and the perception of seniors as being set in their ways (Hummert, Garstka, Shaner, & Strahm, 1994). These perceptions get transmitted at all levels of society and become entrenched as negative age-based stereotypes. The stereotypes then become manifest in communication behavior in what Ryan and colleagues refer to as the communication predicament of aging (Ryan, Hummert, & Boich, 1995). One might ask whether such a predicament is experienced by elderly Puerto Rican individuals when interacting with younger Puerto Rican adults. On the one hand, elderly Puerto Ricans are treated by younger generations with respect and are viewed as a source of stability and wisdom (Neary & Mahoney, 2005); on the other hand, there are potential intergenerational and intercultural forces that may subvert these positive values of aging. Namely, younger adult caregivers, having been raised in American schools and society, may have acculturated into the dominant group's stereotyping of aging. At present, there appears to be little research addressing this possibility. Some authors suggest that Latino caregivers view their family members with dementia in terms of a regression to childhood, a stereotype that has frequently been noted in Anglo-American caregiving (Kemper, 1992). Gallagher-Thompson et al. (2000a, p. 161) described this as a belief "that the brain 'dries up' leading to behaviors *como un nino* (childlike)." Such beliefs can have a negative impact on the communication behaviors toward the person with dementia. For example, Levkoff and colleagues cited one Puerto Rican caregiver who described her mother with dementia "in childlike terms as her 'little one' who had her 'little room' and wore her 'little clothes'. In explaining why she did not allow her mother to do household chores, she said, 'it [would be] like ordering a little girl around'" (1999, p. 342).

Although the negative age-based stereotypes identified in Anglo-American culture may not be as prevalent among families whose members retain a strong Puerto Rican cultural identity, other perceptions they hold about aging or dementia may have a deleterious effect on the person with dementia and those involved in his or her care. Several authors have noted the perception of dementia by the Hispanic community as a mental illness that is due to age (Levkoff et al., 1999), craziness, or having bad blood in the family (Henderson & Gutierrez-Mayka, 1992). Because of the social stigma and shame associated with having a family member with dementia (Henderson, 1996), families may try to shield the person from the outside world, delay seeking professional assessment and services, and become socially isolated and depressed (Dilworth-Anderson et al., 2002; Gallagher-Thompson et al., 2000b, 2003b). Ironically, while such "protective" measures are taken to preserve the dignity of the family, they may in fact undermine the dignity and self-worth of the person with dementia by restricting his or her interpersonal interactions with family, friends, and others in the community (Ponton, 2001).

An additional concern is the potential for stereotypes based not only on age but also on culture to influence how formal health-care providers interact with persons from another cultural or ethnic group (Hinton, 2002; Ponton, 2001). The multicultural milieu of long-term care in North America presents significant challenges to realizing positive interpersonal interactions between staff and residents. Language barriers are a reality for many facilities, and even when staff and residents share a common language, substantial differences in worldview due to ethnicity, religion, or other life experiences are a breeding ground for interpersonal conflict (Small & Montoro-Rodríguez, 2006; Small, Geldart, Gutman, & Clarke Scott, 1998).

Intervention Strategies

There is a paucity of research on interventions with Latino family care-givers (though see Gallagher-Thompson et al., 2000a, 2001, 2003a, 2004). Intervention research involving Anglo-American caregivers has indicated benefits of providing psychoeducational or cognitive–behavioral train-ing, for example, teaching skills to caregivers for resolving interpersonal conflict or coping skills to deal with negative emotions and depression (Gallagher-Thompson et al., 2000a). Empirically supported interven-tions for Anglo-American caregivers that focus on communication are even rarer, and none exist for ethnic minorities. Nevertheless, a variety of suggestions and considerations for meeting the challenges of caregiving in the Puerto Rican context are tentatively offered below in anticipation that future research will investigate their value and effectiveness. Using a multidimensional framework of ethnicity (Barth, 1994), we anticipate that any intervention for Puerto Ricans would have to integrate interpersonal, familial, and community aspects related to the provision of care. Therefore, suggestions need to address individual challenges or resources (religious beliefs, illness representations, etc.), *compadrazo* (family and network sup-port), and the potential impact of organizations, policies, health services, and structural arrangements affecting the history of Puerto Rican families (such as migration patterns). Among these integrated recommendations, we consider the following:

- The importance of *early* intervention and provision of support ser-vices to Puerto Rican caregivers is critical, given that they may expe-rience greater burden compared to other ethnic caregivers.
- Because of circular migration, there is a need for services and educa-tion about Alzheimer's disease and caregiving that are linguistically and culturally tailored to the Puerto Rican caregiving experience, illness perceptions and beliefs, and values associated with well-being and quality of care. This can be accomplished through partnership with community leaders and by training care staff and support agen-cies about cultural norms.
- Similarly, when designing interventions for Puerto Rican caregivers, the extent to which caregivers and persons with Alzheimer's disease are bilingual or bicultural should be determined. An individual may be bicultural and have allegiance to both cultures, albeit in differ-ent domains. In this case, they may be perceived by others as having completely acculturated, because they accommodate to whom they are talking (i.e., they do not show the other culture in their attitudes, etc.). In addition, intergenerational differences should be kept in

mind as an adult child caregiver or family member may have acculturated more than the person with dementia.

- Because more Puerto Rican elders (than other Latino elders) live with
spouses or other family members, it is important to bring to their
attention the challenges associated with switching roles (parent/
child; homemaker, financial provider), and how one can maintain
one's own and the other person's dignity despite taking on unfamiliar and perhaps uncomfortable roles. In this regard, the stigma often
associated with dementia in Latino groups may lead to social isolation, and this needs to be respectfully addressed by noting the consequences of such isolation on the dignity and well-being of persons
with dementia and their caregivers.

- It is also recommended that health professionals attempting to serve
Puerto Rican caregivers address individual religious values and
other cultural beliefs emanating from the Catholic faith tradition,
so that caregivers can attribute and reconceptualize their experience
with Alzheimer's disease as a brain disorder and not feel unnecessary guilt, stigma, or embarrassment about it.

- For Puerto Rican caregivers, reliance on filial support would entail
putting the family over any one individual. In this regard, it would
seem crucial to include all relevant and interested family members
when providing caregiver interventions (Gallagher-Thompson et al.,
2000b, 2003b).

- Approaches to communication emphasizing connecting with the
person with dementia and supporting his or her personhood (e.g.,
Perry and O'Connor, 2002; Small et al., 1998) resonate with the
concept of *personalismo* and, therefore, should be considered when
training caregivers to effectively communicate.

- Certain communication strategies have been found to facilitate positive interactions between Anglo-American caregivers and persons
with Alzheimer's disease (Small & Perry, 2005; Small et al., 2003).
For example, eliminating distractions, using simpler sentence structure, and asking "yes" and "no" (rather than open-ended) questions
enhances communication, whereas using a slower than normal speech
rate does not. The appropriateness of these strategies needs to be
examined through the Puerto Rican cultural lens, and their effectiveness should be put to the test in Puerto Rican caregiving contexts.

Concluding Remarks

One of the main components of the stress–health process applied to caregiving for those with dementia focuses on the management of emotional

responses through coping, adaptation, and adjustment processes (Cohen, Kessler, & Gordon, 1995). Both formal and informal systems of care benefit when caregivers, care recipients, and their family/social and physical environments are able to integrate their responses so as to minimize negative outcomes and maximize "successful adaptation." Recent conceptual frameworks for interventions with caregivers seek to identify those dimensions necessary for effective programs (Schultz et al., 2000). However, for practitioners and human service providers, the simultaneous occurrence of various participants, situations, structures, and processes makes it difficult to identify effective interventions and to single out specific sources responsible for successful and positive emotional responses. For example, Latina caregivers may have accurate information about Alzheimer's disease but fail to choose to implement an effective coping strategy, and conversely, advanced behavioral skills may not be useful if the caregivers do not identify or diagnose the problem correctly. Furthermore, deciding which responses and outcomes are beneficial positive emotional responses, or recognizing them as "successful," is problematic and a value-driven task (Matthews, Zeidner, & Roberts, 2002). To better serve caregivers, we need to inquire about their criteria and consider those values and beliefs associated with dementia, such as social embarrassment and stigma or the idea that burden and distress are a necessary price for growth, as part of a religious system that perceives poverty and suffering as means of personal purification and spiritual development. A culturally competent model would then address Latina caregivers' behavioral responses as based not only on their appraisal of objective needs and availability of family resources, but also on moral judgments and ethical or religious principles. What constitutes an effective and successful outcome is driven by these interactions among value-laden criteria for care of family members.

The dearth of research on interventions with Latino family caregivers and, in particular, with Puerto Rican families makes more urgent the endeavor of identifying cultural dimensions as key features of interventions for ethnocultural groups. The aim is to understand factors that contribute to positive outcomes and their role in ameliorating the hardships and deleterious effects experienced by caregivers of people with dementia. Puerto Ricans share some similar cultural patterns with other Latin and Hispanic Americans; however, they also have a distinct sociocultural tradition and heritage. They are one of the most economically deprived, "hard-to-reach," and "underserved" populations in the United States. Clearly, any attempt to understand the range of choices and behavioral patterns among Puerto Rican caregiving families will present a challenge for community organization's staff, managers, and professionals. At the same time, the benefits derived from endeavoring to improve the quality of life of Puerto Rican caregivers and those they care for should be sufficient impetus to live up to this challenge.

References

Alicea, M. (1990). Dual home bases: A reconceptualization of Puerto Rican migration. *Latino Studies Journal, 1*, 78–98.

Alzheimer's Association. (2004a). *Families care: Alzheimer's caregiving in the United States 2004.* Chicago: Alzheimer's Association and National Alliance for Caregiving.

Alzheimer's Association. (2004b). *Hispanic/Latinos and Alzheimer's Disease.* Chicago: Alzheimer's Association.

Aranda, M. P., & Knight, B. G. (1997). The influence of ethnicity and culture on the caregiver stress and coping process: A sociocultural review and analysis. *Gerontologist, 37*, 342–354.

Aranda, M. P., Villa, V. M., Trejo, L., Ramirez, R., & Ranney, M. (2003). El Portal Latino Alzheimer's Project: Model program for Latino caregivers of Alzheimer's disease-affected people. *Social Work, 48*(2), 259–271.

Ayalon, L., & Arean, P. A. (2004). Knowledge of Alzheimer's disease in four ethnic groups of older adults. *International Journal of Geriatric Psychiatry, 19*, 51–57.

Barth, F. (1994). Enduring and emerging issues in the analysis of ethnicity. In H. Vermeulen & C. Govers (Eds.). *The anthropology of ethnicity* (pp. 11–32). Amsterdam: Het Spinhuis.

Beyene, Y., Becker, G., & Mayen, N. (2002). Perception of aging and sense of well-being among Latino elderly. *Journal of Cross-Cultural Gerontology, 17*, 155–172.

Brewer, J. (2005). Carousel conversation: Aspects of family roles and topic shift in Alzheimer's talk. In B. Davis (Ed.), *Alzheimer talk, text and context: Identifying communication enhancements* (pp. 87-101). New York: Palgrave Macmillan.

Calderon, V., & Tennstedt, S. L. (1998). Ethnic differences in the expression of caregiver burden: Results of a qualitative study. *Journal of Gerontological Social Work, 30*(1–2), 159–178.

Calderon-Rosado, V., Morrill, A., Chang, B., & Tennstedt, S. (2002). Service utilization among disabled Puerto Rican elders and their caregivers. *Journal of Aging and Health, 14*(1), 3–23.

Casa Juan Diego. (2005). *Roots of the Catholic worker movement: Emmanuel Mounier and personalism.* Retrieved September 12, 2005, from www.cjd. org/paper/roots/remman.html

Cauce, A., & Domenech-Rodríguez, M. (2002). Latino families: Myths and realities. In J. Contreras, K. Kerns, &. A. Neal-Barnett (Eds.), *Latino children and families in the United States* (pp. 1–25). Westport, CT: Praeger.

Chun, K. M., Balls Organista, P., & Marin, G. (2003). *Acculturation: Advances in theory, measurement, and applied research.* Washington, DC: American Psychological Association.

Cohen, S., Kessler, R. C., & Gordon, L. U. (1995). Strategies for measuring stress in studies of psychiatric and physical disorders. In S. Cohen, R. C. Kessler, & L. U. Gordon (Eds.), *Measuring stress: A guide for health and social scientists* (pp. 3–26). New York: Oxford University Press.

Connell, C. M., & Gibson, G. D. (1997). Racial, ethnic, and cultural differences in the dementia caregiving: Review and analysis. *Gerontologist, 37,* 355–364.

Coon, D. W., Rubert, M., Solano, N., Mausbach, B., Kraemer, H., Arguelles, T., et al. (2004). Well-being, appraisal, and coping in Latina and Caucasian female dementia caregivers: Findings from the REACH study. *Aging & Mental Health, 8*(4), 330–345.

Cortes, D. E. (2003). Idioms of distress, acculturation, and depression: The Puerto Rican experience. In K. Chun, P. Balls-Organista, & G. Marin (Eds.), *Acculturation: Advances in theory, measurement and applied research* (pp. 207–222). Washington, DC: American Psychological Association.

Cox, C., & Monk, A. (1990). Minority caregivers of dementia victims: A comparison of Black and Hispanic families. *The Journal of Applied Gerontology, 9,* 340–354.

Cox, C., & Monk, A. (1993). Hispanic culture and family care of Alzheimer's patients. *Health and Social Work, 18*(2), 92–100.

Cuadrado, M., & Lieberman, L. (2002). *Traditional family values and substance abuse: The Hispanic contribution to an alternative prevention and treatment approach.* New York: Kluwer/Plenum.

Delgado, M. (1995). Puerto Rican elders and natural support systems: Implications for human services. *Journal of Gerontological Social Work, 24*(1/2), 115–130.

Dilworth-Anderson, P., & Gibson, B. E. (2002). The cultural influence of values, norms, meanings, and perceptions in understanding dementia in ethnic minorities. *Alzheimer Disease and Associated Disorders, 16*(Supp. 2), S56–S63.

Dilworth-Anderson, P., Williams, I. C., & Gibson, B. (2002). Issues of race, ethnicity, and culture in caregiving research: A 20-year review (1980–2000). *Gerontologist, 42,* 237–272.

Edwards, A. B., Cherry, R. L., & Peterson, J. (2000). Predictors of misconceptions of Alzheimer's disease among community dwelling elderly. *American Journal of Alzheimer's Disease, 15,* 27–35.

Gallagher-Thompson, D., Arean, P., Coon, D., Menéndez, A., Takagi, K., Haley, W. et al. (2000a). Development and implementation of intervention strategies for culturally diverse caregiving populations. In R. Schulz (Ed.), *Handbook on dementia caregiving: Evidence-based interventions for family caregivers* (pp. 151–186). New York: Springer.

Gallagher-Thompson, D., Arean, P., Rivera, P., & Thompson, L. W. (2001). Reducing distress in Hispanic family caregivers using a psychoeducational intervention. *Clinical Gerontologist, 23*(1/2), 17–32.

Gallagher-Thompson, D., Coon, D. W., Solano, N., Ambler, C., Rabinowitz, Y., & Thompson, L. W. (2003a). Change in indices of distress among Latino and Anglo female caregivers of elderly relatives with dementia: Site-specific results from the REACH National Collaborative Study. *The Gerontologist, 43*(4), 580–591.

Gallagher-Thompson, D., Haynie, D., Takagi, K., Valverde, I., & Thompson, L. W. (2000b). Impact of an Alzheimer's disease education program: Focus on Hispanic families. *Gerontology & Geriatrics Education, 20*(3), 25–40.

Gallagher-Thompson, D., Singer, L. S., Depp, C., Mausbach, B. T., Cardenas, V., & Coon, D. W. (2004). Effective recruitment strategies for Latino and Caucasian dementia family caregivers in intervention research. *American Journal of Geriatric Psychiatry, 12*(5), 484–490.

Gallagher-Thompson, D., Solano, N., Coon, D., & Arean, P. (2003b). Recruitment and retention of Latino dementia family caregivers in intervention research: Issues to face, lessons to learn. *Gerontologist, 43*(1), 45–51.

Gonzales Ramos, G., Zayas, L. H., & Cohen, E. V. (1998). Child-rearing values of low-income, urban Puerto Rican mothers of preschool children. *Professional Psychology: Research and Practice, 29*, 377–382.

Hall, E. T. (1976). *Beyond culture.* Garden City, NY: Anchor Press.

Henderson, J. N. (1996). Cultural dynamics of dementia in a Cuban and Puerto Rican population in the United States. In G. Yeo & D. Gallagher-Thompson (Eds.), *Ethnicity and the dementias* (pp. 153–166). Washington, DC: Taylor & Francis.

Henderson, J. N., & Gutierrez-Mayka, M. (1992). Ethnocultural themes in caregiving to Alzheimer's patients in Hispanic families. *Clinical Gerontologist, 11*, 59–74.

Hinton, L. (2002). Improving care for ethnic minority elderly and their family caregivers across the spectrum of dementia severity. *Alzheimer Disease and Associated Disorders, 16*(Supp. 2), S50–S55.

Hinton, L., Franz, C., Yeo, G., & Levkoff, S. (2005). Conceptions of dementia in a multiethnic sample of family caregivers. *Journal of the American Geriatrics Society, 53*(8), 1405–1410.

Hinton, L., & Levkoff, S. (1999). Constructing Alzheimer's: Narratives of lost identities, confusion and loneliness in old age. *Culture, Medicine and Psychiatry, 23*, 453–475.

Hummert, M., Garstka, T. A., Shaner, J. L., & Strahm, S. (1994). Stereotypes of the elderly held by young, middle-aged, and elderly adults. *Journal of Gerontology: Psychological Sciences, 49*(5), 240–249.

Janevic, M. R., & Connell, C. M. (2001). Racial, ethnic, and cultural differences in the dementia caregiving experience: Recent findings. *Gerontologist, 41*, 334–347.

Kanellos, N. (1994). *The Hispanic Almanac: From Columbus to corporate America.* Detroit, MI: Visible Ink Press.

Kemper, S. (1992). Language and aging. In F. I. M. Craik & T. A. Salthouse (Eds.), *The handbook of aging and cognition* (pp. 213–269). Mahwah, NJ: Lawrence Erlbaum.

Knight, B., & McCallum, T. (1998). Heart rate reactivity and depression in African-American and White dementia caregivers: Repression or positive coping? *Aging & Mental Health, 2*, 212–221.

Kosloski, K., Schaefer, J., Allwardt, D., Montgomery, R. J. V., & Karner, T. X. (2002). The role of cultural factors on clients' attitudes toward caregiving, perceptions of service delivery, and service utilization. In R. J. V. Montgomery (Ed.), *A new look at community-based respite programs: Utilization, satisfaction, and development (pp. 65–88)*. New York: Haworth Press.

Krause, N., & Goldenhar, L. M. (1992). Acculturation and psychological distress in three groups of elderly Hispanics. *Journal of Gerontology: Social Sciences, 47*(6), S279–S288.

Levkoff, S., Levy, B., & Weitzman, P. F. (1999). The role of religion and ethnicity in the help seeking of family caregivers of elders with Alzheimer's disease and related disorders. *Journal of Cross-Cultural Gerontology, 14*, 335–356.

Matthews, G., Zeidner, M., & Roberts, R. D. (2002). *Emotional intelligence: Science and myth*. Boston: Massachusetts Institute of Technology.

Mausbach, B. T., Coon, D. W., Depp, C., Rabinowitz, Y. G., Wilson-Arias, E., Kraemer, H. C. et al. (2004). Ethnicity and time to institutionalization of dementia patients: A comparison of Latina and Caucasian female family caregivers. *Journal of the American Geriatrics Society, 52*, 1077–1084.

Montoro-Rodríguez, J., & Kosloski, K. (1998). The impact of acculturation on attitudinal familism in a community of Puerto Rican Americans. *Hispanic Journal of Behavioral Sciences, 20*(3), 376–391.

Montoro-Rodríguez, J., Kosloski, K., & Montgomery, R. (2003). Evaluating a practice-oriented service model to increase the use of respite services among minorities and rural caregivers. *The Gerontologist, 43*(6), 916–924.

Morycz, R. K. (1994). Clinical implications of different caregiving relationships for patients with dementia. *Seminars in Speech and Language, 15*(3), 206–215.

Moss-Morris, R., Weinman, J., Petrie, K. J., Horne, R., Cameron, L., & Buick, D. (2002). The revised illness perception questionnaire (IPQ-R). *Psychology and Health, 17*(1), 1–16.

Mounier, E. (1954). *Be not afraid: Studies in personalist sociology*. New York: Harper.

Murray, J., Schneider, J., Banerjee, S., & Mann, A. (1999). EUROCARE: A cross-national study of co-resident spouse carers for people with Alzheimer's disease: II—A qualitative analysis of the experience of caregiving. *International Journal of Geriatric Psychiatry, 14*(8), 662–667.

Neary, S. R., & Mahoney, D. F. (2005). Dementia caregiving: The experiences of Hispanic/Latino caregivers. *Journal of Transcultural Nursing, 16*(2), 163–170.

Ortiz, V. (1995). The diversity of Latino families. In R. E. Zambrana (Ed.), *Understanding Latino families: Scholarship, policy and practice (pp. 18–39)*. Newbury Park, CA: Sage.

Patterson, T. L., Semple, S. J., Shaw, W. S., Yu, E., He, Y., Zhang, M. Y. et al. (1998). The cultural context of caregiving: A comparison of Alzheimer's caregivers in Shanghai, China and San Diego, California. *Psychological Medicine, 28*, 1071–1084.

Perry, J., & O'Connor, D. (2002). Preserving personhood: (Re)membering the spouse with dementia. *Family Relations, 51*, 55–62.

Petrie, K. J., & Weinman, J. A. (1997). *Perceptions of health and illness: Current research and application*. London: Harwood Academy.

Pinquart, M., & Sorensen, S. (2005). Ethnic differences in stressors, resources, and psychological outcomes of family caregiving: A meta-analysis. *The Gerontologist, 45*(1), 90–106.

Ponton, M. O. (2001). Hispanic culture in the United States. In M. O. Ponton & J. Leon-Carrion (Eds.), *Neuropsychology and the Hispanic patient* (pp. 15–38). Mahwah, NJ: Lawrence Erlbaum.

Roberts, J. S., & Connell, C. M. (2000). Illness representations among first-degree relatives of people with Alzheimer disease. *Alzheimer Disease and Associated Disorders, 14*(3), 129–136.

Roberts, J. S., Connell, C. M., Cisewski, D., Hipps, Y., Demissie, S., & Green, R. C. (2003). Differences between African Americans and Whites in their perceptions of Alzheimer Disease. *Alzheimer Disease and Associated Disorders, 17*(1), 19–26.

Ryan, E. B., Hummert, M. L., & Boich, L. H. (1995). Communication predicaments of aging: Patronizing behavior toward older adults. *Journal of Language and Social Psychology, 14*, 144–166.

Sabogal, F., Marin, G., & Otero-Sabogal, R. (1987). Hispanic familism and acculturation: What changes and what doesn't? *Hispanic Journal of Behavioral Sciences, 9*, 397–412.

Sanchez-Ayendez, M. (1998). The Puerto Rican family. In C. H. Mindel, R. W. Habenstein, & J. R. Wright (Eds.), *Ethnic families in America* (4th ed., pp. 199–222). New York: Prentice Hall.

Schiaffino, K. M., Shawaryn, M. A., & Blum, D. (1998). Examining the impact of illness representations on psychological adjustment to chronic illnesses. *Health Psychology, 17*, 262–268.

Schulz, R., Gallagher-Thompson, D., Haley, W., & Czaja, S. (2000). Understanding the interventions process: A theoretical/conceptual framework for intervention approaches to caregiving. In R. Schultz (Ed.), *Handbook of dementia caregiving* (pp. 33–60). New York: Springer.

Schulz, R., O'Brien, A. T., Bookwala, J., & Fleissner, K. (1995). Psychiatric and physical morbidity effects of dementia caregiving: Prevalence, correlates, and causes. *The Gerontologist, 35*, 771–791.

Seigel, J. (1999). Demographic introduction to Racial/Hispanic elderly populations. In T. Miles (Ed.), *Full color aging: Facts, goals, and recommendations for America's diverse elders* (pp. 1–19). Washington, DC: The Gerontological Society of America.

Sink, K. M., Covinsky, K. E., Newcomer, R., & Yaffe, K. (2004). Ethnic differences in the prevalence and pattern of dementia-related behaviors. *Journal of the American Geriatrics Society, 52*, 1277–1283.

Skelton, J. A., & Croyle, R. T. (1991). *Mental representations in health and illness*. New York: Springer.

Small, J. A., Geldart, K., & Gutman, G. (2000). Communication between individuals with dementia and their caregivers during activities of daily living. *American Journal of Alzheimer's Disease and Other Dementias, 15*(5), 291–302.

Small, J. A., Geldart, K., Gutman, G., & Clarke Scott, M. (1998). The discourse of self in dementia. *Ageing and Society, 18*, 291–316.

Small, J. A., Gutman, G., Makela, S., & Hillhouse, B. (2003). Effectiveness of communication strategies used by caregivers of persons with Alzheimer's disease during activities of daily living. *Journal of Speech, Language, and Hearing Research, 46*, 353–367.

Small, J. A., & Montoro-Rodríguez, J. (2006). Conflict resolution strategies in assisted living and nursing home facilities. *Journal of Gerontological Nursing. 32*(1), 39-45.

Small, J. A., & Perry, J. (2005). "Do you remember?" How caregivers question their spouses who have Alzheimer's disease and the impact on communication. *Journal of Speech, Language, and Hearing Research, 48*, 125–136.

Starns, M. K., Karner, T. X., & Montgomery, R. J. V. (2002). Exemplars of successful Alzheimer's demonstration projects. In R. J. V. Montgomery (Ed.), *A new look at community-based respite programs: Utilization, satisfaction, and development* (pp. 141–175). New York: Haworth Press.

Tennstedt, S. L., Chang, B., & Delgado, M. (1998). Patterns of long-term care: A comparison of Puerto Rican, African-American, and Non-Latino White elders. *Journal of Gerontological Social Work, 30*(1/2), 179–199.

U.S. Census Bureau. (2000). *The older population in the United States: March, 2000.* (Current Population Reports.) Washington, DC, U.S. Bureau of the Census, Population Division.

U.S. Department of Commerce. (1997). *Census facts for Hispanic Heritage month* (Press Release No. CB-97FS.10). Washington, DC: U.S. Government Printing Office.

U.S. Department of Commerce. (2003). *The Hispanic population in the United States: March 2002.* (Population Characteristics, June 2003.) Washington, DC: U.S. Government Printing Office.

U.S. Library of Congress. (2004, April 22). *Puerto Rican and Cuban immigration.* Retrieved May 10, 2005, from http://memory.loc.gov/learn/features/immig/introduction.html

Valle, R. (1988). *Caregiving across cultures. Working with dementia illness and ethnically diverse populations.* Washington, DC: Taylor & Francis.

Valle, R., Cook-Gait, H., & Tazbaz, D. (1993). *The cross-cultural Alzheimer dementia caregiver comparison study.* Paper presented at the 46th Gerontological Society of America. New Orleans, LA.

Yaffe, K., Fox, P., Newcomer, R., Sands, L., Lindquist, K., Dane, K. et al. (2002). Patient and caregiver characteristics and nursing home placement in patients with dementia. *Journal of the American Medical Association, 287*(16), 2090–2097.

Zayas, L. H., & Palleja, J. (1988). Puerto Rican familism: Considerations for family therapy. *Family Relations, 37*, 260–264.

CHAPTER 19

Working with Cuban American Families

TRINIDAD ARGÜELLES AND SOLEDAD ARGÜELLES

Periods of Migration and Geographical Concentrations

The Hispanic American population constitutes the largest growing minority group in the United States (U.S. Census Bureau, 2000). Although Cuban Americans currently make up the third largest Hispanic American group in the United States (after Mexican Americans and Puerto Ricans; Therrien & Ramirez, 2000), they are one of the most influential minority groups in the history of this country. Through the years, Cubans have tended to migrate to the United States in definite periods of time, beginning with the 19th century with the first significant migration, and to current times.

They began to immigrate to the United States in the late 1890s, during the time of the Spanish–American War. Many Cubans who immigrated at the end of the 19th century came to the United States to organize insurgent groups against the *colonizadores* (the Spaniard Crown). This experience, as described by Portes and Stepick (1993), represented the first major event to unite the destinies of the two countries: Cuba and the United States. During that time, Cubans settled for a decade in two Floridian cities, Tampa and Key West, and opened businesses, some of which have made a mark in their local economies that has lasted for centuries (i.e., tobacco business in Tampa).

311

It was not until the 1920s that Cubans would again immigrate to the United States, and this time mostly to the cities of Miami, Florida, and New York. Miami was geographically closer to the island and was similar in climate, architecture, and weather, while New York offered job opportunities. This influx of Cubans was due to the election of Gerardo Machado, who, although elected democratically as the Cuban President, decided to modify the constitution so he could remain in power indefinitely. Once again, Cubans migrated to their "neighbor country" (Portes & Stepick, 1993).

Between the 1920s and 1959, Cubans, although in lesser numbers, came to the United States in search of seasonal jobs (i.e., sugarcane workers, baseball players, musicians, and other blue-collar workers who came looking for economic prosperity). In the year 1959, a significant Cuban immigration took place. Thousands of Cubans, estimated to be approximately 10% of the island's population, abandoned or were forced to leave by the Cuban authorities upon the rise of the Fidel Castro regime, which by all accounts was not an elected government, and since its beginnings had repressed civil liberties for Cubans. This wave of Cuban exiles continued through the 1960s with the "freedom flights," where many Cubans left the island on airplane charter flights, or with the early rafters who occasionally arrived at the shores of the United States, settling primarily in Miami, New Jersey, and New York. These Cubans arrived in the United States searching for the civil liberties and economic opportunities they had just lost.

As the years passed, government oppression on the island increased, culminating in a mass exodus in 1980 with the Mariel Boatlift, when approximately 125,000 Cubans came to the United States in boats owned by Cuban Americans residing in the United States. This operation was conceived by Fidel Castro, whereby he allowed Cuban exiles to bring their family members, many of whom had been waiting for decades for a Cuban permit, from Cuba to the United States. In exchange for allowing these Cubans to immigrate to the United States, the Cuban government would board nonpolitical prisoners, murderers, mentally ill patients, and many others who were considered undesirable onto the exiles' vessels, to be shipped onto the shores of Key West. Most of the Cubans who arrived in the 1980 exodus settled in the Miami-Dade, Florida, area.

Yet another significant wave of Cuban exiles occurred in the early 1990s during the Clinton Administration, when numerous rafters arrived at the United States. For the first time ever since 1959, the Cuban refugees were not allowed to remain after being intercepted on the ocean. Thousands of them were sent to Guantanamo Bay, which houses an American military base. This period gave rise to the "wet/dry foot" policy in 1994 that stated that Cubans could apply for political asylum only if they reached American soil. If they were intercepted on the ocean, they would be returned to the island, a drastic change from prior procedures. Before 1994, the Cuban Adjustment Act of 1966 made it easier for Cubans to remain in the United States, even when they did not reach American waters on their own. This change in policy has drastically slowed Cuban immigration and has limited it to those who win a U.S. government sponsored visa lottery to come to the United States.

Cuban American Elders

In Miami-Dade county, Florida, there has been a need to address minority residents of Hispanic background, who constituted about 57% of the population (U.S. Census Bureau, 2000), with 55% of those over 60 years of age of Hispanic descent (Florida Department of Elder Affairs, 2001), close to 90% of whom are Cuban or of Cuban American descent. Cubans in the United States constitute about 1.2 million residents, about 52% of whom live in Miami-Dade county alone, and the rest primarily reside in Tampa, Key West, New Jersey, and New York.

Acculturation has been an interesting phenomenon for Cuban Americans. It would appear that by Cubans having American friends, by birth rates being lower than most other Hispanics (about two children per household; Aponte & Barnes, 1995), and by having the largest income per household of any other Hispanics, they have been significantly acculturated to the American culture. Nonetheless, Cuban Americans have not fully assimilated into the American culture; they maintain their unique festivals (i.e., Carnival Miami), speak their native tongue (even in second and third generations). This nostalgia has been witnessed even among the rich and famous Cuban Americans, such as Hollywood actor Andy García and singer/composer Gloria Estefan.

The acculturation process has also been delineated by the different immigration waves. Cubans who immigrated in the late 1890s to the 1920s, for the most part, either acculturated completely to the point of becoming fully Americanized and assimilated into the U.S. society or they returned to Cuba. Many of the descendants of these groups still reside in the Tampa area, and most have been fully immersed into American society. Interestingly, the acculturation process for Cubans who arrived in the United States beginning in 1959 has been quite different. A significant number of these Cubans maintain Spanish as either their sole or primary tongue. Furthermore, these Cuban "cohorts" would love to visit the island, and many do so in spite of their rejection of the Cuban government. They overcome many obstacles currently in place so that they can visit their family members. Cuban immigrants have managed to successfully adjust to the dominant culture and proudly keep their Cuban roots, as so graciously depicted in the "I Love Lucy" comedy series, where Ricky Ricardo appears, a Cuban-born musician in real life, and on the series, a successful entrepreneur and at the same time a modern American husband. Cuban Americans in Miami, for example, manage to blend both cultures to the point that they do not see a problem in becoming American citizens and still celebrating their Cuban Independence Day, or having their daughters and granddaughters (who were probably born in the United States) participate in beauty pageants such as Miss Florida (part of the Miss USA pageant) or Miss Cuba in Exile Pageant, a completely Cuban American pageant.

The Traditional Cuban Family

Traditionally, the extended family has played an important role within Cuban American family structures. Upon arriving in the United States and being faced with the geographical reality of living in a big country and experiencing geographical separation from their relatives, Cuban American families appear to have now turned into a "modified nuclear family." This means that the nuclear family and the extended family might not necessarily reside under one roof as they traditionally did in Cuba; nonetheless, they still share many of same duties and responsibilities. Traditional Cuban families are composed of intergenerational households, with mother, father, children, grandparents, and in-laws, and some other more distant relatives (i.e., aunts, uncles, and cousins) who might reside under the same roof or in close proximity. Yet, once in the United States, Cuban families evolved into a modified version of this, where family members might live close but not under the same roof (i.e., in an efficiency next door, or in a duplex next to them).

Importance of the Nuclear and Extended Family

In Cuban families, single parents frequently rely on the guidance and support of fictive kin (i.e., neighbors and relatives), similar to many African American families. For example, for them, the saying, "Who is your brother? Your closest neighbor" (in Spanish, ¿Quién es tu hermano?, Tu vecino más cercano), is really a truism. Furthermore, the idea of *compadres-comadres* (Godparents to the children by way of Baptism) is taken very seriously, whereby independent of the religious affiliation, these individuals become "true members of the family" from the baptism on. Cuban families tend to be enmeshed, and this at times causes surprise from the dominant culture. A Cuban male, for example, might reside at home, living with his parents until age 30 or so until he decides to get married; this would rarely be the case in a White non-Hispanic family. Living at home for longer periods of time also prevails with Cuban women, and sometimes, Cuban American young adults attend the local university or college instead of going away to college, because their parents do not encourage them or place guilt on them, so they do not go.

The enmeshed family phenomenon can also be viewed in the caregiving field. Sometimes, females (daughters or daughters-in-law) might be the primary caregivers. They might find themselves abandoning their jobs or simply sacrificing any rest/leisure time to care for an ill older relative instead of placing him or her in an assisted living facility or nursing home. As a whole, Cuban American families tend to care for their ill, older relatives (Mintzer et al., 1992) for longer periods of time than their White non-Hispanic counterparts. Because women are often the primary caregivers, this responsibility often forces them to leave their jobs or drastically reduce their work hours, which will later impact their lifestyles drastically and even contribute to depression because they are indirectly leaving their support system of work and friends.

Because Cuban families tend to be pretty enmeshed, they at times overprotect a family member with dementia, making it hard for them to let anyone else inside the family system, even those trying to help. It is not uncommon for Cuban children not to allow the nurse assistant to bathe parents with dementia, because they feel that no strangers should do this.

Gender Roles

Although Cuban culture might be perceived as *"machista"* (male dominated or oriented), historically, Cuban women have had a central role in the family. They do not only share the child-rearing responsibilities with husbands and other family members, but they also share the responsibility of passing on the "patriotic torch." Independent of whether the family resides on the island or in the United States, it is usually the mother that teaches them to become conscious about their nationality and patriotic identity. This sense of patriotism is passed on for generations, even in the United States, where sometimes even second-generation Cubans, when asked about their ethnicity or nationality, might simply respond "I am Cuban American," or "I was born here to Cuban or to Cuban American parents."

In addition to being active mothers, wives, and patriots, many Cuban women also hold jobs. The number of working Cuban American women has drastically increased. In 1959, for example, about 13% of Cuban women were employed; this number increased to about 42% in 2001 (Institute for Cuban and Cuban American Studies, 2003).

Decision-Making Authority

Decisions within Cuban families are usually entertained among the family members, where even the children have a voice. This becomes more complex in the United States, where you might have family members making decisions who might not communicate effectively with one another due to language barriers or simply different concepts of reality due to generation gaps or place of birth. Ultimately, although it might be both parents who would make decisions for the family, the female's input is heavily weighted. One could say that Cuban families are matriarchal, whereby the father would often leave the responsibility of the children's upbringing entirely to the mother so he can concentrate in being the primary breadwinner. It is common for Cuban mothers to say to their kids, "ask your father for permission to go out," and then have the father turn around and say, "No, ask your mother, she knows best." There is even a saying among Cubans: "Who has the last word in the house?" and the answer is "the husband, who says to the wife, 'yes, my dear.'" Gender roles are also important when making decisions related to placement and treatment of an individual with dementia. For example, it is common for families to appoint daughters or daughters-in-law to be responsible for carrying out the treatment plan (Mintzer et al., 1992).

Cuban Caregivers in the Context of Hispanic Caregivers

Cuban Americans are similar to other Hispanics or Latinos in a number of ways but are unique in others. According to Bernal (1982), for example, Cubans are different from other Hispanics in terms of class, greater degree of European and African ancestry, and most of all, a unique historical connection with powerful nations (i.e., Spain, the United States, and the former Soviet Union). This geopolitical reality that includes Cuba's proximity to the United States has made Cubans feel very "special" and that they can overcome any catastrophe with the sense of being Cuban, including dealing with dementia. Cubans make light of situations that would otherwise be very hard to bear (*choteo*), allowing them to take matters more lightly and with less stress (Bernal, 1982). The constant joking, paraphrasing, and "*tuteo*" (speaking in colloquial second-person singular) are just some of the unique traits of the Cuban American cultural heritage that must be taken into account when providing mental health assistance.

Religiosity or Spirituality Within the Cuban Community: Its Role in Mental Health

Although Cuban Americans mostly self-identify as Roman Catholics, in practice, many either do not fully practice the religion or practice it in conjunction with other religious belief systems, such as *Santería*. *Santería* is in itself a religion and is a perfect example of the syncretism of the Yoruban Nigerian cult of the Orishas and the Roman Catholic cult of the Saints that Cubans inherited from the Spaniards. This marriage between the two religions allowed the African slaves living in Cuba and their descendents to worship two religions at a time by basing its manifestation not so much in the one God that most monotheist religions worship, but indeed in the polytheism manifestation of the many saints or *orishas*. This practice has transcended this group and is now practiced fully by any Cuban sector, including the exile community. Each Roman Catholic saint has an equivalent saint in the Santería rite. These orishas are perceived as healers or powers that will cure or alleviate the "crazy person." In fact, the word *demented, demente* in Spanish, has the connotation of "crazy" or "being crazy." As a result, it carries a stigma. Furthermore, Cubans generally do not trust the mental health system, because the Castro regime has used psychiatry and other related professions to torture and control dissidents and keep the anti-Castro movement in the dark. The stigma plus the lack of trust in the mental health system are also evident in the exile community, and many families of patients with dementia may find refuge in the practice of this Afro-Cuban religion or in other alternative types of treatment or religions (i.e., herbal medicine). Traditionally, it is more acceptable to seek assistance from a *Santero* or religious leader than to consult a psychiatrist, especially concerning illnesses such as dementia that might carry an aura of curse or bad luck into the family. Recently though, the Protestant religions, especially the Evangelical ones, have become popular within Cuban communities, both on the island and in the United States. They also contribute to the belief of the Cuban people that the omnipotence of God is also shown in God's power to heal the mind.

Intervention Strategies and Cuban Caregivers of Dementia Patients

The psychological, physical, and economic strains of caregiving for a family member with a dementia diagnosis have been supported by multiple research findings. Caregivers of dementia patients are at risk for suffering clinical depression, anxiety, and many other medical conditions (Bass, Noelker, & Rechlin, 1996; Schulz et al., 1997). Although the difficulties of being a caregiver are significant regardless of demographic variables such as gender, ethnicity, and economic status, it is important to address these variables in order for effective interventions to be developed. Furthermore, the identification of ethnicity as a key factor in the treatment of psychological distress has been a phenomenon of the second half of the 20th century. According to Shibutani and Kwan, an ethnic group is "those who conceive of themselves as alike by virtue of their common ancestry, real or fictitious, and who are so regarded by others" (1965, p. 23). Furthermore, McGoldrick suggested that "ethnicity is a powerful influence in determining identity" (1982, p. 5). The last two references allude to the importance of taking an individual's ethnicity into consideration when treating his or her medical or psychological symptoms; the case of caregivers of patients with dementia is no exception. When developing effective interventions for this particular group of individuals, identifying their ethnic groups and targeting specific techniques or strategies to that specific group are important in providing them with the support they need. In spite of the myth that ethnic minorities are not "psychologically minded," it is currently known that if the appropriate measures are taken into account in order to facilitate treatment fidelity and symptom reduction, they could benefit from psychological treatment modalities. In the case of Cuban American caregivers, some of the factors that should be taken into consideration include levels of acculturation (i.e., spoken language and years in the United States); family and gender roles; demographic characteristics of the interventionist; and other issues related to trust. It is recommended that every step taken toward effective intervention with Cuban American caregivers needs to include at least the four factors listed above.

According to Aponte and Barnes (1995), determining the acculturation level of an individual is important, because it will assist the interventionist to better understand the patient's view of him- or herself, monitor the intervention success, and assess the service utilization patterns and the overall understanding of how patients present their symptoms. The second important factor to be understood when working with Cuban American families is family roles. Because it is important for Cuban American families to maintain their value system, respecting the roles that family members play is crucial; these could be based on gender, generation, or any type of status. The third factor to be taken into consideration when providing psychotherapeutic support to Cuban American caregivers, is that interventionists must be attuned to how their ethnicity and the ethnicity of their patients interrelate. It is important for Cuban American caregivers to feel that professionals treating them are empathetic toward their stress and understand their acculturation, immigration history, and family roles. Oftentimes, Cuban American caregivers will prefer a bilingual professional to treat them. Data reveal that with different groups of His-panics, although there is a tendency to prefer bilingual therapists, depend-ing on the patients' level of acculturation, the preference is mediated by such factors as years of experience or competency levels of the therapists. In the case of Cuban Americans, the therapist's respect toward their politi-cal and religious views is highly cherished in the therapeutic relationship.

Therapeutic Interventions That Support Family
Caregivers of Individuals with Dementia

A review of the literature related to treatment of Cuban American caregiv-ers revealed a paucity of evidence-based modalities for specific groups of individuals. It appears that most of the data have been captured on either a mixed ethnic sample (combining several Hispanic groups), on a younger cohort than most Cuban American caregivers, and on cohorts that have been treated for symptoms or stressors not related to caregiving. Studies specifically on Cuban American caregivers of individuals with dementia are difficult to find.

Support groups have been found to be beneficial for Hispanics of all ages. Specifically, Vasquez and Han (1995) suggested that, if they are conducted by ethnically competent facilitators, support groups could be instrumental in enhancing Hispanics' self-esteem, trust, and intimacy issues, and in assisting with identity issues. Moreover, other interventions were identified as being effective in treating depressive symptomatology in elders, not specific to Cuban or Hispanic elders. Grant (1995) found that psychodynamic, behavioral, cognitive-behavioral, and interpersonal ther-apies have been successful in the treatment of depressive symptoms. He also stated that some of the issues that need to be taken into consideration when working with elders are similar to those that are important when working with ethnic minorities. The psychoeducational model described by Morano and Bravo (2002) is an attempt to study effective modalities to assist Hispanic caregivers of individuals with Alzheimer's disease. This detailed program was implemented with Hispanics from several Spanish-speaking countries who reside in the United States, and it mainly provided information to caregivers regarding disease symptoms and resources.

Also related to the specifics of intervention in the elderly, Argüelles, Klausner, Argüelles, and Coon (2003) highlighted the fact that family therapy in late-life families is slightly different than family therapy in adult families. Issues of loss of autonomy and value conflicts appear to be of special interest in older persons. Finally, these authors discussed the fam-ily therapy modality utilized by the Resources for Enhancing Alzheim-er's Caregiver Health I (REACH I) project at the Miami site. Structural

Ecosystems Therapy (SET) was augmented by a technological intervention (Computer Telephone Integration System [CTIS]). Together with a White non-Hispanic population, the REACH I intervention at the Miami site was tested in a population of Cuban American caregivers of patients with Alzheimer's disease. REACH I represented one of the first attempts to identify and test interventions that are specially targeted to a Cuban American sample, instead of the often used "Hispanic" sample, encompassing a mix of many groups of Hispanics. This approach agrees with the suggestion made by Harwood and colleagues (1998) that it is preferable to research Hispanic groups separately.

Description of SET

SET combines two major theoretical family therapy approaches: structural family therapy (Minuchin & Fishman, 1981) and the social ecological approach/ecosystemic approach (Bronfenbrenner, 1986). This treatment modality was developed by Szapocznik and associates (1997) using a sample of Hispanic and African American adolescents diagnosed with conduct disorder. Through the years, SET has been utilized when treating other populations, but the REACH I sample represented the first time that this modality was tested on an older Cuban American sample of caregivers of Alzheimer's patients, and in conjunction with the CTIS component. SET consisted of many of the factors that were discussed above as being key when working with Cuban American or Hispanic individuals: high regard for family values and for extended familial ties (including friends, neighbors, and others who help); respect for family roles; and engaging with the family members, taking into account their acculturation levels. SET seemed to be a perfect fit for Cuban American families taking care of an Alzheimer's patient. For a more comprehensive description of the intervention, the reader can review Argüelles et al. (2003).

Description of the CTIS

For a more comprehensive description of the CTIS, please refer to Argüelles and von Simson (1999). This system was utilized by the REACH I project and entailed a screen phone with text and voice integrated with computers features. The screen phones were installed in the caregivers' homes, and they allowed caregivers to access menu-driven capabilities. Thanks to the CTIS, caregivers were able to participate in on-the-phone support groups, access resources such as respite services, and enhance communication with their friends and family members.

Outcomes of the REACH I SET + CTIS Treatment Modality

Data revealed that caregivers who participated in this therapeutic modality experienced amelioration of depressive symptoms after 6 months of treatment. Additionally, there was evidence that after 18 months of participating in the SET + CTIS treatment, Cuban American husbands and daughters benefited more than their White non-Hispanic counterparts, or than other relatives (Eisdorfer et al., 2003).

Also from the REACH I SET + CTIS treatment group are the research findings of Bank, Argüelles, Rubert, Eisdorfer, and Czaja (in press). This study explored the on-the-phone discussion group experience using the CTIS system and revealed that most caregivers, both White non-Hispanic and Cuban American, reported that participating in these discussion groups was beneficial to them. They reported that they obtained emotional support and practical tips from other caregivers, as well as enhanced their social needs.

The specific interactional communication and behavioral patterns of the SET family therapy modality used in the REACH I project were studied by Mitrani and Czaja (2000) in their report of the project's clinical observations. Furthermore, Mitrani, Feaster, McCabe, Czaja, and Szapocznik (2005) adapted the well-known Structural Family Systems Rating that assesses the patterns of interactions important in the SET therapy modality of the REACH I project.

End-of-Life Issues

Important issues related to life and death are often difficult to discuss, even in cultures that are future oriented and that practice preventive medicine. These issues become more challenging to handle for cultures, such as the Cuban American culture, that are so present oriented. In Cuba, for example, the only advanced planning for funeral arrangements is the purchasing of the *Panteón* and the *Osario*. The *Panteón* is the family's own cemetery plot or land so they can bury loved ones. The *Osario* (ossuary or charnel house) is a unique feature of the islander's burial system whereby about 3 years after the person has been buried, the family receives a citation from the cemetery to unbury the person's remains, and these are then placed in a smaller coffin or *osario* that can also be owned by the deceased person's family. The ritual that takes places 3 years after the person's burial is very important, because it is a reality check, whereby the entire family needs to come to grips with the fact that the person is deceased, and the family members have to meet and appoint a family member who will actually "identify the remains" and "transfer them from the big coffin to the small one." This ritual is nonexistent in the exiled community, because Cuban Americans are not buried this way in the United States. Furthermore, the process of acquiring the plot in the cemetery is looked upon more like a business transaction, and even the funeral arrangements, which in Cuba are the duty of the surviving family members, become at times the person's own prearranged burial.

Other issues, including a living will and advance directives, are challenging subjects to be discussed within Cuban families, especially when dealing with individuals with dementia, because the families are often in denial or perceive the dementia as part of the aging process, and they hope for a recovery that will not occur. Also, because of their present-oriented culture, Cuban Americans do not believe that they will ever need to make these decisions or arrangements. Furthermore, they operate as a culture with the belief that whatever happens will happen anyhow, so it does not matter whether or not you prepared in advance for it. Another issue related to death and dying or end-of-life issues is bargaining. This bargaining usually includes bargaining with God for either a cure or more time to live.

Resources for Families

There are many resources available for family members. Unfortunately, some are only available in English, which makes it harder for the older Cuban American cohort to understand or have access to them, but others are either bilingual (English and Spanish) or are made available to them through third parties. Other ways of disseminating information through the community is to utilize local advocacy and community organizations or entities that serve this community. In Miami-Dade county, for example, organizations such as the Hispanic Coalition on Aging, the local chapter of the Alzheimer's Assocation, the local Area Agency on Aging, the Alzheimer's Disease Initiative (ADI), the University of Miami's Memory Disorders Clinic, and the Wien Center for Alzheimer's Disease and other Related Dementia are some of the resources that are available to caregivers who seek assistance and orientation, not only in terms of educational materials and information in both English and Spanish, but also in terms of diagnosis, treatment, and evaluation of their loved ones, and support systems (e.g., local support groups) available for the caregivers. Other resources have been research projects serving the community at a local level but funded nationally, such as REACH I and II projects, Cognitive Rehabilitation Projects, and Medication Adherence Projects. The community and its infrastructure have also joined the cause and assisted the researchers via their local radio shows, providing open forums to speak about dementia and educate minority communities, especially the Cuban American radio, which is a vibrant part of that community.

Some of the resources' available via the Internet are as follows:

Alzheimer's Association (www.alz.org): Bilingual resources

Alzheimer's Disease Education and Referral Center (www.ADEAR): For professionals and caregivers (bilingual resources), comprehensive resources

European Alzheimer's organization (www.Alzheimer-europe.org): Multilingual resources, very general information

Family caregiver alliance (www.caregiver.org): Comprehensive bilingual resources

National Hispanic Coalition on Aging (www.nhcoa.org): Lots of resources having to do with legislation and assistance

Universo Médico (www.universomedico.com.mx): For professionals, paraprofessionals, and family members (in Spanish, from Mexico)

Practical Suggestions

The following are suggestions that could serve as a guide to practitioners when treating Cuban American caregivers of individuals with Alzheimer's disease or Cuban American elders, in general:

1. Pay special attention to issues related to acculturation, immigration history, political views, and family roles.
2. Do not assume psychopathology or prejudge out of the ordinary behaviors (i.e., Santeria beliefs), but instead, assess them within a Cuban American context.
3. Be accepting of more extreme emotional expressions (i.e., a loud tone of voice).
4. Although speaking Spanish is not a must, a bilingual interventionist is the preferred choice of professional. A second choice is a professional who might not be bilingual but attempts to speak Spanish.

Conclusions and Future Directions

Although recent efforts to develop effective strategies to assist the caregivers of individuals with Alzheimer's disease are proving to be successful, it appears that treatment initiatives for Cuban Americans could be further explored and enhanced. It will be interesting to follow the generational trajectory of Cuban Americans and how the coming generations continue to react and deal with issues related to Alzheimer's disease. Also, as psychopharmacological interventions become more prevalent and efficient in treating Alzheimer's disease, the role that psychological interventions, especially family interventions, will play in the overall treatment plan is worth being explored. Finally, the continuous role of technology-driven interventions might prove to be increasingly popular. As Cuban Americans continue to have access to technology, this population will become increasingly open to using it as an aid to success. Overall, continuous refinement of interventions and discovery of appropriate ways to disseminate the results appear to be two major goals for the interventionist who treats Cuban American caregivers of individuals with Alzheimer's disease.

References

Aponte, J. F., & Barnes, J. M. (1995). Impact of acculturation and moderator variables on the intervention and treatment of ethnic groups. In J. F. Aponte, R. Y. River, & J. Wohl (Eds.), *Psychological interventions and cultural diversity* (pp. 19–39). Boston: Allyn & Bacon.

Argüelles, S., Klausner, E., Argüelles, T., & Coon, D. (2003). Family interventions to address the needs of the caregiving system. In D. W. Coon, D. Gallagher-Thompson, & L. Thompson (Eds.), *Innovative interventions to reduce dementia caregiver distress: A clinical guide* (pp. 99–118). New York: Springer.

Argüelles, S., & von Simson, A. (1999). Innovative family and technological interventions for encouraging leisure activities in caregivers of persons with Alzheimer's disease. *Activities, Adaptation, and Aging, 24*(2), 83–99.

Bank, A., Argüelles, S., Rubert, M., Eisdorfer, E., & Czaja, S. J. (in press). The value of telephone support groups among ethnically diverse caregivers of persons with dementia. *The Gerontologist*.

Bass, D. M., Noelker, L. S., & Rechlin, L. R. (1996). The moderating influence of service use on negative caregiving consequences. *Journal of Gerontology: Social Sciences, 51B*, S121–S131.

Bernal, G. (1982). Cuban families. In M. McGoldrick, J. K. Pearce, & J. Giordano (Eds.), *Ethnicity and family therapy* (pp. 187–207). New York: Guildford Press.

Bronfenbrenner, U. (1986). Ecology of the family as a context for human development: Research perspectives. *Developmental Psychology, 22*, 723–742.

Eisdorfer, C., Czaja, S. J., Loewenstein, D. A., Rubert, M. P., Argüelles, S., Mitrani, V. B. et al. (2003). The effect of a family therapy and technology-based intervention on caregiver depression. *The Gerontologist, 43*, 521–531.

Florida Department of Elder Affairs. (2001). *Florida county profile. Dade County.* Tallahassee: Author.

Grant, R. W. (1995). Interventions with ethnic minority elderly. In J. F. Aponte, R. Y. Rivers, & J. Wohl (Eds.), *Psychological interventions and cultural diversity* (pp. 109–144). Boston, MA: Allyn & Bacon.

Harwood, D. G., Barker, W. W., Cantillon, M., Loewenstein, D. A., Ownby, R., & Duara, R. (1998). Depressive symptomatology in first-degree family caregivers of Alzheimer disease patients: A cross-ethnic comparison. *Alzheimer Disease and Associated Disorders, 12*, 340–346.

Institute for Cuban American Studies. (2003). *Cuba's women: Numbers tell the story.* Online database of information. Cuba On-Line.

Loewenstein, D. A. & Eisdorfer, C. (1992). Issues in geriatric research. In L. K. Hsu & M. Hersen (Eds.), *Research in psychiatry: Issues, strategies, and methods.* New York: Plenum Press.

McGoldrick, M. (1982). Ethnicity and family therapy: An overview. In M. McGoldrick, J. K. Pearce, & J. Giordano, *Ethnicity and family therapy* (pp 3–30). New York: Guilford Press.

Mintzer, J., Rubert, M., Loewenstein, D., Gamez, E., Millor, A., Quinteros, R. et al. (1992). Daughters caregiving for Hispanic and non-Hispanic Alzheimer patients: Does ethnicity make a difference? *Community Mental Health Journal, 28*(4), 293–301.

Mitrani, V. B., & Czaja, S. J. (2000). Family-based therapy for family caregivers: Clinical observations. *Aging and Mental Health, 4*, 200–209.

Mitrani, V. B., Feaster, D. J., McCabe, B. E., Czaja, S. J., & Szapocznik, J. (2005). Adapting the Structural Family Systems Rating to assess the patterns of interaction in families of dementia caregivers. *The Gerontologist, 45*, 445–455.

Morano, C. L., & Bravo, M. (2002). A psychoeducational model for Hispanic Alzheimer's disease caregivers. *The Gerontologist, 42*, 122–126.

Portes, A., & Stepick, A. (1993). Enter the Cubans. In A. Portes & A. Stepick (Eds.), *City on the edge. The transformation of Miami* (pp. 89–107). Berkeley and Los Angeles: University of California Press.

Schulz, R., Newson, J., Mittelmark, M., Burton, L., Hirsh, C., & Jackson, S. (1997). Health effects of caregiving: The caregiver health effects study, an ancillary study of the cardiovascular health study. *Annals of Behavioral Medicine, 19*, 110–116.

Shibutani, T., & Kwan, K. M. (1965). *Ethnic stratification.* New York: Macmillan.

Szapocznik, J., Kurtines, W. M., Santisteban, D. A., Pantín, H., Scopetta, M., Mancilla, Y. et al. (1997). The evolution of structural ecosystemic theory for working with Latino families. In J. G. García & M. C. Zea (Eds.), *Psychological interventions and research with Latino populations* (pp. 166–190). Boston: Allyn & Bacon.

Therrien, M., & Ramirez, R. R. (2000). *The Hispanic population in the United States: March 2000* (Current Population Reports, P20-535). Washington, DC: U.S. Census Bureau.

U.S. Census Bureau. (2000). *State and county quick facts.* (Data derived from Population Estimates, 2000 Census of Population and Housing). Washington, DC: Author.

Valle, R. (1989). Cultural and ethic issues in Alzheimer's disease family research. In E. Light & B. D. Lebowitz (Eds.), *Alzheimer's disease. Treatment and family stress: directions for research* (DHHS Publication No. ADM 89-1569, pp. 122–153). Washington, DC: U.S. Government Printing Office.

Vasquez, M. J. T., & Han, A. L. (1995). Group interventions and treatment with ethnic minorities. In J. F. Aponte, R. Y. Rivers, & J. Wohl (Eds.), *Psychological interventions and cultural diversity* (pp. 109–144). Boston, MA: Allyn & Bacon.

CHAPTER 20

Working with Mexican American Families

MELISSA A. TALAMANTES, LAURA TREJO, DANIEL JIMENEZ,
AND DOLORES GALLAGHER-THOMPSON

Background

We celebrate and uncertainly face the challenges of the burgeoning population of older people in the United States. Over a decade ago we wrote the
chapter entitled *Service Delivery Issues and Recommendations for Working
with Mexican American Family Caregivers* in the first edition of this volume and now are encouraged to report in this revision that considerably
more literature is available on Mexican American and other Latino caregivers. In this chapter, the reader can expect the following: (a) an updated
overview of the demographics on older Hispanic/Latino people and caregivers and how family caregivers are effected by caregiving responsibilities;
(b) an increased understanding of the role of Hispanic/Latino families in
care provision for relatives with dementia; (c) an examination of barriers
to care and service needs; and (d) an exploration of issues of cultural competency and available resources for caregivers, service providers, and the
general community.

The unprecedented growth in the number of older adults is evident
as the numbers of Latino older adults continue to escalate (U.S. Department of Health and Human Services, Administration on Aging [USD-
HHS, AoA], 2003). The number of older Latino adults (of any ethnicity) is

327

estimated to increase from 1.5 million in 2000 to 2.9 million in 2010 and 13.8 million in 2050 (Hayward & Zhang, 2001). In particular, Mexican American elders are the largest cohort and the fastest growing (USDHHS, AoA, 2003). These demographic trends show that increasing caregiving demands will greatly influence Latino communities in the United States.

The 2000 Census indicated that over 70% of older Latino adults live in four states—California (27%), Florida (16%), New York (9%), and Texas (20%); twice as many live with other relatives, and nearly one third more reported needing help from others for personal care compared to the total senior population (USDHHS, AoA, 2003). These factors highlight various unique needs this population may face, including long-distance caregiving, intergenerational family structures that demand family-based interventions, and challenges associated with accessing affordable, accessible, and acceptable care from providers trained to work with a population affected by dementia.

Authors of a report on family caregiving in the United States conducted by the National Alliance for Caregiving (NAC) and the American Association for Retired Persons (NAC & AARP, 1997; NAC & AARP, 2004) noted that family members provide some type of care to at least 70% of persons with dementia who live at home (NAC & AARP, 1997). They also noted that minorities, unemployed, and caregivers with less income experience significant financial difficulties (NAC & AARP, 1997). Over 27% of Latino households provide informal caregiving to an impaired friend or family member. Latino caregivers are mainly women around 40 years of age in the sandwich generation caring for older relatives and for children under the age of 18 (NAC & AARP, 1997; USDHHS, AoA, 2003). Caregivers caring for elders with more disabilities experience their own physical or mental health problems, and there is no evidence that family caregivers alone can provide care to elders with significant chronic illness (Aranda & Knight, 1997). Contrary to existing speculation and beliefs about extensive Latino social support, actual studies have found that Latino caregivers have identified fewer networks for support (Phillips, Torres de Ardon, Komnenich, Killeen, & Rusinak, 2000). Other research indicates that many Latino elders do not believe that they have a caregiver available to them in the future should they require care (Talamantes, Cornell, Espino, Lichtenstein, & Hazuda, 1996), and they report less social support compared to other cultural groups (Adams, Aranda, Kemp, & Takagi, 2002). This finding is interesting in view of other research emphasizing Mexican American caregivers' desire to provide care for their disabled family members in the home (Mausbach et al., 2004; Johnson, Schwiebert, Alvarado-Rosenmann, Pecka, & Shirk, 1997).

Most current research on Latino caregivers has used nonprobability sampling methods and a wide range of measures of psychological well-being that often cannot be directly compared (Aranda & Knight, 1997; Dilworth-Anderson, Williams, & Gibson, 2002; Talamantes & Aranda, 2004). Despite these limitations, the available research indicates that Latinos experience greater psychological distress and depression as a result of caregiving responsibilities when compared to other ethnic groups (Adams et al., 2002; Cox & Monk, 1993; Friss, Whitlatch, & Yale, 1990; Talamantes & Aranda, 2004).

The Role of Caregivers in Caring for Family Members Affected by Dementia

Mexican American caregivers will be faced with many challenges as a result of the increased illness and functional disability experienced by elder Mexican Americans (Angel, Angel, Aranda, & Miles, 2004; Bryant, Shetterly, Baxter, & Hamman, 2002; Peek, Ottenbacher, Markides, & Ostir, 2000). There exists an increased prevalence of vascular dementia for Latinos (Haan et al., 2003). More critical are the comorbid diseases and disabilities that can increase caregiver responsibilities (Haan et al., 2003). For example, diabetes rates are 30% higher in Latino and American Indian populations (Flores et al., 2002). As such, persons affected with diabetes may experience many disease complications, such as infections, amputations, retinopathy, and renal dialysis, resulting in the need for more physical care by caregivers (Flores et al., 2002). Compounded with increased physical disabilities and dementia, caregivers will need to seek other resources to help with the care demands they will face. Additionally, elders with lower education and income report poorer functioning (Jolicoeur & Madden, 2002; Zunker & Cummins, 2004). Researchers from the Hispanic Established Population for Epidemiological Studies of the Elderly (H-EPESE) found that although Mexican American elders may have serious physical and cognitive impairments, they remained living in the community rather than in institutions (Angel et al., 2004). Thus, caregivers may be caring for family members later through their illnesses. Despite ongoing research and more information regarding caregiving, Mexican American caregivers do not generally access formal dementia evaluation for affected family members or avail themselves of available resources until the dementia has progressed to a late stage (Morano & Bravo, 2002; Neary & Mahoney, 2005; Wallace, Campbell, & Lew-Ting, 1994).

What is it about Mexican American cultural values, beliefs, and norms that may influence caregiving patterns? Research indicates that Mexican American elders continue to rely on family to provide support (Angel &

Angel, 1998; Jolicoeur & Madden, 2002). Cultural factors, such as filial piety and gender expectations, social support, and acculturation, are critical to how caregivers may view their role as caregivers (Robinson-Shurgot & Knight, 2004).

Familismo (familism) supports a family-centered collectivism (as opposed to individualism). In other words, *familismo* encompasses solidarity and the sense of duty and loyalty that one feels toward family members (Sabogal, Marin, Otero-Sabogal, Marin, & Perez-Stable, 1987). Consequently, *familismo* is expected to mediate the effects of ethnicity on social support and burden. Caregivers with high familism values are, in theory, more willing to care for family members with dementia, because they are more loyal and accepting of family duties. These caregivers are expected to report less perceived burden and fewer depressive symptoms (Robinson-Shurgot & Knight, 2004).

There is evidence that lower levels of income and education, coupled with the lack of information about dementia diagnoses and limited access to treatment, place added stress on caregivers and may increase the likelihood of their experiencing significant depression and pessimism (Adams et al., 2002). Regardless of the number of adult children available to provide care, Mexican American elders are reported to have scored the lowest on perceived social support (Adams et al., 2002). These findings are contrary to previous studies, which noted that Latino familial (filial) obligations and care expectations were strong when caring for their elders (Dilworth-Anderson et al., 2002; Gallagher-Thompson, Talamantes, Ramirez, & Valverde, 1996). Thus, being from a large family may be either a positive or negative influence on the caregiver's mood and function.

Cultural influences affecting caregivers who care for family members with dementia may yield both positive and negative beliefs regarding the nature of the dementia (Dilworth-Anderson & Gibson, 2002). In a qualitative study examining illness meanings, Dilworth et al. (2002) discuss reasons why Hispanic caregivers may attribute the presence of dementia to experiencing a difficult life. For example, a Hispanic caregiver shared that her mother's use of alcohol and her difficult life may have contributed to her dementia. Positive dimensions of caregiving that may be in alignment with cultural values and beliefs include life satisfaction, mastery, and personal gain; thus, the investigators emphasize the importance of developing interventions that evaluate the caregiver's view of their caregiving situation in relationship to satisfaction, burden, and coping (Morano, 2003). In one study, researchers found that less acculturated Latina caregivers reported more positive aspects in caregiving and were also less likely to institutionalize their affected family member with dementia compared to

Latina caregivers who were more acculturated (Mausbach et al., 2004). A study by Robinson-Shurgot and Knight (2004) conducted among Latino caregivers from the Los Angeles, California, area found that acculturation did not affect caregiver distress directly, but it indirectly influenced it through the cultural value *familismo*, which was correlated with burden. Acculturation also affects other cultural values that have a direct effect on caregiver burden and emotional distress.

Interventions to Assist Mexican American Caregivers

Gallagher-Thompson and colleagues have been at the forefront of developing and testing the efficacy of psychoeducational support groups for Latino caregivers, the primary purpose of which is to teach caregivers cognitive and behavioral skills for coping and managing frustrations in caregiving (Gallagher-Thompson, Areán, Rivera, & Thompson, 2001; Gallagher-Thompson, Solano, Coon, Areán, 2003b; Gallagher-Thompson et al., 2004). Their Older Adult and Family Center (OAFC) developed the Coping with Caregiving (CWC) intervention as a way to reduce the stress experienced by caregivers. It is a skill-building, psychoeducational group intervention based on the cognitive behavioral theories of Beck (Beck, Rush, Shaw, & Emery, 1979) and Lewinsohn (Lewinsohn, 1974; Lewinsohn, Muñoz, Youngren & Zeiss, 1986). In line with these theories, negative mood is thought to be reduced by addressing and challenging negative thoughts and attitudes and by increasing positive reinforcement by using more adaptive social behaviors (Lewinsohn, 1974; Lewinsohn et al., 1986).

The CWC teaches a number of mood management skills based on these principles in a small group format, with six to eight caregivers (with one skilled leader) who meet weekly for 90 min, over a period of 6–16 weeks. Duration depends on goals of the class and content areas to be covered. For example, most research studies use the 12–16 week format in order to achieve more lasting results; but in a community-based agency where staff time is limited, the six-session CWC emphasizing one or two sets of skills might be preferred. To reduce negative mood, an emphasis is placed on learning how to relax in stressful situations; appraise the care-receiver's behavior more realistically; and communicate more assertively. To increase positive mood, classes teach how to understand the relationship between mood and activities and help the caregiver to develop strategies to do smaller, everyday pleasant activities on a more regular basis.

There are five components to the full-length intervention. The *behavioral management* component teaches caregivers how to manage problematic or disruptive behaviors of the care-receiver. Relaxation techniques are used to help caregiver's better cope with these problems. *Cognitive reappraisal* teaches caregivers how to change unhelpful thinking about themselves as caregivers and their caregiving situation. Thought patterns are modified to become adaptive. *Communication skills* help the caregivers to better communicate with their loved one, with doctors, and with others about their needs. Assertiveness training is part of this component. *Increasing everyday pleasant events* teaches caregivers how to incorporate pleasurable events in everyday life to improve mood. They are asked to identify pleasant events that can be done alone and those that can be shared with the care receiver. *Planning for the future* is the fifth and final component. Caregivers prepare for different options for care as their loved one's illness progresses, and there is open discussion regarding end-of-life care. The course of the full-length program is described below.

Module	Topic area
Class 1	Education about dementia, stress, and understanding difficult behaviors
Classes 2–5	Instruction and practice with Trigger–Behavior–Reaction paradigm to modify behavior problems of the care-receiver
Classes 6–8 and 11–12	Instruction and practice with changing unhelpful thoughts, improving communication with family members and the health-care system (how to get the help needed), and increasing everyday pleasant activities
Classes 9–10	Planning for future needs (e.g., advance directives; placement issues)
Classes 13–16	Practice in skill maintenance

The CWCs were designed to be small (three to nine participants) and interactive. The goal of the class series is to develop a valuable set of skills through practice inside and outside the classroom and by receiving constructive feedback by the group facilitators. It was specifically tailored to meet the needs of the Hispanic/Latino caregivers in the community after its initial success with Caucasian caregivers. The OAFC has implemented this program in separate projects. The first version of the class was implemented in the multisite Resources for Enhancing Alzheimer's Caregiver Health (REACH) program with much success (Gallagher-Thompson et al., 2003a). The OAFC site in Palo Alto, California, enrolled 105 Latino caregivers, who were predominately of Mexican origin; about half participated in the 12 week CWC program. Following the success of the initial REACH project, the principal investigators reunited to do REACH II. This time, the overall program incorporated many elements of the CWC intervention (e.g., cognitive appraisals and behavior management), but it was packaged differently. REACH II included telephone support groups and in-home, one-on-one counseling sessions, but no small face-to-face groups were used. Over 500 caregivers (about one-fourth were of Mexican origin) were enrolled, and about half were successfully taught the skills contained in REACH II. The second iteration of the intervention is being used in the Stress Management Project at the time of this writing, with promising feedback from the caregivers involved. Preliminary data indicate the success of this program on a number of caregiver distress indices (Gallagher-Thompson, personal communication, August 30, 2005). Half of the Latino caregivers have been enrolled to teach them the skills of the CWC, while the other half of the group was randomized to a control condition. Analysis of pre- and post-change on indices of depression, stress, and caregiver burden indicates that those in the CWC improved more, overall, than those in the telephone support condition. Taken together, these studies suggest that the CWC is an empirically validated treatment that is flexible enough to meet the needs of large numbers of Latino caregivers. It has been shown to effectively reduce the stress caregivers feel, and it has provided them with the tools and resources to cope with their situation (Gallagher-Thompson et al., 2003b).

Barriers to Successful Intervention

Despite the encouraging results, there have been a number of obstacles the OAFC staff has had to overcome. Being part of the government (Veteran's Administration) and Stanford University, participants were hesitant to enroll. To overcome this initial distrust, partnerships with community health-care agencies were developed and maintained over time, which proved to be invaluable. The majority of participants who enrolled in the projects came through referrals from agencies already serving the Latino community with whom OAFC staff had developed strong bonds of mutual trust (Gallagher-Thompson et al., 2004).

Once participants were enrolled, staff noticed that some of the issues being dealt with are unique to this population. For example, some caregivers were dealing with immigration issues that further complicated the intervention. Others were reluctant to admit to symptoms of burden, because this implied that they did not accept their role and were not grateful for what the care receiver had done for them earlier in life. Most of these caregivers were also experiencing role strain; most were married, had children under the age of 18 still living in the house, and were employed, in addition to their caregiving responsibilities.

These caregivers also had preconceived erroneous notions about Alzheimer's disease. Many believed that it was attributed to *locura* (craziness), *nervios* (nerves), a punishment from God, the result of poor nutrition, a normal part of aging, or a stress earlier in life (e.g., a family tragedy or migration; Levy, Hillygus, Lui, & Levkoff, 2000; Ortiz, Simmons, & Hinton, 1999). These caregivers tended to interpret Alzheimer's-like symptoms more multidimensional, encompassing religious, spiritual, and environmental domains. They were more likely to use folk models to explain Alzheimer's disease symptomatology and view it as a normal part of aging (Gray, Jimenez, Tong, & Gallagher-Thompson, under review). Therefore, effective intervention programs need to expose the myths caregivers have of the disease so that stress management for the caregiver becomes a more viable intervention approach.

A key barrier contributing to Latino caregivers' awareness and ability to access health and social services is limited English proficiency skills. The inability to speak English has been empirically associated with less care seeking and reduced access to services (Flores et al., 2002). Examples of how this can create barriers include: (a) difficulty in making appointments and accessing basic information about the visit, when they seek care or services; (b) the inability to communicate adequately with health or social service staff; and (c) reduced client/patient satisfaction with cross-language communications leading to a reluctance to return to the agency and the inability to understand or follow through with health recommendations, such as medication compliance, nutrition, and physical activity requirements. Latino elders and their caregivers living in rural communities (e.g., along the West Texas/Mexico border) have less access to specialists, greater difficulty with transportation, and more economic disparities than their non-Hispanic White counterparts or Latinos living in large cities (Borders, 2004). In each case, availability of bilingual/bicultural staff can greatly facilitate their enrollment.

Listed below are other considerations to keep in mind while working with the Latino community. The literacy level of the client should be assessed. Not being able to read may be a source of shame that can cause reluctance to join groups and can provide a roadblock to the "homework" required in a program like the CWC. An understanding of their beliefs about why they are caregivers; beliefs about male and female roles in the family; the use of family support and the satisfaction with it; and their use of religious coping should all be recognized. An access issue is whether adult children can provide transportation to appointments due to their inability to get time off work (Borders, 2004).

Here are some suggestions for working effectively with Mexican American caregivers. First, educate them about the causes, symptoms, and treatment of memory problems—beware of the word *dementia*. Provide materials in English and Spanish, and inform them of other community resources (e.g., adult day care) that could be very helpful. Second, be open to incorporating their use of religious coping into their work with you. Most professionals shy away from this, but for many Latinos, faith-based beliefs and practices are strong sources of coping and support. Third, take into account the person's literacy level and be creative with it. For example, use role-play situations where they can practice communication, and teach relaxation techniques that do not rely on reading. Fourth, challenge their beliefs surrounding the use of services, especially the feelings of guilt. Fifth, suggest pleasant activities and help them take notice of the ones they have already been using. Sixth, involve *la familia* whenever possible—not just the primary caregiver. Seventh, provide services in the client's preferred language; ask, do not assume it is Spanish. Eighth, do not be overly "formal" with Latino caregivers, instead, encourage *platicar*, informal sharing of information at the start of sessions, both in groups and one-on-one. Finally, be positive and inspire hope for the future. Many Latina caregivers are significantly depressed but respond well to treatments that empower them and give them tools to better manage their everyday lives.

Moving Toward Cultural Competency in Service Delivery to Mexican American Caregivers and Making Use of the Available Resources

Achieving cultural competency from an interpersonal to an organizational level is a process that must be achieved over time (Evans, 1997; Talamantes & Aranda, 2004). However, for some service providers, the belief is that cultural competency can never be truly realized. With this in mind, service providers committed to providing culturally competent services to Mexican American and other Hispanic/Latino caregivers should avail themselves of the existing training materials and cultural experts and brokers knowledgeable about service delivery issues within their respective communities. In the monograph on *Cultural Competency in Working with Family Caregivers*, Talamantes and Aranda (2004) suggested that certain critical elements that distinguish between the fact approach and attitude/skill approach to cultural competency and the knowledge, attitudes, and skill domains needed for effective care should be incorporated into any curricular models and intervention plans with Mexican American caregivers. Core concepts are recommended for understanding how the cultural systems of caregivers and care recipients operate and move beyond the traditional domains of race and ethnicity. Careful consideration of how other factors, such as the role of caregiver to care receiver (spouse, adult–child, etc.), gender, socioeconomic status, social support, health-care issues, geographic location (rural or urban), play an important role in the assessment of caregivers and delivery of services to caregivers. Detailed analysis of this cross-cultural approach is available through the Family Caregiver Alliance (Family Caregiver Alliance, 2004 [www.caregiver.org]). Fortunately, model community-based programs that serve Latino caregivers exist and effectively provide services to this group (Aranda, Villa, Trejo, Ramirez, & Ranney, 2003).

El Portal Latino Alzheimer's Project is an example of a model dementia network program (Aranda et al., 2003). Since its beginning in 1992 to provide dementia-specific services to elder Latinos and their caregivers, the practice strategies of El Portal to ensure effective collaborative partnerships that foster multidisciplinary, interorganizational, community-based networks serving a defined geographic area continue to promote service access and delivery to this historically underserved population. El Portal as a care network for people with dementia provides an array of culturally sensitive and linguistically competent services to caregivers and their family members. Examples of services include care management, adult day care, respite, legal assistance, transportation, and support groups. In addition to these client-level service innovations, the demonstration project is credited with encouraging the local Alzheimer's Association to establish a satellite office in the heart of East Los Angeles, becoming the first major health advocacy group to have a presence in a predominately ethnic minority community. A discussion of service utilization, consumer satisfaction, and program development strategies resulting from the Administration on Aging Alzheimer's Disease Demonstration Grants to State programs, which includes the work of El Portal and others, such as the SeaMar project in Seattle, Washington, can be found in Montgomery (2002).

In closing, it is important to include comments regarding language and outreach strategies. Any type of translation of caregiver assessment tools and informational resources (educational brochures, media, etc.) should undergo a vigorous cross-cultural adaptation and translation process to examine cultural equivalency of the concepts. Conceptual translation rather than word-for-word literal translations should be done using back-translation and validation techniques. This process ensures the accuracy of conceptual and contextual uniformity of the meaning of the tool or resource. Consideration of the range of literacy levels of Latino caregivers must be addressed when developing research and caregiver educational materials (Talamantes & Aranda, 2004).

The importance and use of community brokers and experts has been widely discussed in the literature (Valle, 1989) for learning more about the culture and for conducting outreach efforts. The use of culturally appropriate strategies, consistent and continuous community outreach strategies, and genuine commitment for providing services to Hispanic/Latino caregivers will influence caregivers' response to the target program (AoA, 2001; Aranda et al., 2003; Gallagher-Thompson et al., 2004; Talamantes & Aranda, 2004). Providers are encouraged to test these strategies for work within their own communities. Among the most consistent successful outreach strategies include using local Spanish-language media, conducting brief informal talks at already scheduled events in the community, using a dedicated bilingual telephone helpline, reaching out to the faith-based organizations and local small business or Latino Chamber of Commerce, if available. An important outreach message to communicate to Latino caregivers is that services are there to complement (not replace) their personal care (Montgomery, 2002). In brief, despite the many challenges encountered in working with Mexican American caregivers, the rewards are great. As a group, they are extremely responsive to a broad range of intervention programs tailored to meet their needs, when offered in a linguistically and culturally competent manner. Response rates and indices of improvement have been similar to those found in earlier studies with Caucasian family caregivers; this is very encouraging to service providers and researchers alike and should pave the way for future development of novel intervention programs for this growing population of Latino family caregivers.

Acknowledgment

This research was partially supported by grant #AG 18784 from the National Institute on Aging and grant #IIRG-01-3157 from the National Office of the Alzheimer's Association, Chicago, Illinois, to Dolores Gallagher-Thompson, Principal Investigator, and 3 PO1 AG018784-04S1 from the National Institute on Aging as a supplement to the above-mentioned grant.

References

Adams, B. M., Aranda, M. P., Kemp, B. J., & Takagi, K. (2002). Ethnic and gender differences among Anglo American, African-American, Japanese-American and Mexican-American spousal caregivers of persons with dementia. *Journal of Clinical Geropsychology*, 8(4), 279–301.

Administration on Aging. (2001). *Achieving cultural competence: A guidebook for providers of services to older Americans and their families.* Washington, DC: U.S. Department of Health and Human Services. Retrieved July 12, 2005 from http://aoa.dhhs.gov/minorityaccess/guidebook2001

Angel, J. L., & Angel, R. J. (1998). Aging trends, Mexican Americans in the Southwestern USA. *Journal of Cross-Cultural Gerontology, 13,* 281–290.

Angel, J. L., Angel, R. J., Aranda, M. P., & Miles, T. P. (2004). Can the family still cope? *Journal of Aging and Health, 16*(3), 338–354.

Aranda, M. P., & Knight, B. G. (1997). The influence of ethnicity and culture on the caregiving stress and coping process: A sociocultural review and analysis. *The Gerontologist, 37,* 342–354.

Aranda, M. P., Villa, V. M., Trejo, L., Ramirez, R., & Ranney, M. (2003). El portal Latino Alzheimer's project: Model program for Latino caregivers of Alzheimer's disease-affected people. *Social Work, 48,* 259–271.

Beck, A. T., Rush, A. J., Shaw, B. F., & Emery, G. (1979). *Cognitive therapy of depression.* New York: Guilford Press.

Borders, T. F. (2004). Rural community-dwelling elders' reports of access to care: Are there Hispanic versus non-Hispanic white disparities? *The Journal of Rural Health, 20*(30), 210–220.

Bryant, L. L., Shetterly, S. M., Baxter, J., & Hamman, R. F. (2002). Modifiable risks of incident functional dependence in Hispanic and non-Hispanic White elders: The San Luis Valley Aging and Health study. *The Gerontologist, 42,* 690–697.

Cox , C., & Monk, A. (1993). Hispanic culture and family care of Alzheimer patients. *Health and Social Work, 18,* 92–99.

Dilworth-Anderson, P., & Gibson, B. E. (2002). The cultural influence of values, norms, meanings, and perceptions in understanding dementia in ethnic minorities. *Alzheimer's disease and Associated Disorders, 16*(Supp. 2), S56–S63.

Dilworth-Anderson, P., Williams I. C., & Gibson, B. E. (2002). Issues of race, ethnicity, and culture in caregiving research: A 20-year review (1980–2000). *The Gerontologist, 42,* 237–272.

Evans, J. (1997). *Journey towards cultural competency: Lessons learned.* National MCH Resource Center on Cultural Competency. Austin, TX: Texas Department of Health.

Family Caregiver Alliance. (2003). *Women and caregiving: Facts and figures.* Fact sheet prepared by the National Center on Caregiving at Family Caregiver Alliance and reviewed by Phyllis Mutschler, PhD, Executive Director, National Center on Women and Aging, Brandeis University.

Flores, G., Fuentes-Afflick, E., Barbot, O., Carter-Pokras, O., Claudio, L., Lara, M. et al. (2002). The health of Latino children: Urgent priorities, unanswered questions, and a research agenda. *Journal of the American Medical Association, 288,* 82–90.

Friss, L., Whitlatch, C. J., & Yale, R. (1990). *Who's taking care? A profile of California's family caregivers of brain-impaired adults.* San Francisco: The Family Survival Project.

Gallagher-Thompson, D., Areán, P., Rivera, P., & Thompson, L. W. (2001). A psychoeducational intervention to reduce stress in Hispanic family caregivers: Results of a pilot study. *Clinical Gerontologist, 23,* 17–32.

Gallagher-Thompson, D., Coon, D. W., Solano, N., Ambler, C., Rabinowitz, Y., & Thompson, L. W. (2003a). Change in indices of distress among Latino and Anglo female caregivers of elderly relative with dementia: Site-specific results from the REACH national collaborative study. *The Gerontologist, 43,* 580–591.

Gallagher-Thompson, D., Singer, L. S., Depp, C., Mausbach, B. T., Cardenas, V., & Coon, D. W. (2004). Effective recruitment strategies for Latino and Caucasian dementia family caregivers in intervention research. *American Journal of Geriatric Psychiatry, 12*(5), 484–490.

Gallagher-Thompson, D., Solano, N., Coon, D., & Areán, P. (2003b). Recruitment and retention of Latino dementia family caregivers in intervention research: Issues to face, lessons to learn. *The Gerontologist, 43,* 45–51.

Gallagher-Thompson, D., Talamantes, M., Ramirez, R., & Valverde, I. (1996). Service delivery issues and recommendations for working with Mexican American family caregivers. In G. Yeo & D. Gallagher-Thompson (Eds.), *Ethnicity and the dementias.* Washington, DC: Taylor & Francis, pp.137–152.

Gray, H. L., Jimenez, D. E., Tong, H. Q., & Gallagher-Thompson, D. (in review). Ethnic differences in beliefs regarding Alzheimer's disease among dementia family caregivers. *American Journal of Geriatric Psychiatry.*

Haan, M. N., Mungas, D. M., Gonzalez, H. M., Ortiz, T. A., Acharya, A., & Jagust, W. J. (2003). Prevalence of dementia in older Latinos: Stroke and genetic factors. *Journal of the American Geriatrics Society, 51,* 169–177.

Hayward, M. D., & Zhang, Z. (2001). Demography of aging: A century of global change, 1950–2050. In R. H. Binstock & L. K.George (Eds.), *Handbook of aging and the social sciences* (pp. 69–85). San Diego, CA: Academic Press.

Johnson, R. A., Schwiebert, V. L., Alvarado-Rosenmann, P., Pecka, G., & Shirk, N. (1997). Residential preferences and eldercare views of Hispanic elders. *Journal of Cross-Cultural Gerontology, 12,* 91–107.

Jolicoeur, P. M., & Madden, T. (2002). The good daughters: Acculturation and caregiving among Mexican-American women. *Journal of Aging Studies, 16*(2), 107–120.

Levy, B., Hillygus, J., Lui, B., & Levkoff, S. (2000). The relationship between illness attributions and caregiver burden: A cross-cultural analysis. *Journal of Mental Health and Aging, 6,* 213–225.

Lewinsohn, P. M. (1974). A behavioral approach to depression. In R. J. Friedman & M. M. Katz (Eds.), *The psychology of depression: Contemporary theory and research* (pp. 157–178). New York: Wiley.

Lewinsohn, P. M., Muñoz, R. F., Youngren, M. A., & Zeiss, A. M. (1986). *Control your depression.* New York: Prentice Hall.

Mausbach, B. T., Coon, D. W., Depp, C., Rabinowitz, Y. G., Wilson-Arias, E., Kraemer, H. C. et al. (2004). Ethnicity and time to institutionalization of dementia patients: A comparison of Latina and Caucasian female family caregivers. *Journal of the American Geriatrics Society, 52*(7), 1077–1084.

Montgomery, R. J. V. (2002). *A new look at community based respite programs: Utilization, satisfaction, and development.* New York: Haworth Press.

Morano, C. L. (2003). Appraisal and coping: Moderators or mediators of stress in Alzheimer's disease caregivers. *Social Work Research, 27*, 116–128.

Morano, C. L., & Bravo, M. (2002). A psychoeducational model for Hispanic Alzheimer's disease caregivers. *The Gerontologist, 42*(1), 122–126.

National Alliance for Caregiving and American Association of Retired Persons. (1997). *Family caregiving in the U.S.: Findings from a national survey.* Final Report.

National Alliance for Caregiving and American Association of Retired Persons. (2004). *Caregiving in the U.S.*

Neary, S. R., & Mahoney, D. F. (2005). Dementia caregiving: The experiences of Hispanic/Latino Caregivers. *Journal of Transcultural Nursing, 16*, 163–170.

Ortiz, A., Simmons, J., & Hinton, W. L. (1999). Locations of remorse and home-lands of resilience: Notes on grief and sense of loss of place of Latino and Irish-American caregivers of demented elders. *Culture, Medicine, & Psychiatry, 23*, 477–501.

Peek, M. K., Ottenbacher, K. J., Markides, K. S., & Ostir, G. V. (2003). Examining the disablement process among older Hispanic adults. *Journal of Gerontology: Social Sciences, 57*, 413–425.

Phillips, L. R., Torres de Ardon, E., Komnenich, P., Killeen, M., & Rusinak, R. (2000). The Mexican American caregiving experience. *Hispanic Journal of Behavioral Sciences, 22*, 296–311.

Robinson-Shurgot, G., & Knight, B. G. (2004). Preliminary study investigating acculturation, cultural values, and psychological distress in Latino caregivers of dementia patients. *Journal of Mental Health and Aging* (in press).

Sabogal, F., Marin, G., Otero-Sabogal, R., Marin, B. V., & Perez-Stable, E. J. (1987). Latino familism and acculturation: What changes and what doesn't? *Latino Journal of Behavioral Sciences, 9*, 397–412.

Talamantes, M. A., & Aranda, M. P. (2004). *Cultural competency in working with family caregivers.* San Francisco, CA: Family Caregiving Alliance.

Talamantes, M. A., Cornell, J., Espino, D. V., Lichtenstein, M. J., & Hazuda, H. P. (1996). SES and ethnic differences in perceived caregiver availability among young-old Mexican Americans and Non-Hispanic Whites. *The Gerontologist, 36*(1), 88–99.

U.S. Department of Health and Human Services, Administration on Aging. (2003). *Snapshot: A statistical profile of Hispanic older Americans aged 65+.* Washington, DC: Author.

Valle, R. (1989). Cultural and ethnic issues in Alzheimer's disease family research. In E. Light & B. D. Lebowitz (Eds.), *Alzheimer's disease treatment and family stress: Directions for research* (pp.122–154). Washington, DC: National Institute of Mental Health.

Wallace, S. P., Campbell, K., & Lew-Ting, C. (1994). Structural barriers to the use of formal in-home services by elderly Latinos. *Journal of Gerontology, 49*, S253–S263.

Zunker, C. L., & Cummins, J. J. (2004). Elderly health disparities on the U.S. Mexico border. *Journal of Cross-Cultural Gerontology, 19*, 13–25.

Working with Gay, Lesbian, Bisexual,
and Transgender Families

CHAPTER 21

Working with Gay, Lesbian, Bisexual, and Transgender Families

DAVID W. COON AND MARY H. BURLESON

The majority of accounts to date exploring lesbian, gay, bisexual, and transgender (LGBT) caregiving appear in the HIV/AIDS literature and describe outcomes associated with the LGBT community's response to the AIDS epidemic (e.g., Fredriksen, 1999; Wight, 2002). However, results from several surveys in larger U.S. cities (i.e., New York, San Francisco, San Jose, California) are emerging that provide data on LGBT caregivers to older adults (Cantor, Brennan, & Shippy, 2004; Hoctel, 2002; Outword Online, 2000; Reiter, 2003). The data suggest that LGBT caregivers provide similar kinds of care as heterosexual caregivers, but that both LGBT caregivers and recipients experience sexual-orientation-based discrimination that is a barrier to service utilization. These barriers are probably even worse in areas without established LGBT communities (Coon & Zeiss, 2003a).

In this chapter, we take the position that until LGBT caregivers no longer experience the discrimination and social isolation that create barriers to receiving competent care, professional ethics demand that providers increase both their understanding of issues LGBT caregivers face and their competence in providing LGBT caregiver referrals and services. In this chapter, we provide an overview of key issues related to LGBT caregiving that appear in the literature and provide program developers and practitioners with a framework to help bridge the gap between research and practice and to assist in translating information about LGBT caregivers. Readers desiring more detail and a thorough review of these issues should see Cahill, South, and Spade (2000), Cantor et al. (2004), Coon (2003), Coon and Zeiss (2003b).

Defining LGBT: Issues for Service Provision and Research

Today's LGBT caregivers encompass a diverse group in terms of ethnicity, race, language, national origin, and physical challenges, crossing both cohort and cultural boundaries. Many of them, especially older LGBT caregivers, do not self-identify to service providers (Cahill et al., 2000), which can negatively impact the quality of care they receive. The number of LGBT caregivers is unknown, and efforts to estimate their numbers based on prevalence of LGBT individuals in the general population are complicated by the complexities in LGBT definitions and issues around self-identification (e.g., Fox, 1996). Knowing the number of LGBT caregivers could improve planning and delivery of services but is not required to maximize competence in the development and implementation of effective services for LGBT caregivers. Simply ignoring issues of sexual orientation and LGBT discrimination permits heterosexism to guide service provision, limiting professionals' ability to serve all types of caregivers (Coon, 2003; Coon & Zeiss, 2003b). Therefore, professionals need ongoing training and consultation that helps increase their awareness of the sociocultural contexts that impact LGBT caregivers and enhance their professional competence for service provision.

Sociocultural Contexts Surrounding LGBT Caregiving

Sociocultural context substantially influences LGBT caregivers' beliefs and expectations about dementia, illness, and family caregiving, as well as their perceptions of caregiver burden and stress, the appropriateness of help-seeking behavior, and the palatability of existing services (e.g., Coon, Ory, & Schulz, 2003; Gallagher-Thompson et al., 2003b). Several components of the larger sociocultural context emerge in unique ways for LGBT caregivers and warrant additional consideration. These include issues related to *Cultural, Historical, Employment* (and related contexts), *Social Support*, and *Spiritual* (CHESS) contexts. The CHESS framework (Coon, 2001) provides guidelines for researchers, administrators, program developers, and practitioners to approach culturally competent assessment of LGBT caregiving situations. Table 21.1 briefly illustrates some of these issues and their impacts, as viewed through the CHESS framework. For

Table 21.1 The Chess Framework: Issues and Impacts in LGBT Caregiving

Acronym	Examples of issues and impacts
C Cultural context	Cultural contexts vary in openness about sexuality, acceptable forms of sexuality, and ramifications of violating prohibitions. Cultural attitudes may influence whether LGBT caregivers withhold or alter information, avoid personal contact, or opt for more anonymous services to protect themselves or preclude family interference. Cultural context is related to use of nontraditional health care; service providers must be open and informed about these methods in order to enhance goal alignment with clients.
H Historical context	Relevant historical events and processes include changes in societal attitudes about sexuality and the HIV/AIDS epidemic. Historical changes differentially affect older and younger cohorts of LGBT caregivers in ways that impact their knowledge about and willingness to utilize services.
E Employment, financial, and legal contexts	Impacts of caregiving on employment are compounded by discrimination against LGBT employees. Lack of legal protection for LGBT partners prevents access to health benefits and allows for interference by blood relatives or facility personnel in visiting rights and decision making.
S Social support context	Service providers should avoid the inaccurate stereotypical view that older LGBT persons are childless or alone; LGBT support networks include both family of origin and family of choice. Future cohorts of caregiving gay or bisexual men may have smaller support networks due to losses from HIV/AIDS; thus, they may need more assistance.
S Spiritual context	Because LGBT caregivers and recipients must often uphold, adapt, or discard religious doctrine and spiritual beliefs discordant with their sexual orientation, religious coping may be turned to less frequently or perceived as being less effective. In areas with large LGBT populations, churches and temples may exist to serve the LGBT community; in other areas, institutionalized religion may not provide effective support or may actively discriminate against them.

relevant reviews and discussion of the material in Table 21.1, see Cahill and colleagues (2000), Coon (2003), Coon and Zeiss (2003b).

Exploring and Overcoming Potential Barriers to Service Utilization

Identifying barriers to LGBT caregiver service utilization is another essential tool to increase service providers' awareness and competence. While family caregivers from all backgrounds can face many barriers to service utilization across their caregiving careers, LGBT caregivers typically encounter additional obstacles. These obstacles can be found across multiple levels of service provision and intervention, from those targeting individuals and families all the way to the policy levels on Capitol Hill, and the theme of discrimination and intolerance is woven throughout (DiPlacido, 1998; Herek, Gillis, & Cogan, 1999). The DISCuSS model (Coon, 2001) is a framework to help providers identify barriers and develop or implement strategies to overcome them at each level: *Discrimination* (hatred and intolerance), *Individual/Interpersonal* level, *System/Organizational* level, *Community* level, and *System and Social policy* levels. Table 21.2 illustrates examples of barriers and strategies at each level. Readers interested in more information should see Cahill and colleagues (2000), Coon (2003), and Coon and Zeiss (2003b), for relevant reviews and discussion.

Table 21.2   DISC(u)SS Framework: Exploring and Overcoming Service Utilization Barriers

Acronym	Examples of Barriers	Examples of Current or Potential Strategies to Overcome Barriers
D **Discrimination, Insensitivity, Harassment (throughout levels)**	Fears of discrimination, including hate crimes, loss of employment, and social stigma, stop many LGBT caregivers and care recipients from seeking services.Health-care providers, nursing homes, and senior centers sometimes discriminate against LBGT clients, who then retreat from seeking care.Heterosexism, ageism, and HIV/AIDS-related discrimination combine to affect many LGBT caregivers.	Provide a safe place where LGBT caregivers can talk openly. Honor LGBT staff members' rights to privacy, and assign staff to work with caregivers based on competence, rather than LGBT identity.Remain mindful of the pervasive impact of discrimination; adopt a zero tolerance policy for discrimination, and apply it uniformly; adopt inclusive language and challenge discriminatory language in both verbal and written communications.

(continued)

Table 21.2 (continued)

Acronym	Examples of Barriers	Examples of Current or Potential Strategies to Overcome Barriers
I **Individual/** **Interpersonal** **level**	Caregiver–care-recipient dyads may be differentially "out" across different contexts. Sociocultural contexts may influence caregivers' self-identification. The additional stress of coming out may be too much for a caregiver to handle. Internalized homophobia may impede caregivers and care recipients seeking help from LGBT-specific resources. LGBT caregivers may be suspicious of agencies and professionals.	Learn to work effectively across a continuum of "outness." Respect individuals' levels of outness and self-identification in light of their sociocultural contexts. Openly discuss limits to confidentiality and strategies to protect privacy. Provide referrals to LGBT-sensitive informal and formal care resources. Recognize that LGBT suspicion of health-care and social services professionals may be realistic, based on past experiences.
S **System/** **Organizational** **level**	Health-care systems, insurance companies, and service agencies often have discriminatory policies. Few organizations provide domestic partner benefits. Care-related decision-making power is often automatically given to biological relatives. LGBT partners may be denied visitation rights. LGBT applicants for long-term care may be discriminated against.	Educate staff about LGBT resources for caregiving, and request feedback from clients about these referrals. Create a "safe place" symbol to indicate that agencies are sympathetic to and have received training in working with the LGBT community. Foster staff participation at continuing education presentation, consultation, and formal staff trainings on LGBT topics.
C(u) **Community** **level**	Many geographic regions and municipalities have minimal protection for LGBT persons. Some communities (e.g., religious-based) actively reject LGBT members. Some segments of LGBT communities hold racist or ageist attitudes that deter some LGBT caregivers from accessing available LGBT-specific services. Ageism in LGBT communities may limit availability of formal support for LGBT elders and caregivers.	Encourage communities to take advantage of the inclusive definition of the National Family Caregiver Support Program (NFCSP) for needs assessment and service development. Promote stronger ties between LGBT community agencies and agencies working under NFCSP to ensure LGBT needs are included in outreach. Rally LGBT communities to develop broadly inclusive LGBT-sensitive caregiving-related services. Promote use of "safe place" symbol.

(continued)

Table 21.2 (continued)

Acronym	Examples of Barriers	Examples of Current or Potential Strategies to Overcome Barriers
S S System/Social Policy level	Even decades-long LGBT partnerships are often not recognized by government entities.Lack of recognition may lead to inability for partners to access Social Security spousal benefits, disability benefits, and retirement benefits.LGBT couples do not receive tax benefits (e.g., marital deductions, spousal exemptions for gift and estate taxes); hence, they have fewer financial resources in late life.LGBT couples do not receive equal treatment in Medicaid spend-down.	Encourage and support LGBT representation and full involvement in White House Conference on Aging to help LGBT older adults.Train home-care assistants in LGBT awareness and competence to ease LGBT access to mainstream home health services.Build partnerships with LGBT organizations to create local systems of caregiver support.

Extending Recent Interventions to Future Work with LGBT Caregivers

Recent research reviews have been unable to identify the one best intervention to ease family caregiver distress and enhance well-being (e.g., Bourgeois, Schulz, & Burgio, 1996; Coon et al., 2003; Dunkin & Anderson-Hanley, 1998; Kennet, Burgio, & Schulz, 2000; Pusey & Richards, 2001). This may be due in part to the diverse sociocultural contexts and backgrounds of caregivers for those with dementia and the varying courses dementia may take with care recipients. Nevertheless, several promising programs have proven effective in reducing caregiver emotional distress or burden and are seen as useful by caregivers. The promising intervention approaches identified to date tend to develop caregivers' skills to effectively manage care recipients' problem behaviors or their own stress levels (e.g., Burgio et al., 2003; Gallagher-Thompson et al., 2003a; Teri, Logsdon, Uomoto, & McCurry, 1997); modify physical and social environments of the caregiving dyad to help support its activities (Gitlin et al., 2003); capitalize on technological approaches, such as telephone-based or online support, combined with skill-focused education (e.g., Eisdorfer et al., 2003; Steffen, Mahoney, & Kelly, 2003); and integrate multiple program components, such as individually tailored caregiver counseling, support, and education (e.g., Mittelman, Roth, Coon, & Haley, 2004). However, no research to date has examined the effectiveness of these interventions with LGBT caregivers.

Although few formal services exist that target LGBT older adults, caregivers, or care recipients, practices that focus on LGBT sensitive information and referral, published material, and face-to-face and online support groups (Coon, 2003; Reiter, 2003) are increasing around the United States. LGBT older adults in the recent New York survey most frequently cited social and emotional support as the type of support they needed; and in response to being questioned about why the LGBT community should help its senior members, most participants indicated the community is best at caring for its own. This may be a reflection of the persistent discrimination and insensitivity experienced by LGBT individuals (Cantor et al., 2004). LGBT face-to-face support groups for caregivers of older adults, particularly those with memory impairment, have become available in a number of areas in the country, with several sponsored by local Alzheimer's Association chapters (Ceridwyn, 2002; Gollance, 2003; Levine & Altman, 2002). In general, LGBT caregiver support groups provide a haven in which to share concerns and get support without the added burden of masking one's sexual orientation, identity, and relationships.

The final framework presented in this chapter is intended to assist LGBT support group leaders, but it can be easily adapted for other populations. The SURE 2 Framework (*Sharing* and *Support, Unhelpful thinking* and *Understanding, Reframes* and *Referrals*, and *Education* and *Exploration*) has been used successfully in an LGBT caregiver support group in San Francisco and also can be extended to LGBT individual, couple, and group counseling arenas (see Coon & Zeiss, 2003b, for additional information). This approach is built from an empowerment perspective and integrated with basic cognitive and behavioral therapy (CBT) methods (Beck, Rush, Shaw, & Emery, 1979; Lewinsohn, Muñoz, Youngren, & Zeiss, 1986).

In a typical SURE 2 support group meeting, members first *share* their concerns with other members, and an "agenda" is developed by the group for topics to be covered during the rest of the meeting, when informational and emotional *support* will be the focus. Members help each other identify thinking or behaviors that are *unhelpful* while acknowledging and *understanding* that it is easy to be caught up in negative patterns of thought and action. SURE 2 caregivers are encouraged to *reframe* their thinking and change behavior through basic problem solving, positive reframing, and other CBT techniques, and to elicit ideas for doing so from the group. These ideas include identification of unique obstacles facing LGBT caregivers, such as the challenges of managing "outness" effectively and the difficulty in finding LGBT-sensitive services, along with the sharing of *referrals* when competent professionals and organizations are identified. Each meeting includes an *education* component, with topics ranging from caregiving- and dementia-related research findings to information about upcoming seminars or presentations by local organizations. Group members *explore* each others' recent experiences with alternative coping strategies or referrals, and finally, they explore and decide on strategies or referrals to try before their next meeting.

The SURE 2 framework was developed in response to several concerns that appear specific to LGBT caregivers (Coon & Zeiss, 2003b; Levine & Altman, 2002), beyond the concerns they share with their heterosexual counterparts (e.g., acceptance of the disease process, information on services, grief and loss):

- When biological family members need care, LGBT caregivers can experience insensitivity and ignorance on the part of other family members who automatically assume that because they are "single," they can handle a larger share of caregiving responsibilities. This perspective ignores LGBT primary partnerships or nontraditional family relationships. In the New York survey, one third of almost 350 LGBT older adults reported that family members expected more caregiving responsibilities of them, because they were LGBT and assumed they had fewer explicit family responsibilities—an assumption that was typically false (Cantor et al., 2004).
- Such expectations can ultimately force LGBT caregivers either "out of the closet" or further "in the closet," exacerbating caregiver stress, negatively impacting their family-of-choice relationships, and diminishing positive aspects of caregiving.
- Prior experience with HIV/AIDS caregiving, particularly among gay-identified men, creates both knowledge and skill with regard to the caregiving career but can also lead to burnout and tap into a deep well of grief for community members who have lost so many from their support networks.
- Some LGBT caregivers may be asked to care for an individual who once disowned them. These caregivers may be asked to endure ongoing overt or subtler forms of homophobia from the care recipient and other family members during the course of caregiving.
- Conflicts at work can arise when employers minimize the importance of caregiving responsibilities to LGBT partners or lifelong friends.
- LGBT caregivers frequently face homophobia in home health and long-term care settings, with some institutions impeding LGBT caregivers' access to their partners or refusing to allow LGBT partners to openly express affection for fear that heterosexual staff, patients, or family members will become uncomfortable.

- LGBT partners may have to endure ongoing conflicts with biological relatives over substitute decision making, given the limitations of various local, state, and federal laws, and particularly when relevant legal documents are not in place. By contrast, they also can experience complete withdrawal of biological family members, now that the gay or lesbian partnership can no longer be avoided or denied.

Moreover, the lack of a single best intervention for dementia caregivers may also be due to the multiple levels of obstacles family caregivers face in today's world. These obstacles, in turn, can be directly tied to the corresponding need for multiple levels of intervention (i.e., interventions at the individual/interpersonal, systems/organizational, community, and systems/social policy levels). These interventions, programs, and services should build on strategies aimed at the obstacles to LGBT caregiver service utilization mentioned earlier and create purposeful linkages between successful interventions identified within each level (Emmons, 2001). Table 21.3, drawn from earlier work (Coon, 2003; Coon & Zeiss, 2003b), provides examples of existing and suggested types of intervention programs and services categorized by intervention level. Clearly, this list needs ongoing review and expansion in order to foster the development and integration of effective services for LGBT caregivers.

Table 21.3 DISC(u)SS Framework: Program and Service Examples by Level of Intervention

Acronym	Examples of Current or Potential Programs and Services
D Discrimination, Insensitivity, Harassment	Adopt a zero tolerance policy for discrimination across all levels of service provision and apply to all employees and volunteers. Challenge discriminatory language, thinking, behavior, and policies; adopt inclusive language in conversations and printed materials.Increase opportunities for students in social and health-care programs to receive education, training, and supervision experiences related to LGBT clients and issues.
I Individual/ Interpersonal level	Distribute LGBT-sensitive information and referral for caregivers. Develop, market, and help facilitate face-to-face and online support groups for LGBT caregivers.Develop and support LGBT caregiver respite weekends.Implement LGBT caregiver skill training workshops to provide information and teach caregivers to effectively navigate legal, financial, and service delivery barriers.Create caregiver and care recipient education and support groups for LGBT friends and partners.

(continued)

Table 21.3 (continued)

Acronym	Examples of Current or Potential Programs and Services
S System/ Organizational level	Conduct in-service training for national and local staff of senior and LGBT advocacy agencies on unique needs of LGBT seniors, care recipients, and caregivers.Pool resources and develop partnerships between LGBT community-based organizations, senior service organizations, health-care organizations, and Area Agencies on Aging (AAA) to create more effective pathways of care for LGBT caregivers and their care recipients.Incorporate LGBT information into program intake and survey information (particularly important is the identification of opportunities to share such information anonymously).
C(u) Community level	Adopt LGBT media and community/service campaigns to increase LGBT caregiver awareness of available resources. Persuade professional organizations to support media and community service campaigns to increase provider knowledge of the distinct needs of LGBT older adults and caregivers.Encourage newly forming LGBT retirement communities to incorporate community education, training, and support interventions to help inform the entire retirement community about caregiving.
S S System/Social Policy level	Recognize LGBT families through adoption of spousal benefits, disability benefits, retirement benefits for same-sex partners, and elimination of unequal treatment in "Medicaid spend-down."Train home-care assistants in LGBT awareness and competence to ease LGBT access to mainstream home health services.Revise the Family and Medical Leave Act to include same-sex partners.Champion the National Family Caregiver Support Program's broad definition of "family" that can help support services for LGBT caregivers and friends and partners providing care to LGBT seniors.Enlarge government and private foundation support for needs assessments, caregiver intervention research, and demonstration projects targeting the LGBT community. Require LGBT sensitivity training as part of state- and federal-supported programs for seniors and their caregivers. Include sexual orientation in all antidiscrimination policies protecting employment, public housing, and access and delivery of services.Back the Joint Commission on the Accreditation of Healthcare Organizations' (JCAHO) addition of respect for "residents' habits and patterns of living (including lifestyle choices related to sexual orientation)" to the requirements in its accreditation manual for assisted living facilities.

Concluding Comments

Professionals and organizations working with LGBT caregivers need to expand their mission beyond merely increasing their awareness of some LGBT-related issues and barriers to developing competence in the design and administration of effective interventions across multiple levels, from daily individual practice to national policies that impede LGBT individuals' ability to meet their caregiving demands. By raising awareness of the array of unique issues and contexts LGBT caregivers face and building professional competence through ongoing education, training, and consultation, they can become the change agents and change agencies needed to effectively serve LGBT care recipients and their caregivers.

Finally, this chapter has purposely focused on many of the challenges encountered by LGBT caregivers. However, professionals must also celebrate the diversity of LGBT community members and recognize that LGBT caregivers and care recipients alike often experience great joys that counterbalance the hardships and obstacles described herein. Caregivers in the recent New York survey mentioned throughout the chapter reported that caring for either a family of origin or family of choice member also nurtured them spiritually or emotionally, gave them a sense of purpose, or made them a better person (Cantor et al., 2004). As one LGBT caregiver shared not too long ago with his LGBT support group, "We often talk about that book [Kath Weston's *Families We Choose: Lesbians, Gays, Kinship*]. My family is really both: it's my nuclear, my blood family, and it's the gay and lesbian family Todd and I chose together here in the city and from back home, years ago. Many of them are still with us. They are our champions" (Coon & Zeiss, 2003b, p. 289).

References

Beck, A. T., Rush, A. J., Shaw, B. F., & Emery, G. (1979). *Cognitive therapy of depression*. New York: Guilford Press.

Bourgeois, M. S., Schulz, R., & Burgio, L. (1996). Intervention for caregivers of patients with Alzheimer's disease: A review and analysis of content, process, and outcomes. *International Journal of Human Development, 43*, 35–92.

Burgio, L.D., Stevens, A., Guy, D., Roth, D.L., & Haley, W.E. (2003). Impact of two psychosocial interventions on White and African American family caregivers of individuals with dementia. *The Gerontologist, 43*, 568–579.

Cahill, S., South, K., & Spade, J. (2000). *Outing Age: Public policy issues affecting gay, lesbian, bisexual and transgender elders*. New York: The Policy Institute of the National Gay and Lesbian Task Force Foundation. Retrieved from www.ngltf.org

Cantor, M. H., Brennan, M., & Shippy, R. A. (2004). *Caregiving among older lesbian, gay, bisexual and transgender New Yorkers.* New York: National Gay and Lesbian Task Force Policy Institute.

Ceridwyn, N. (2002, Spring). Finding LGBT resources on Alzheimer's. *Dimensions (Newsletter of the Mental Health and Aging Network).*

Coon, D. W. (2001, March). LGBT caregivers: Obstacles and innovations in care. In A. Stevens, *Advancing the care of people with Alzheimer's Disease through the use of technology: Innovative case management techniques in home healthcare.* Symposium conducted at the First Joint Conference of the American Society on Aging and The National Council on the Aging, New Orleans, LA.

Coon, D. W. (2003). *Lesbian, gay, bisexual and transgender (LGBT) issues and family caregiving.* San Francisco, CA: Family Caregiver Alliance National Center on Caregiving. Retrieved February 27, 2006, from www.caregiver.org/caregiver/jsp/content_node.jsp?nodeid=981

Coon, D. W., Ory, M. G., & Schulz, R. (2003). Family caregivers: Enduring and emergent themes. In D. W. Coon, D. Gallagher-Thompson, & L. Thompson (Eds.), *Innovative interventions to reduce dementia caregiver distress: A clinical guide* (pp. 3–27). New York: Springer.

Coon, D. W., & Zeiss, L. M. (2003a, January). Caring for families we choose: Intervention issues with LGBT caregivers. In D. W. Coon, *Dementia caregiving interventions: Intersections of gender, sexual orientation and culture.* Symposium conducted at the National Multicultural Conference and Summit III, Los Angeles, CA.

Coon, D. W., & Zeiss, L. M. (2003b). The families we choose: Intervention issues with LGBT caregivers. In D. W. Coon, D. Gallagher-Thompson, & L. Thompson (Eds.), *Innovative interventions to reduce dementia caregiver distress: A clinical guide* (pp. 267–295). New York: Springer.

DiPlacido, J. (1998). Minority stress among lesbians, gay men, and bisexuals: A consequence of heterosexism, homophobia, and stigmatization. In G. Herek (Ed.), *Psychological perspectives on lesbian and gay issues: Vol. 4. Stigma and sexual orientation: Understanding prejudice against lesbians, gay men, and bisexuals* (pp. 138–159). Thousand Oaks, CA: Sage.

Dunkin, J. J., & Anderson-Hanley, C. (1998). Dementia caregiver burden: A review of the literature and guidelines for assessment and intervention. *Neurology, 51*(Supp. 1), S53–S60.

Eisdorfer, C., Czaja, S. J., Loewenstein, D. A., Rubert, M. P., Argüelles, S., Mitrani, V. B. et al. (2003). The effect of a family therapy and technology-based intervention on caregiver depression. *The Gerontologist, 43,* 521–531.

Emmons, K. M. (2001). Behavioral and social science contributions to the health of adults in the United States. In B. D. Smedley & S. L. Syme (Eds.), *Promoting health: Intervention strategies from social and behavioral research* (pp. 254–321). Washington, DC: National Academy Press.

Fox, R. (1996). Bisexuality in perspective: A review of theory and research. In B. Firestein (Ed.), *Bisexuality: The psychology and politics of an invisible minority* (pp. 263–291). Thousand Oaks, CA: Sage.

Fredriksen, K. L. (1999). Family caregiving responsibilities among lesbians and gay men. *Social Work, 44,* 142–155.

Gallagher-Thompson, D., Coon, D., Solano, N., Ambler, C., Rabinowitz, R., & Thompson, L. (2003). Change in indices of distress among Latina and Anglo female caregivers of elderly relatives with dementia: Site specific results from the REACH National Collaborative Study. *The Gerontologist, 43,* 580–591.

Gallagher-Thompson, D., Hargrave, R., Hinton, L., Arean, P., Iwamasa, G., & Zeiss, L. M. (2003). Interventions for a multicultural society. In D. Coon, D. Gallagher-Thompson, & L. W. Thompson (Eds.), *Innovative interventions to reduce dementia caregiver distress: A clinical guide* (pp. 50–73). New York: Springer.

Gitlin, L.N., Winter, L., Corcoran, M., Dennis, M., Schinfeld, S., & Hauck, W. (2003). Effects of the home environmental skill-building program on the caregiver–care recipient dyad: Six-month outcomes from the Philadelphia REACH initiative. *The Gerontologist, 43,* 532–546.

Gollance, R. (2003, Spring). Groups support gay men and lesbians facing challenges of caring for aging parents. *Dimensions (Newsletter of the Mental Health and Aging Network), 10,* 7–8.

Herek, G. M., Gillis, J. R., & Cogan, J. C. (1999). Psychological sequelae of hate crime victimization among lesbian, gay, and bisexual adults. *Journal of Consulting and Clinical Psychology, 67,* 945–951.

Hoctel, P. D. (2002, January–February). Community assessments show service gaps for LGBT elders. *Aging Today, 23*(1), 5–6.

Kennet, J., Burgio, L., & Schulz, R. (2000). Interventions for in-home caregivers: A review of research 1990 to present. In R. Schulz (Ed.), *Handbook on dementia caregiving: Evidence-based interventions for family caregivers* (pp. 61–125). New York: Springer.

Levine, J. A., & Altman, C. (2002, Winter). Collaborating to support lesbian and gay caregivers for people with Alzheimer's. *Outword (Newsletter of the Lesbian & Gay Aging Issues Network), 8,* 3, 7–8.

Lewinsohn, P. M., Muñoz, R. F., Youngren, M. A., & Zeiss, A. M. (1986). *Control your depression.* New York: Prentice Hall.

Mittelman, M., Roth, D. L., Coon, D. W., & Haley, W. E. (2004). Sustained benefit of supportive intervention for depressive symptoms in Alzheimer's caregivers. *American Journal of Psychiatry, 161,* 850–856.

Outword Online. (2000, August). San Jose, Calif.: Local needs assessment looks at LGBT elders. American Society on Aging's *Outword Online.* Retrieved February 27, 2006, from http://www.asaging.org/networks/LGAIN/outword_online/2000/outaug.cfm

Pusey, H., & Richards, D. (2001). A systematic review of the effectiveness of psychosocial interventions for carers of people with dementia. *Aging & Mental Health, 5,* 107–119.

Reiter, B. (2003). New web-based outreach supports LGBT caregivers locally, nationally. *Outword, 9*(3), 1, 6.

Steffen, A., Mahoney, D. F., & Kelly, K. (2003). Capitalizing on technological advances. In D. W. Coon, D. Gallagher-Thompson, & L. Thompson (Eds.), *Innovative interventions to reduce dementia caregiver distress: A clinical guide* (pp. 189–209). New York: Springer.

Teri, L., Logsdon, R. G., Uomoto, J., & McCurry, S. M. (1997). Behavioral treatment of depression in dementia patients: A controlled clinical trial. *Journal of Gerontology B: Psychological Science and Social Science, 52,* 159–166.

Wight, R. G. (2002). AIDS caregiving stress among HIV-infected men. In B. J. Kramer & E. H. Thompson, Jr. (Eds.), *Men as caregivers: Theory, research, and service implications* (pp. 190–212). New York: Springer.

Appendix: Additional Resources

Administration on Aging

(Web site: www.aoa.dhhs.gov/prof/aoaprog/caregiver/careprof/progguid-ance/resources/nfcsp_resources_guide.asp)

Access the Web site to read the National Family Caregiver Support Program (NFCSP) Resource Guide for the Aging Network; especially, see chapter 8, "Designing the NFCSP in the Context of Diverse Caregiver Populations."

American Society on Aging

Phone: 415-974-9600

Web site www.asaing.org/lgain

Outword is the newsletter of the Lesbian and Gay Aging Issues Network (LGAIN). *Outword Online* is a monthly e-mail update designed to bring members of the American Society on Aging's LGAIN timely announcements and occasional brief articles relevant to aging issues for lesbians, gays, bisexuals, and transgender folk.

Family Caregiver Alliance

690 Market St., Suite 600, San Francisco, CA 94104

Phone: 415-434-3388 and 800-445-8106

e-mail: info@caregiver.org

Web site: www.caregiver.org

The report "LGBT Caregiving: Frequently Asked Questions" is available free online at www.caregiver.org/factsheets/lgbt_FAQ.html. The report "Legal Issues for LGBT Caregivers" is available free online at www.care-giver.org/factsheets/lgbt_legal.html.

Gay and Lesbian Medical Association
459 Fulton Street, Suite 107, San Francisco, CA 94102
Phone: 415-255-4547
e-mail: info@glma.org
Web site: www.glma.org

Gay Men's Health Crisis
The Tisch Building, 119 West 24 Street, New York, NY 10011
Phone: 212-367-1000
Web site: www.gmhc.org

Gay Yellow Pages
Web site: www.gayellowpages.com)

Go to "Organizations/Resources: Age-Group and Senior Focus." This provides a national directory of programs and groups for LGBT older adults.

Lambda Legal Defense Fund
120 Wall Street, Suite 1500, New York, NY 10005-3904
Phone: 212-809-8585; fax: 212-809-0055
Web site: www.lambdalegal.org

LGBT Caring Community Program and Online Support Group
www.caregiver.org/lgbt-sptgroup.html)

National Association on HIV over Fifty
Web site at www.hivoverfifty.org
Also see "Bibliography on Caregiving."

National Center for Lesbian Rights (NCLR)
870 Market St., Suite 570, San Francisco, CA 94102
Phone: 415-392-6257
Web site: www.nclrights.org

National Gay and Lesbian Task Force
1325 Massachusetts Ave., NW, Suite 600, Washington, DC 20005-4171
Phone: 202-393-5177
Web site: www.ngltf.org

New Leaf Outreach to Elders (Formerly GLOE/Gay & Lesbian Outreach to Elders)

The New Leaf Outreach to Elders is located in San Francisco, California. Additional information can be obtained by phone (415-255-2937) or by visiting the Web site (www.newleafservices.org).

Old Lesbians Organizing for Change
P.O. Box 980422, Houston, TX 77098
Web site: www.oloc.org

Pride Senior Network
22 W. 23rd St., 5th Floor, New York, NY 10010
Phone: 212-675-1936
Web site: www.pridesenior.org

Senior Action in a Gay Environment
305 Seventh Avenue, 16th Fl., New York, NY 10001;
Phone: 212-741-2247
Web site: www.sageusa.org

Senior Pages
Web site: www.seniorpages.com

Click on "Gay Seniors" for a listing of national organizations that support LGBT older adults.

Transgender Aging Network
Web site: www.forge-forward.org/TAN

UCSF AIDS Health Project Monograph Series
See P. Zeifert, M. Leary, A. A. Boccellari. (1995). *AIDS and the impact of cognitive impairment: A treatment guide for mental health providers* (No. 1). San Francisco: University of California San Francisco.

PART V

Community Partnerships for Support of Ethnic Elders and Families

CHAPTER 22

Reaching Diverse Caregiving Families Through Community Partnerships

ELIZABETH S. EDGERLY AND THERESA SULLIVAN

In 2005, over 4.5 million Americans were estimated to have Alzheimer's disease (Hebert, Scherr, Bienias, Bennett, & Evans, 2003) and that number is projected to reach to between 11 and 16 million by 2050. Increasing age is the greatest risk factor for Alzheimer's, with as many as one in ten individuals over the age of 65 and 48% of those 85 years and older affected (Evans et al., 1989). Overall, the population of those 65 and older will double by 2050 (Hebert et al., 2003). The trend of living longer will clearly contribute to the huge increases in the number of persons impacted by dementing illness. Of course, this only represents the individuals impacted by the disease. When we consider that one in ten Americans has a family member with the disease and one in three is concerned about someone who is impacted, we can see the major impact of dementia on our communities (Alzheimer's Association, 1992).

Another trend that will change the face of Alzheimer's is the increasing diversity of our society. By the year 2050, projections indicate that there will be twice as many White/Anglo elders, four times as many African American elders, seven times the number of Hispanic/Latino elders, 6.5 times the number of Asian and Pacific Islander elders, and 3.5 times the number of American Indian elders. By 2050, African Americans, Latinos, and Asian and Pacific Islanders (APIs) will represent 30% of the population over age 65 as compared to 15% of the 65 and older population in 1990 (Hobbs, 2001). This shift to an increasingly older and more diverse society points to the need for greater services for those impacted by dementing illnesses and their families.

In this chapter, we will highlight the current literature on the unique needs of diverse caregivers of persons with dementia, identify potential models for programs to serve these needs, and describe two successful programs utilizing different models for community outreach and service delivery. Where possible, we present data to support the use of a particular model. Our literature search revealed limited published information on successful programs for diverse caregivers of persons with dementia. Experience tells us that there are many more failed attempts than successes in developing service programs that are effective in reaching diverse families affected by dementia. We hope that with greater focus on this topic, and with the sharing of best practices, this can be much improved. To this end, we will outline elements of two successful programs involving partnerships that we believe would do well in replication.

A review of the literature reveals the following: there are many more commonalities than differences among caregivers of persons with dementia with diverse backgrounds. Appreciation, understanding, and respect for these differences are keys to developing a successful dementia program. Because of the differences in culture, language, and preferences for programs, a one-size-fits-all program is unlikely to meet the needs across ethnic and racial groups.

Findings on How Caregivers Differ by Ethnicity

In their report, "Racial and Ethnic Differences in Family Caregiving in California," the authors found that cultural values and beliefs influence families' decisions about using formal support services (Giunta, Chow, Scharlach & Dal Santo, 2004). Barriers to service utilization were identified by the caregivers interviewed as including poor service quality, services not available, services not being offered by "people who are like" the caregiver, and language barriers (Giunta et al., 2004). The El Portal Alzheimer's Project found that the primary reason that families in the Latino community of Los Angeles did not seek services was that they did not know where to go (Aranda, Villa, Trejo, Ramirez, & Ranney, 2003). Some community agencies have developed interorganizational collaborations to begin breaking down the barriers to the utilization of services by diverse caregiving families. Social service and health-care organizations that are identified as "mainstream" can establish relationships and build trust within diverse communities by developing and enhancing partnerships with grassroots organizations that have a demonstrated history of being responsive to families' needs for support.

The majority of primary caregivers, regardless of ethnicity, receive little help from formal service providers (Cox, 1999). The most common reasons were the perception that help was not needed or that appropriate services were not available (Giunta et al., 2004). However, as the disease progresses and the intensity of care increases, primary caregivers are increasingly likely to report unmet needs and to seek help from formal service providers (Navaie-Waliser et al., 2001).

Researchers have found variations by culture and ethnicity in caregivers' experience of workload, burden, needs, and desire for help (Janevic & Connell, 2001). African Americans, for example, report a heavier caregiver workload than do White caregivers, and they report greater unmet needs. Navaie-Waliser et al. (2001) also found that the intensity of the care provided was not mitigated by the receipt of formal care services. Despite this, Black caregivers were less likely to report difficulty with caregiving. Hispanic caregivers in the Narvaie-Waliser et al. study were no different from White caregivers in terms of their workload or unmet needs. While caregivers from diverse communities often express a greater need for formal support services than White caregivers, minority caregivers utilize significantly fewer services than White caregivers. Formal service utilization differs by ethnicity (Giunta et al., 2004); African Americans and White caregivers are significantly more likely to use services than Latino or Asian and Pacific Island (API) caregivers. The greater the language and cultural barriers, the less likely diverse families are to seek services.

Despite the widely held view that diverse caregivers get more help from those around them, a review of the literature by Dilworth-Anderson and colleagues did not support this (Dilworth-Anderson, Williams, & Gibson, 2002). Instead, they found that diverse caregivers rely on different helpers than do White caregivers but do not receive more help than White caregivers. White caregivers rely on help provided primarily by close family members, whereas diverse families receive help from extended family and friends. African American and Latino caregivers tend to report stronger values of filial support (i.e., giving back to their elders) than do White caregivers (Connell & Gibson, 1997; Lee & Sung, 1997; Sanchez, 1992). African American and Latino caregivers also report lower levels of caregiver stress and a greater reliance on religion as a coping strategy (Levkoff, Levy, & Weitzman 1999).

Culture plays a role in the coping strategies used by diverse caregivers as well as the caregivers' perception of the situation. Cultural values, beliefs, and norms about caregiving as well as a sense of obligation to take care of one's elders appears to foster a more positive view of caregiving and the role of the caregiver in diverse communities. This sense of pride and fulfillment of an obligation, not surprisingly, could serve to decrease diverse caregivers' sense of need for help. A clear understanding of and respect for this would potentially alter how we promote the use of certain formal services. For example, service providers often encourage caregivers to "take care of yourself" by utilizing respite care services, such as adult day care and in-home care, in order to "take a break" from the round-the-clock caregiving required by the person with dementia. While these reasons may have validity (certainly caregiver wellness impacts the well-being of the person with dementia), it may be misguided as an approach to encourage participation from diverse caregivers. Consider this: if a caregiver believes it is his or her filial duty to care for an elder with dementia, and he or she derives pride and a sense of self-worth from the role, the caregiver is less likely to use services solely to receive respite for him- or herself. It may be more culturally appropriate to highlight the benefits for the person with dementia, such as time out with others for the social stimulation or activities that are therapeutic for the person with dementia, such as reminiscing or developing new interests and hobbies.

Dementia Care Networks: an Interorganizational Statewide Collaboration

In 1992, the State of California awarded a federal demonstration grant[1] to the Los Angeles Chapter of the Alzheimer's Association to develop innovative programs for underserved persons with dementia and their caregivers, which created the El Portal project to identify and address unmet service needs among Latino communities. This project was replicated in an African American community in 1997 and again in three Asian populations in 2000. The Asian communities included Chinese, Vietnamese, and Japanese families at two sites, one in Santa Clara County serving Chinese and Vietnamese caregivers and the other in Los Angeles County serving Chinese and Japanese caregivers. These demonstration projects replicated the successful "El Portal" Dementia Care Network model.

Each dementia care network has four principles in its guiding philosophy: first, the community must become involved in the development and oversight of the project; second, the community has a strong sense of what will work and should be empowered to individualize the program to match local beliefs and strengths; third, the project should include capacity building, not just service provision; and, fourth, there will be a reciprocity in learning between the Alzheimer's Association and the partnering community agencies. The Association learns how to provide culturally appropriate services to the targeted community, and the local providers learn about dementia care, and how to address caregivers' needs.

In each dementia care network, the local Alzheimer's Association chapter partnered with the local Area Agencies on Aging (AAA) and ethnic health and social service organizations in order to offer culturally competent dementia services and outreach. This interorganizational collaboration focuses on developing dementia competence in culturally competent, trusted community agencies, and sponsoring care advocates to work in the partner agencies. The partner agencies, in turn, serve as advisors in helping to develop the cultural competency in the Alzheimer's Association's staff, volunteers, and Board members.

In the Asian Dementia Care Network demonstration sites, the Alzheimer's Association selected local ethnic health and social service providers to provide outreach and care coordination services to Chinese, Vietnamese, and Japanese persons with dementia and their families. The sites involved in the project in Los Angeles were the Little Tokyo Service Center serving the Japanese community and the Chinatown Service Center serving the Chinese community. In San Jose, the John XXIII Multiservice Center served Vietnamese and Chinese families. Each of these partners was a well-established, trusted institution in the community. Following the dementia care network model, the partner agencies recruited and hired bilingual/bicultural care advocates to conduct in-depth home-based assessments, to provide information and referrals, to connect families to diagnostic, support, and community-based services, and to provide community education and outreach. Care advocates are the linchpin of a dementia care network, assisting families in navigating bureaucracy, proactively helping them to access services, and becoming a general community resource for other professionals serving ethnic communities who are interested in learning how to provide dementia services. The Alzheimer's Association provided intensive dementia-related training and clinical supervision to the care advocates in collaboration with the partner agencies and provided caregiver support groups, educational workshops, professional training, and safe return services to community providers and families in the program.

Families were targeted through a variety of outreach activities, including media (newsletters, ethnic newspapers, television and radio interviews), community educational workshops, and word of mouth. Interested families received a home visit during which the care advocate established rapport with the family, provided information about memory loss and dementia, and offered referrals to community resources, including diagnostic evaluations. Families also received assistance identifying appropriate providers and subsidizing respite care. Families were encouraged to hire individuals to provide care in the home or to use day care or overnight respite services in the community. Care advocates completed a thorough assessment of the caregiver's situation, needs, level of burden, and coping strategies during the home visit.

Each dementia care network relied on information gathered from needs assessments or focus groups to tailor the services to the needs of the community. For the Asian Dementia Care Networks, six focus groups were conducted with a total of 68 Asian caregivers of persons with dementia to determine their attitudes toward dementia and Alzheimer's disease, common challenges and needs, and recommendations for how to promote culturally sensitive dementia care services. Four recommendations emerged from the groups: (a) to actively promote dementia care services through ethnic media, retail locations, the Internet, and e-mail; (b) to expand access and availability of caregiver support groups for Asian caregivers; (c) to expand in-home supportive services for caregivers; and (d) to broaden service offerings to reach additional Asian families.

Over a period of seven years, the El Portal Dementia Care Network in Los Angeles reached nearly 7,000 service users through care management, support groups, counseling, legal advocacy and planning, translation assistance during medical evaluations, and respite services (Cherry & Trejo 2003). To reach these families, thousands of outreach and education contacts were made through media and public events. Consistent with El Portal, clients served through the Dementia Care Networks were predominantly female (70%), about half living with spouses and about three-quarters over age 75, with 33% over age 85. In this project, 12% of the persons with dementia lived alone, and 77% spoke a language other than English. Participants generally had low incomes, with 30% reporting incomes under $8,000 and only seven percent reporting incomes higher than $30,000.

Family Caregiver Alliance: Ethnic Outreach Program

The Ethnic Outreach Program at Family Caregiver Alliance (FCA) in San Francisco offers another example of an interorganizational model that seeks to reduce barriers to accessing services and increase families' utilization of community resources. FCA is the San Francisco Bay Area Caregiver Resource Center and the National Center on Caregiving. FCA was the original model for eleven California Caregiver Resource Centers that provide the following services: information about diagnosis and care options, emotional support, and consultation on care planning, links to community programs, legal/financial consultation, respite services, counseling, as well as a broad range of publications and educational programs for families and professionals. FCA developed the Ethnic Outreach Program to meet the needs of diverse families by increasing internal cultural competency, developing partnerships with community organizations to conduct outreach and education, and following up by providing direct services by trained bicultural and bilingual staff members who represented the targeted communities.

FCA launched the Ethnic Outreach Program (EOP) with private funding in 1992 to implement outreach strategies and develop community partnerships with key service providers in the African American, Chinese, and Latino communities. The objectives of the program were to build the capacity of the organization (FCA) to work effectively with families and providers in diverse communities; develop and distribute culturally appropriate and language-specific educational materials; raise the level of awareness about dementia and caregiving among service providers in grassroots community agencies in the San Francisco Bay Area; increase the resources available to caregivers through collaboration with these community agencies; and provide a range of culturally sensitive and linguistically appropriate support services to families.

The premise was based on the concept that an effective interorganizational collaboration would begin with building cultural competency within the lead organization and, thereby, more effectively reaching out and partnering with culturally identified community organizations to assist these agencies in building their dementia capacity to assess needs and coordinate services for family caregivers and persons with dementia.

Three outreach specialist positions were funded over a five-year period, following which the program was integrated into FCA's core services programs. The responsibilities of the outreach specialist positions included building and maintaining relationships with the ethnic communities and grassroots organizations, providing in-service professional education, and forming planning committees with key providers to develop educational workshops for families on dementia care, caregiving strategies to reduce stress, and long-term care planning.

One of the challenges in reaching underserved communities is the lack of understanding about dementia and the resulting misperceptions about dementia care (Gallagher-Thompson, Solano, Coon, & Areán, 2003). Ongoing outreach efforts of the EOP included community education programs that were repeated every 6 months to continue reaching and informing professional and family caregivers about caregiving issues and to create a consistent presence in the communities by FCA. Greater community awareness and recognition of FCA resulted in increased calls for assistance from the community at large by 10% each year over 5 years, with the highest percentage in increased calls from families from the targeted communities. The baseline in 1991 of calls from caregivers who identified themselves as African American, Asian, Latino, or other Non-White was 18%. By 1995, the percentage of callers from diverse communities had grown to 36% of total callers. Most callers were able to speak with one of the bilingual or bicultural outreach specialists for an initial intake interview and resource consultation. Other bilingual or bicultural staff members were also available to provide information and referral and follow-up support.

The outreach specialists also provided a broad range of direct services, including in-home assessments, care planning consultations, counseling, and support to families. FCA was also able to provide financial assistance to families who could benefit from respite services. The outreach specialists identified appropriate resources in the community and assisted families in accessing and coordinating services. Implementing the program effectively required that the outreach specialists spend at least half of their time out in the community conducting outreach and education and the other half of their time providing direct services to families in their homes, in the FCA offices, or in shared space from community agencies.

The caregiver assessment data over the first 3 years of the Ethnic Outreach Program showed that caregivers from diverse communities were no more likely to rely on family and friends for help than the general caregiving population (Family Caregiver Alliance, 1993). The greatest needs identified by the caregivers who were served were information and education (78%), emotional support (41%), and respite care (35%). Over time, the increasing numbers of families seeking help from what was considered a mainstream agency demonstrated the effectiveness of the outreach efforts. The 6-month follow-up assessments showed that families were increasingly using formal support services, understood better what their care planning options were, and felt more confident that support was available.

Lessons Learned

Lesson 1: Recruit Bilingual and Bicultural Staff

Both the Alzheimer's Association Dementia Care Network and the Family Caregiver Alliance Ethnic Outreach Program recruited and trained bilingual and bicultural staff to play a central role in outreach and program delivery. The outreach specialists or care advocates who will be developing relationships, building trust, and maintaining visibility in the community and who will be providing direct services will be most effective if they represent the ethnicity of the communities they wish to serve. These individuals should have the language skills and cultural capacity to identify with the culture in order to earn the trust and respect of the community. It is more important to hire bilingual/bicultural staff with strong communication and relationship-building skills, and experience working within the community than it is to have specific experience in caregiving and dementia care. This recommendation is consistent with those of Gallagher-Thompson, Solano, Coon, and Areán (2003) in their article on the recruitment of diverse (in this case, Latino) caregivers for research. While we recognize that recruiting for research is different from recruiting for patient and family services, we believe that the comparison is justifiable.

In many instances, it can be extremely difficult to find someone with both cultural expertise and dementia experience. The focus in both projects was on finding enthusiastic bicultural/bilingual individuals with strong ties to the community and then providing them with intensive training in the dementia content area. The specialists underwent training in dementia and caregiving in preparation for developing educational materials and programs. By providing ongoing professional development opportunities and supportive supervision to staff, the organization continued to build and strengthen capacity to deliver culturally appropriate services. The outreach specialists and care advocates in both projects participated in numerous professional development programs in their first year.

Lesson 2: Provide Diversity Training at All Levels

To ensure appropriate representation at all levels and to build the organization's capacity in cultural competency, diversity training needs to be an ongoing effort and must be consistently applied at all levels, including management, board of directors, advisory councils, and direct services staff. Both the Alzheimer's Association and Family Caregiver Alliance engaged in a series of programs that included specifically designed workshops for the Board of Directors and training for managers at all levels; each organization also required all staff to participate in workshops that included exercises in raising cultural sensitivity as well as specific information about values and preferences of families from diverse communities. To be successful, the lead agency must be knowledgeable about the cultural values and beliefs of the community and make it a goal to recruit diverse candidates when filling board or staff positions. Including volunteers who represented the identified communities and who shared their professional expertise was a strong influence on changing the face of these organizations in the community. Both the Alzheimer's Association and FCA found it is crucial to the success of the program to recruit board and advisory council members from diverse communities to act as ambassadors to community and grassroots organizations.

Lesson 3: Utilize Linguistically and Culturally Appropriate Tools and Materials

Both highlighted projects developed new educational materials in different languages. In the FCA project, 500 introductory packets were sent to community organizations and included a cover letter with a brief overview of the organization and an introduction to the program, offering an in-person outreach meeting or an in-service orientation, and promising a follow-up call. In the first year, FCA offered a series of five culturally appropriate and language-specific fact sheets; program brochures were also translated into Chinese and Spanish for dissemination to family members, which proved to be an effective way to enhance the outreach efforts. Similarly, the Alzheimer's Association dementia care networks created new linguistically and culturally appropriate educational workshops with Power Point slides and handouts and new translated pamphlets and brochures on dementia-related topics.

Language has consistently been identified as a cultural barrier for families to gain awareness and access services. When translating materials, the variety of dialects and the history of the countries of origin in the community must be taken into consideration. Furthermore, an emphasis on conceptual translation rather than literal translation is essential (Gallagher-Thompson et al., 2003). In the Alzheimer's Association project, care advocates experienced difficulty translating some items in the standardized assessment tools. For instance, one item during the intake asked "how have you (*the caregiver*) grown as a person." Not only were the respondents confused by this question, but the care advocates were as well. Idiomatic expressions such as this demonstrate the need for conceptual versus literal translation. Similarly, there were two items on the intake form, the first of which asked the caregiver about their "competence" as a caregiver, and the second asked about their "confidence" as a caregiver. In Vietnamese, both "competence" and "confidence" are translated identically, which resulted in the participants being asked the same question twice.

Care should also be taken with the appearance and style of the marketing materials, as the design and presentation will have different appeal for different cultures. It is important to be mindful of the photos displayed in brochures and other marketing tools, to be sure they represent the target population. Distribution of marketing and informational materials should include health fairs, medical clinics, senior centers, churches, and non-traditional service providers, such as community centers, shop owners, banks, and alternative health providers.

Lesson 4: Understanding Attitudes, Beliefs,
and Values About Dementia is Essential

The focus groups conducted by the Alzheimer's Association revealed that many of the Asian caregivers surveyed viewed dementia as a normal part of aging: "It's (Alzheimer's disease) a part of the natural process of aging." Others described it as something shameful: "For Chinese people, some might think Alzheimer's is a shameful word, your family members will feel embarrassed." Some also expressed doubt about the value of formal services or existing treatments: "For a brain illness like Alzheimer's, we can only be sympathetic, caring and ready to help." Others expressed confusion about the causes of dementia and discomfort with the terminology used to describe and discuss the disease: "Forgetfulness is one word. It is more pleasant to the ear. Dementia is not as nice. And Alzheimer's is the worst." Appreciating these attitudes and beliefs is a key component to creating effective and culturally appropriate materials and services for diverse families (Gallagher-Thompson et al., 2003).

Lesson 5: Launch a Media Campaign

In both projects, the media played a central role in attracting attention and raising awareness about dementia in general and the programs in particular. Media campaigns were conducted targeting newspapers, radio, and television stations serving the communities of interest. Press releases, public service announcements, and personal interest articles in the appropriate language were prepared and disseminated to local media. In the FCA project, personal contacts were made with media representatives to follow up on the materials sent. In the first 2 years of the Ethnic Outreach Program, FCA conducted 19 radio and television interviews in different languages and was mentioned 12 times in culturally specific community newspapers. The Alzheimer's Association received 25 calls from Chinese-speaking caregivers following a television interview about dementia and the API project. Both projects found the ethnic media to be receptive to promoting awareness of the programs offered, and these efforts proved widely effective in reaching diverse families.

Lesson 6: Identify Potential Community Partners

Bailey and Koney (1996) outlined strategies of creating interorganizational community-based partnerships to strategically address community needs. Their model emphasizes community involvement, interactive structure between collaborating agencies, system development, and other components to successful collaborations. While the two projects differed in terms of their structure, both embodied the elements of successful inter-organizational partnerships. In the Alzheimer's Association program, the chapter replicated the "El Portal Dementia Care Network" model that builds dementia capacity within an ethnically oriented community agency by supporting a professional position within that agency. Services were primarily delivered in the community by the partner agency that was already well known to the target community and had strong connections with other grassroots providers and community-based organizations. In the FCA program, the organization first focused on building internal cultural capacity and then reached out to numerous grassroots agencies in the community to help the identified community partner agencies develop their internal knowledge about dementia and competency in dealing with the topic of caregiving. Grassroots and community organizations that are gatekeepers to the targeted communities were identified by researching specific categories of resources, including health care, social service and family services organizations, community centers, senior centers, and churches. Participating in professional coalitions and consortiums was an effective way of expanding the network of contacts to build interorganizational partnerships to collaborate to best serve the needs of families. The outreach specialists in the FCA model and the care advocates in the Alzheimer's Association model made themselves consistently present in the community. They continued to ask their contacts and the consumers where families traditionally went to seek help, and more and more providers were added to the outreach list, such as dentists, pharmacists, spiritual healers, and herbalists.

Lesson 7: Offer in-Service Training and Community Orientations

While reaching out to community contacts, the FCA outreach specialists offered an on-site meeting with interested recipients to provide an overview of the program, describe services available to their constituents, and offer in-service training on specific topics related to dementia and caregiving issues for staff who provide direct support to families. Ten percent of the initial recipients responded with invitations for an on-site meeting or an in-service training. Those who did not respond to the introductory packet were followed-up with a telephone call to provide a personal introduction and invitation to learn more about the program. The response rate steadily increased to 25% as personal introductions were made, and a series of outreach visits, in-service trainings, and community orientations were conducted. These contacts served to extend the reach by building trust with the key providers in the community. In the first 2 years, in-service trainings were provided to 49 community organizations. Orientations were provided at 24 different professional coalitions or consortiums of agencies. More than 1,500 individual professionals participated over a 2-year period.

Similarly, the Alzheimer's Association's Dementia Care Network sought to enhance community capacity to serve people with dementia through providing training programs for a cross section of professionals from the targeted community. Multiple professional training events were offered, reaching audiences ranging from physicians and attorneys to family caregivers and home-care workers. Wherever possible, the Alzheimer's Association and Family Caregiver Alliance collaborated their outreach efforts by cosponsoring community education programs.

Lesson 8: Build Dementia Care Capacity with Key Providers

From the greater list of identified community contacts in the targeted communities, the key providers will emerge through their motivation to engage in the process and by their growing awareness of the needs of caregiving families in their communities. Key providers will be those who have an established trust within the community and a sincere interest in collaborating to reach and inform families about dementia and related caregiving issues. The Alzheimer's Association care advocates are employed by agencies with established community trust. Part of their role is to provide dementia care training and consultation to colleagues in their agencies so that the organization's overall dementia care capacity is enhanced. Ideally, however, the key providers should represent a range of organizations within the community, including health-care programs, social service agencies, churches and faith-based organizations, home care, adult day care, and others who serve families.

Lesson 9: Involve the Community

Another key element to successful collaborations is community input. For both interorganizational projects, advisory committee members met regularly to discuss the program, address issues, identify additional partner agencies, and plan for how to sustain funding in future years. Key providers were also invited to participate on planning committees to collaborate on the development and implementation of family education programs.

Given their knowledge of the needs expressed by their constituent families, these key providers assisted in developing the curriculum for community workshops to expand awareness about memory loss, behavior changes, the impact on families, and resources available to help. Using terms that were non-threatening to the community proved to be more successful in drawing an audience, for instance, "memory loss" instead of dementia or Alzheimer's disease or "caring for an aging family member" instead of the term *caregiving*, which is not easily identified within different cultures and languages. Experts in the field of dementia and caregiving who are bilingual and bicultural were invited to speak at these cosponsored community workshops. Physicians, psychologists, nurses, and social workers who the audience identified with were able to engage families in learning more about care planning and utilizing community resources. Several collaborative community education programs were presented each year, reaching approximately 500 family members annually.

Lesson 10: Deliver on the Promise to Serve

One of the most effective marketing and outreach methods is to deliver on the promises made in the community to provide supportive services to families who are referred from collaborating agencies or who learned about the programs through the community workshops or materials disseminated in the neighborhoods. FCA's Ethnic Outreach Program staff was well prepared to deliver a range of services that were culturally sensitive and tailored to the needs of individual families. The Alzheimer's Association provided training, supervision, and support to staff employed by the partner agencies and worked over time to develop internal capacity. Both FCA and the Alzheimer's Association had an established history of developing, providing, and modifying services to be responsive to the gaps between needs identified by families and services offered by trained professionals that included in-home psychosocial caregiver assessments, care planning consultations, respite assistance, counseling, and support groups. At FCA, psycho-educational workshops and groups designed to reduce caregiver distress were also adapted to be culturally and linguistically appropriate.

By increasing public awareness about dementia and caregiving, and increasing families' knowledge about community resources available, service utilization steadily increased by 10% annually over a period of 5 years. The referral sources identified by families calling FCA to seek help included primarily health-care and social services organizations (35%), and "word of mouth" (32%) was identified nearly as frequently. FCA learned that delivering on your promise to provide user-friendly services and effective interventions goes a long way to increase word-of-mouth referrals.

Conclusion

We described two interorganizational models that were effective in reaching families caring for loved ones with dementia in ethnic communities. Partnering with community and grassroots organizations is key to creating successful programs for diverse caregivers of persons with dementia. The essential ingredients are a long-term commitment to serve, strong community partnerships, a consistent presence and involvement in the community, and the capacity to appreciate cultural differences in attitudes, beliefs, and values about dementia and caregiving. Because it is a struggle to sustain ongoing funding for building services and outreach efforts, interorganizational partnerships and collaborations will extend the reach of the resources available to provide such services. By utilizing a variety of public awareness efforts, including the offering of culturally and linguistically appropriate literature, ethnic-specific media campaigns, and community education programs, Family Caregiver Alliance and the Alzheimer's Association saw significant increases in the numbers of ethnically diverse families served. The two models offer different approaches to the structure of staffing: one created internal staff positions and the other provided support to positions in the partnering agencies. They demonstrated similar capacity-building efforts in developing cultural sensitivity internally and in building dementia care capacity in community organizations. Both models demonstrated effectiveness in building collaborative relationships in the community and in serving increasing numbers of diverse families in each successive year. The keys to success included building trust in the community, exchanging knowledge with grassroots providers, and following up with a consistent presence and ability to provide quality culturally appropriate services.

Note

1. This project was supported, in part, by a grant (no. 90AZ2787) from the Administration on Aging, Department of Health and Human Services, Washington, DC 20201. Grantees undertaking projects under government sponsorship are encouraged to freely express their findings and conclusions. Points of view or opinions do not, therefore, necessarily represent the official Administration on Aging policy. This project was also supported by the California Department of Aging, through Contract Number CT-0405-21, and the Alzheimer's Association Los Angeles, Riverside, and San Bernardino Counties Chapter.

References

Alzheimer's Association. (1992). Unpublished Gallup poll survey of 1,015 individuals. Alzheimer's Association, Los Angeles, Riverside, and San Bernardino (2004). *Dementia Care Network Replication Manual.*

Aranda, M. P., Villa, V. M., Trejo, L., Ramirez, R., & Ranney, M. (2003). El Portal Latino Alzheimer's Project: Model program for Latino caregivers of Alzheimer's disease-affected people. *Social Work, 48*(2), 259–271.

Bailey, D., & Koney, K. M. (1996). Interorganizational community-based collaboratives: A strategic response to shape the social work agenda. *Social Work, 41*(6), 602–611.

Cherry, D. L., & Trejo, L. (2003). El Portal and the dementia care network model. *Dimensions, 10*(4), 3, 8.

Connel, C. M., & Gibson, G. D. (1997). Racial, ethnic, and cultural differences in dementia caregiving: Review and analysis. *The Gerontologist, 37*(3), 355–364.

Cox, C. (1999). Race and caregiving: Patterns of service use by African American and White caregivers seeking Alzheimer's assistance. *American Journal of Gerontological Social Work, 32*, 5–17.

Dilworth-Anderson, P., Williams, I. C., & Gibson, B. E. (2002). Issues of race, ethnicity and culture in caregiving research: A 20-year review (1980–2000). *The Gerontologist, 42*(2), 237–272.

Evans, D. A., Funkenstein, H. H., Albert, M. S., Scherr, P. A., Cook, N. R., Chown, M. J. et al. (1989). Prevalence of Alzheimer's disease in a community population of older persons: Higher than previously reported. *Journal of the American Medical Association, 262*(18), 2552–2556.

Family Caregiver Alliance (1993). *1993 Annual Report,* California Caregiver Resource Centers.

Gallagher-Thompson, D., Solano, N., Coon, D., & Areán, P. (2003). Recruitment and retention of Latino dementia family caregivers in intervention research: Issues to face, lessons to learn. *The Gerontologist, 43*(1), 45–51.

Giunta, N., Chow, J., Scharlach, A. E., & Dal Santo, T. S. (2004). Racial and ethnic differences in family caregiving in California. *Journal of Human Behavior in the Social Environment, 9*(4), 85–109.

Hebert, L. E., Scherr, P. A., Bienias, J. L., Bennett, D. A., & Evans, D. A. (2003). Alzheimer's disease in the U.S. population: Prevalence estimates using the 2000 census. *Archives of Neurology, 60*(8), 1119–1122.

Hobbs, F. B. (2001). *The elderly population.* U.S. Census Bureau, Age and Sex Statistics Branch. Retrieved March 3, 2006, from http://www.census.gov/population/www/pop-profile/elderpop.html

Janevic, M. R., & Connell, C. (2001). Racial, ethnic, and cultural differences in dementia caregiving experiences: Recent findings. *The Gerontologist, 41*(3), 334–347.

Lee, Y. R., & Sung, K. T. (1997). Cultural differences in caregiving motivations for demented parents: Korean caregivers versus American caregivers. *International Journal of Aging and Human Development, 44*, 115–127.

Levkoff, S. E., Levy, B. R., & Weitzman, P. F. (1999). The role of religion and ethnicity in the help seeking of family caregivers of elders with Alzheimer's disease and related disorders. *Journal of Cross-Cultural Gerontology, 14,* 335–356.

Navaie-Waliser, M., Feldman, P. H., Gould, D. A., Levine, C., Kuerbis, A. N., & Donelan, K. (2001). The experiences and challenges of informal caregivers: Common themes and differences among whites, blacks and Hispanics. *The Gerontologist, 41*(6), 733–741.

Sanchez, C. D. (1992). Mental health issues: The elderly Latina. *Journal of Geriatric Psychiatry, 25,* 60–84.

Index